Natsume's
BOOK of FRIENDS

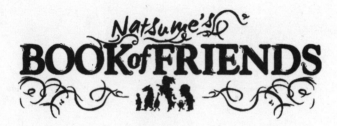

Shojo Beat

Natsume's BOOK of FRIENDS

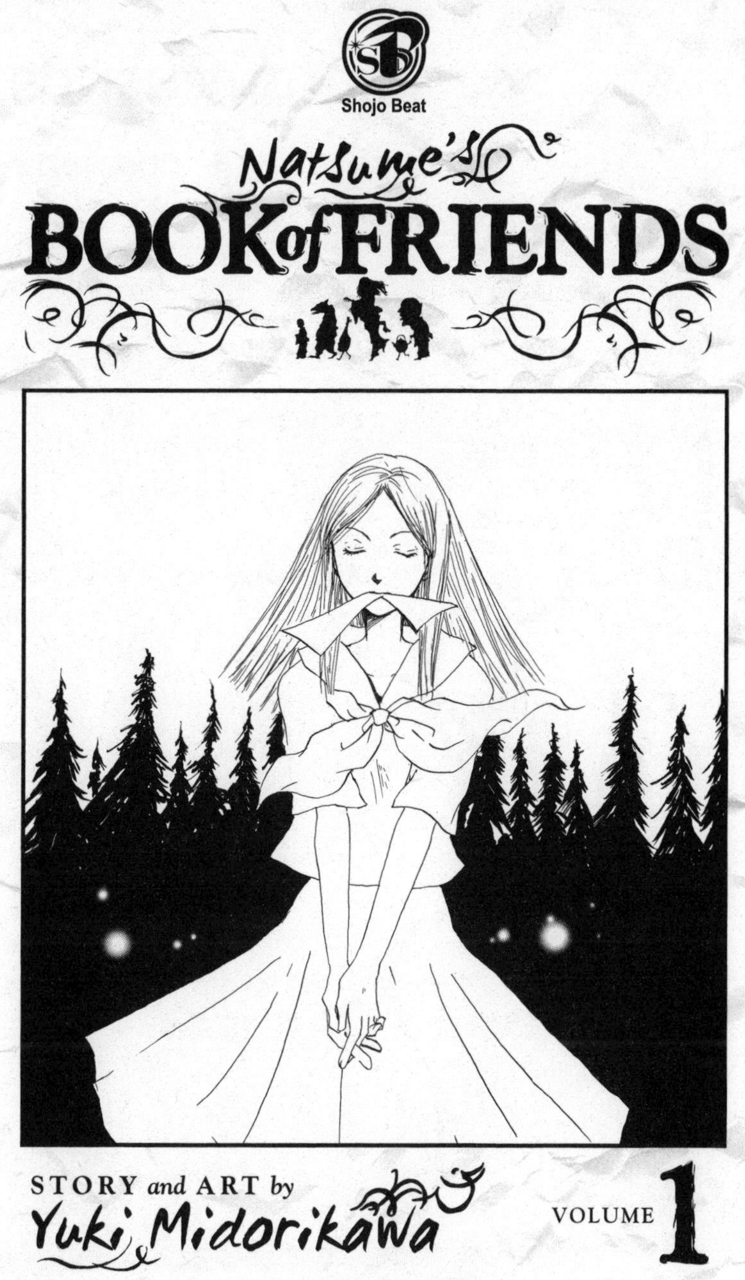

STORY and ART by
Yuki Midorikawa

VOLUME 1

Natsume's
BOOK of FRIENDS

VOLUME 1 CONTENTS

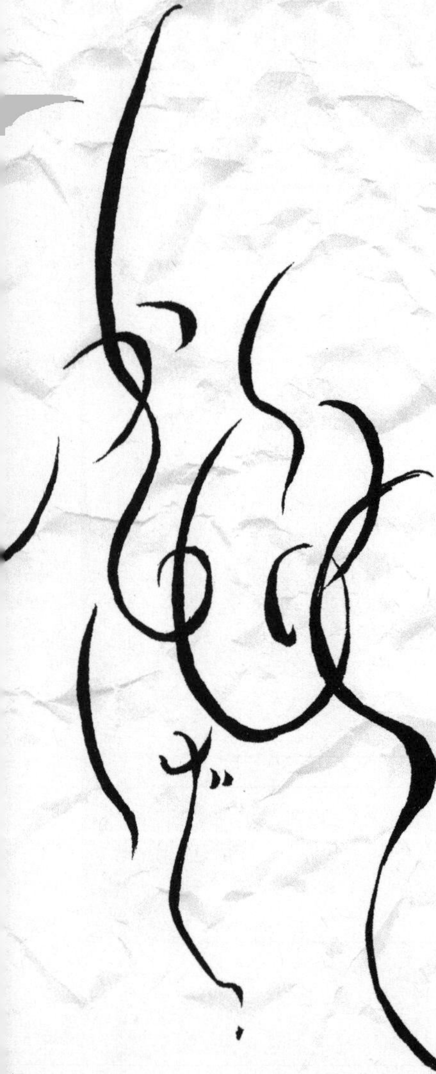

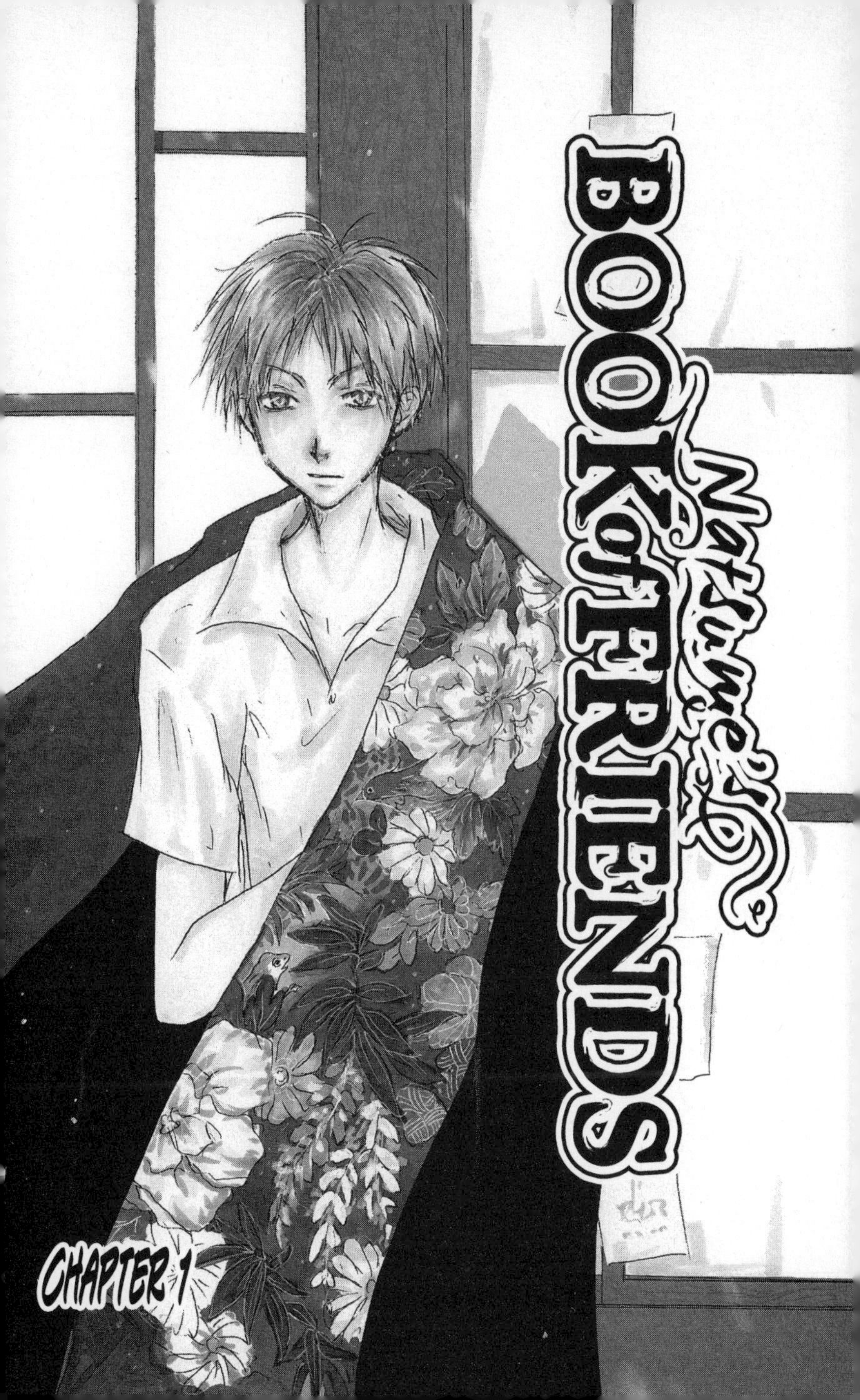
Natsume's BOOK of FRIENDS
CHAPTER 1

WHERE IS SHE?
WHERE DID SHE GO?
HSH
SHF
SHF
SHF
SHF
HSH
IT'S SO HOT!
fwap
fwap
SHF

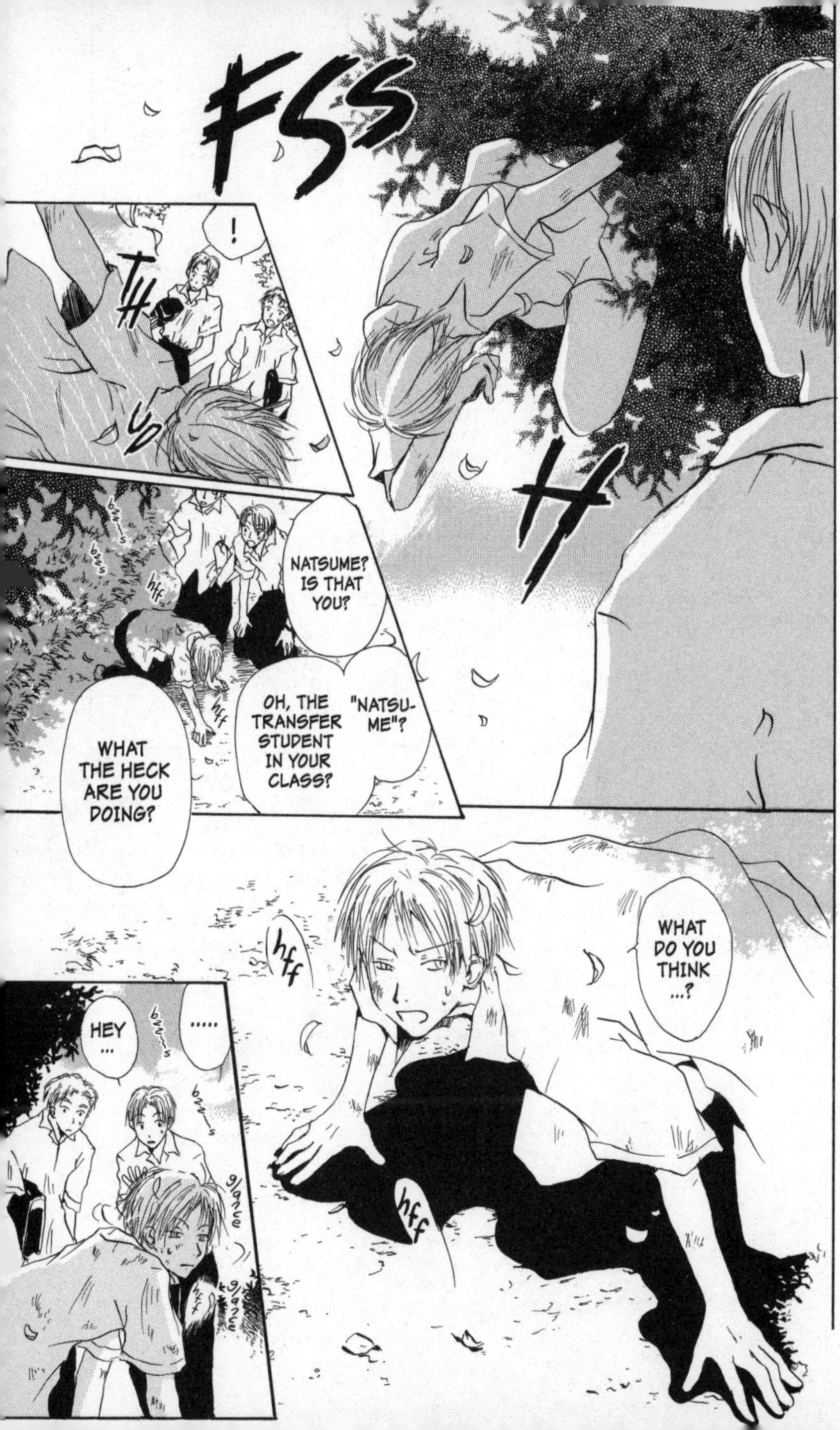
FSS
H
!
THUD
bzz-s
bzz-s
hff
NATSUME? IS THAT YOU?
"NATSU-ME"?
OH, THE TRANSFER STUDENT IN YOUR CLASS?
hff
WHAT THE HECK ARE YOU DOING?
WHAT DO YOU THINK ...?
hff
hff
......
HEY ...
bzz-s
bzz-s
glance
glance
hff

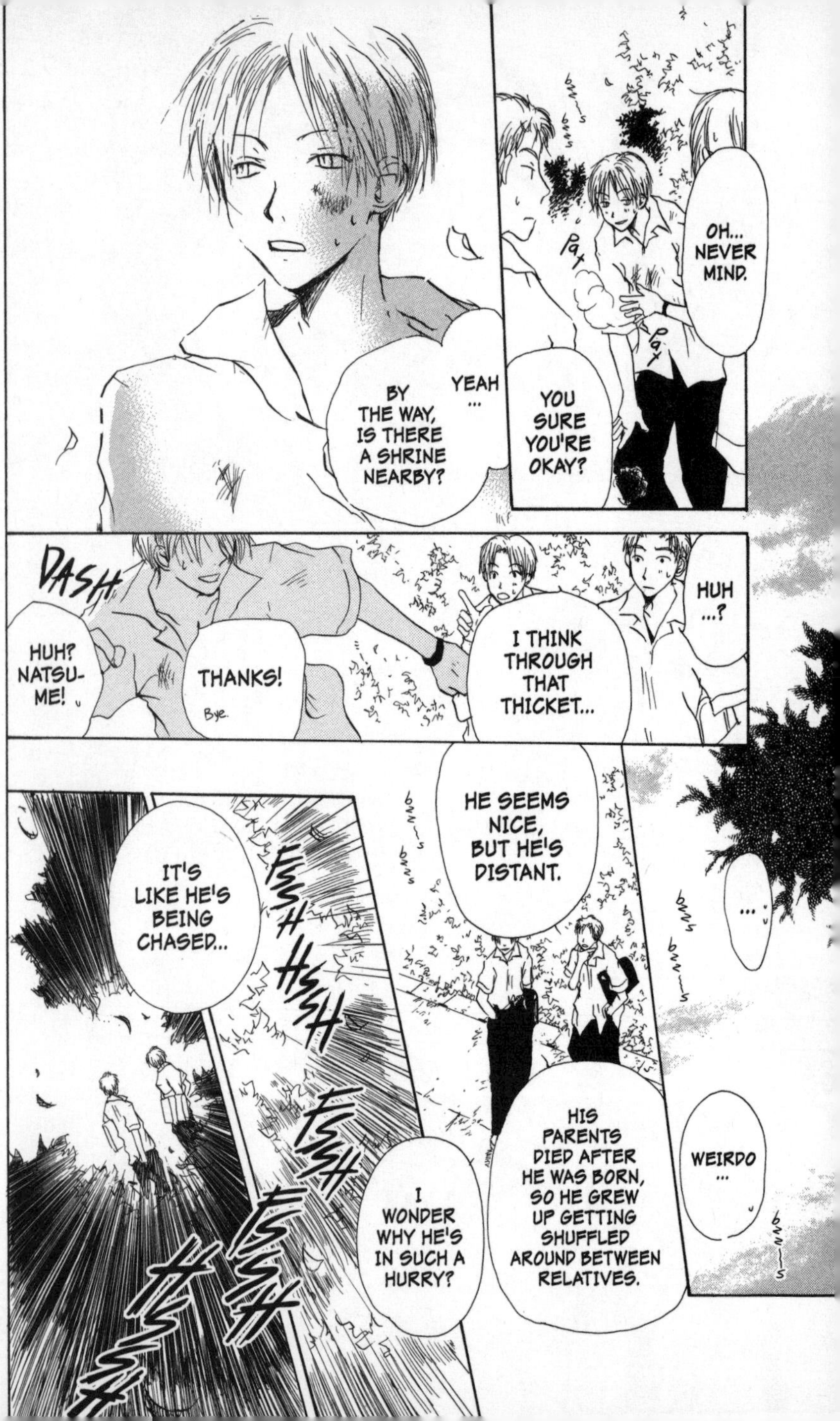
bzz
OH... NEVER MIND.
Pat
Pat
YOU SURE YOU'RE OKAY?
YEAH ...
BY THE WAY, IS THERE A SHRINE NEARBY?
HUH ...?
I THINK THROUGH THAT THICKET...
THANKS!
Bye.
DASH
HUH? NATSU-ME!
...
bzz
HE SEEMS NICE, BUT HE'S DISTANT.
bzz
WEIRDO ...
HIS PARENTS DIED AFTER HE WAS BORN, SO HE GREW UP GETTING SHUFFLED AROUND BETWEEN RELATIVES.
I WONDER WHY HE'S IN SUCH A HURRY?
IT'S LIKE HE'S BEING CHASED...
FSSH HSSH
FSSH
FSSH HSSH

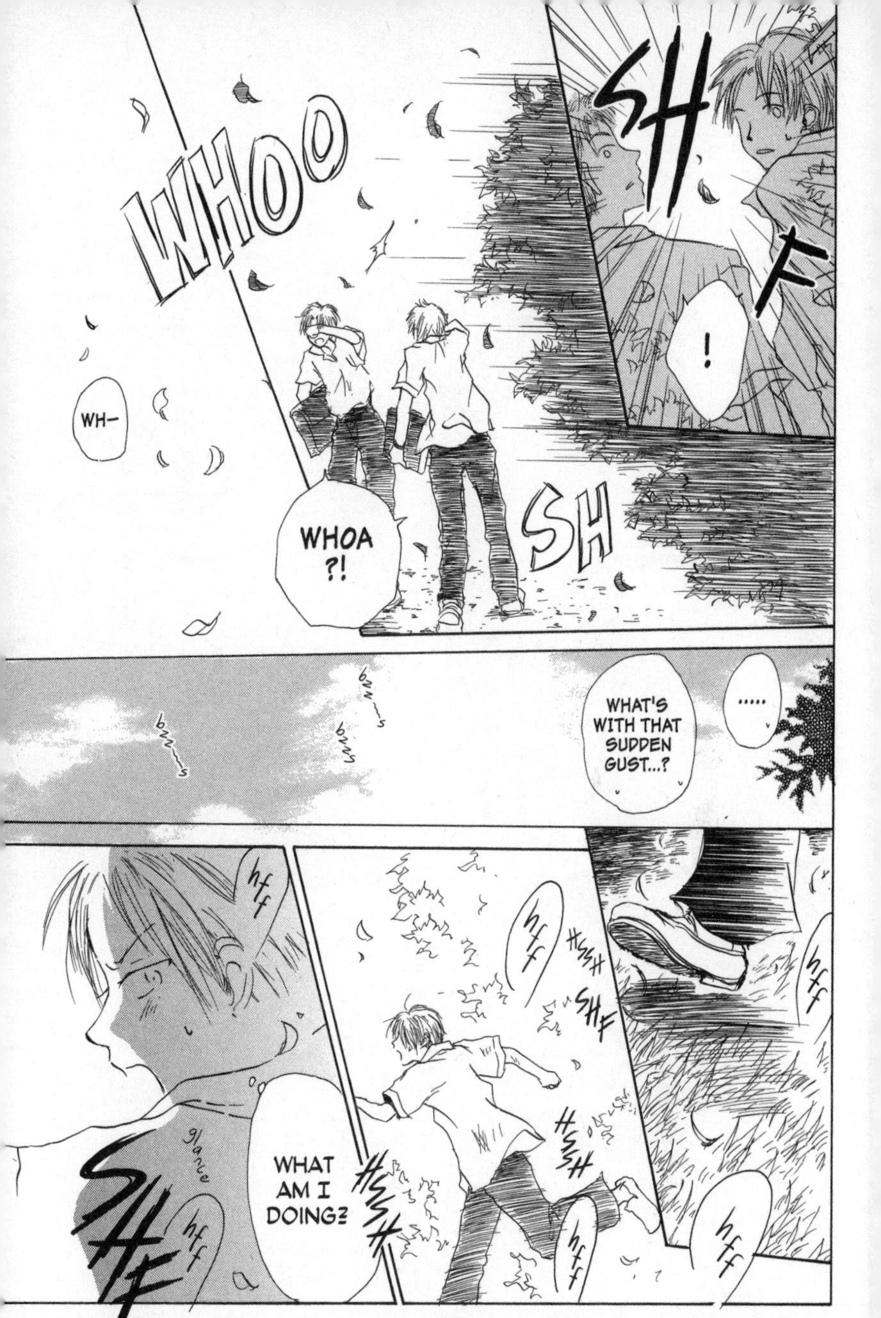
SHF
!
WHOO
WH–
SH
WHOA ?!
......
WHAT'S WITH THAT SUDDEN GUST...?
bzzz
bzzz
bzzz
hff
hff
hff
HSH
SHF
HSH
HSH
hff
hff
WHAT AM I DOING?
glance
SHF
hff

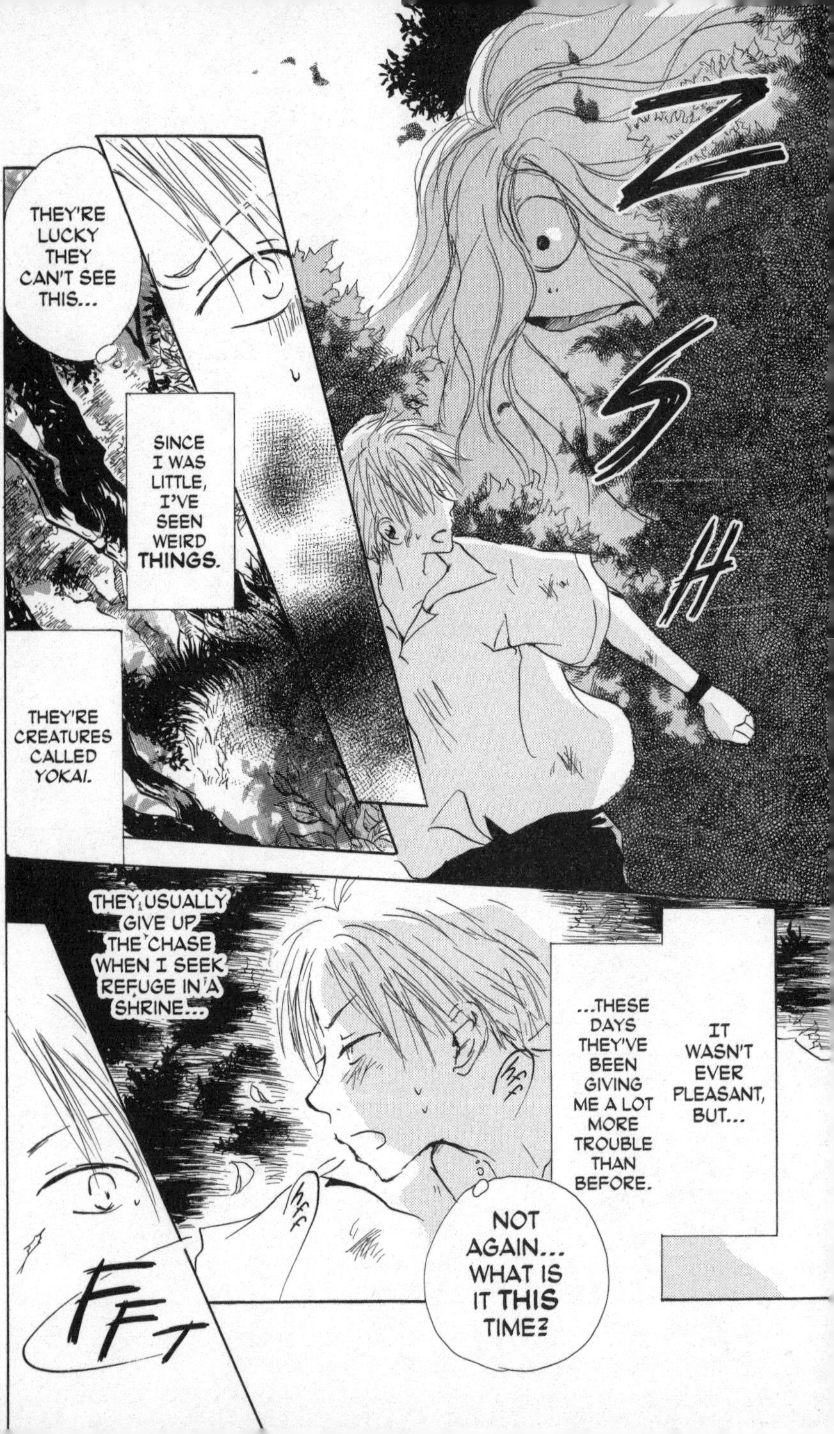
ZSH
THEY'RE LUCKY THEY CAN'T SEE THIS...
SINCE I WAS LITTLE, I'VE SEEN WEIRD THINGS.
THEY'RE CREATURES CALLED YOKAI.
IT WASN'T EVER PLEASANT, BUT...
...THESE DAYS THEY'VE BEEN GIVING ME A LOT MORE TROUBLE THAN BEFORE.
NOT AGAIN... WHAT IS IT THIS TIME?
THEY USUALLY GIVE UP THE CHASE WHEN I SEEK REFUGE IN A SHRINE...
FFT

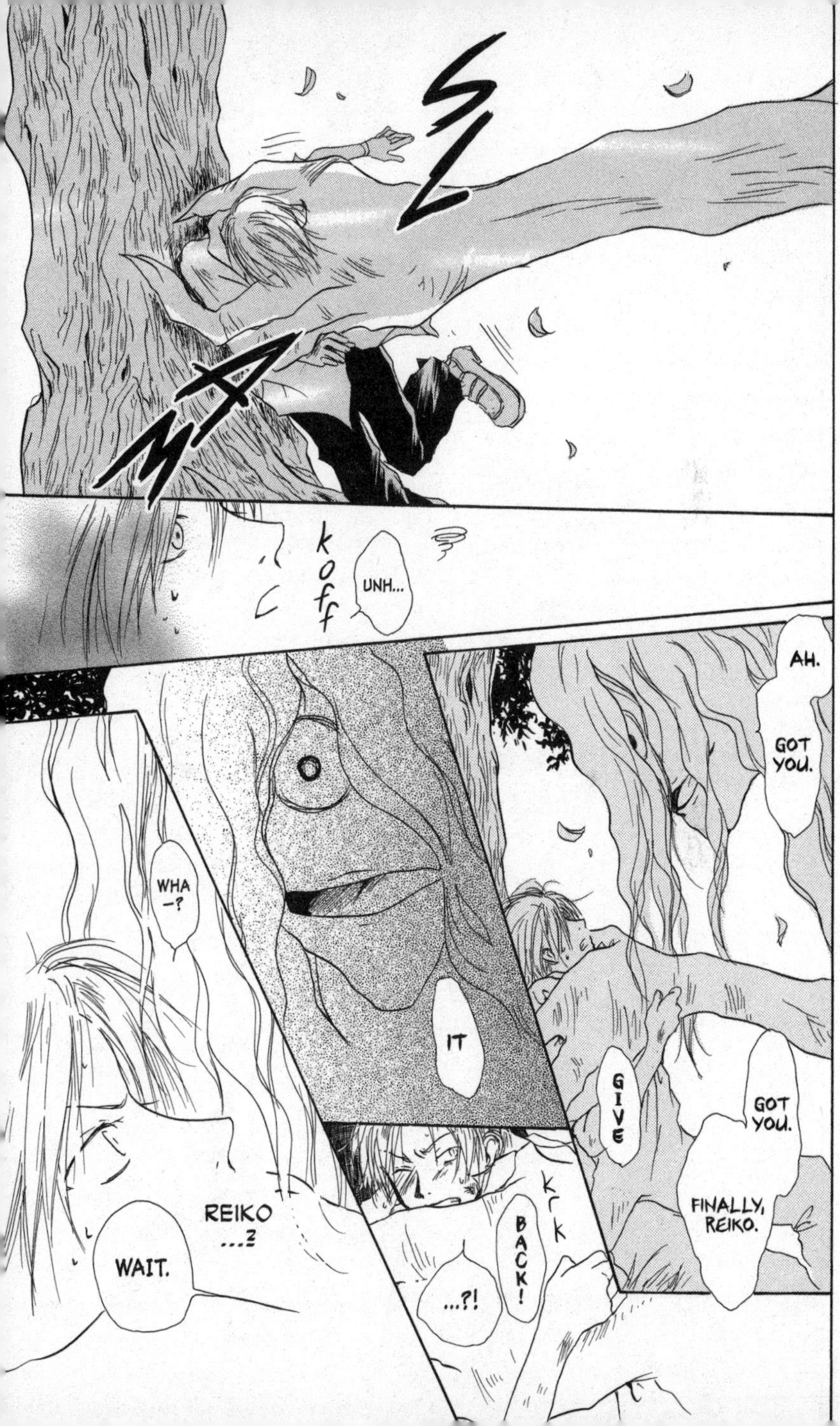
SLAM
koff
UNH...
AH.
GOT YOU.
GOT YOU.
FINALLY, REIKO.
GIVE
IT
krk
BACK!
...?!
WHA—?
REIKO...?
WAIT.

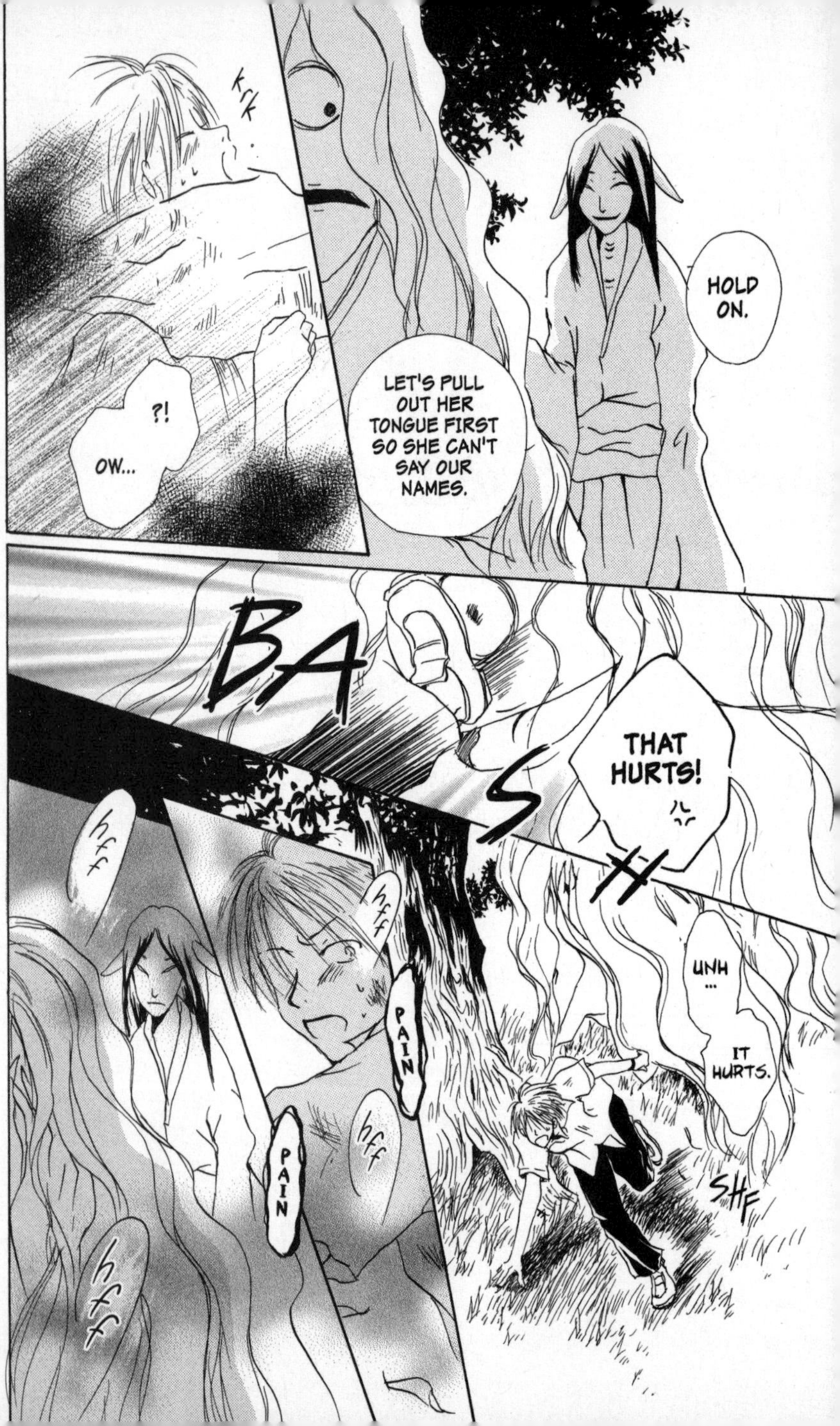
HOLD ON.
LET'S PULL OUT HER TONGUE FIRST SO SHE CAN'T SAY OUR NAMES.
KRK
?!
OW...
BASH
THAT HURTS!
UNH ...
IT HURTS.
SHF
hff
PAIN
hff
PAIN
hff
hff

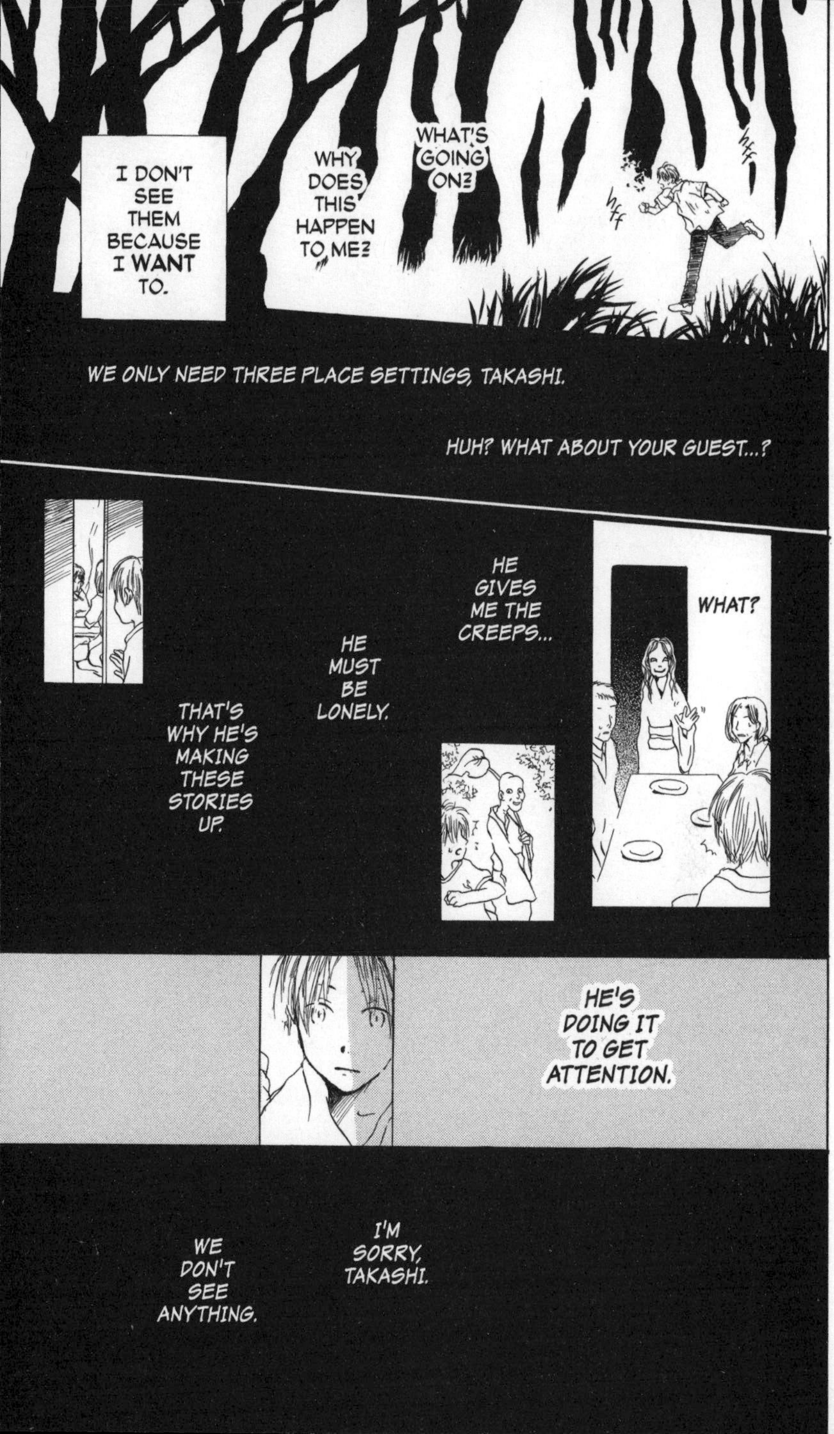
WHAT'S GOING ON?
WHY DOES THIS HAPPEN TO ME?
I DON'T SEE THEM BECAUSE I WANT TO.
WE ONLY NEED THREE PLACE SETTINGS, TAKASHI.
HUH? WHAT ABOUT YOUR GUEST...?
WHAT?
HE GIVES ME THE CREEPS...
HE MUST BE LONELY.
THAT'S WHY HE'S MAKING THESE STORIES UP.
HE'S DOING IT TO GET ATTENTION.
I'M SORRY, TAKASHI.
WE DON'T SEE ANYTHING.

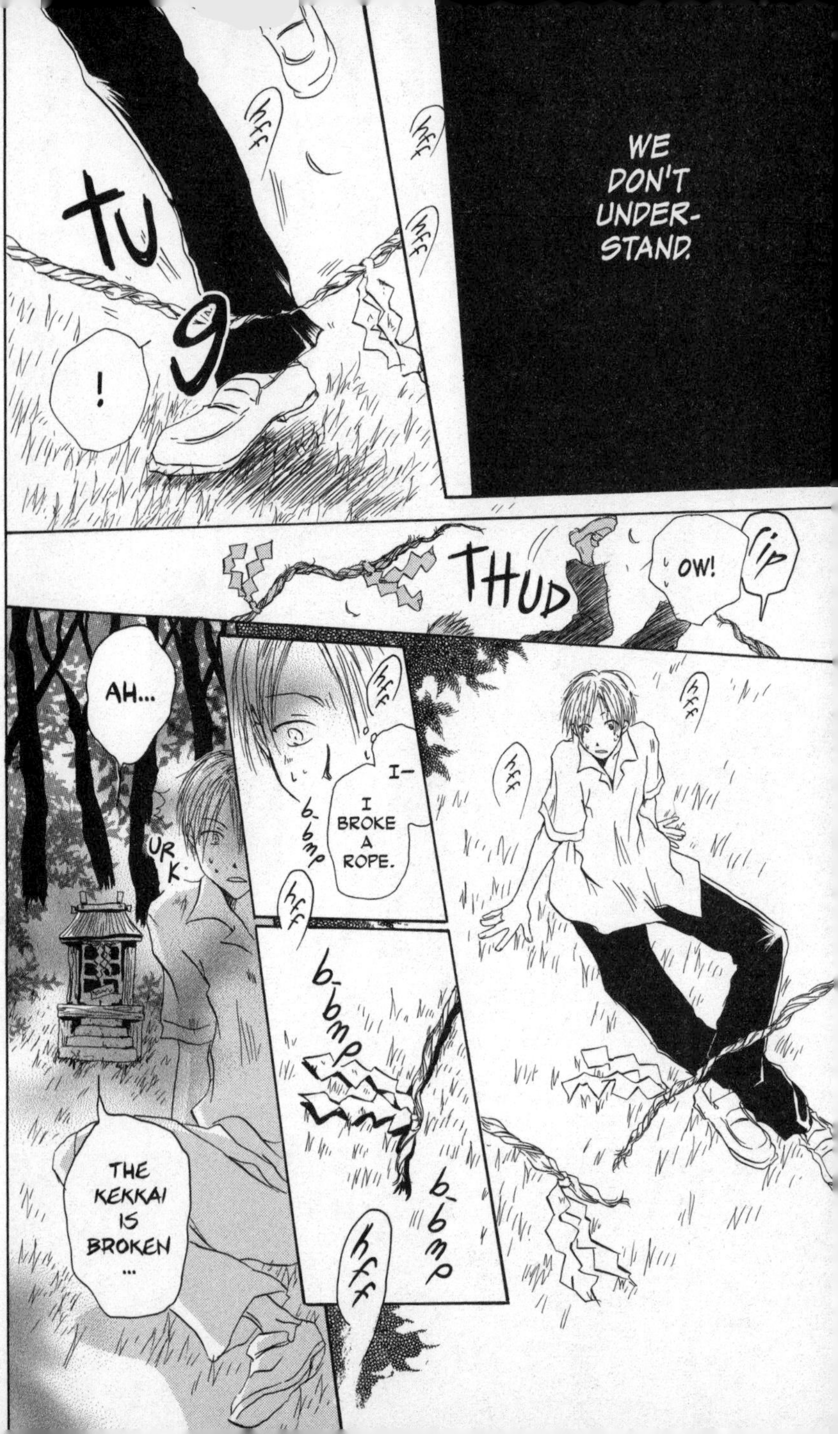
WE DON'T UNDER-STAND.
hff
hff
hff
tug
!
rip
OW!
THUD
hff
hff
hff
I—
I BROKE A ROPE.
b-bmp
hff
b-bmp
b-bmp
hff
AH...
URK
THE KEKKAI IS BROKEN ...

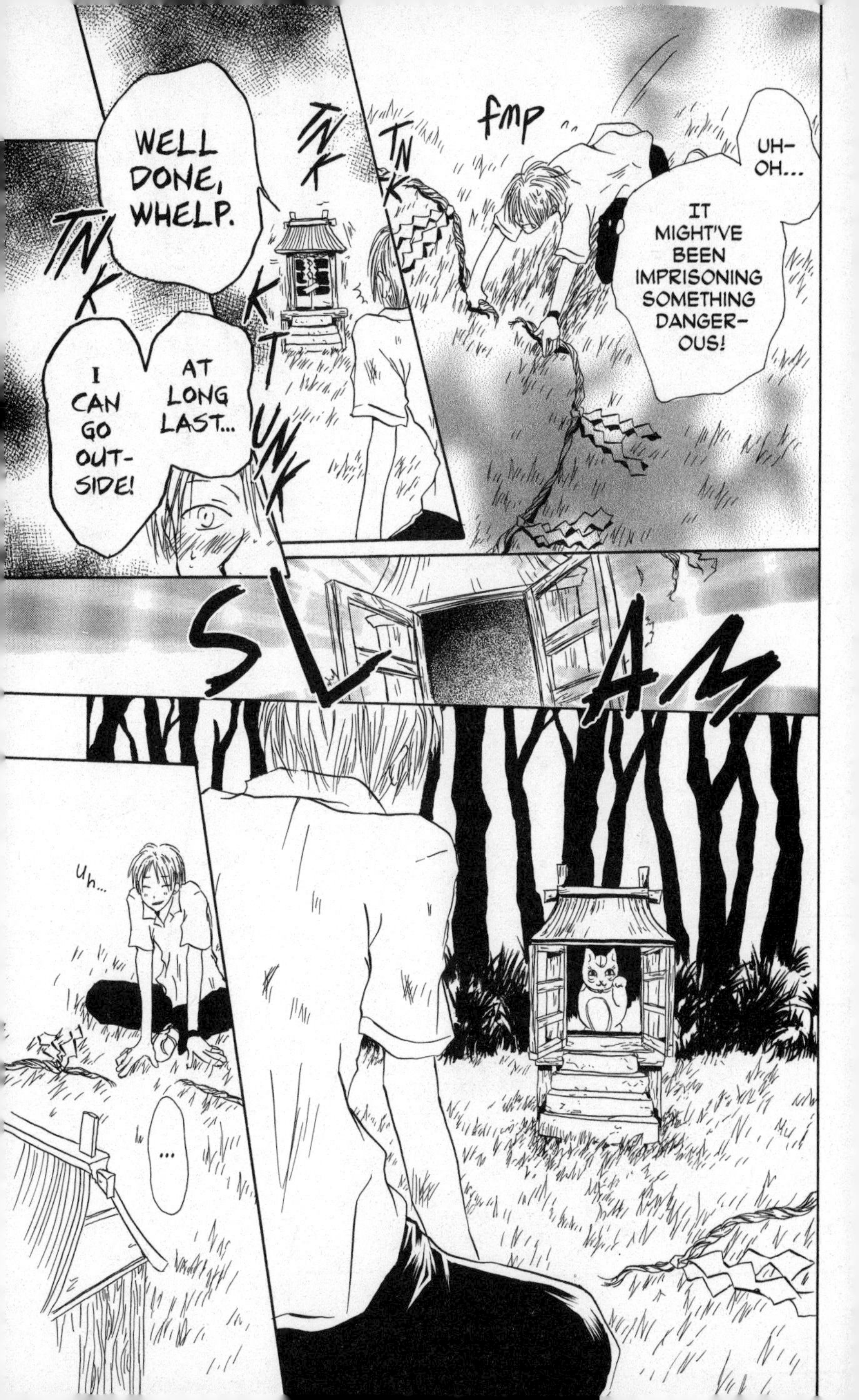

UH-OH...
IT MIGHT'VE BEEN IMPRISONING SOMETHING DANGER-OUS!
fmp
TNK
TNK
WELL DONE, WHELP.
AT LONG LAST...
I CAN GO OUT-SIDE!
TNK
KTUNK
SLAM
Uh...
...

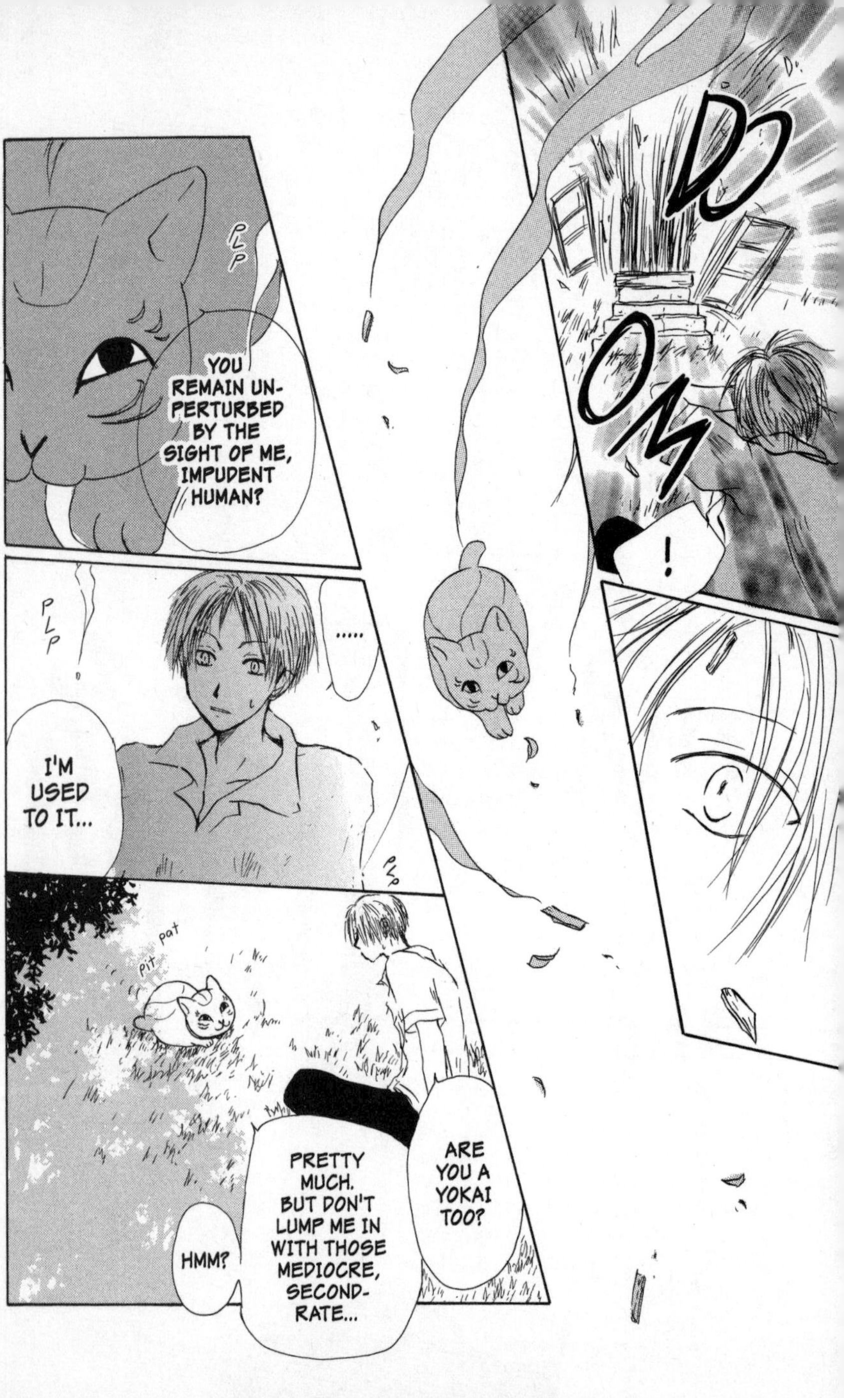
Do.
DOOOM
!
PLP
YOU REMAIN UN-PERTURBED BY THE SIGHT OF ME, IMPUDENT HUMAN?
PLP
.....
I'M USED TO IT...
PLP
pit pat
ARE YOU A YOKAI TOO?
PRETTY MUCH. BUT DON'T LUMP ME IN WITH THOSE MEDIOCRE, SECOND-RATE...
HMM?

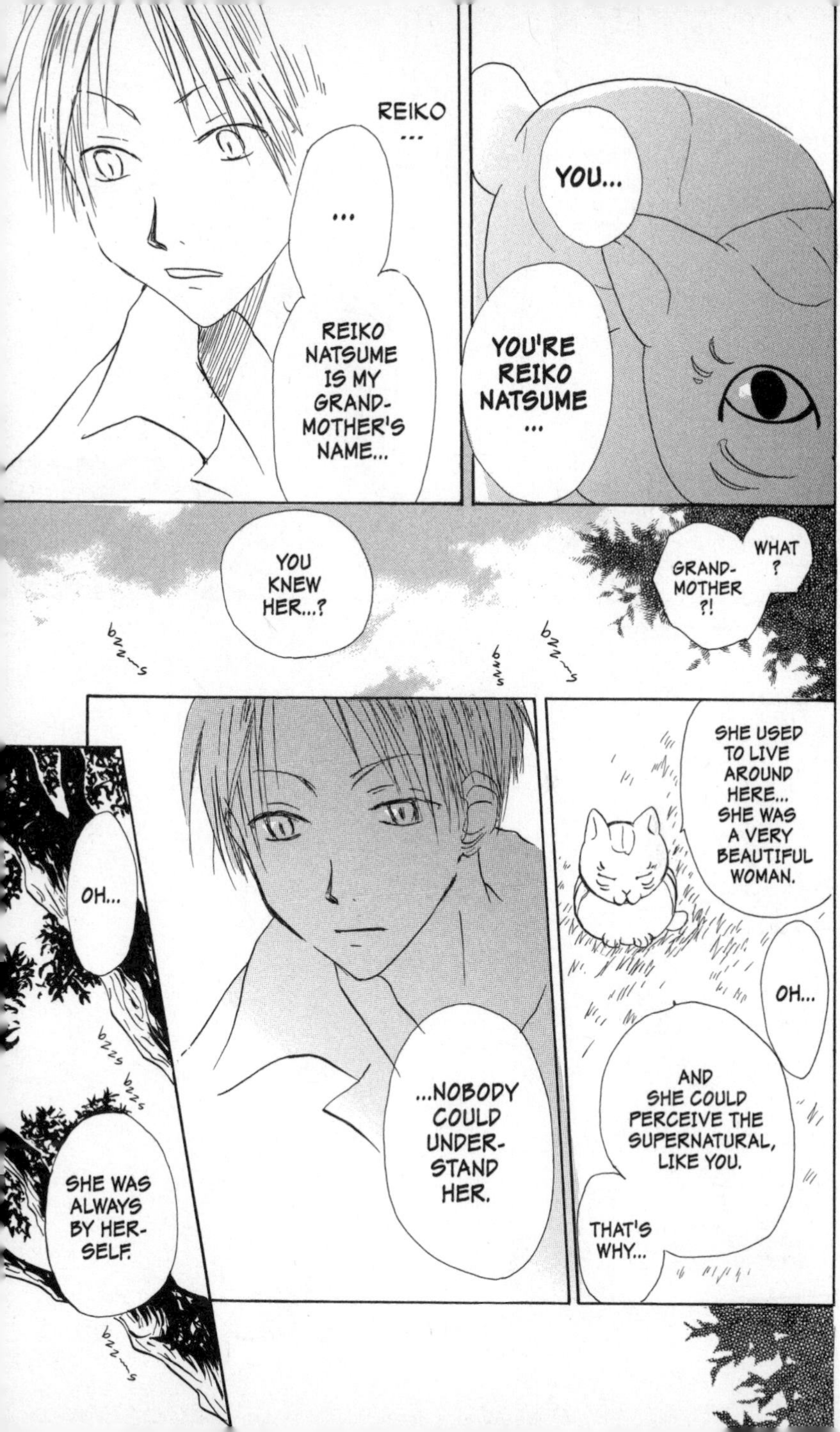
YOU...
YOU'RE REIKO NATSUME ...
REIKO ...
...
REIKO NATSUME IS MY GRAND-MOTHER'S NAME...
WHAT ?
GRAND-MOTHER ?!
YOU KNEW HER...?
bzz~s
bzzs
bzz~s
SHE USED TO LIVE AROUND HERE... SHE WAS A VERY BEAUTIFUL WOMAN.
OH...
AND SHE COULD PERCEIVE THE SUPERNATURAL, LIKE YOU.
THAT'S WHY...
...NOBODY COULD UNDER-STAND HER.
OH...
bzzs
bzzs
SHE WAS ALWAYS BY HER-SELF.
bzz~s

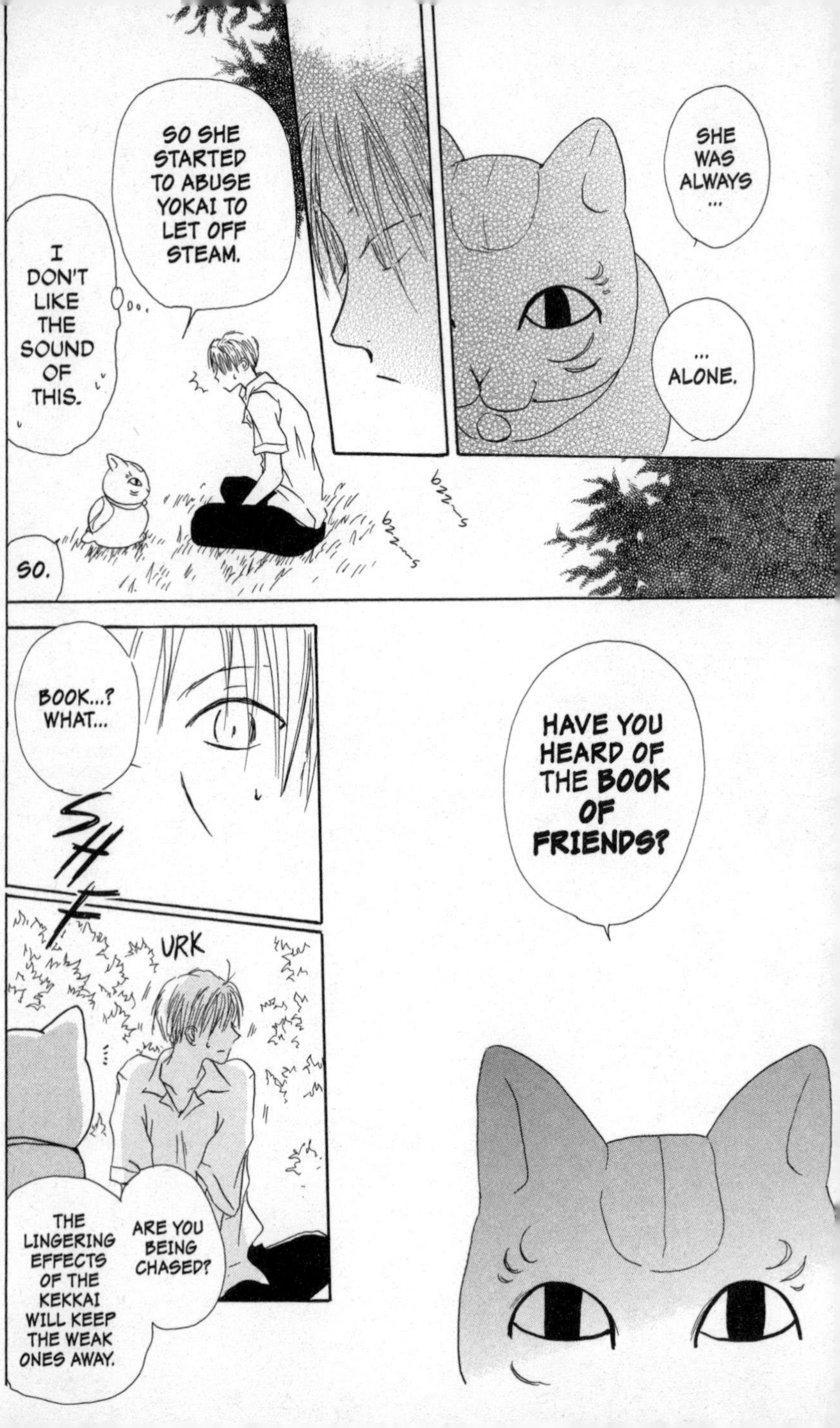
SHE WAS ALWAYS ...
... ALONE.
SO SHE STARTED TO ABUSE YOKAI TO LET OFF STEAM.
I DON'T LIKE THE SOUND OF THIS.
SO.
HAVE YOU HEARD OF THE BOOK OF FRIENDS?
BOOK...? WHAT...
SHH
URK
ARE YOU BEING CHASED?
THE LINGERING EFFECTS OF THE KEKKAI WILL KEEP THE WEAK ONES AWAY.

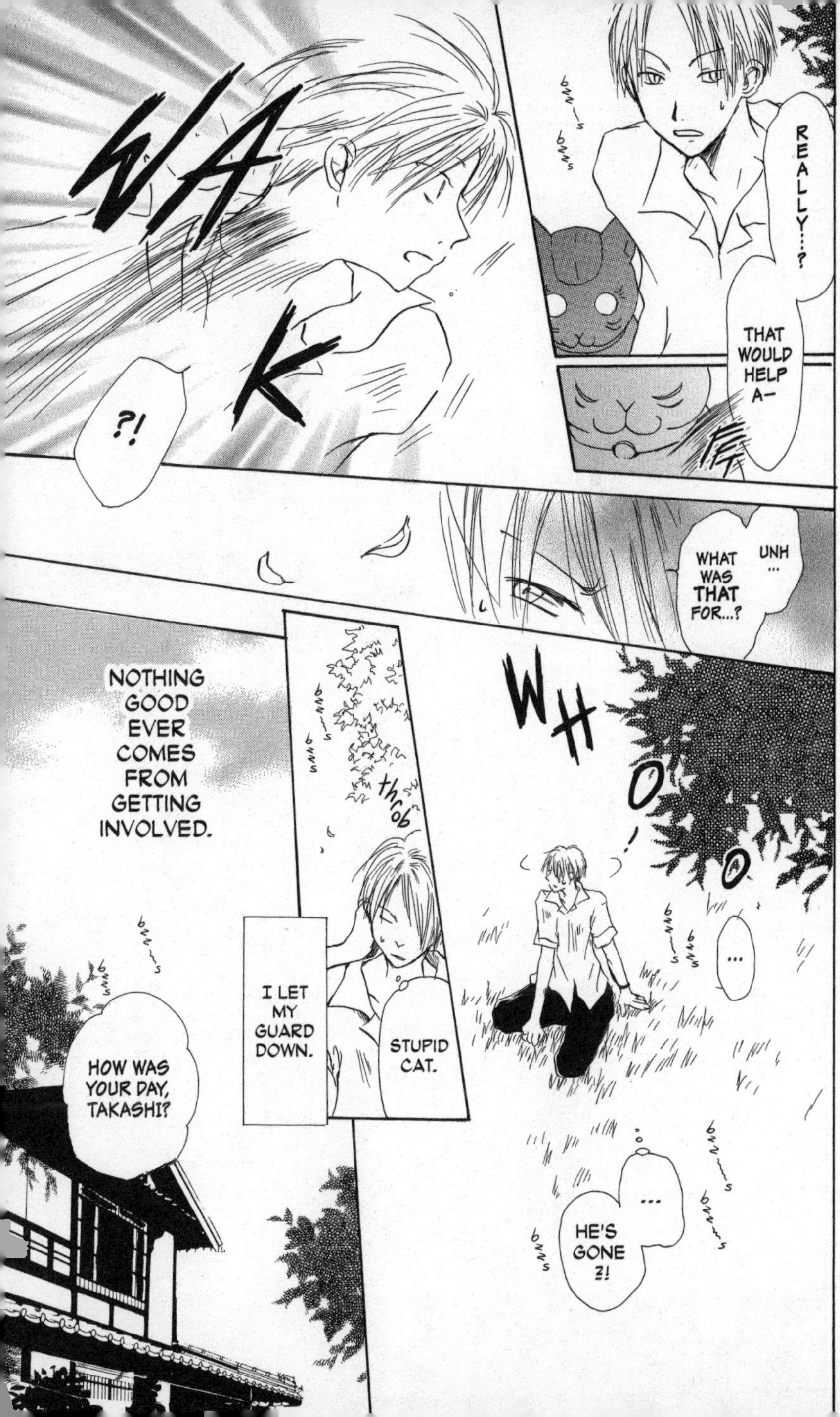
bzz-s bzz-s
REALLY...?
THAT WOULD HELP A—
WAK
?!
UNH...
WHAT WAS THAT FOR...?
WHOOO!
...
bzz-s bzz-s
...
HE'S GONE?!
bzz-s bzz-s
throb
STUPID CAT.
I LET MY GUARD DOWN.
NOTHING GOOD EVER COMES FROM GETTING INVOLVED.
bzz-s bzz-s
HOW WAS YOUR DAY, TAKASHI?

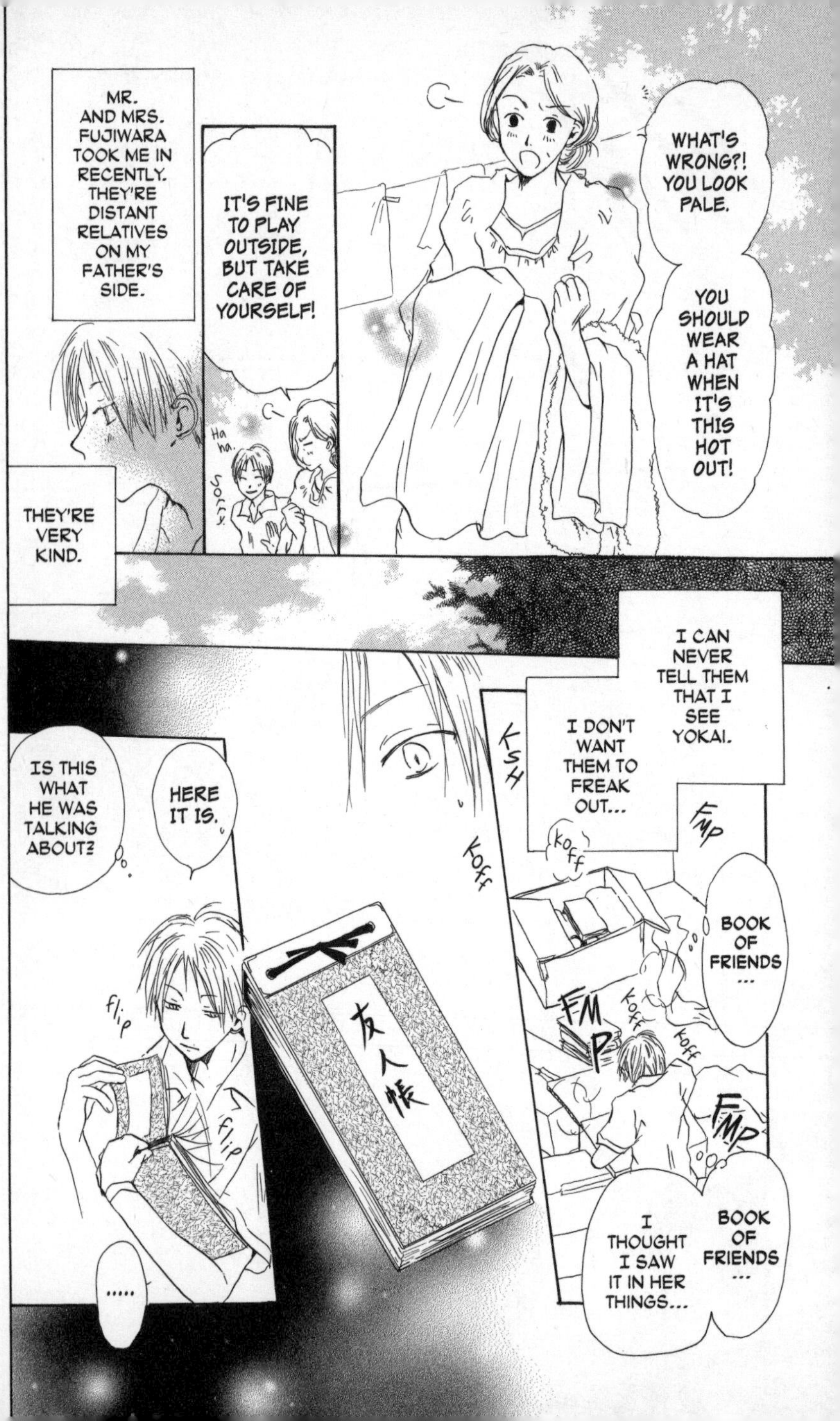
WHAT'S WRONG?! YOU LOOK PALE.
YOU SHOULD WEAR A HAT WHEN IT'S THIS HOT OUT!
IT'S FINE TO PLAY OUTSIDE, BUT TAKE CARE OF YOURSELF!
Ha ha. Sorry.
MR. AND MRS. FUJIWARA TOOK ME IN RECENTLY. THEY'RE DISTANT RELATIVES ON MY FATHER'S SIDE.
THEY'RE VERY KIND.
I CAN NEVER TELL THEM THAT I SEE YOKAI.
I DON'T WANT THEM TO FREAK OUT...
FMP
koff
BOOK OF FRIENDS...
FMP
koff
koff
FMP
BOOK OF FRIENDS...
I THOUGHT I SAW IT IN HER THINGS...
KSH
koff
HERE IT IS.
IS THIS WHAT HE WAS TALKING ABOUT?
友人帳
flip
flip
......

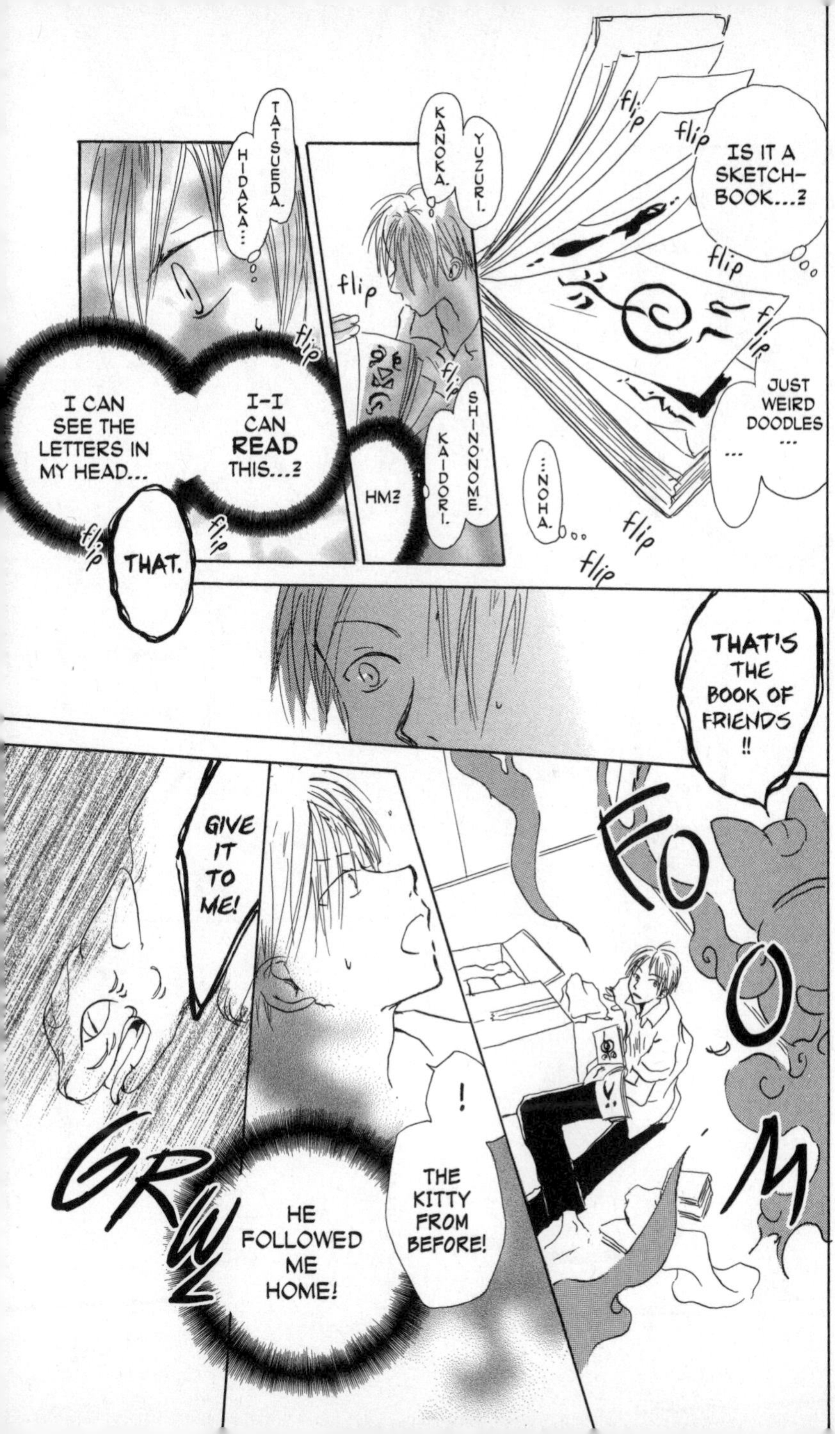
flip
flip
IS IT A SKETCH-BOOK...?
flip
flip
JUST WEIRD DOODLES ......
...NOHA.
flip
flip
YUZURI.
KANOKA.
flip
flip
SHINONOME.
KAIDORI.
HM?
TATSUEDA.
HIDAKA...
flip
I-I CAN READ THIS...?
I CAN SEE THE LETTERS IN MY HEAD...
flip
flip
THAT.
THAT'S THE BOOK OF FRIENDS!!
FOOOM
!
THE KITTY FROM BEFORE!
HE FOLLOWED ME HOME!
GIVE IT TO ME!
GRWL

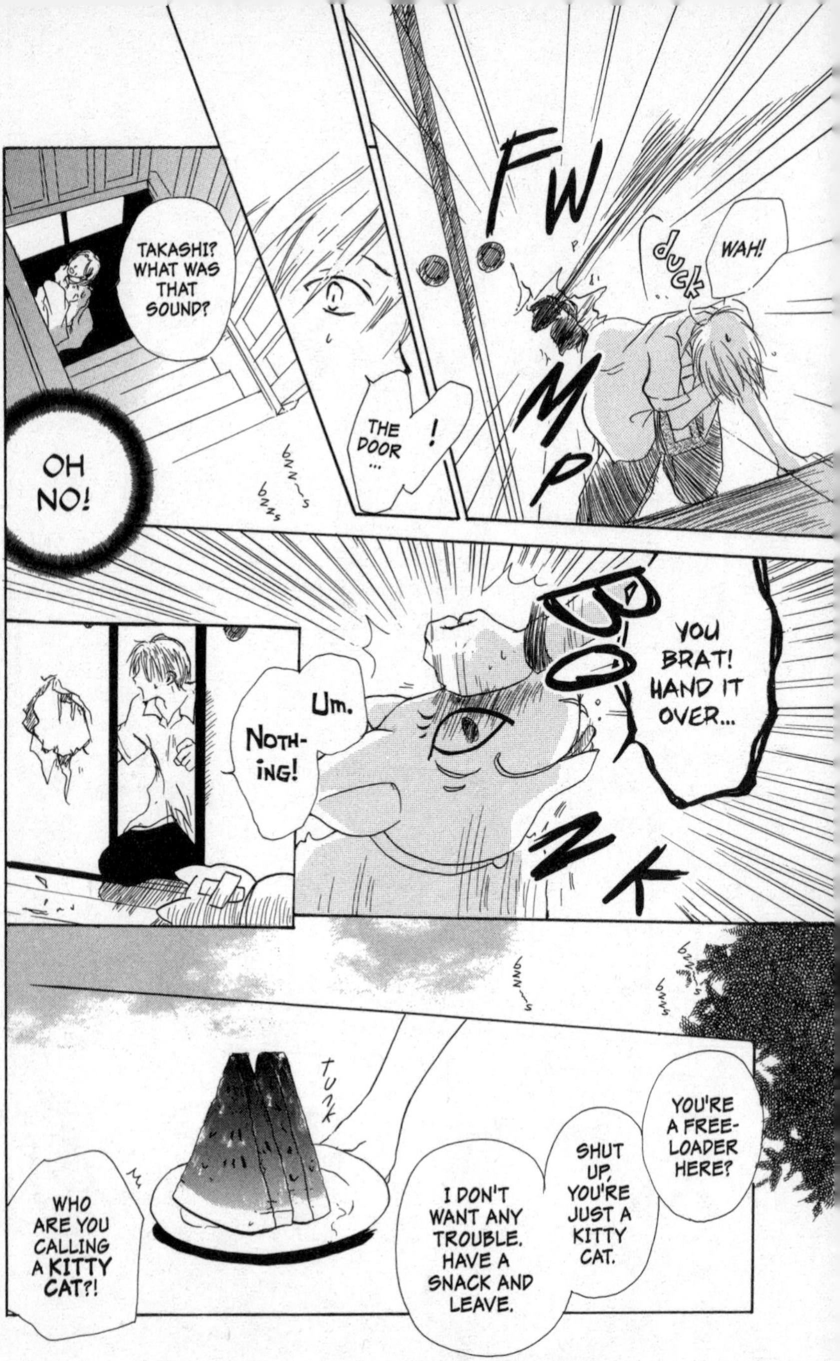
WAH!
duck
FWMP
!
THE DOOR ...
TAKASHI? WHAT WAS THAT SOUND?
bzz~s
bzzs
OH NO!
YOU BRAT! HAND IT OVER...
BONK
Um. NOTHING!
bzz~s
bzzs
TUNK
YOU'RE A FREE-LOADER HERE?
SHUT UP, YOU'RE JUST A KITTY CAT.
I DON'T WANT ANY TROUBLE. HAVE A SNACK AND LEAVE.
WHO ARE YOU CALLING A KITTY CAT?!

01

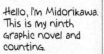

Hello, I'm Midorikawa. This is my ninth graphic novel and counting.

Only one more book until I reach the goal I had when I first started as a manga artist: ten graphic novels to my name. A big thank you to everyone who picked it up, and to all my editors. I'll keep working hard every day to earn your support.

I came up with Natsume for a bi-monthly manga magazine as a story that could work with each episode as a stand alone. It's a memorable manga, the first my current editor and I worked together to create.

I hope you enjoy it.

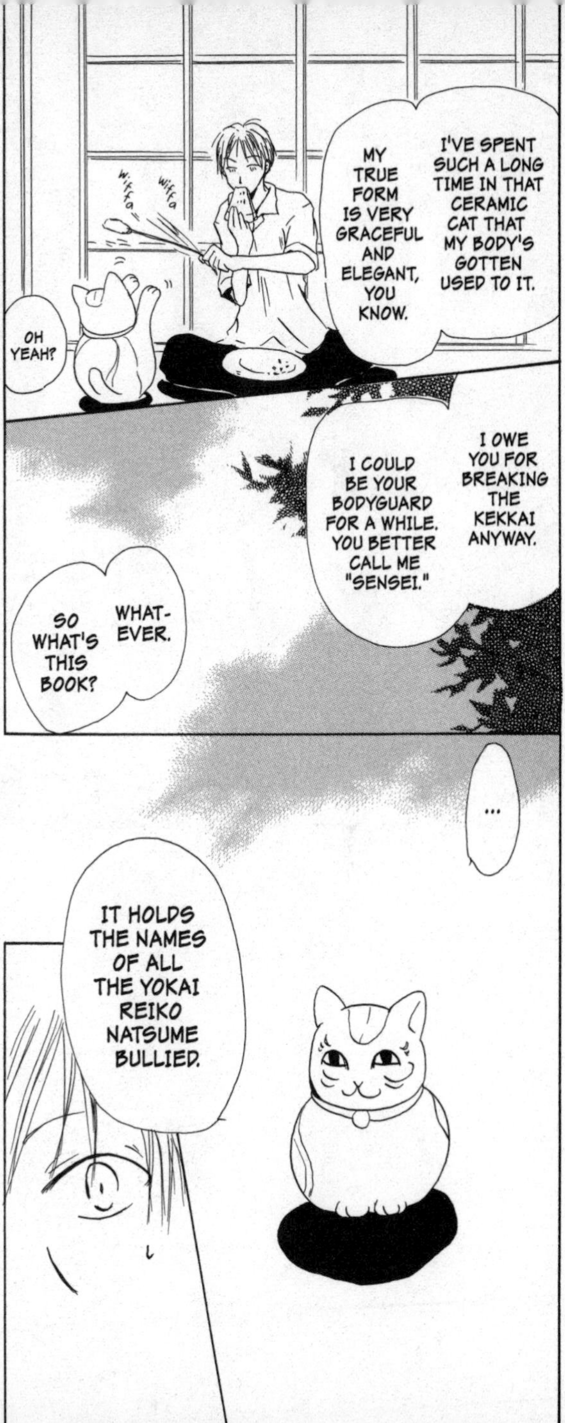
I'VE SPENT SUCH A LONG TIME IN THAT CERAMIC CAT THAT MY BODY'S GOTTEN USED TO IT.
MY TRUE FORM IS VERY GRACEFUL AND ELEGANT, YOU KNOW.
wiffa
wiffa
OH YEAH?
I OWE YOU FOR BREAKING THE KEKKAI ANYWAY.
I COULD BE YOUR BODYGUARD FOR A WHILE. YOU BETTER CALL ME "SENSEI."
WHAT-EVER.
SO WHAT'S THIS BOOK?
...
IT HOLDS THE NAMES OF ALL THE YOKAI REIKO NATSUME BULLIED.

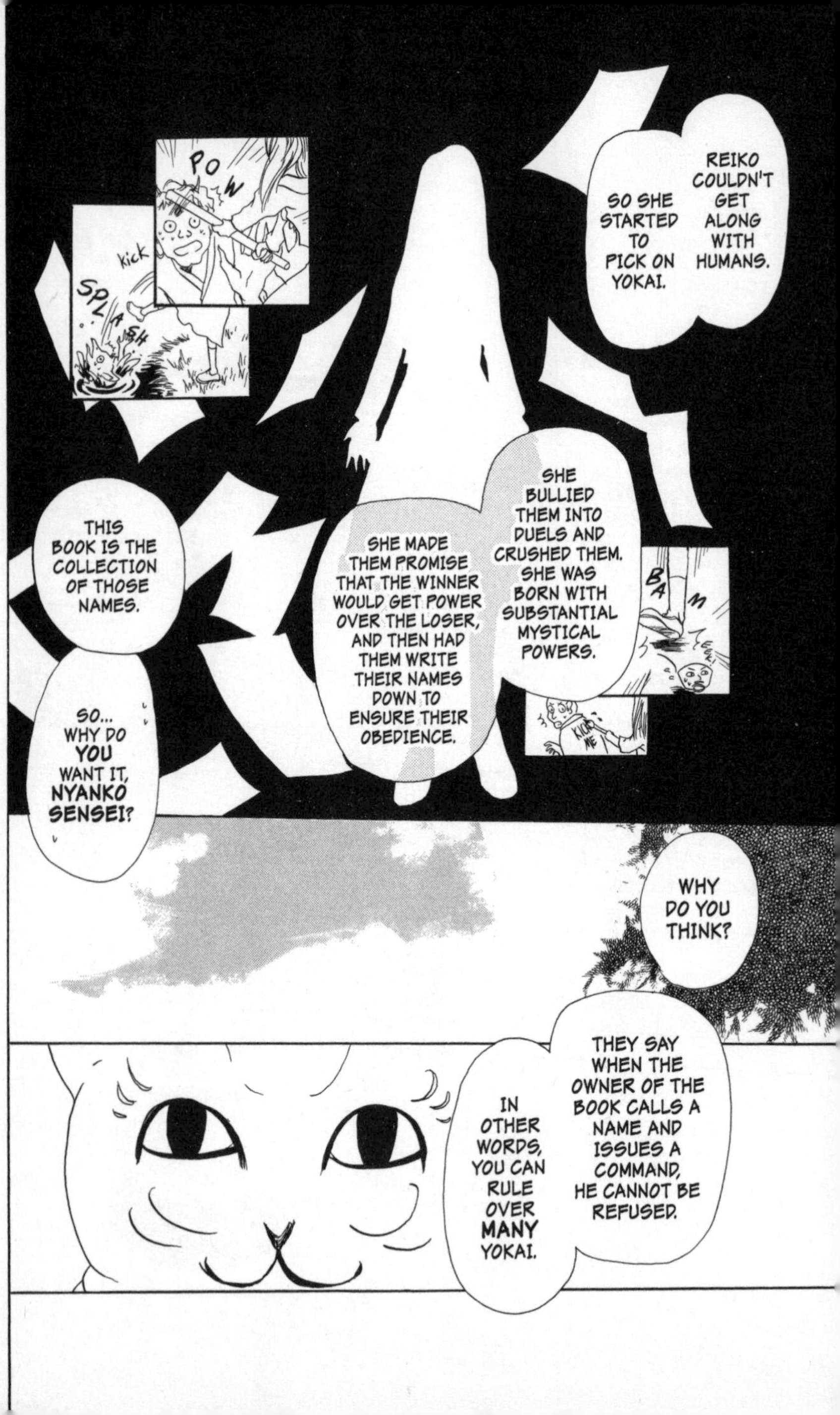
REIKO COULDN'T GET ALONG WITH HUMANS.
SO SHE STARTED TO PICK ON YOKAI.
POW
kick
SPLASH
SHE BULLIED THEM INTO DUELS AND CRUSHED THEM. SHE WAS BORN WITH SUBSTANTIAL MYSTICAL POWERS.
BAM
KICK ME
SHE MADE THEM PROMISE THAT THE WINNER WOULD GET POWER OVER THE LOSER, AND THEN HAD THEM WRITE THEIR NAMES DOWN TO ENSURE THEIR OBEDIENCE.
THIS BOOK IS THE COLLECTION OF THOSE NAMES.
SO... WHY DO YOU WANT IT, NYANKO SENSEI?
WHY DO YOU THINK?
THEY SAY WHEN THE OWNER OF THE BOOK CALLS A NAME AND ISSUES A COMMAND, HE CANNOT BE REFUSED.
IN OTHER WORDS, YOU CAN RULE OVER MANY YOKAI.

02

❋ ~Internal monologues~

I don't really like using them (though I like reading them). Ones that paint a mental image make me especially nervous. That's not because of the difficulties in expression, but because once you can see clearly through a character's head, I can't draw him anymore. I lose my interest when I find out that's all there is. So I try to minimize monologues as much as I can to ones that explain the situation, or that show the closeness (or lack thereof) between two people, for example. Such monologues are fine for female characters, but I prefer that readers don't read every thought and emotion for a male character. It feels like there are fewer monologues the more I care about a character. Now, Natsume is a struggle in that respect. I kept thinking many times that I wouldn't have to suffer like this if only Natsume were a girl. But I wanted to do a story about a boy and his non-human teacher, so I guess it comes with the territory.

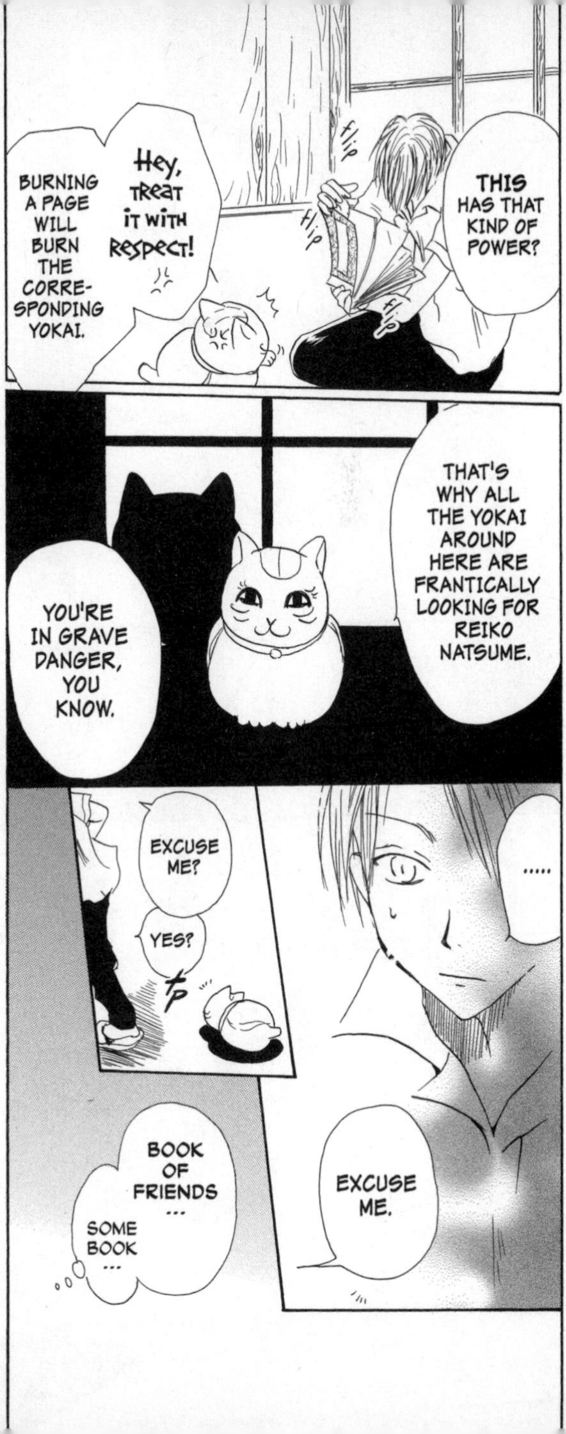
THIS HAS THAT KIND OF POWER?
flip
flip
flip
Hey, TREAT IT WITH RESPECT!
BURNING A PAGE WILL BURN THE CORRESPONDING YOKAI.
THAT'S WHY ALL THE YOKAI AROUND HERE ARE FRANTICALLY LOOKING FOR REIKO NATSUME.
YOU'RE IN GRAVE DANGER, YOU KNOW.
.....
EXCUSE ME.
EXCUSE ME?
YES?
tp
BOOK OF FRIENDS ...
SOME BOOK ...

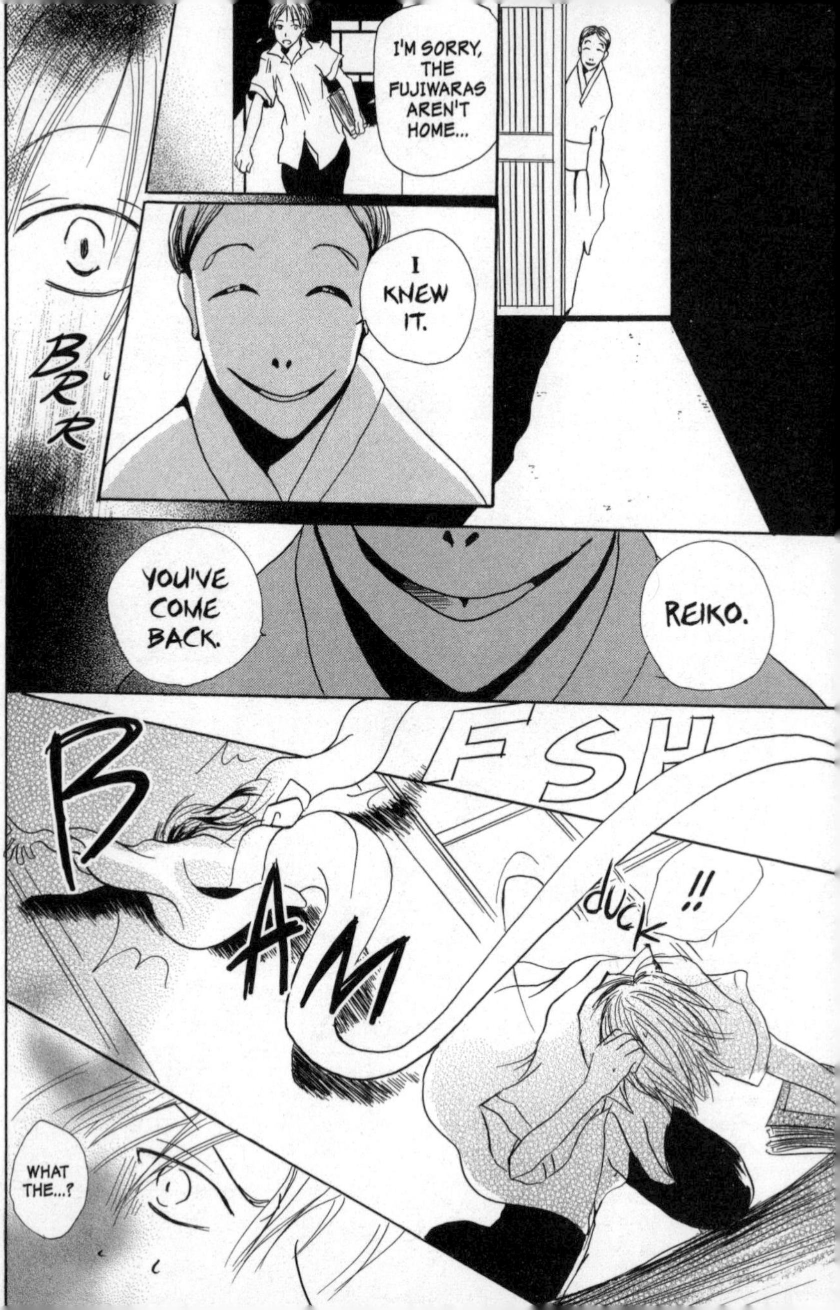
I'M SORRY, THE FUJIWARAS AREN'T HOME...
I KNEW IT.
BRRR
REIKO.
YOU'VE COME BACK.
FSH
duck
!!
BAM
WHAT THE...?

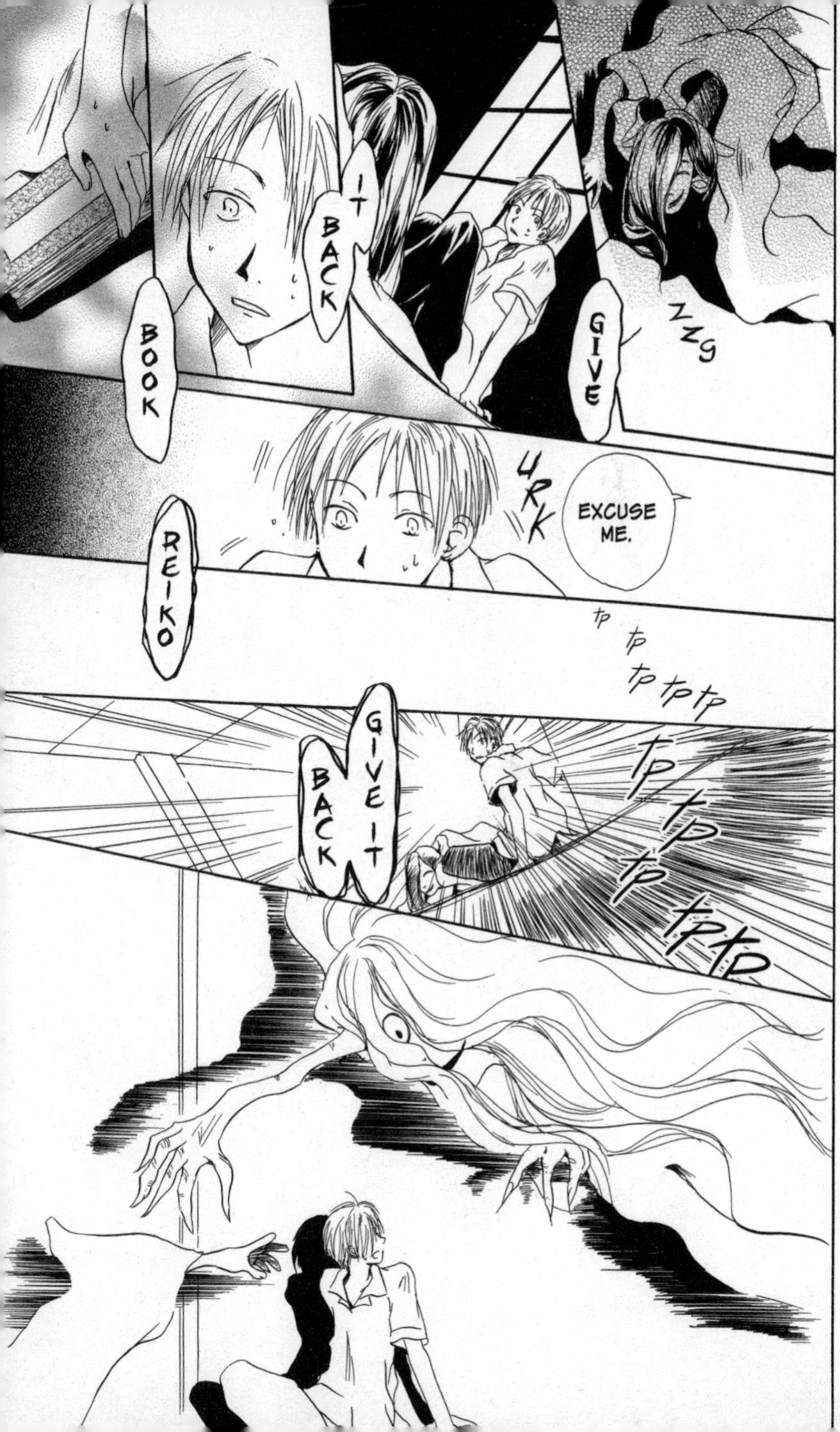
GIVE
ZZZG
IT BACK
BOOK
URK
EXCUSE ME.
REIKO
tp tp tp tp tp
tp tp tp tp tp
GIVE IT BACK
tptptp

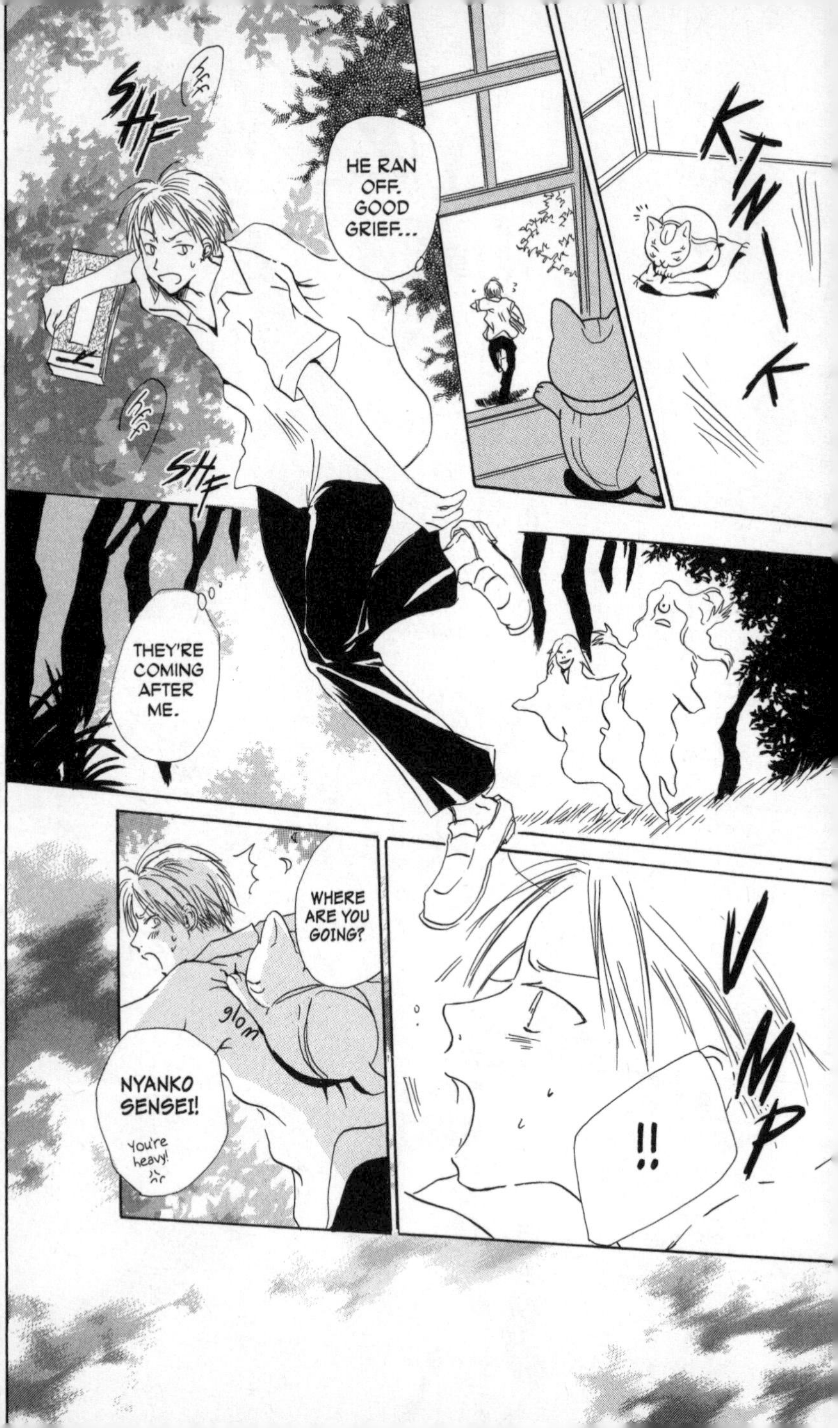
KTNK
HE RAN OFF. GOOD GRIEF...
SHF
HFF
HFF
SHF
THEY'RE COMING AFTER ME.
VMMP
!!
WHERE ARE YOU GOING?
glom
NYANKO SENSEI!
You're heavy!

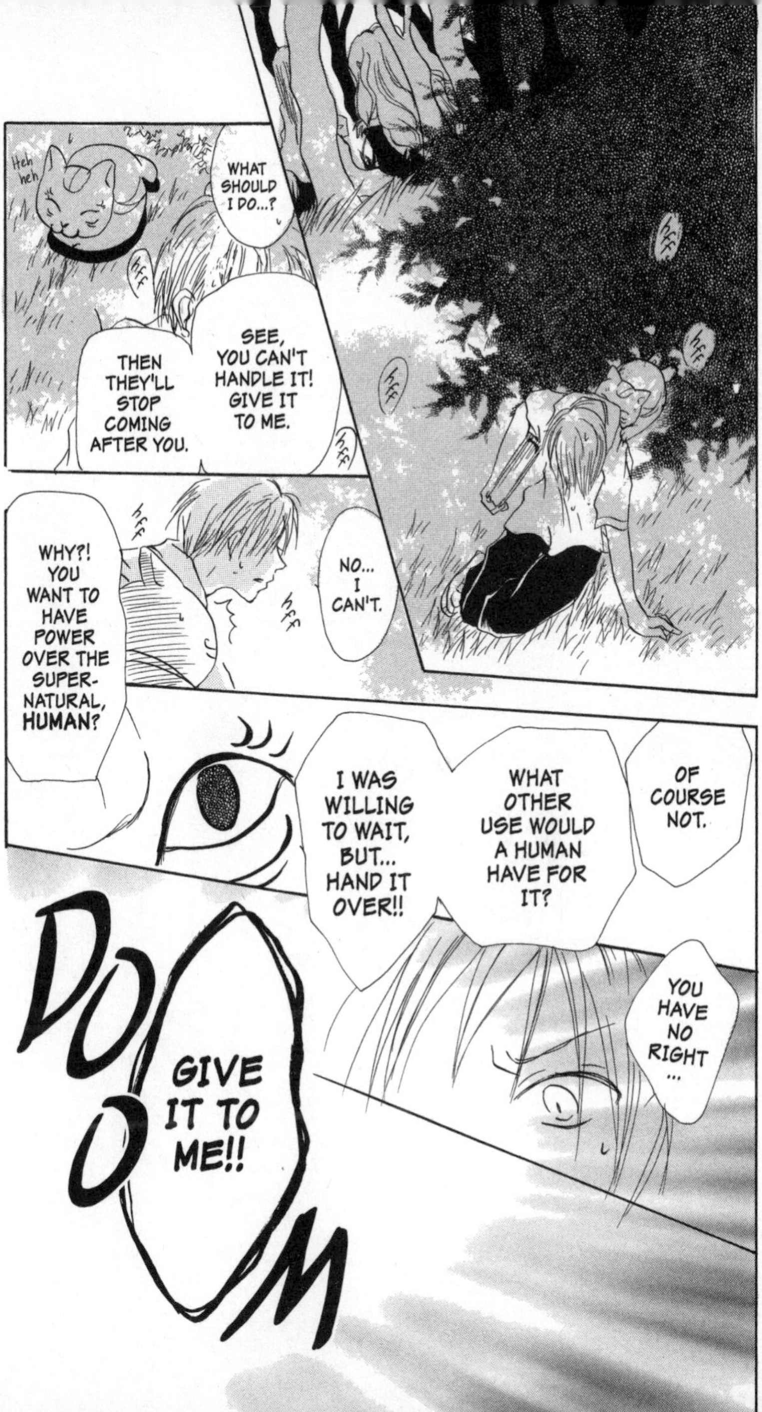
hff
hff
hff
hff
WHAT SHOULD I DO...?
Heh heh
hff
SEE, YOU CAN'T HANDLE IT! GIVE IT TO ME.
THEN THEY'LL STOP COMING AFTER YOU.
NO... I CAN'T.
hff
hff
WHY?! YOU WANT TO HAVE POWER OVER THE SUPER-NATURAL, HUMAN?
OF COURSE NOT.
WHAT OTHER USE WOULD A HUMAN HAVE FOR IT?
I WAS WILLING TO WAIT, BUT... HAND IT OVER!!
YOU HAVE NO RIGHT...
GIVE IT TO ME!!
DOOOM

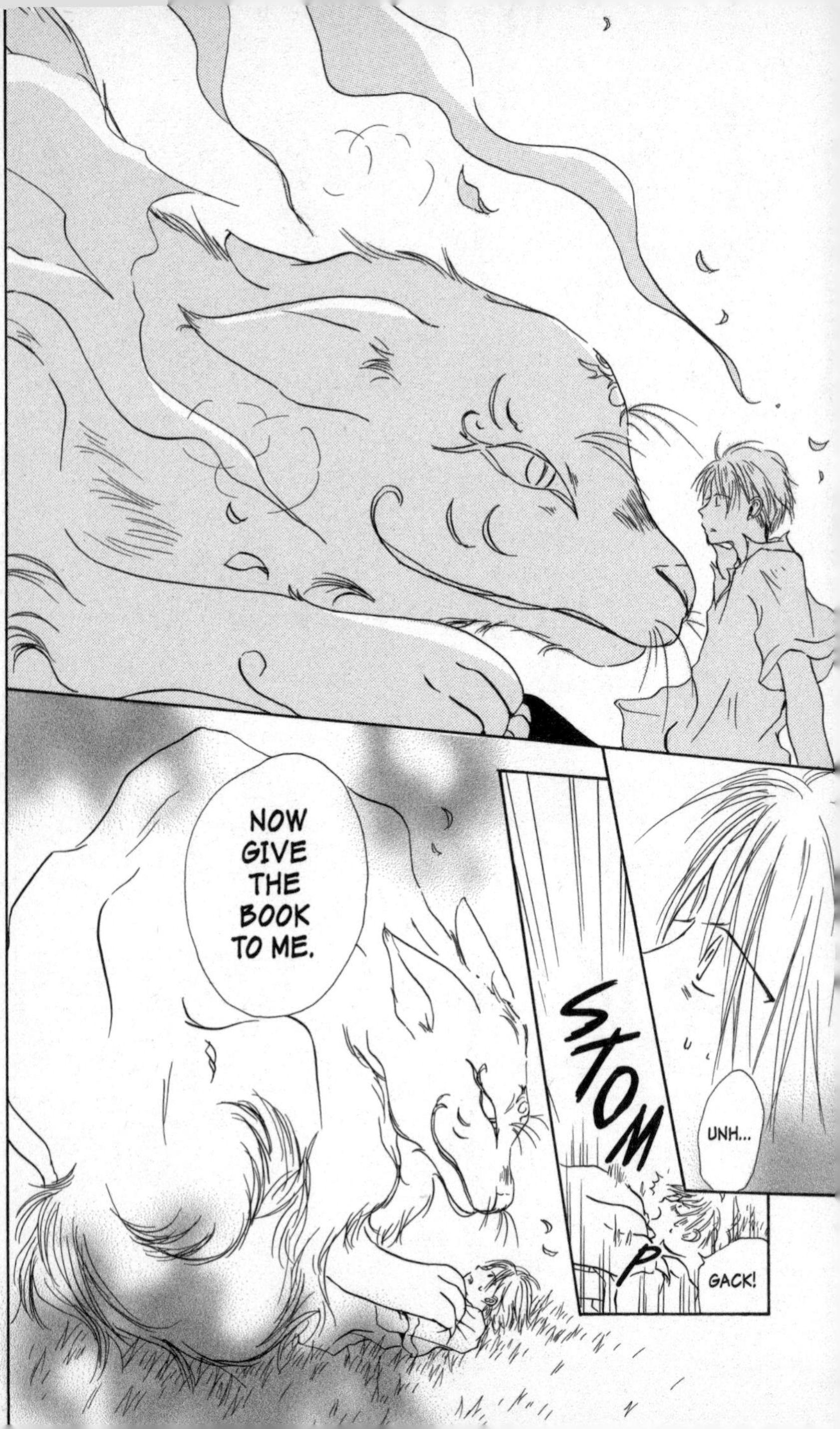
UNH...
NOW GIVE THE BOOK TO ME.
STOMP
GACK!

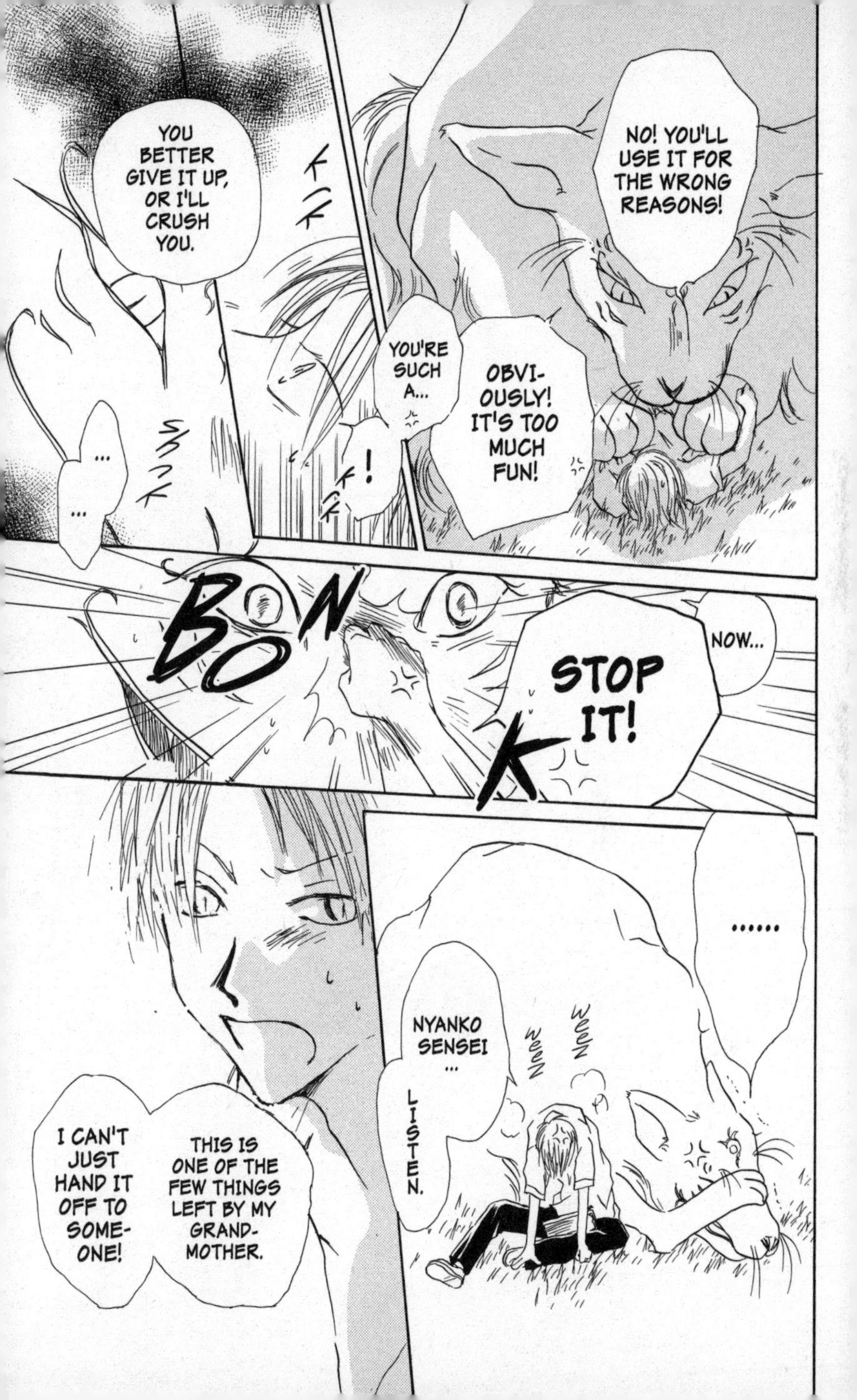

NO! YOU'LL USE IT FOR THE WRONG REASONS!
OBVI-OUSLY! IT'S TOO MUCH FUN!
YOU'RE SUCH A...
KICK!
KICK
YOU BETTER GIVE IT UP, OR I'LL CRUSH YOU.
SMACK
... ...
NOW...
STOP IT!
BONK
......
WEEZ WEEZ
NYANKO SENSEI...
LISTEN.
THIS IS ONE OF THE FEW THINGS LEFT BY MY GRAND-MOTHER.
I CAN'T JUST HAND IT OFF TO SOME-ONE!

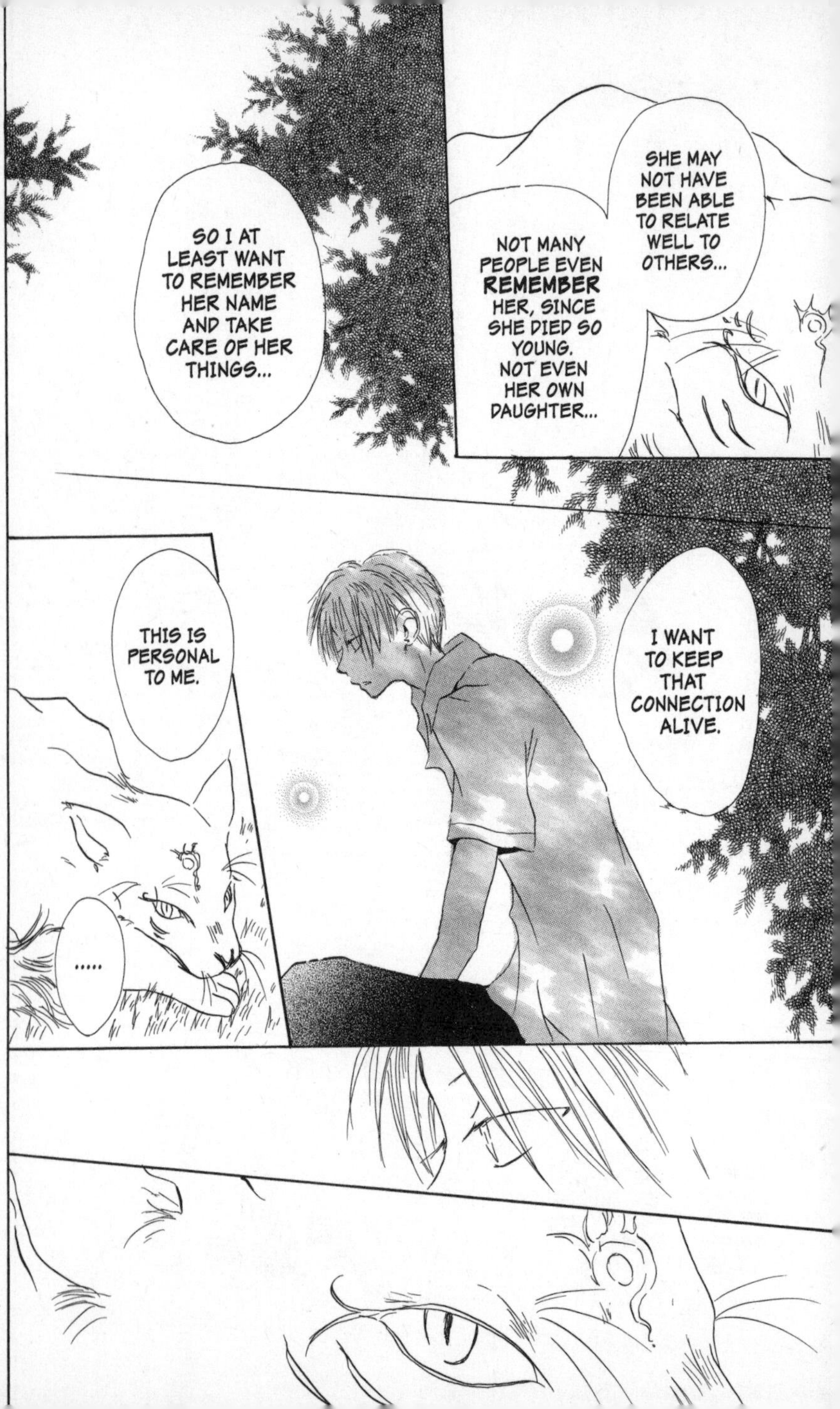
SHE MAY NOT HAVE BEEN ABLE TO RELATE WELL TO OTHERS...
NOT MANY PEOPLE EVEN **REMEMBER** HER, SINCE SHE DIED SO YOUNG. NOT EVEN HER OWN DAUGHTER...
SO I AT LEAST WANT TO REMEMBER HER NAME AND TAKE CARE OF HER THINGS...
I WANT TO KEEP THAT CONNECTION ALIVE.
THIS IS PERSONAL TO ME.
.....

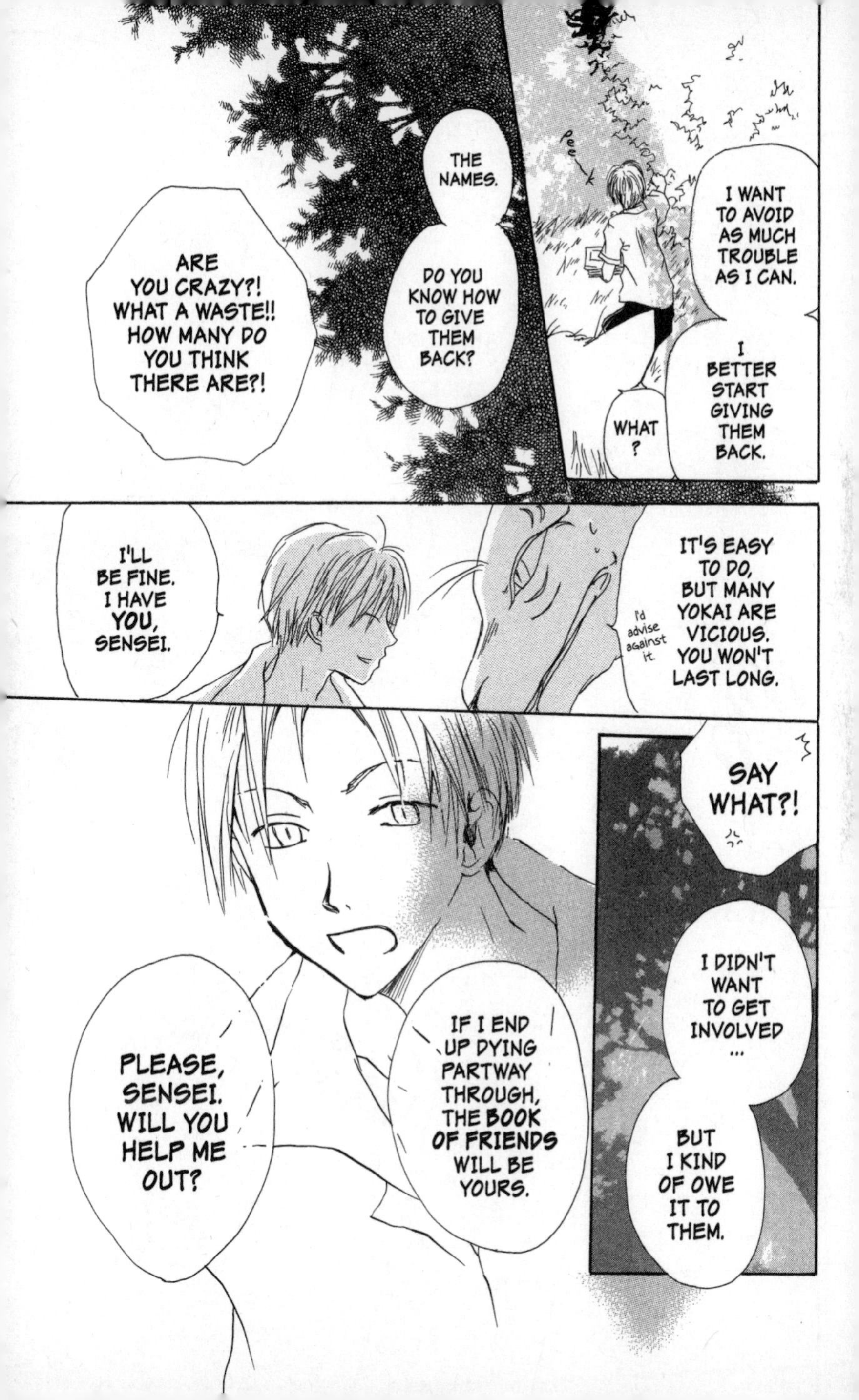
I WANT TO AVOID AS MUCH TROUBLE AS I CAN.
I BETTER START GIVING THEM BACK.
WHAT?
Pee-k
THE NAMES.
DO YOU KNOW HOW TO GIVE THEM BACK?
ARE YOU CRAZY?! WHAT A WASTE!! HOW MANY DO YOU THINK THERE ARE?!
IT'S EASY TO DO, BUT MANY YOKAI ARE VICIOUS. YOU WON'T LAST LONG.
I'd advise against it.
I'LL BE FINE. I HAVE YOU, SENSEI.
SAY WHAT?!
I DIDN'T WANT TO GET INVOLVED...
BUT I KIND OF OWE IT TO THEM.
IF I END UP DYING PARTWAY THROUGH, THE BOOK OF FRIENDS WILL BE YOURS.
PLEASE, SENSEI. WILL YOU HELP ME OUT?

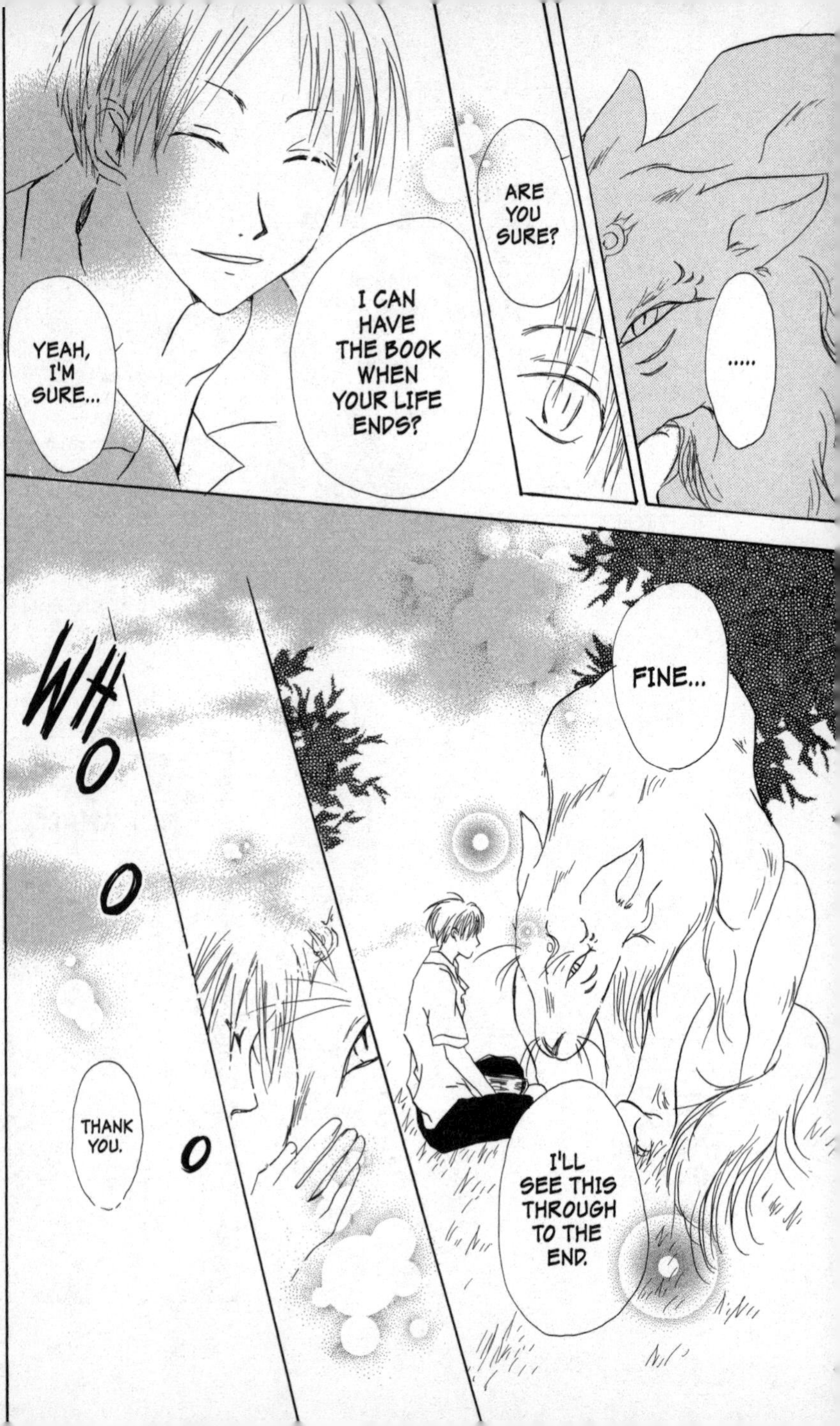
.....
ARE YOU SURE?
I CAN HAVE THE BOOK WHEN YOUR LIFE ENDS?
YEAH, I'M SURE...
FINE...
I'LL SEE THIS THROUGH TO THE END.
WHOOOO
THANK YOU.

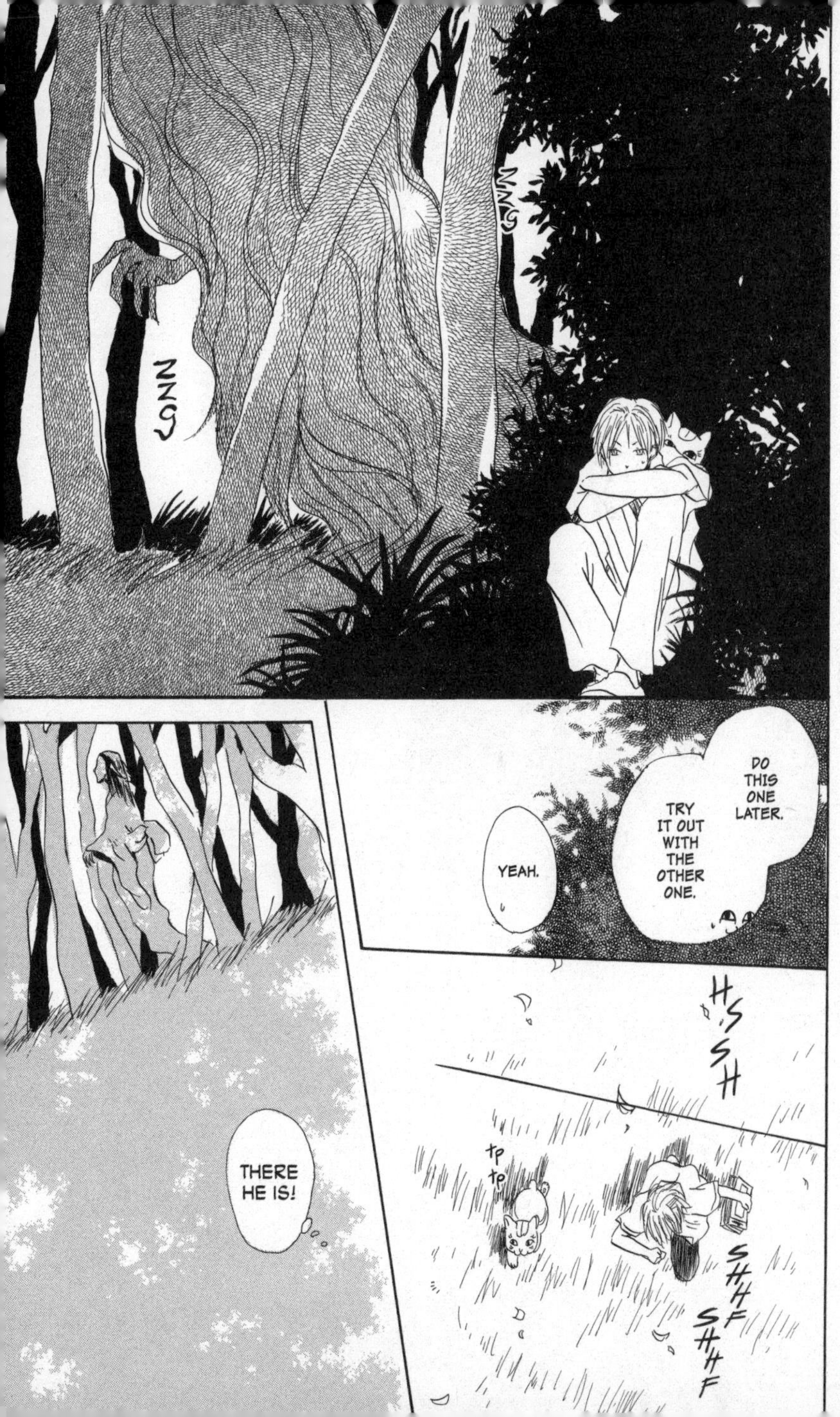
DO THIS ONE LATER.
TRY IT OUT WITH THE OTHER ONE.
YEAH.
HSSH
tp tp
SHHF
SHHF
THERE HE IS!

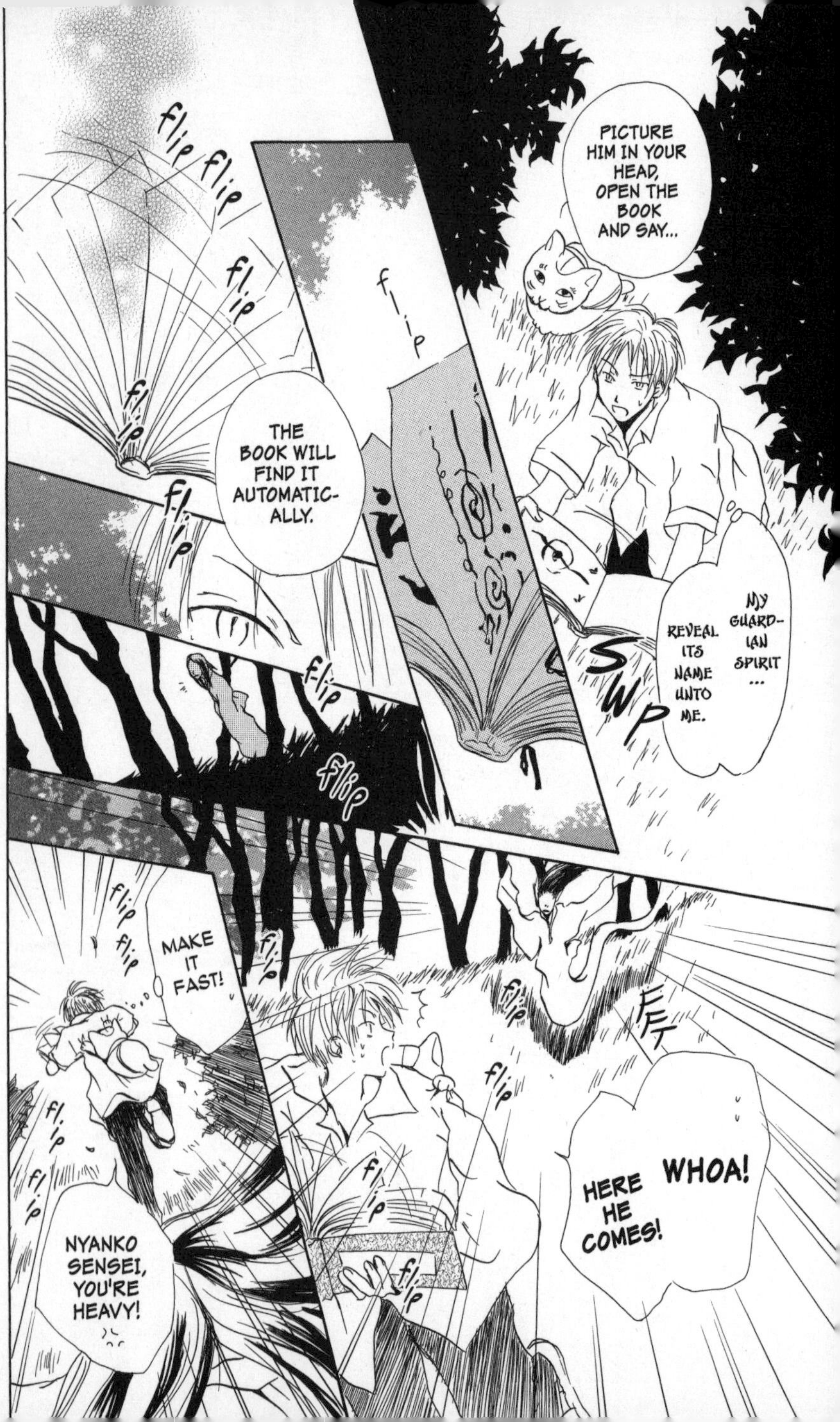
PICTURE HIM IN YOUR HEAD, OPEN THE BOOK AND SAY...
flip flip
flip
flip
flip
MY GUARDIAN SPIRIT...
REVEAL ITS NAME UNTO ME.
SWP
flip
THE BOOK WILL FIND IT AUTOMATICALLY.
flip
flip
WHOA!
HERE HE COMES!
FFT
flip
flip
flip
MAKE IT FAST!
flip flip
flip
flip
NYANKO SENSEI, YOU'RE HEAVY!

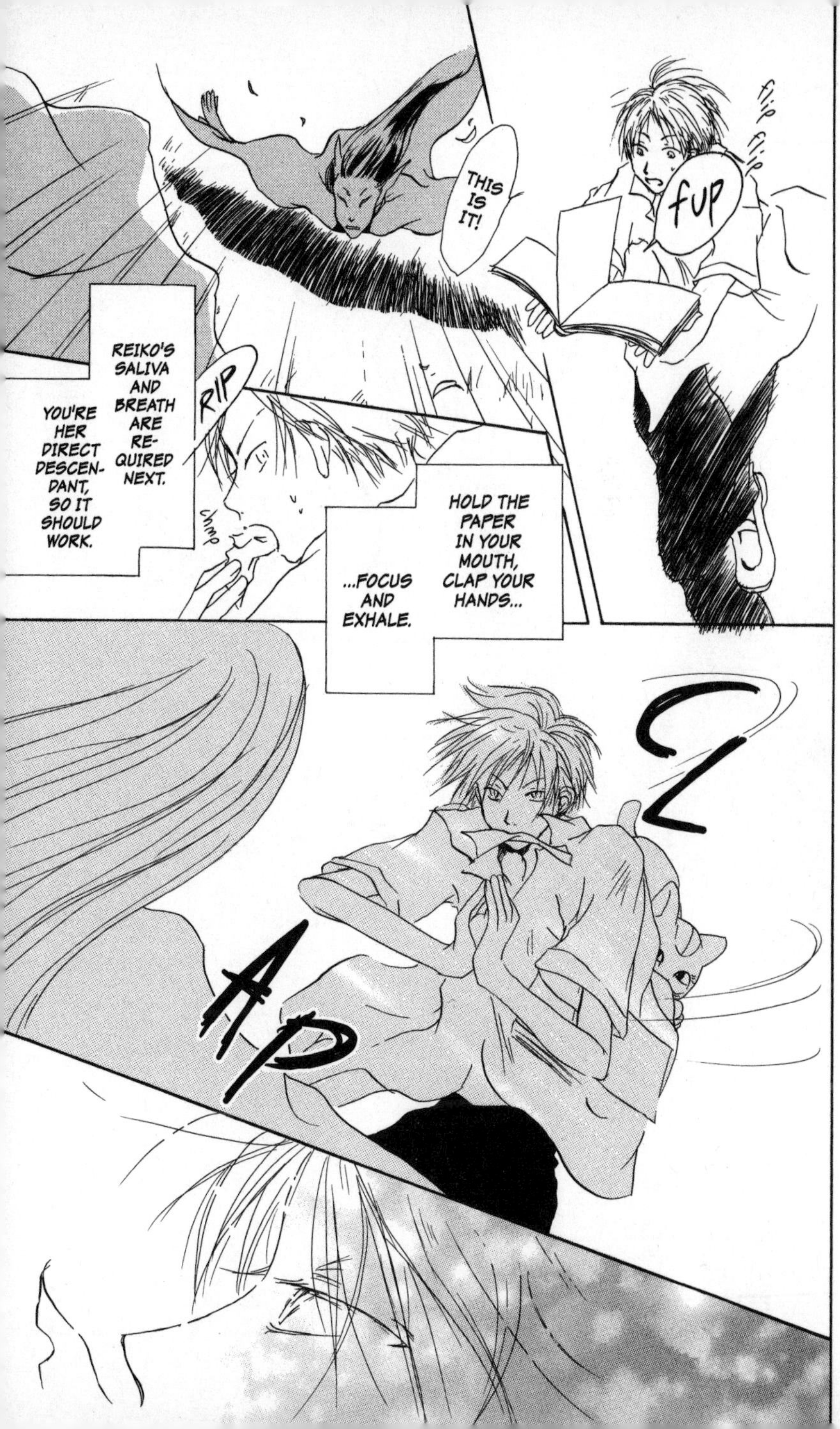
flip flip
fup
THIS IS IT!
RIP
REIKO'S SALIVA AND BREATH ARE RE-QUIRED NEXT.
YOU'RE HER DIRECT DESCEN-DANT, SO IT SHOULD WORK.
chomp
HOLD THE PAPER IN YOUR MOUTH, CLAP YOUR HANDS...
...FOCUS AND EXHALE.
CL
AP

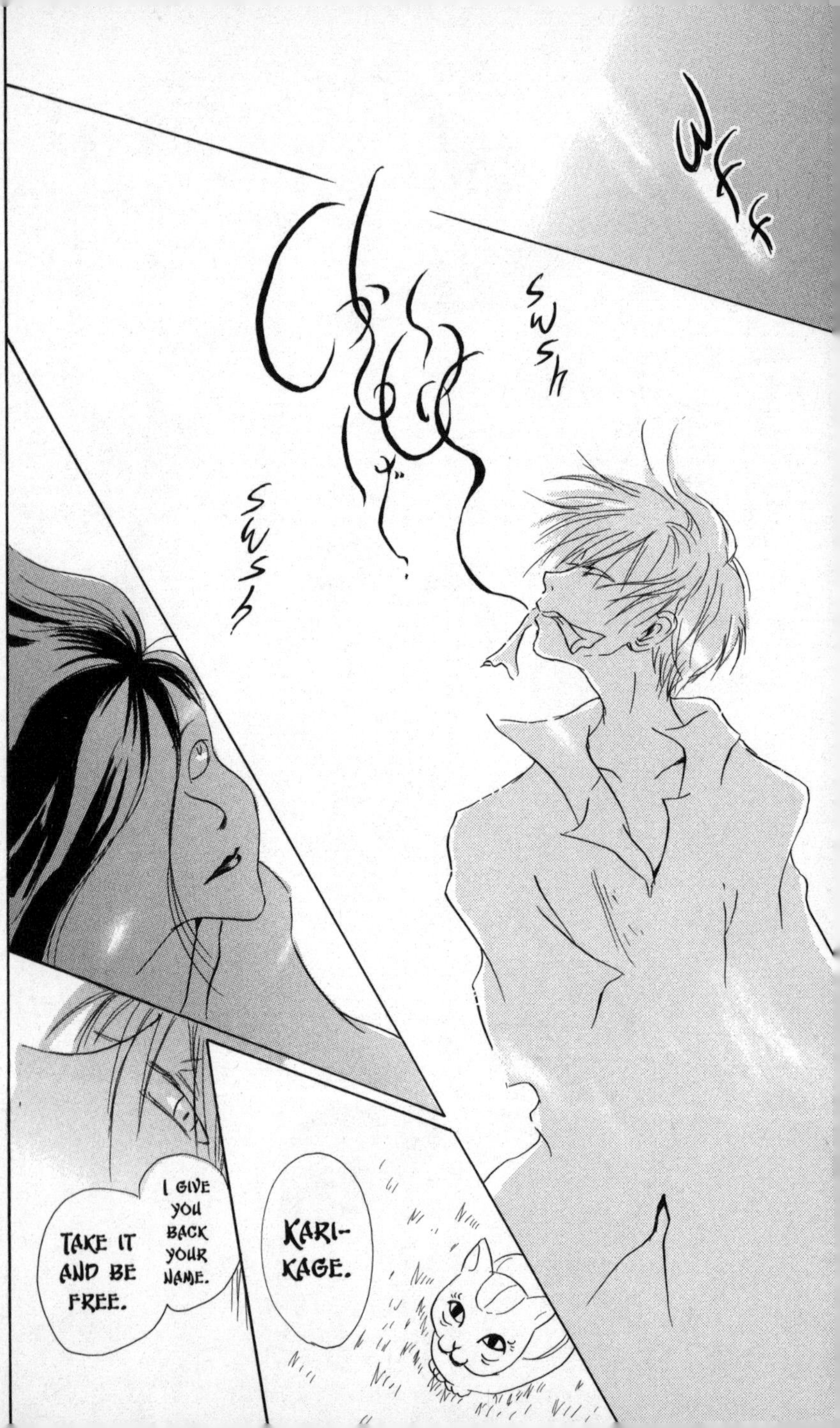
wff
swsh
swsh
KARI-KAGE.
I GIVE YOU BACK YOUR NAME.
TAKE IT AND BE FREE.

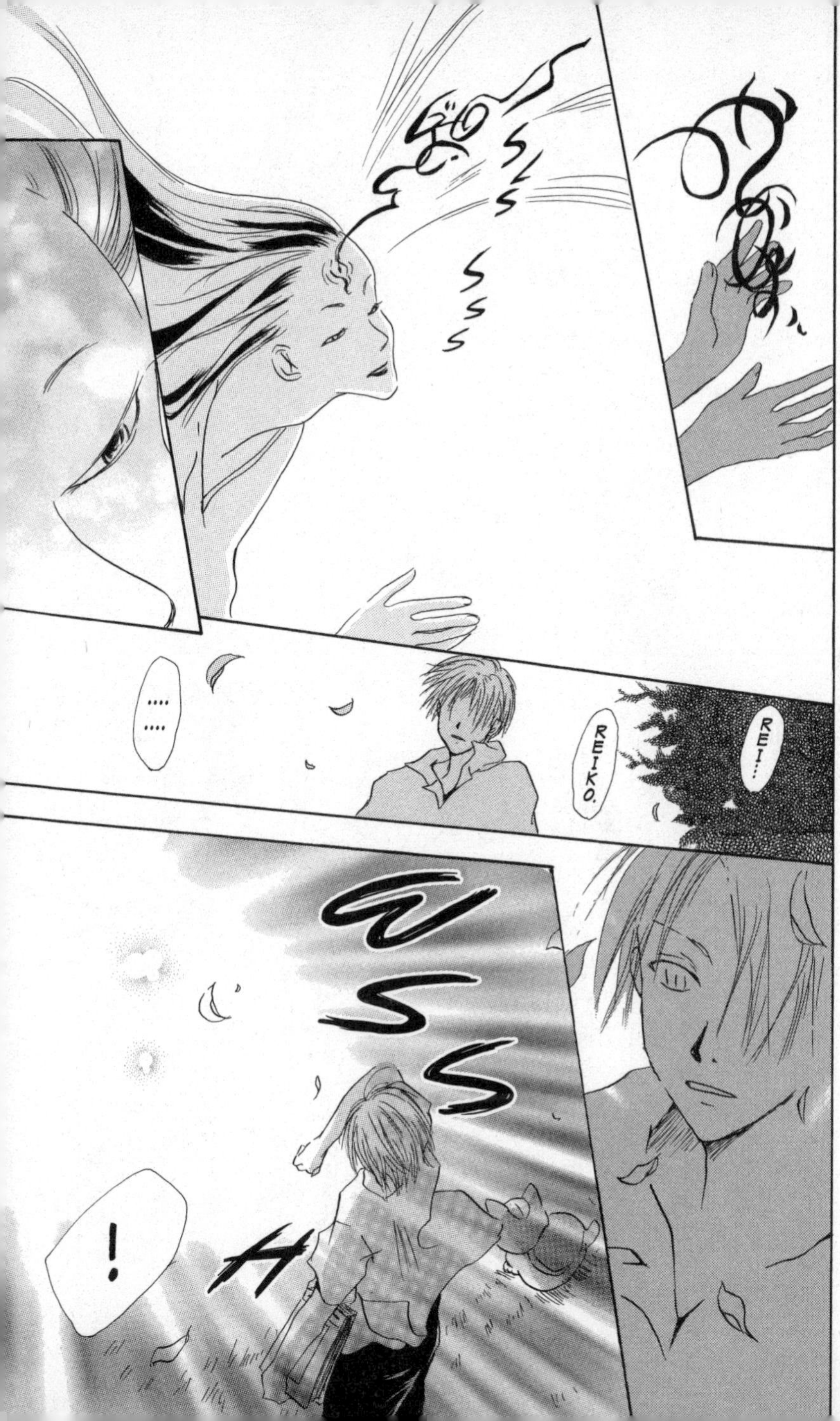
SSSS
REI...
REIKO.
......
......
WSSH
!

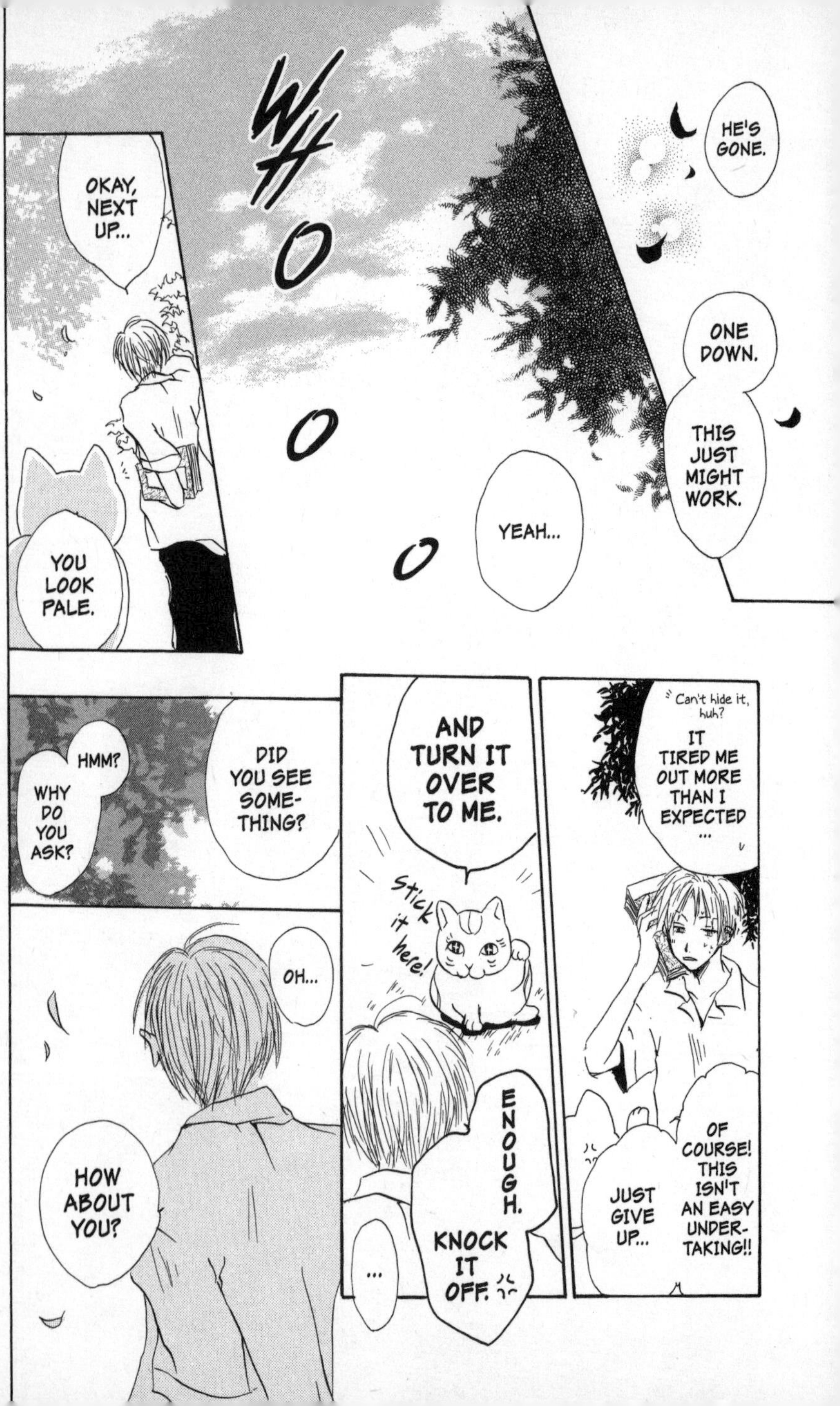
HE'S GONE.
ONE DOWN.
THIS JUST MIGHT WORK.
YEAH...
WHOOO
OKAY, NEXT UP...
YOU LOOK PALE.
Can't hide it, huh?
IT TIRED ME OUT MORE THAN I EXPECTED...
OF COURSE! THIS ISN'T AN EASY UNDER-TAKING!!
JUST GIVE UP...
AND TURN IT OVER TO ME.
Stick it here!
ENOUGH.
KNOCK IT OFF.
...
DID YOU SEE SOME-THING?
HMM?
WHY DO YOU ASK?
OH...
HOW ABOUT YOU?

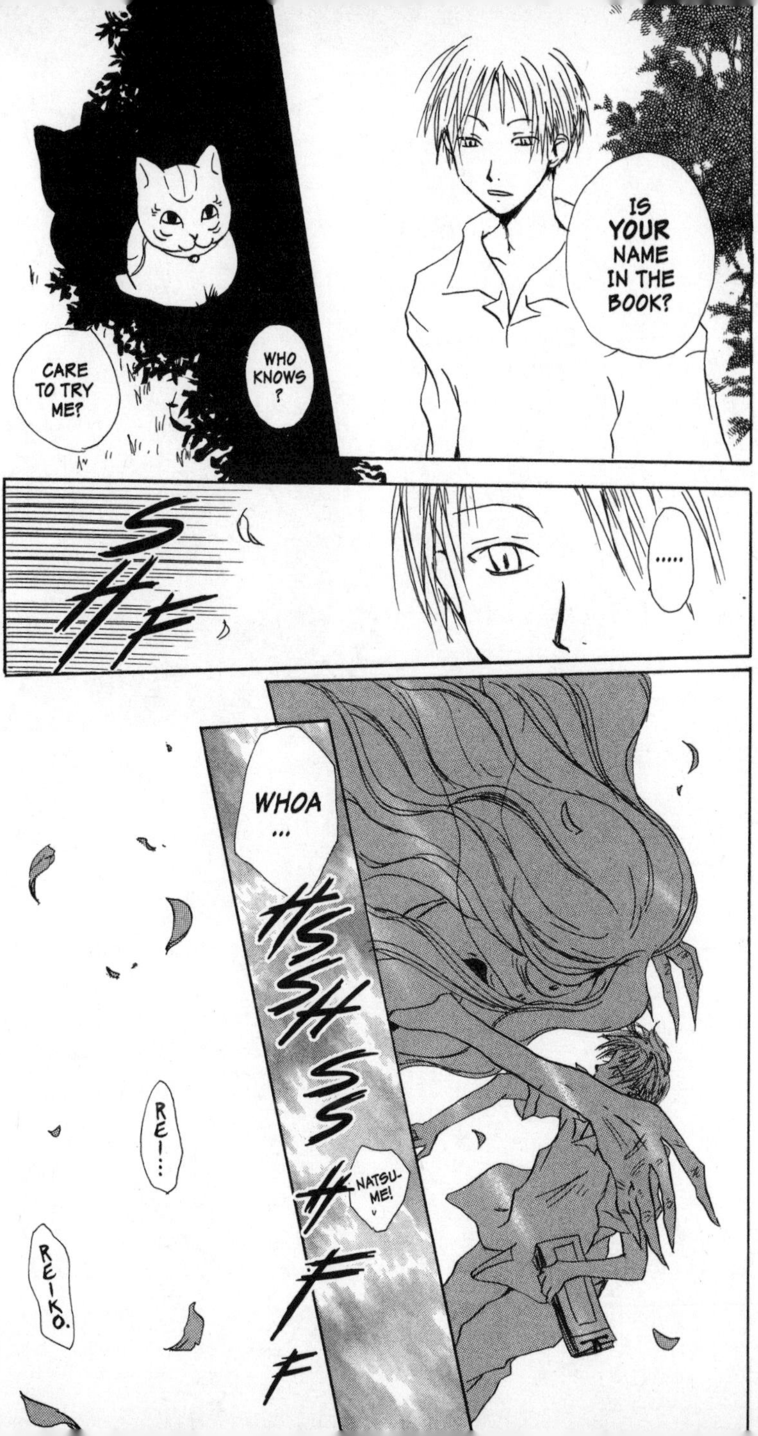
IS YOUR NAME IN THE BOOK?
WHO KNOWS?
CARE TO TRY ME?
SHFF
......
WHOA...
HSSHSSHFF
NATSU-ME!
REI...
REIKO.

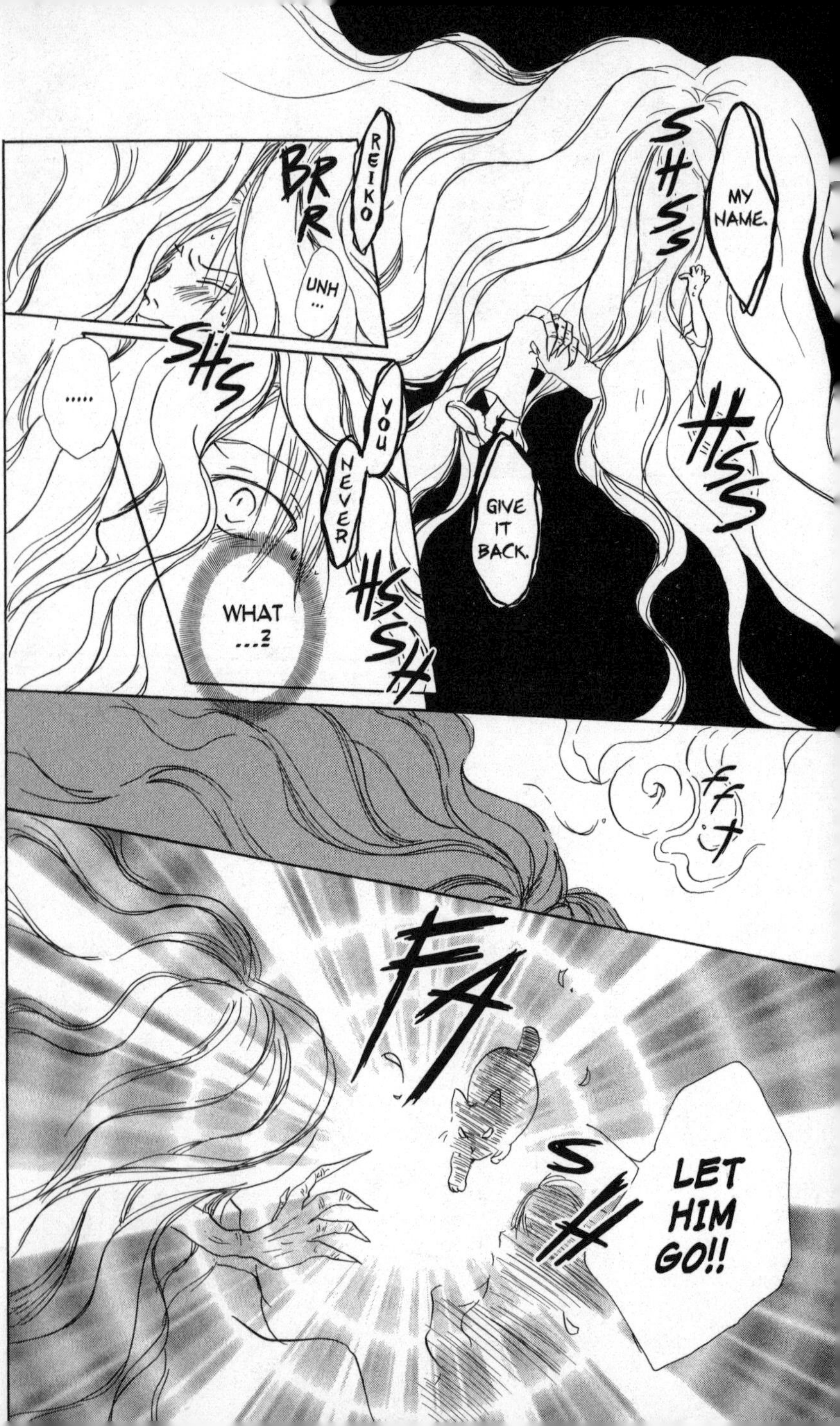
SHSS
MY NAME.
HSS
GIVE IT BACK.
REIKO
BRR
UNH ...
YOU
NEVER
SHS
HSSSH
WHAT ...?
.....
FFT
FA
SH
LET HIM GO!!

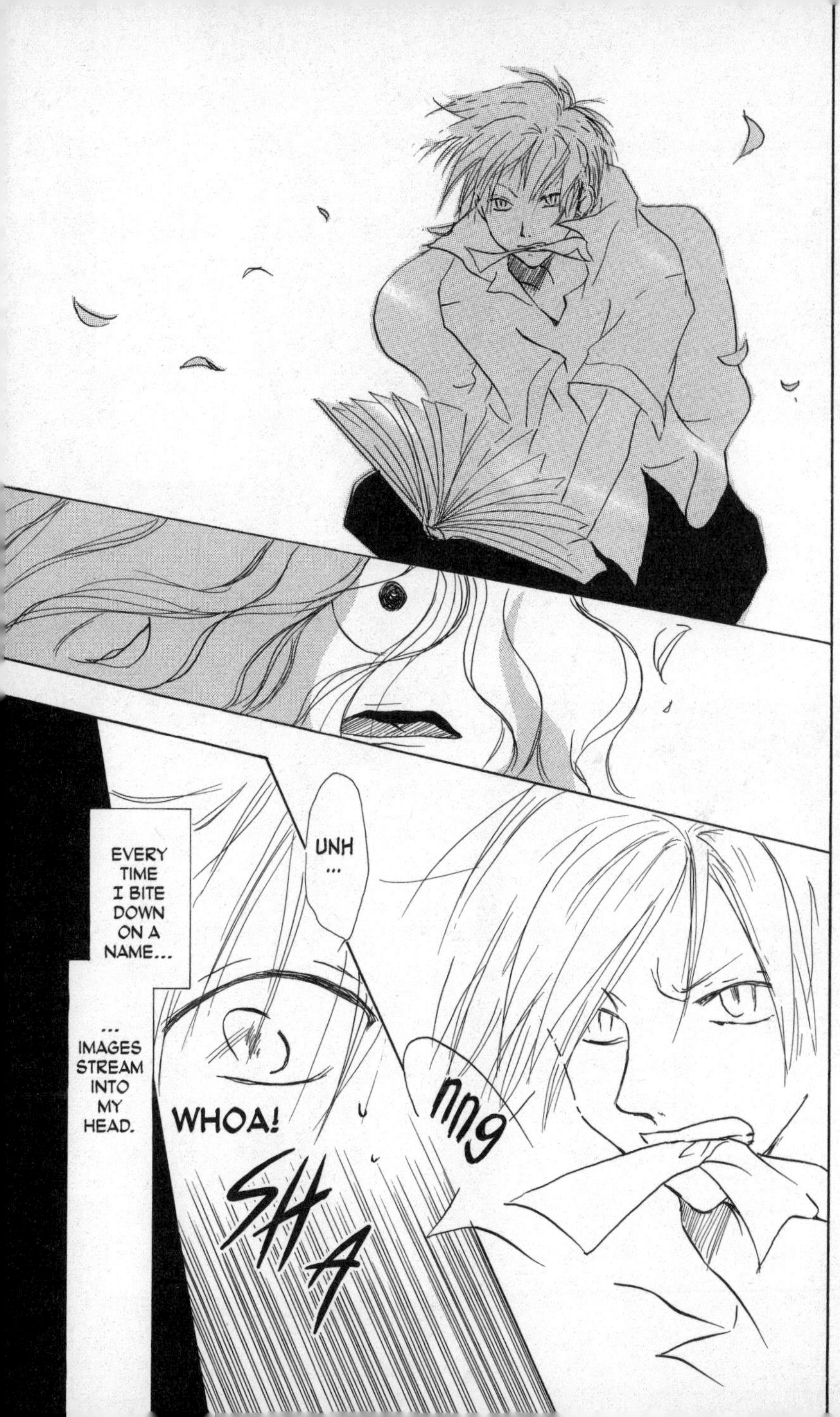
UNH ...
EVERY TIME I BITE DOWN ON A NAME...
nng
WHOA!
...IMAGES STREAM INTO MY HEAD.
SHA

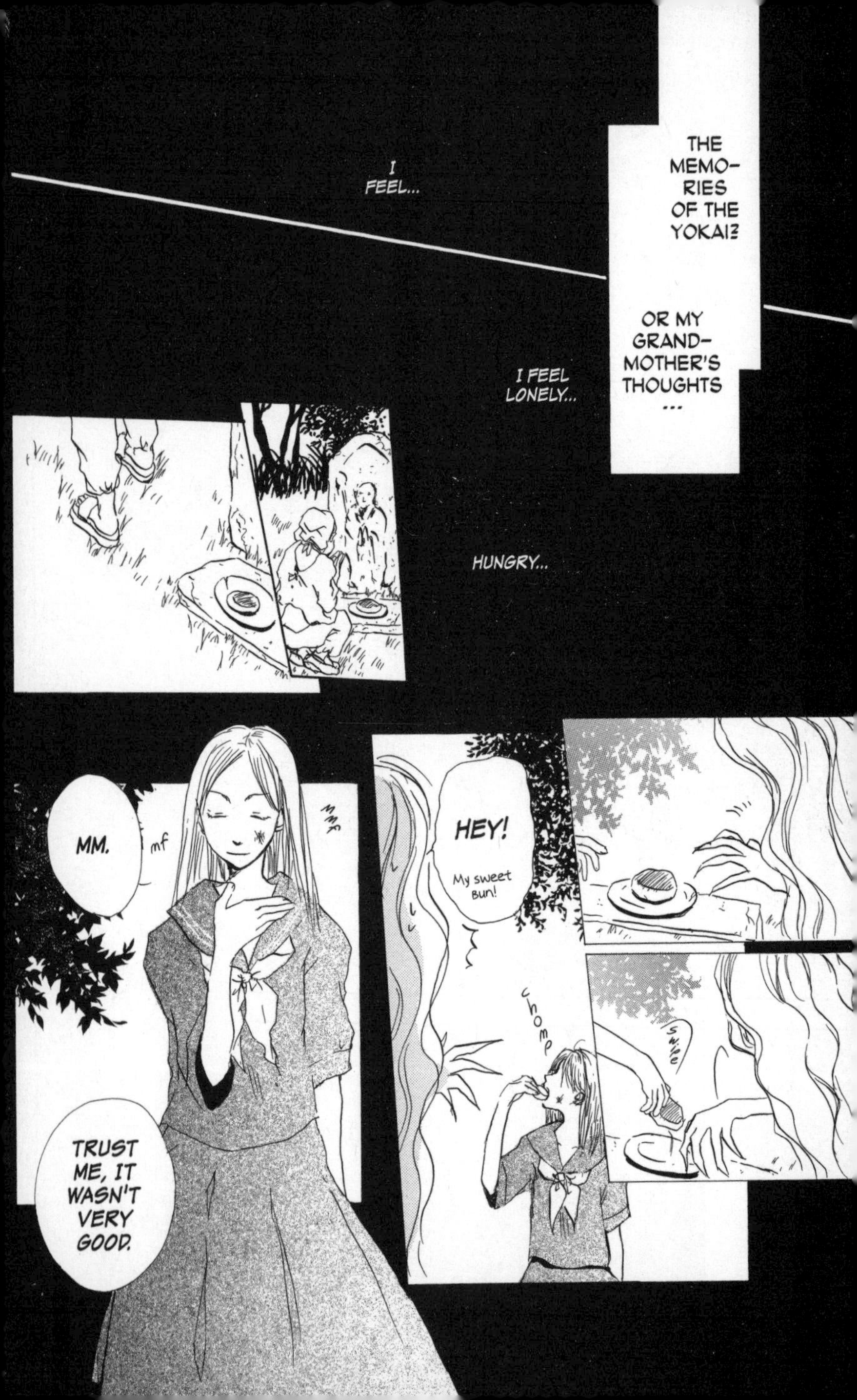
THE MEMORIES OF THE YOKAI?
OR MY GRANDMOTHER'S THOUGHTS...
I FEEL...
I FEEL LONELY...
HUNGRY...
swipe
HEY!
My sweet Bun!
chomp
mmf
mf
MM.
TRUST ME, IT WASN'T VERY GOOD.

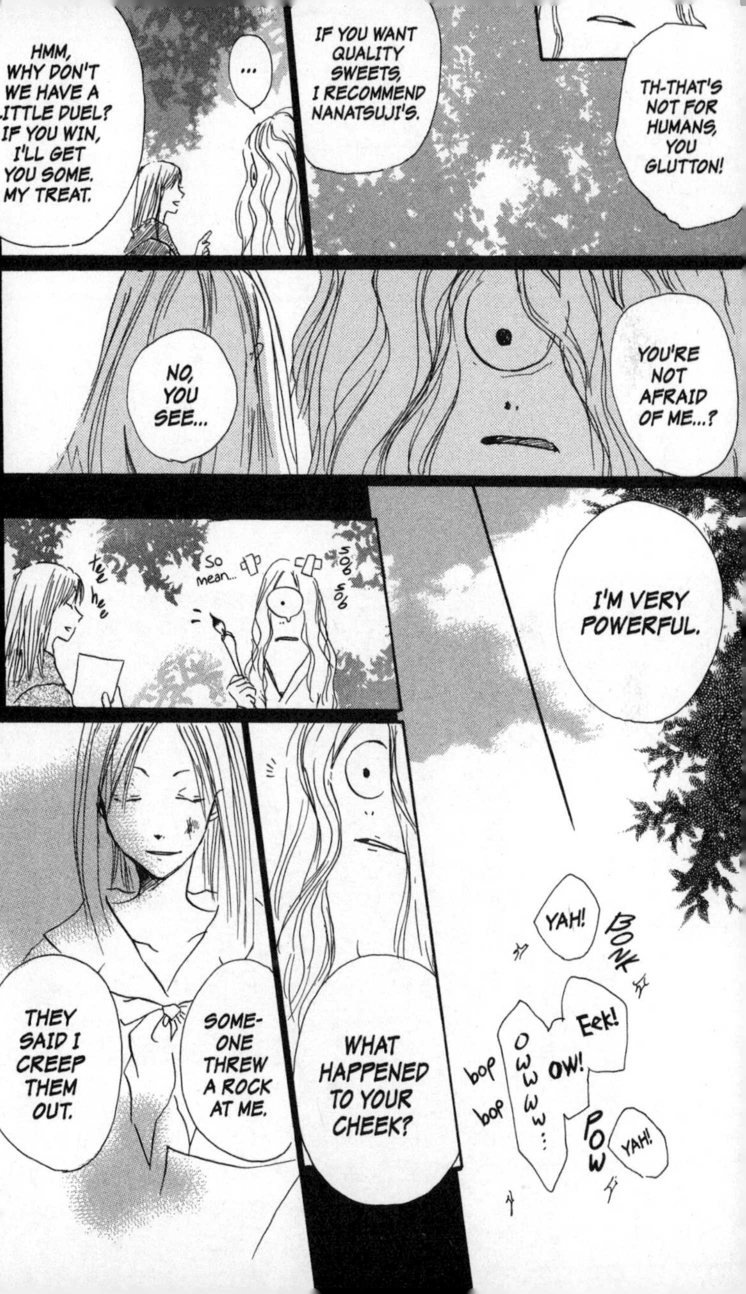
TH-THAT'S NOT FOR HUMANS, YOU GLUTTON!
IF YOU WANT QUALITY SWEETS, I RECOMMEND NANATSUJI'S.
...
HMM, WHY DON'T WE HAVE A LITTLE DUEL? IF YOU WIN, I'LL GET YOU SOME. MY TREAT.
YOU'RE NOT AFRAID OF ME...?
NO, YOU SEE...
I'M VERY POWERFUL.
YAH!
BONK
Eek!
OW!
OWWWW...
bop bop
POW
YAH!
sob sob
So mean...
tee hee
WHAT HAPPENED TO YOUR CHEEK?
SOME-ONE THREW A ROCK AT ME.
THEY SAID I CREEP THEM OUT.

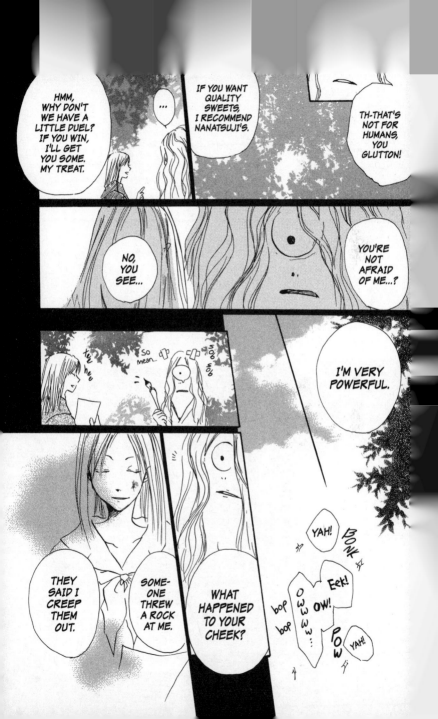

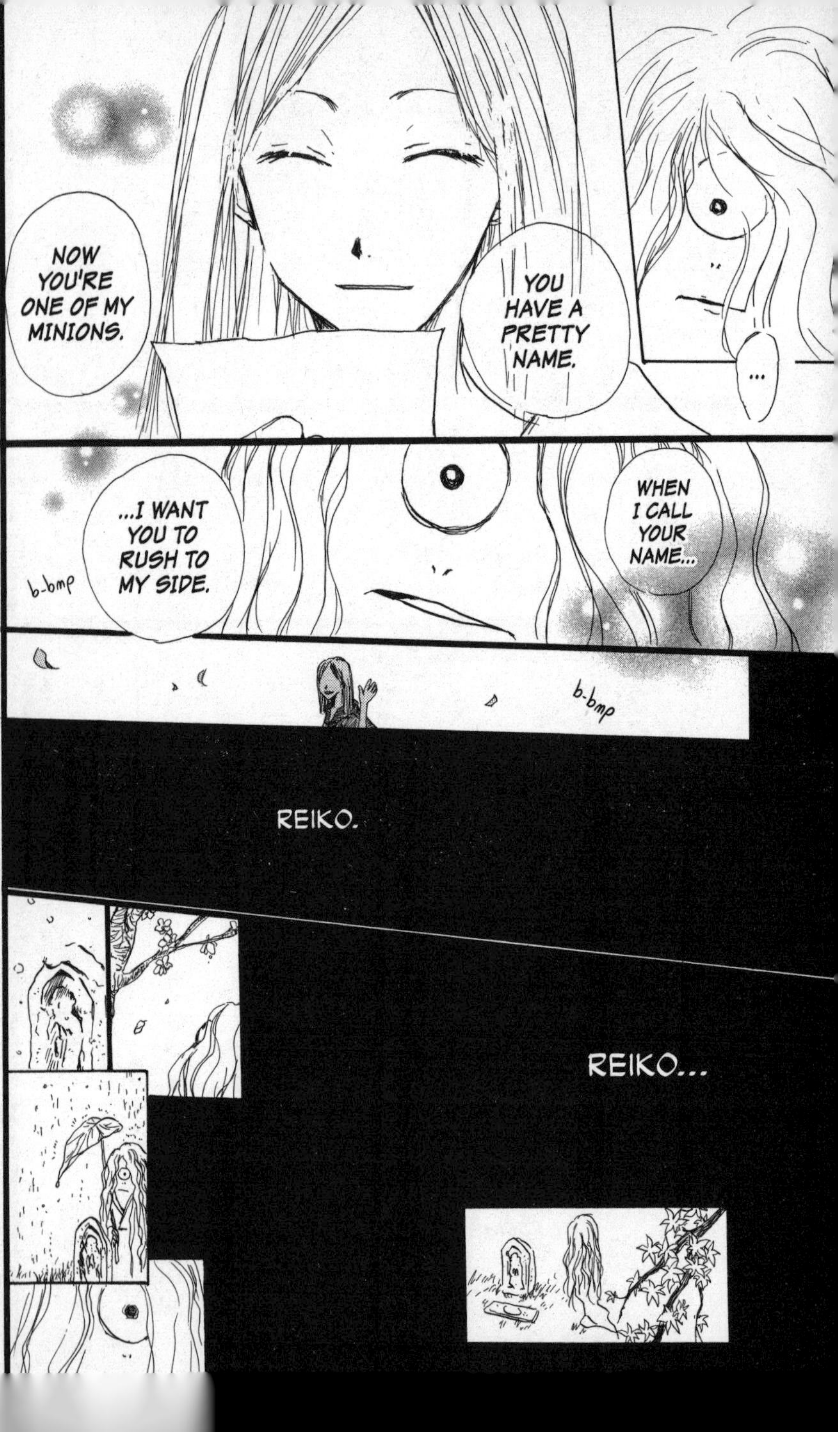
...
YOU HAVE A PRETTY NAME.
NOW YOU'RE ONE OF MY MINIONS.
WHEN I CALL YOUR NAME...
...I WANT YOU TO RUSH TO MY SIDE.
b-bmp
b-bmp
REIKO.
REIKO...

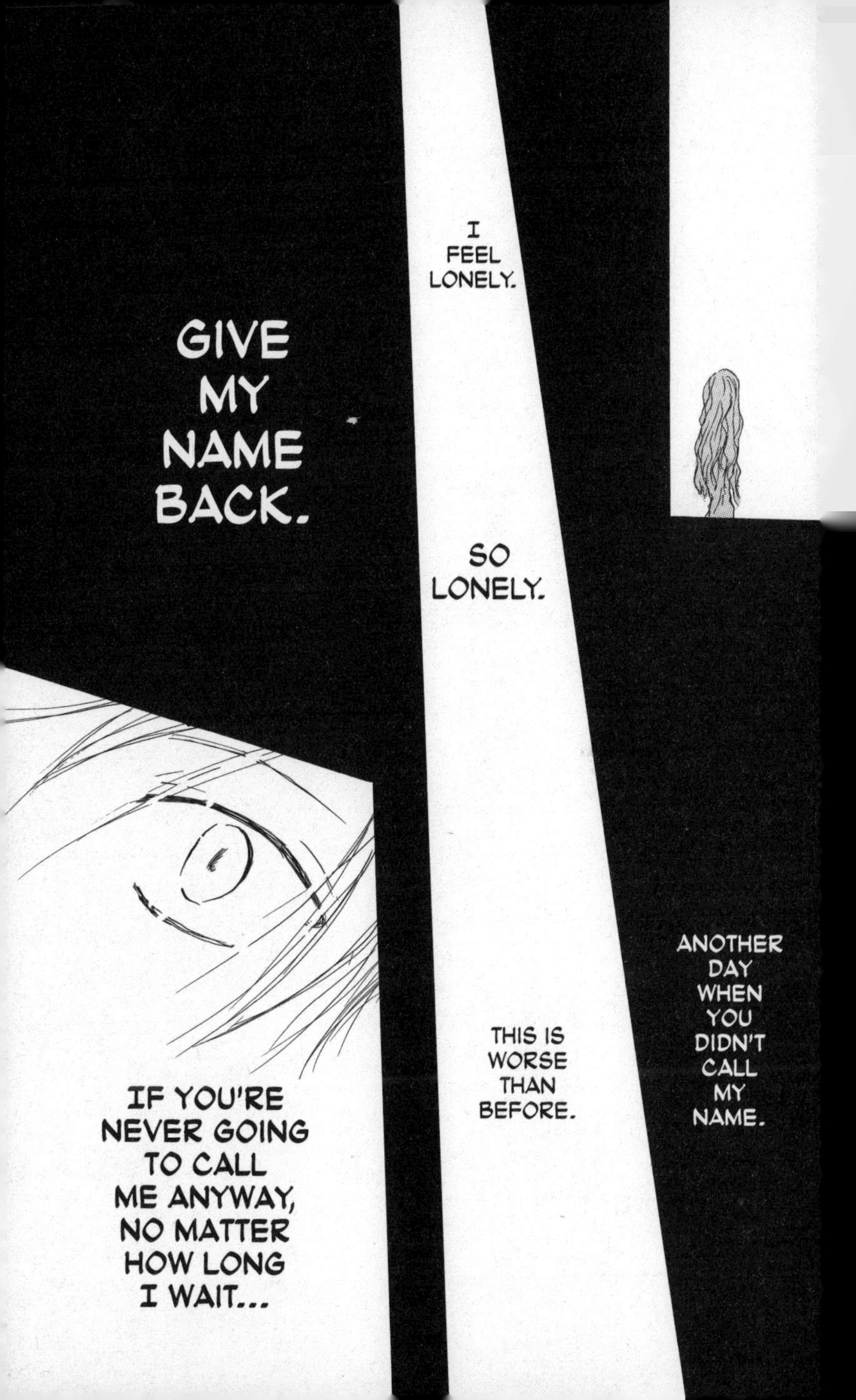
ANOTHER DAY WHEN YOU DIDN'T CALL MY NAME.
I FEEL LONELY.
SO LONELY.
THIS IS WORSE THAN BEFORE.
GIVE MY NAME BACK.
IF YOU'RE NEVER GOING TO CALL ME ANYWAY, NO MATTER HOW LONG I WAIT...

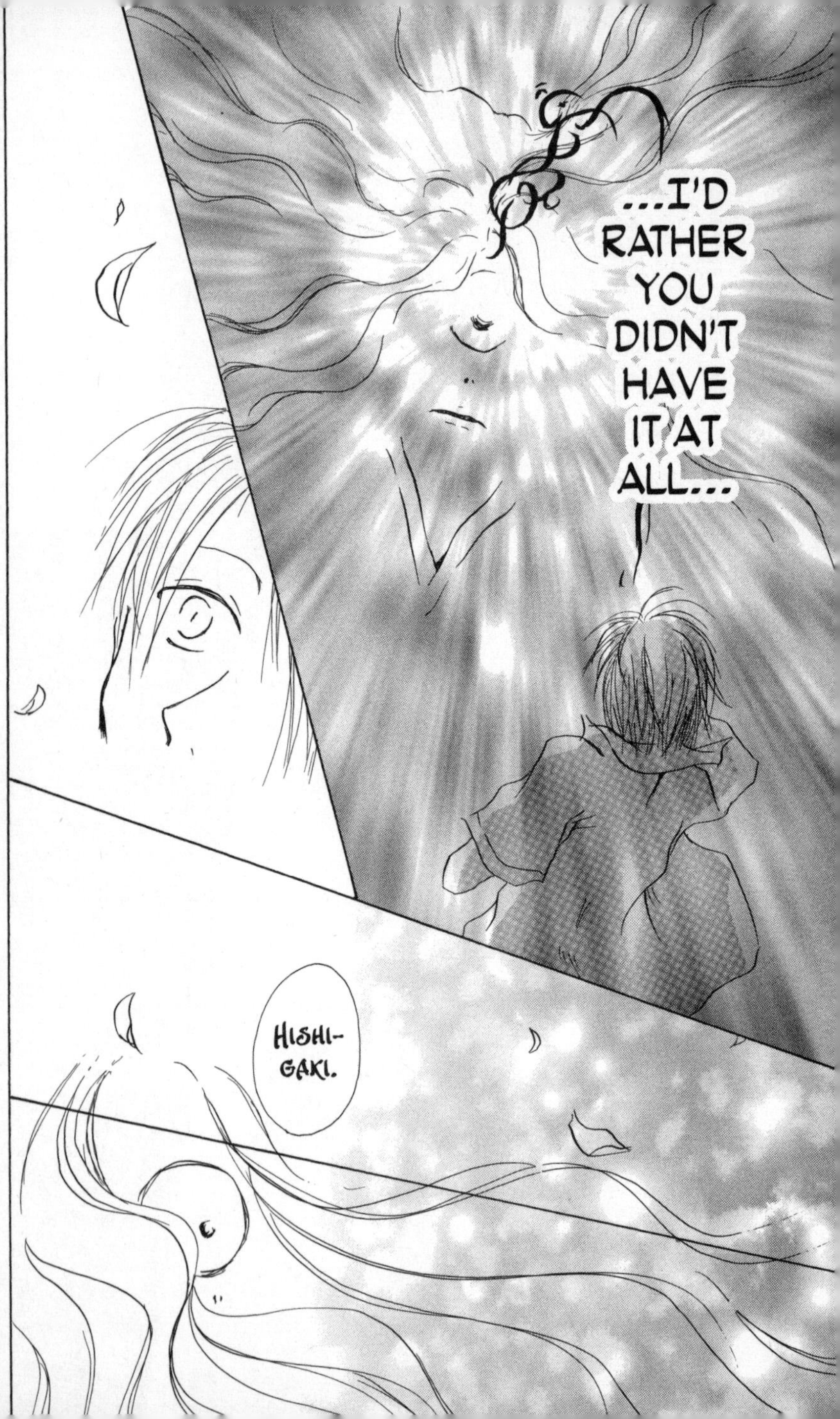
...I'D RATHER YOU DIDN'T HAVE IT AT ALL...
HISHI-GAKI.

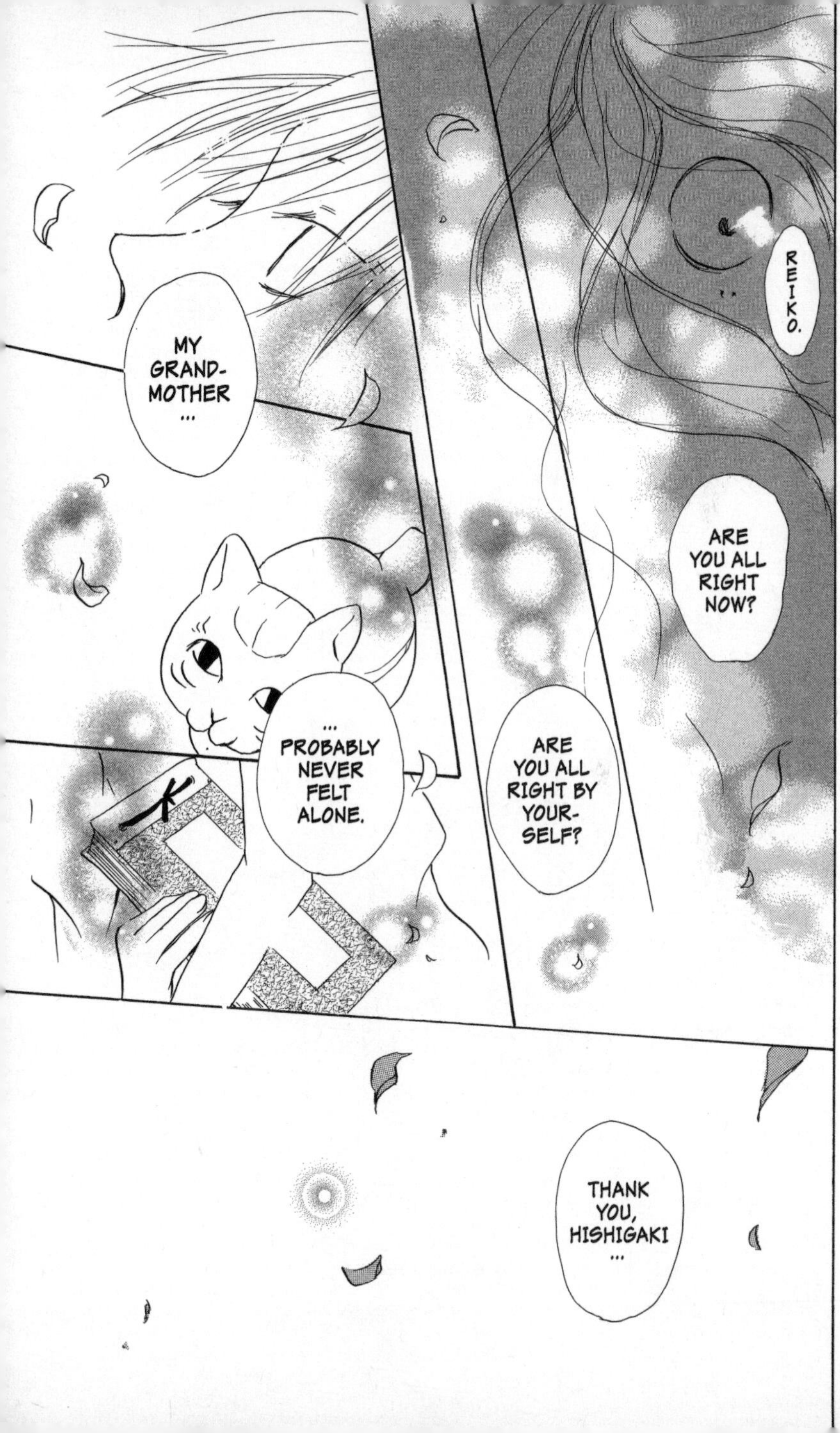
REIKO.
ARE YOU ALL RIGHT NOW?
ARE YOU ALL RIGHT BY YOURSELF?
MY GRANDMOTHER...
...PROBABLY NEVER FELT ALONE.
THANK YOU, HISHIGAKI...

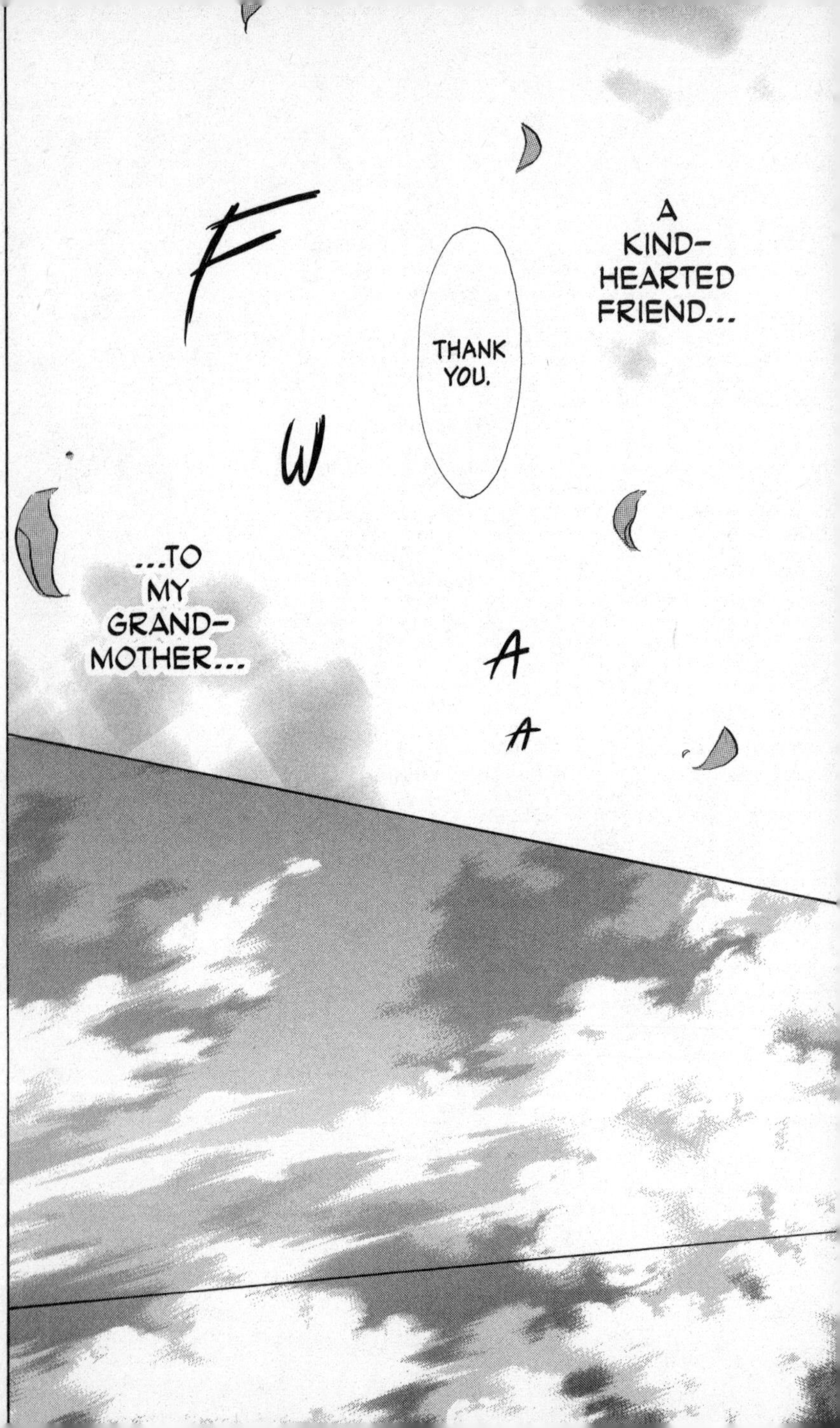
A KIND-HEARTED FRIEND...
THANK YOU.
FWAA
...TO MY GRANDMOTHER...

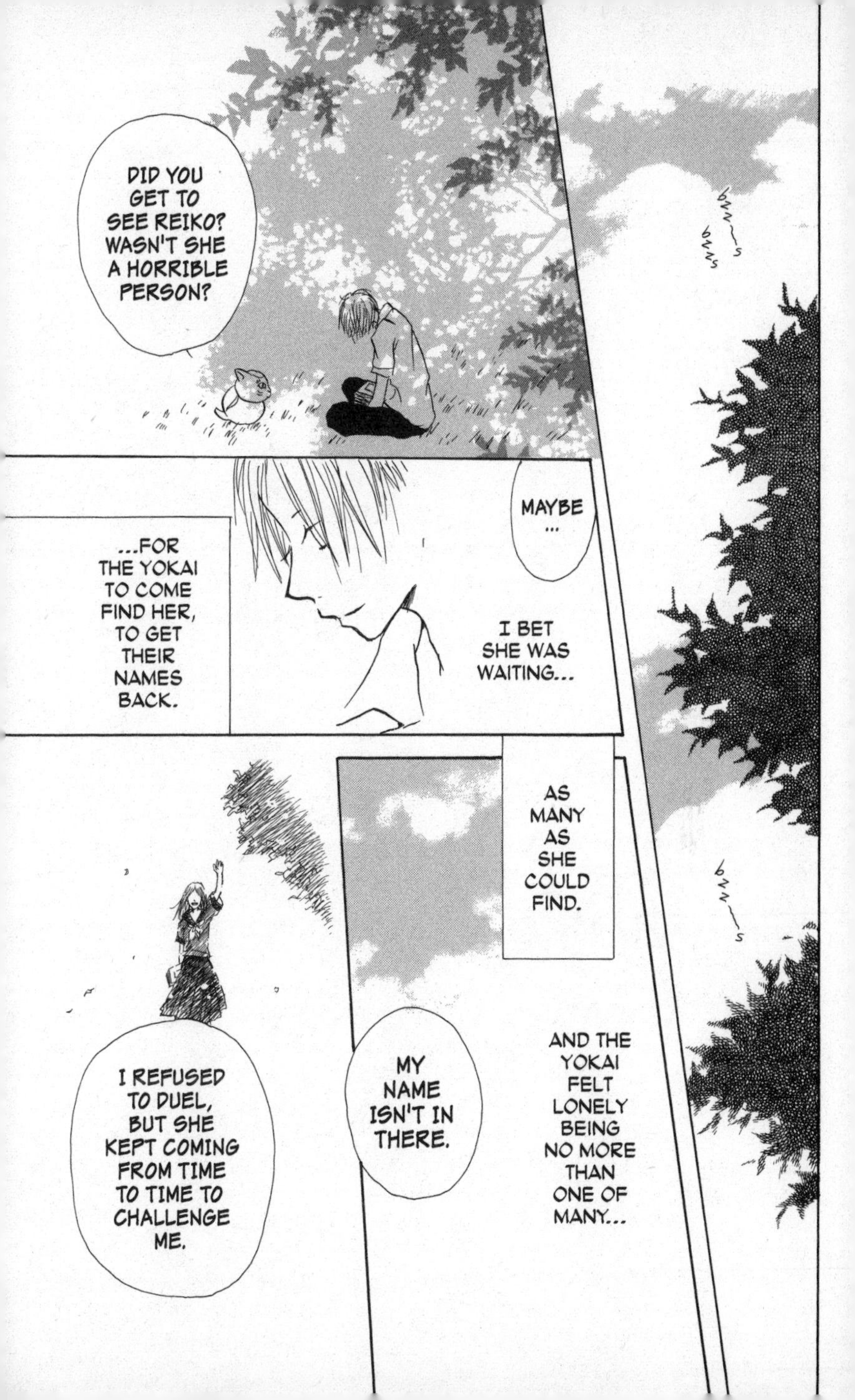
bzz~s
bzz~s
DID YOU GET TO SEE REIKO? WASN'T SHE A HORRIBLE PERSON?
MAYBE...
I BET SHE WAS WAITING...
...FOR THE YOKAI TO COME FIND HER, TO GET THEIR NAMES BACK.
AS MANY AS SHE COULD FIND.
bzz~s
AND THE YOKAI FELT LONELY BEING NO MORE THAN ONE OF MANY...
MY NAME ISN'T IN THERE.
I REFUSED TO DUEL, BUT SHE KEPT COMING FROM TIME TO TIME TO CHALLENGE ME.

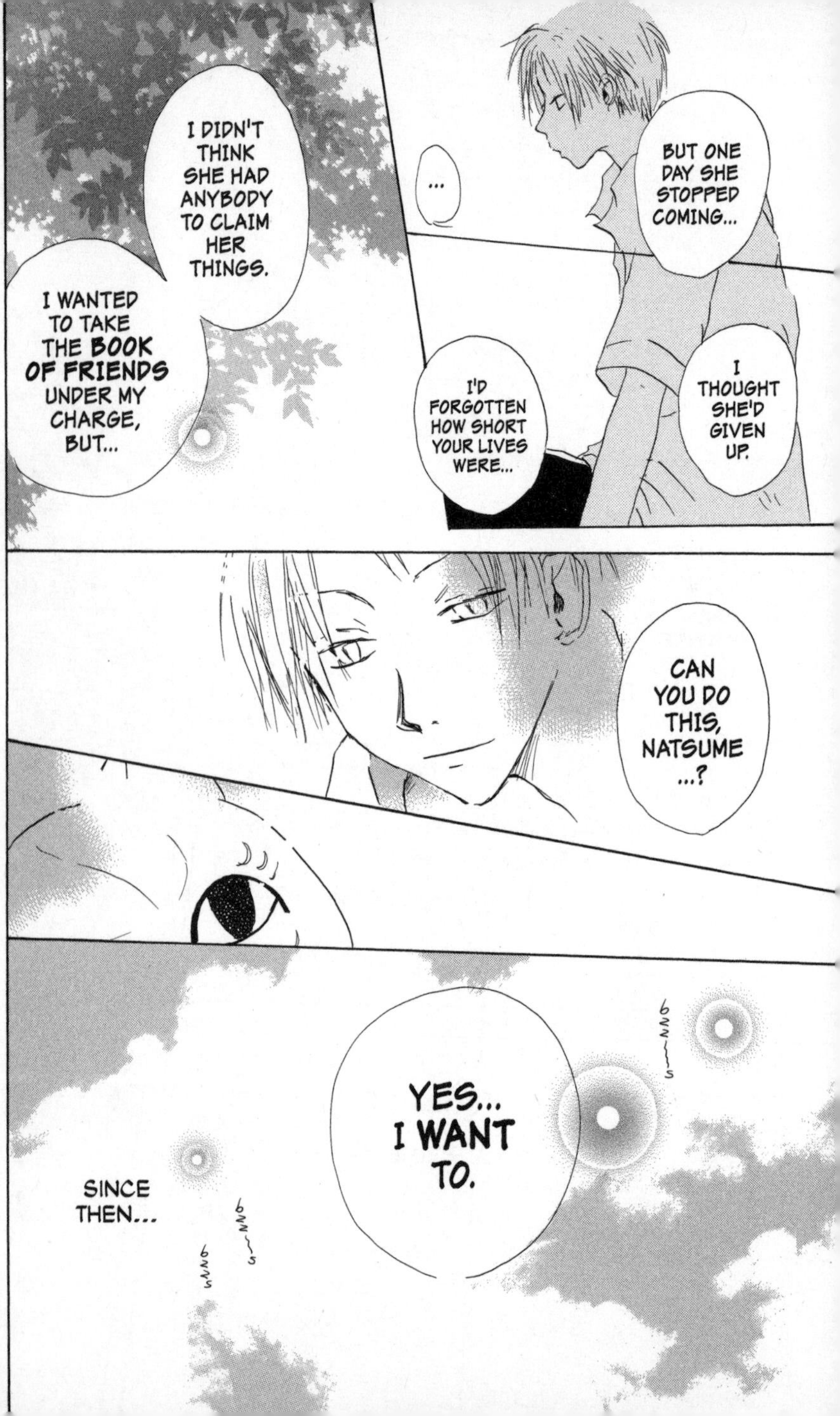
BUT ONE DAY SHE STOPPED COMING...
...
I THOUGHT SHE'D GIVEN UP.
I'D FORGOTTEN HOW SHORT YOUR LIVES WERE...
I DIDN'T THINK SHE HAD ANYBODY TO CLAIM HER THINGS.
I WANTED TO TAKE THE BOOK OF FRIENDS UNDER MY CHARGE, BUT...
CAN YOU DO THIS, NATSUME ...?
YES... I WANT TO.
SINCE THEN...

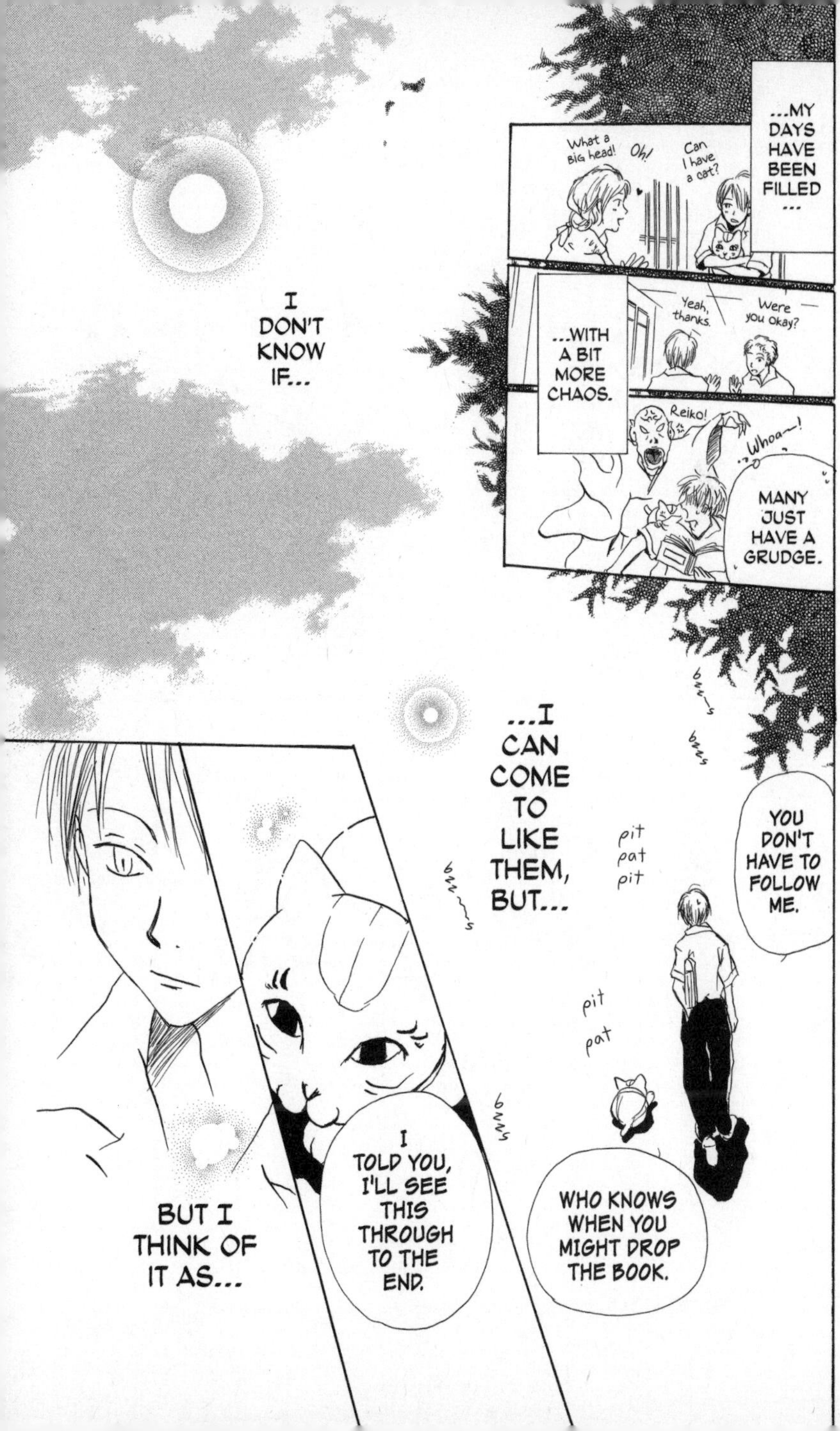
...MY DAYS HAVE BEEN FILLED...
Can I have a cat?
Oh!
What a BIG head!
Were you okay?
Yeah, thanks.
...WITH A BIT MORE CHAOS.
Reiko!
Whoa~!
MANY JUST HAVE A GRUDGE.
I DON'T KNOW IF...
bzz~s
bzzs
...I CAN COME TO LIKE THEM, BUT...
YOU DON'T HAVE TO FOLLOW ME.
pit pat pit
bzz~s
pit pat
WHO KNOWS WHEN YOU MIGHT DROP THE BOOK.
bzzs
I TOLD YOU, I'LL SEE THIS THROUGH TO THE END.
BUT I THINK OF IT AS...

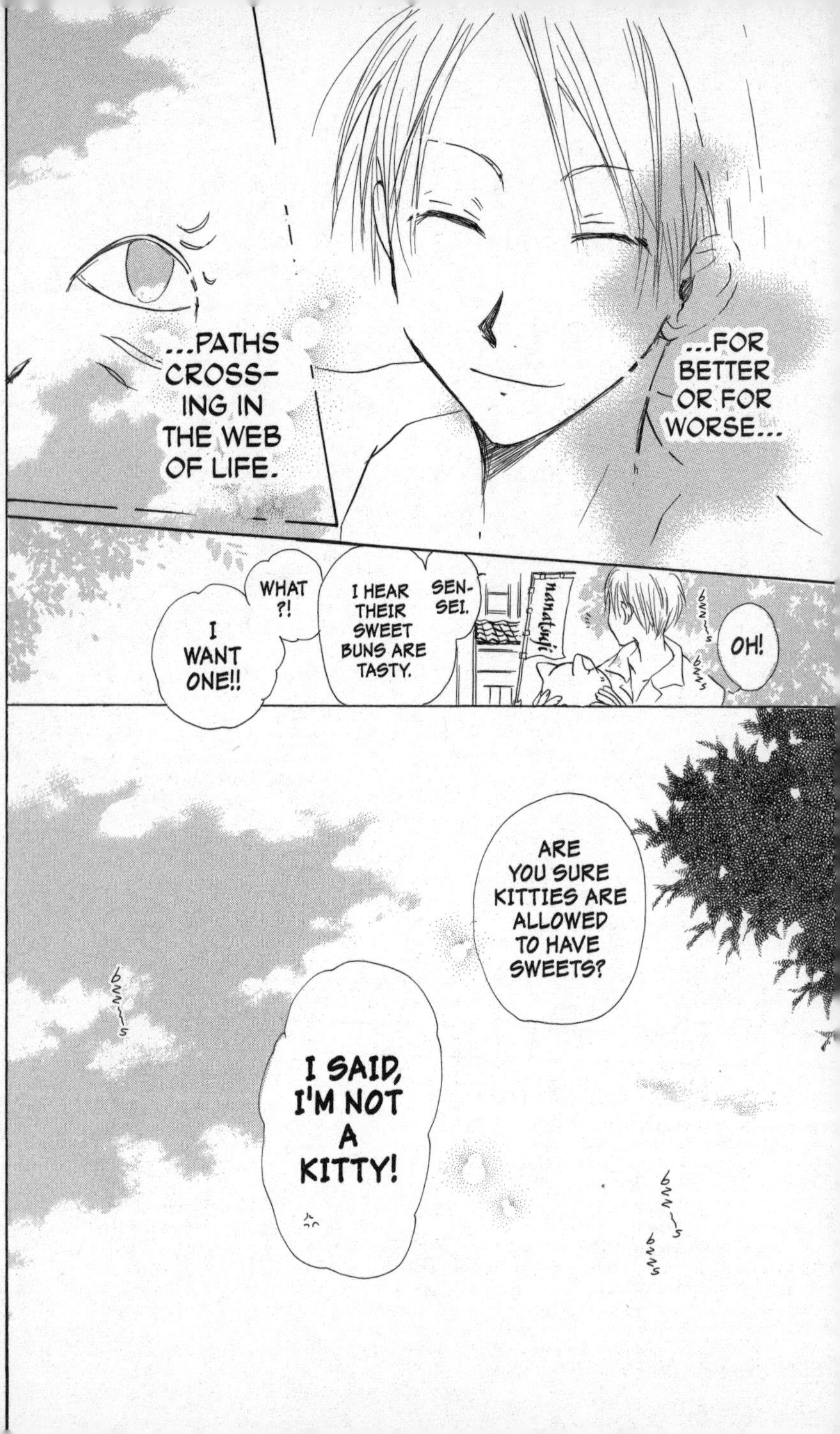
...FOR BETTER OR FOR WORSE...
...PATHS CROSSING IN THE WEB OF LIFE.
OH!
nanatsuji
SEN-SEI.
I HEAR THEIR SWEET BUNS ARE TASTY.
WHAT?!
I WANT ONE!!
ARE YOU SURE KITTIES ARE ALLOWED TO HAVE SWEETS?
I SAID, I'M NOT A KITTY!

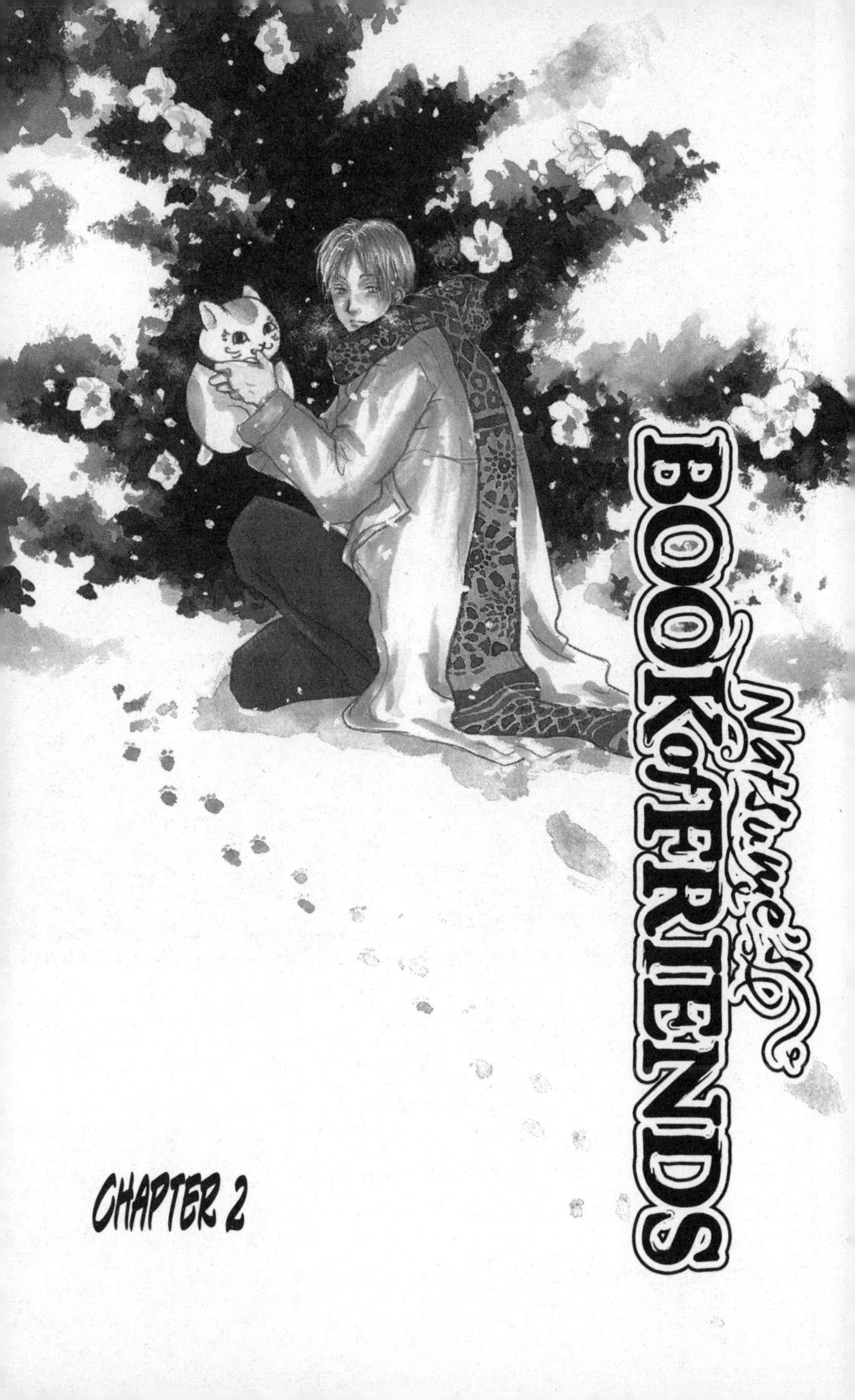
Natsume's
BOOK of FRIENDS
CHAPTER 2

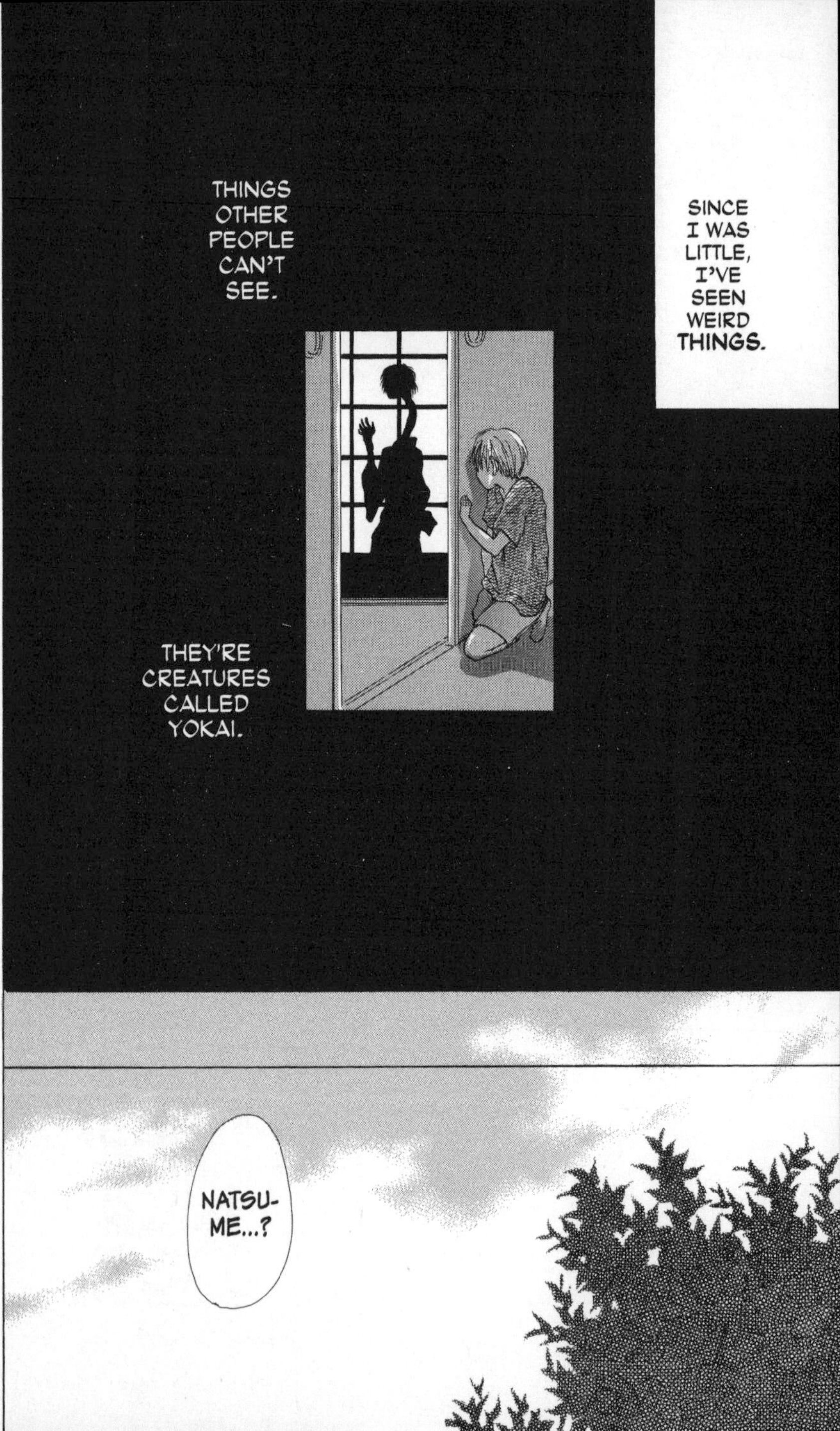
SINCE I WAS LITTLE, I'VE SEEN WEIRD THINGS.
THINGS OTHER PEOPLE CAN'T SEE.
THEY'RE CREATURES CALLED YOKAI.
NATSU-ME...?

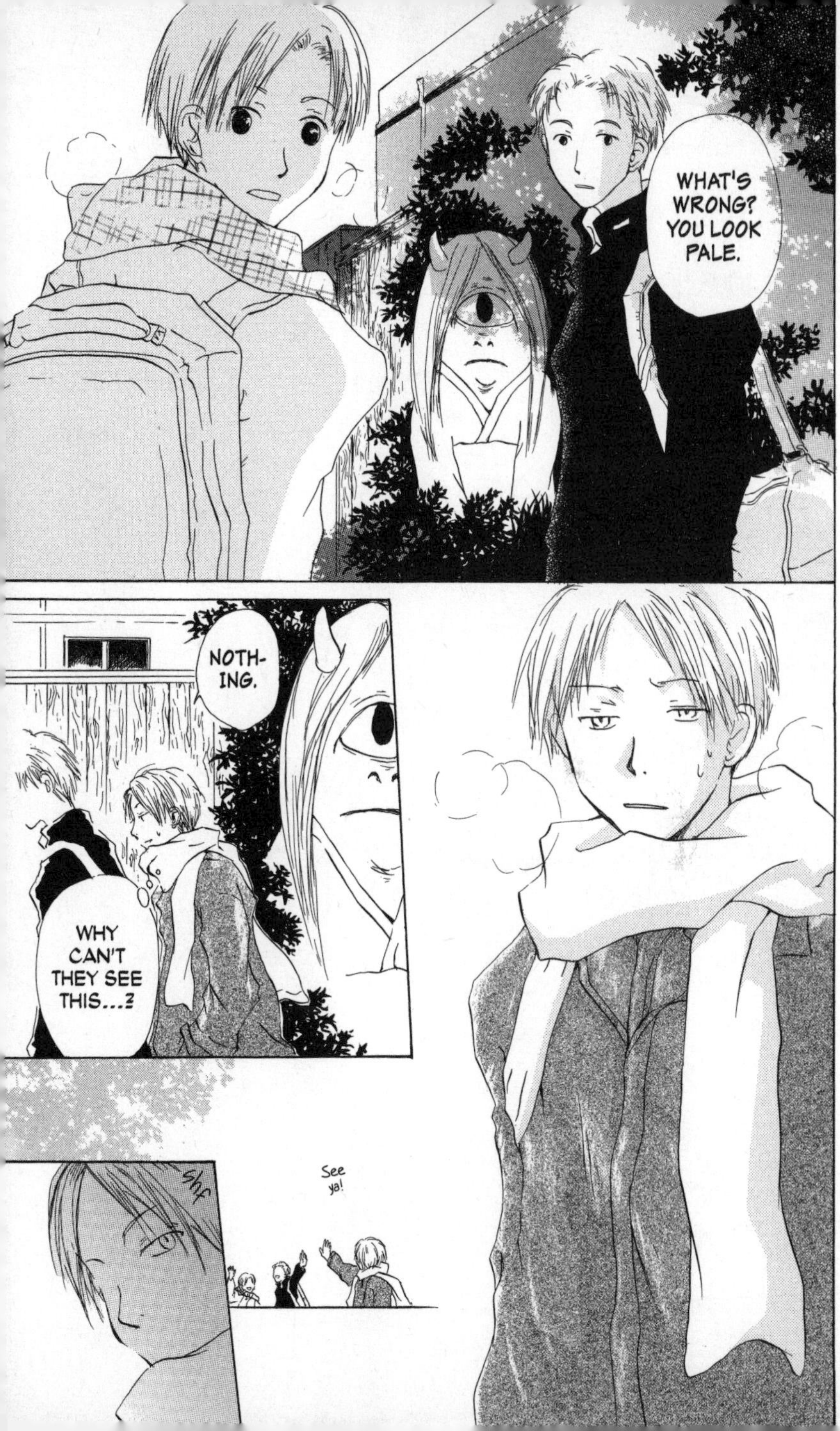
WHAT'S WRONG? YOU LOOK PALE.
NOTH-ING.
WHY CAN'T THEY SEE THIS...?
See ya!
shf

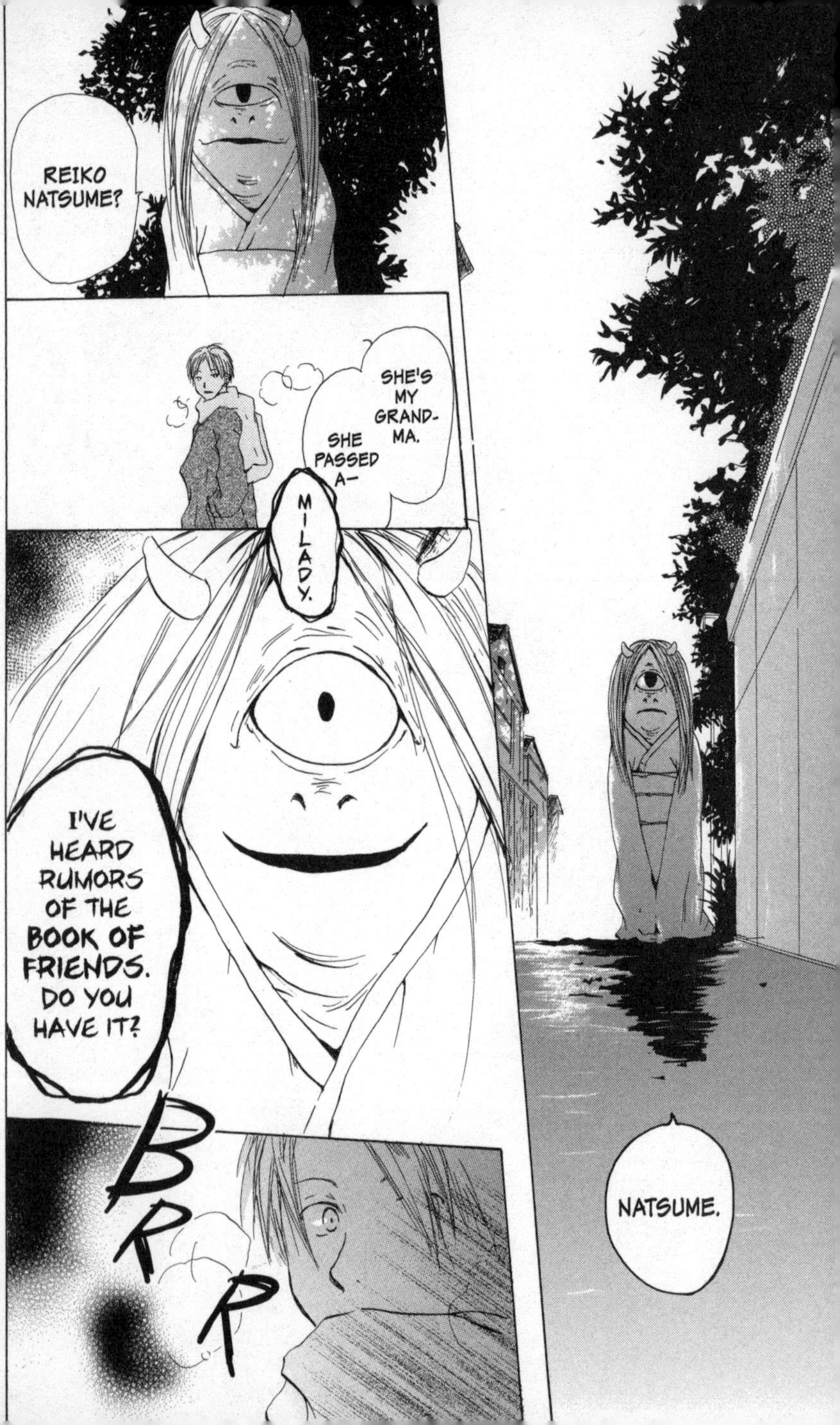
NATSUME.
REIKO NATSUME?
SHE'S MY GRANDMA.
SHE PASSED A—
MILADY.
I'VE HEARD RUMORS OF THE BOOK OF FRIENDS. DO YOU HAVE IT?
BRRR

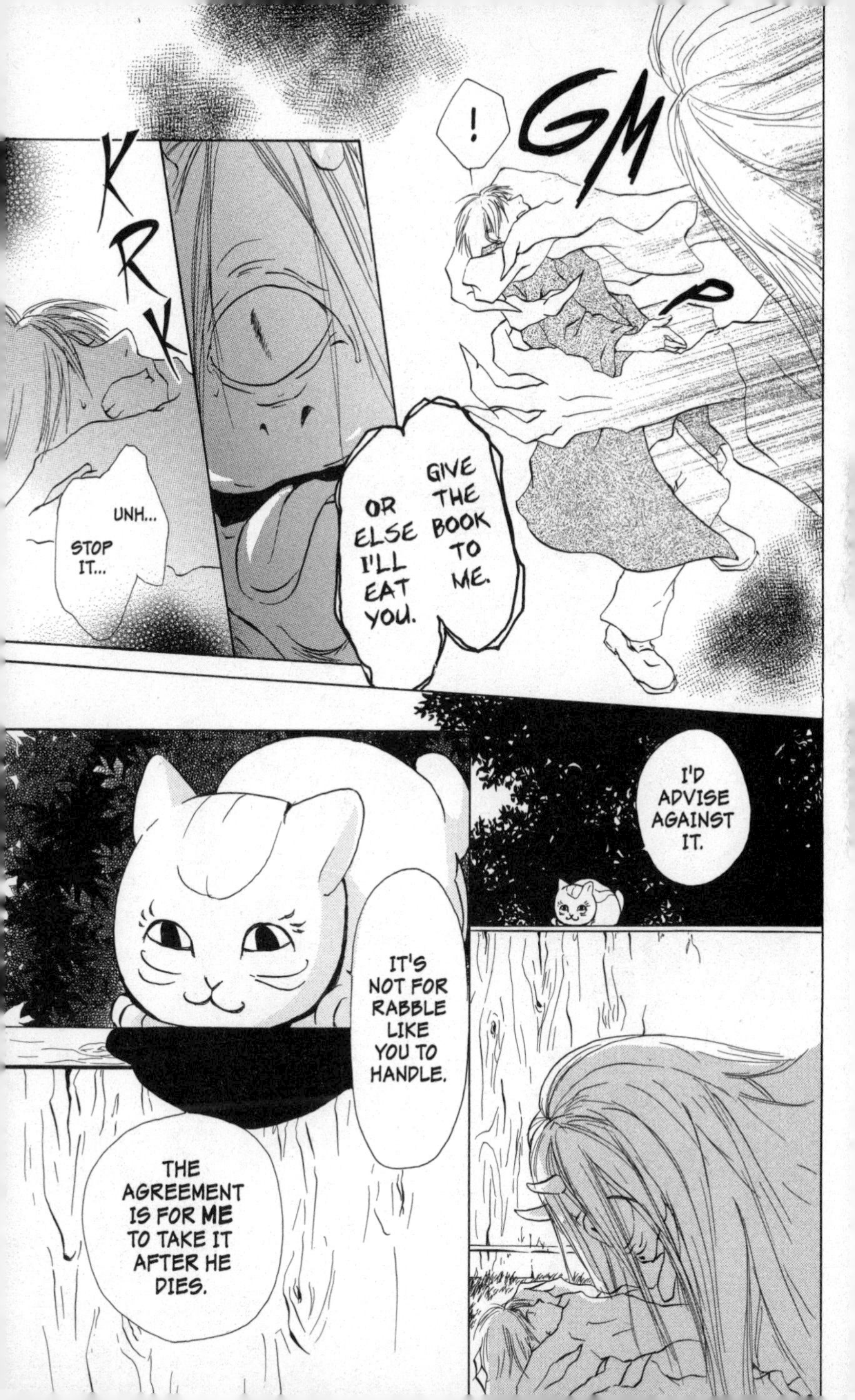
!
GMP
KRK
GIVE THE BOOK TO ME. OR ELSE I'LL EAT YOU.
UNH... STOP IT...
I'D ADVISE AGAINST IT.
IT'S NOT FOR RABBLE LIKE YOU TO HANDLE.
THE AGREEMENT IS FOR ME TO TAKE IT AFTER HE DIES.

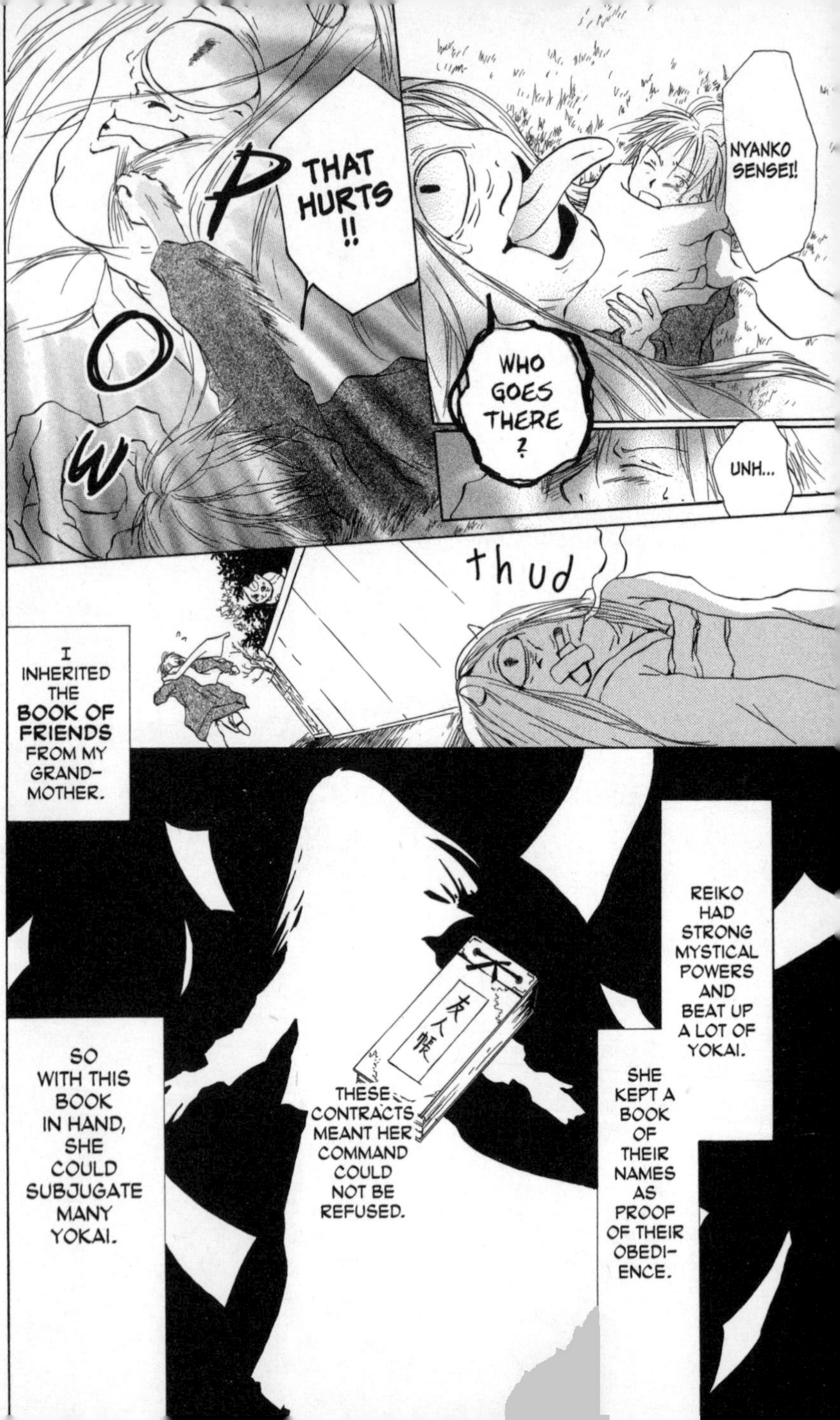
NYANKO SENSEI!
WHO GOES THERE?
UNH...
POW
THAT HURTS!!
thud
I INHERITED THE BOOK OF FRIENDS FROM MY GRANDMOTHER.
REIKO HAD STRONG MYSTICAL POWERS AND BEAT UP A LOT OF YOKAI.
SHE KEPT A BOOK OF THEIR NAMES AS PROOF OF THEIR OBEDIENCE.
友人帳
THESE CONTRACTS MEANT HER COMMAND COULD NOT BE REFUSED.
SO WITH THIS BOOK IN HAND, SHE COULD SUBJUGATE MANY YOKAI.

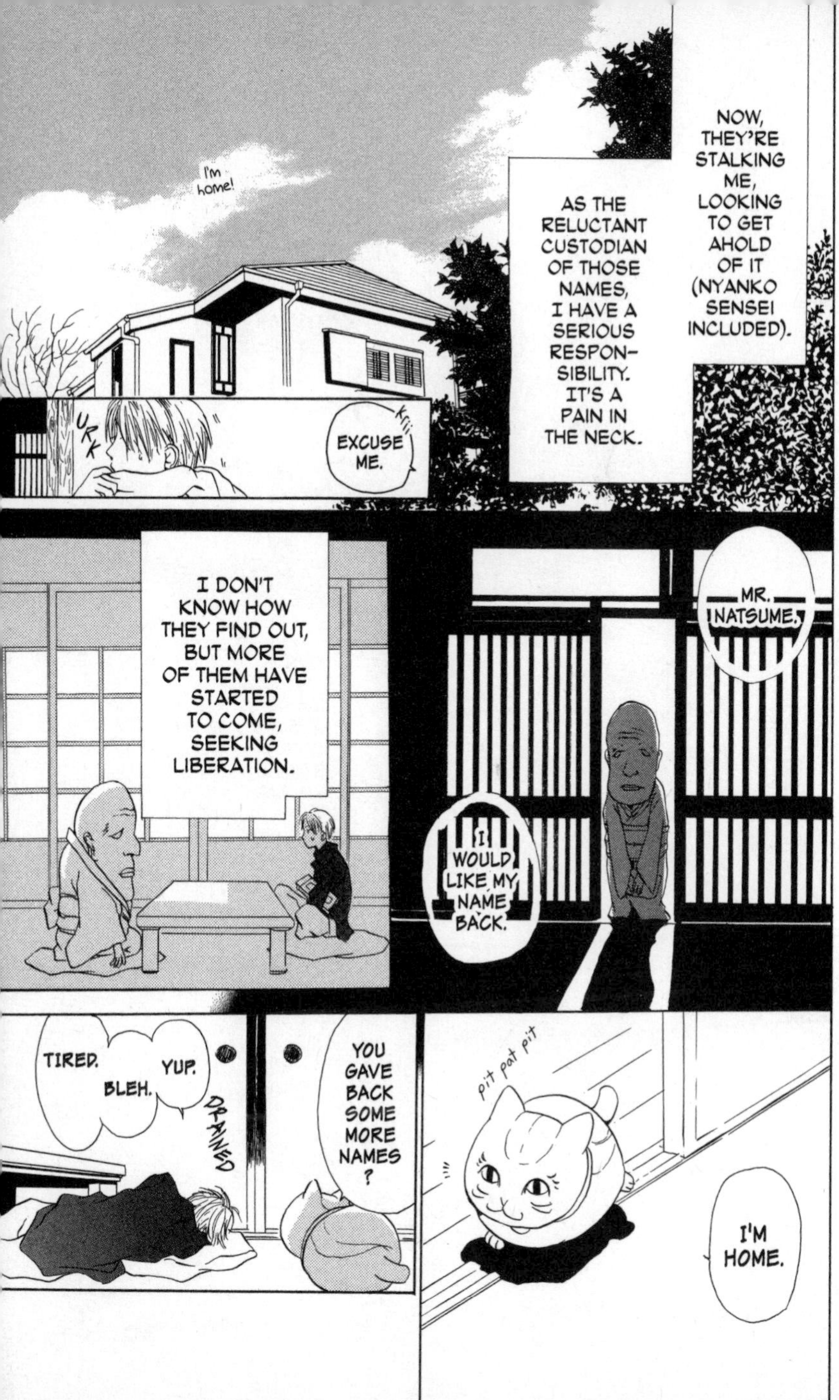
NOW, THEY'RE STALKING ME, LOOKING TO GET AHOLD OF IT (NYANKO SENSEI INCLUDED).
AS THE RELUCTANT CUSTODIAN OF THOSE NAMES, I HAVE A SERIOUS RESPON-SIBILITY. IT'S A PAIN IN THE NECK.
I'm home!
krii
EXCUSE ME.
URK
MR. NATSUME.
I WOULD LIKE MY NAME BACK.
I DON'T KNOW HOW THEY FIND OUT, BUT MORE OF THEM HAVE STARTED TO COME, SEEKING LIBERATION.
pit pat pit
I'M HOME.
YOU GAVE BACK SOME MORE NAMES?
YUP.
TIRED.
BLEH.
DRAINED

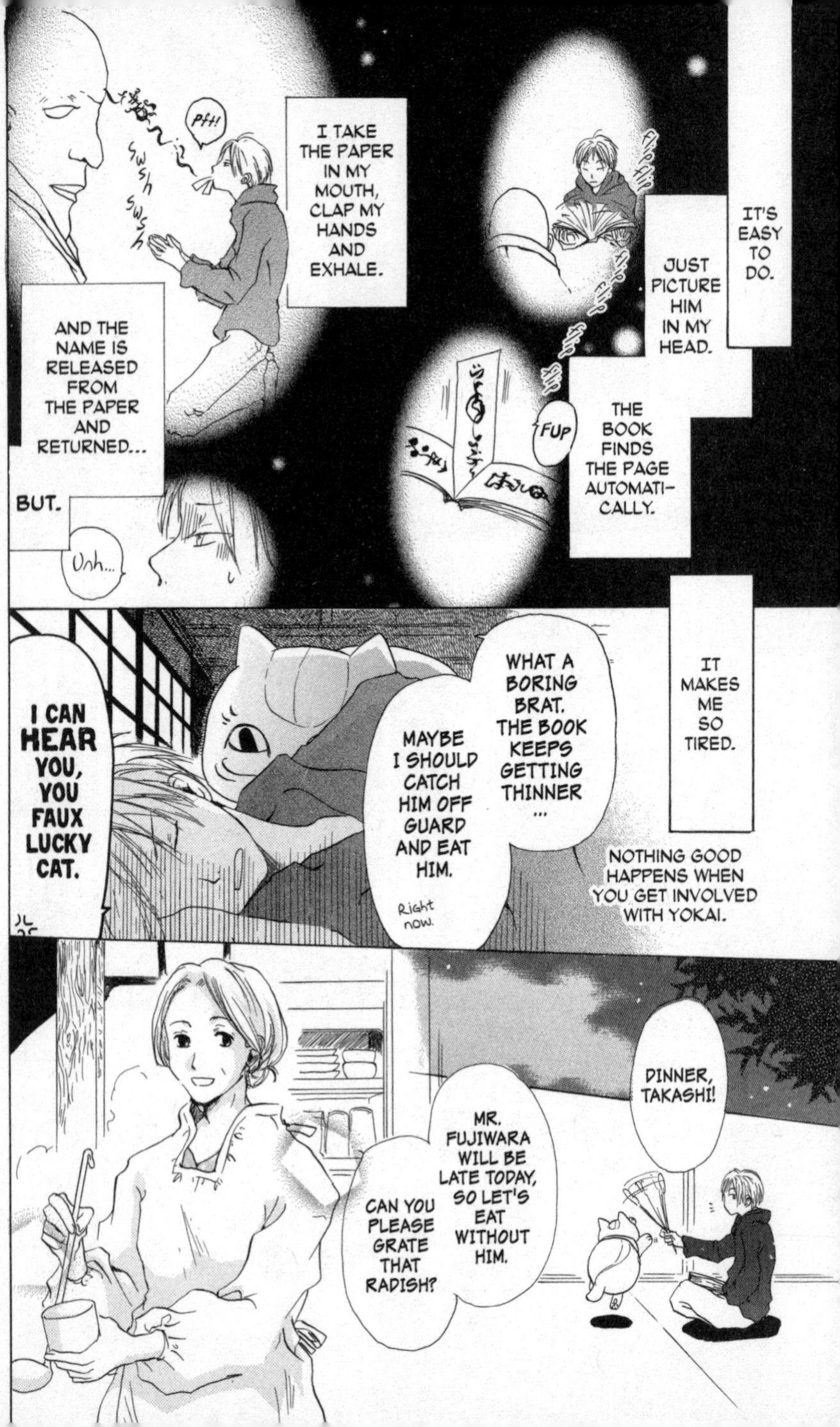
IT'S EASY TO DO.
JUST PICTURE HIM IN MY HEAD.
flip flip
FUP
THE BOOK FINDS THE PAGE AUTOMATICALLY.
I TAKE THE PAPER IN MY MOUTH, CLAP MY HANDS AND EXHALE.
Pff!
swsh swsh
AND THE NAME IS RELEASED FROM THE PAPER AND RETURNED...
BUT.
Unh...
IT MAKES ME SO TIRED.
NOTHING GOOD HAPPENS WHEN YOU GET INVOLVED WITH YOKAI.
WHAT A BORING BRAT. THE BOOK KEEPS GETTING THINNER...
MAYBE I SHOULD CATCH HIM OFF GUARD AND EAT HIM.
Right now.
I CAN HEAR YOU, YOU FAUX LUCKY CAT.
DINNER, TAKASHI!
MR. FUJIWARA WILL BE LATE TODAY, SO LET'S EAT WITHOUT HIM.
CAN YOU PLEASE GRATE THAT RADISH?

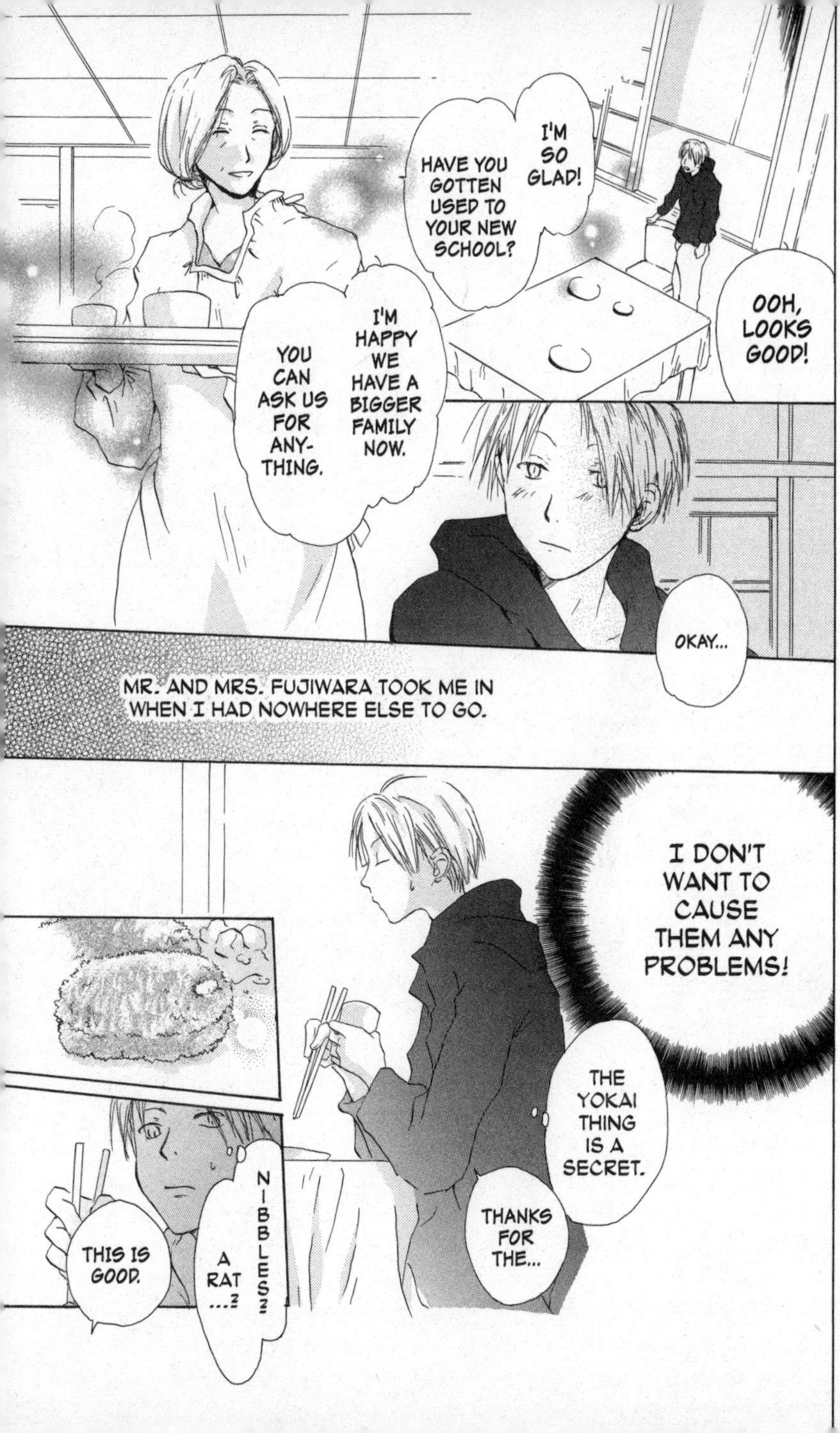
OOH, LOOKS GOOD!
I'M SO GLAD!
HAVE YOU GOTTEN USED TO YOUR NEW SCHOOL?
I'M HAPPY WE HAVE A BIGGER FAMILY NOW.
YOU CAN ASK US FOR ANY-THING.
OKAY...
MR. AND MRS. FUJIWARA TOOK ME IN WHEN I HAD NOWHERE ELSE TO GO.
I DON'T WANT TO CAUSE THEM ANY PROBLEMS!
THE YOKAI THING IS A SECRET.
THANKS FOR THE...
NIBBLES
A RAT...?
THIS IS GOOD.

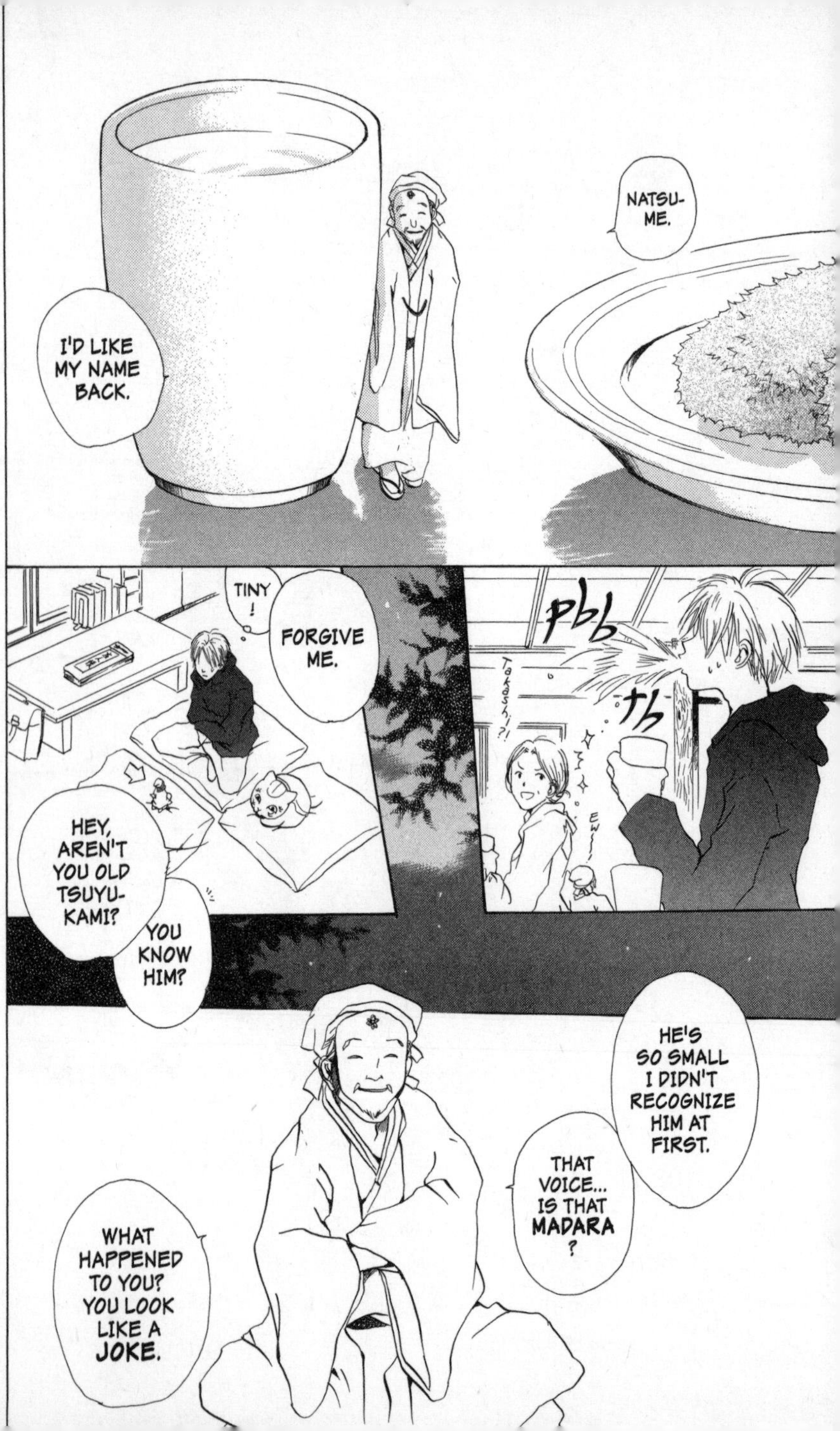
NATSU-ME.
I'D LIKE MY NAME BACK.
pbb
th
Takashi?!
TINY!
FORGIVE ME.
HEY, AREN'T YOU OLD TSUYU-KAMI?
YOU KNOW HIM?
HE'S SO SMALL I DIDN'T RECOGNIZE HIM AT FIRST.
THAT VOICE... IS THAT MADARA?
WHAT HAPPENED TO YOU? YOU LOOK LIKE A JOKE.

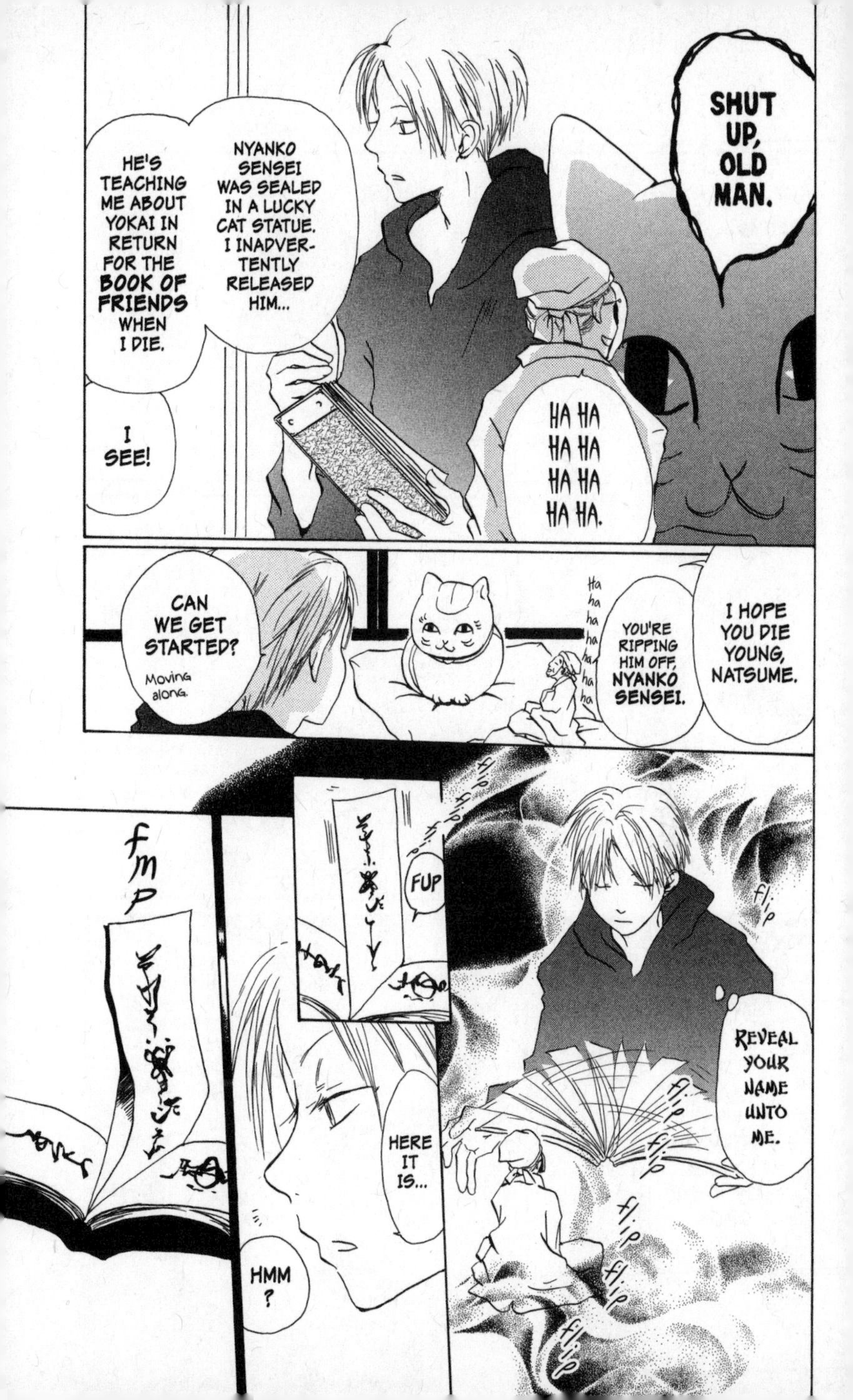
SHUT UP, OLD MAN.
NYANKO SENSEI WAS SEALED IN A LUCKY CAT STATUE. I INADVERTENTLY RELEASED HIM...
HE'S TEACHING ME ABOUT YOKAI IN RETURN FOR THE BOOK OF FRIENDS WHEN I DIE.
HA HA HA HA HA HA HA HA.
I SEE!
I HOPE YOU DIE YOUNG, NATSUME.
YOU'RE RIPPING HIM OFF, NYANKO SENSEI.
Ha ha ha ha ha ha ha ha
CAN WE GET STARTED?
Moving along.
flip flip flip
flip
REVEAL YOUR NAME UNTO ME.
flip flip
flip flip flip
FUP
HERE IT IS...
HMM?
fmp

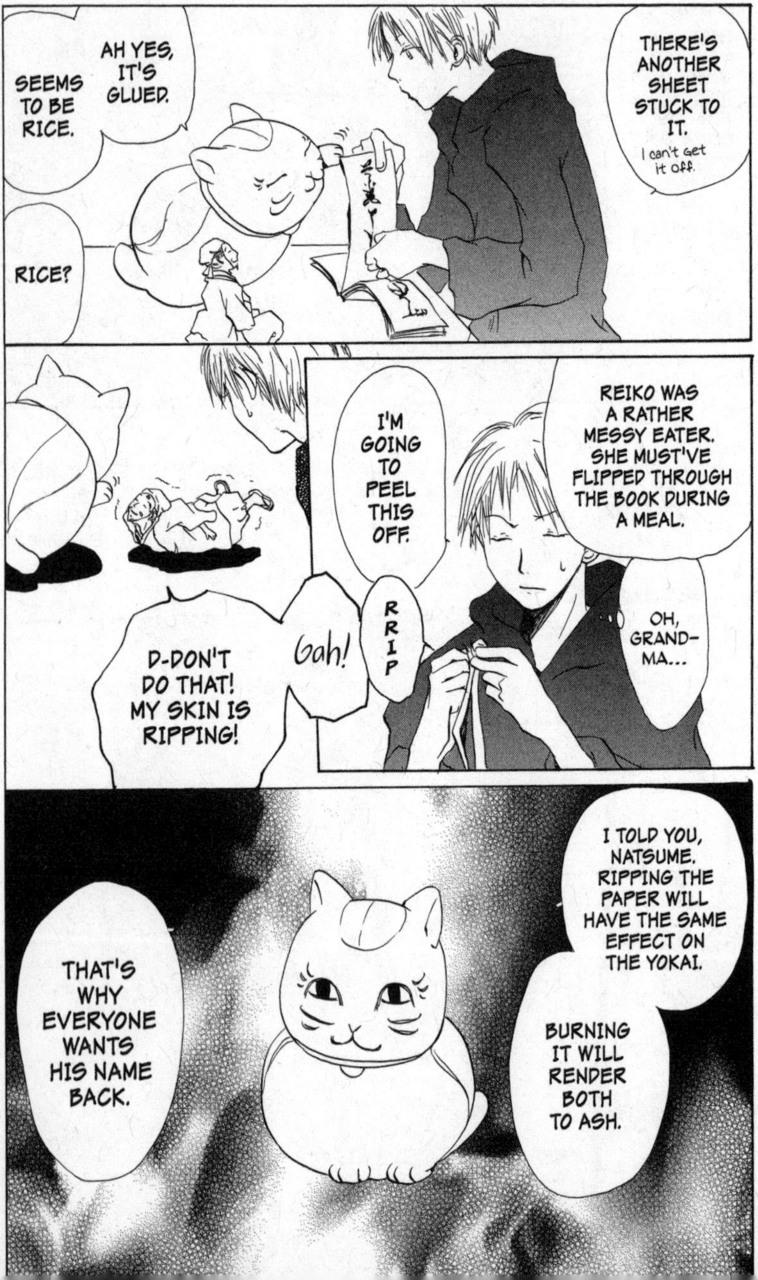
THERE'S ANOTHER SHEET STUCK TO IT.
I can't get it off.
AH YES, IT'S GLUED.
SEEMS TO BE RICE.
RICE?
REIKO WAS A RATHER MESSY EATER. SHE MUST'VE FLIPPED THROUGH THE BOOK DURING A MEAL.
I'M GOING TO PEEL THIS OFF.
OH, GRAND-MA...
RRIP
Gah!
D-DON'T DO THAT! MY SKIN IS RIPPING!
I TOLD YOU, NATSUME. RIPPING THE PAPER WILL HAVE THE SAME EFFECT ON THE YOKAI.
BURNING IT WILL RENDER BOTH TO ASH.
THAT'S WHY EVERYONE WANTS HIS NAME BACK.

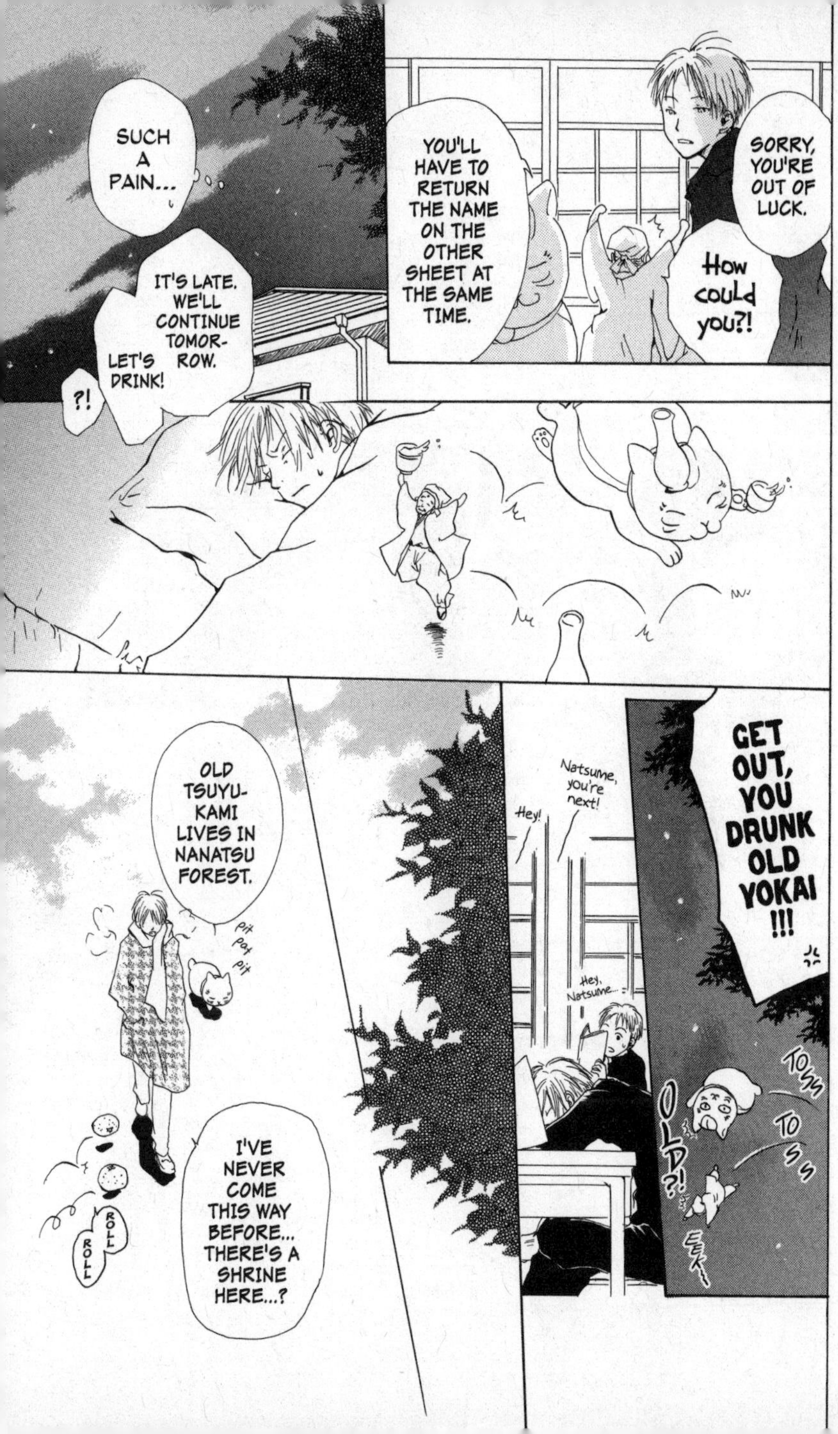
SORRY, YOU'RE OUT OF LUCK.
How could you?!
YOU'LL HAVE TO RETURN THE NAME ON THE OTHER SHEET AT THE SAME TIME.
SUCH A PAIN...
IT'S LATE. WE'LL CONTINUE TOMOR-ROW.
LET'S DRINK!
?!
GET OUT, YOU DRUNK OLD YOKAI!!!
TOSS
TOSS
OLD?!
EEK!
Natsume, you're next!
Hey!
Hey, Natsume...
OLD TSUYU-KAMI LIVES IN NANATSU FOREST.
pit pat pit
ROLL
ROLL
I'VE NEVER COME THIS WAY BEFORE... THERE'S A SHRINE HERE...?

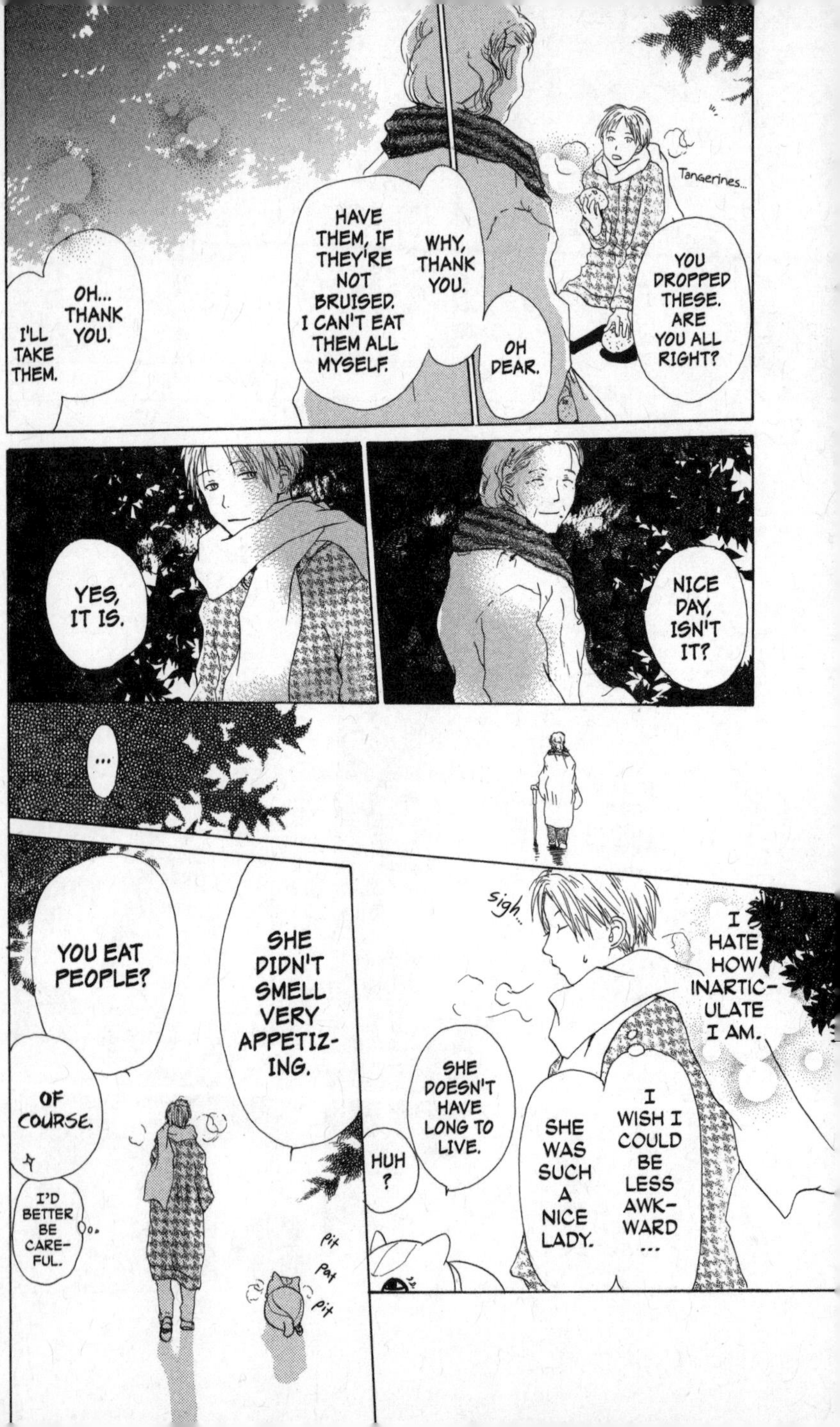
Tangerines...
YOU DROPPED THESE. ARE YOU ALL RIGHT?
OH DEAR.
WHY, THANK YOU.
HAVE THEM, IF THEY'RE NOT BRUISED. I CAN'T EAT THEM ALL MYSELF.
OH... THANK YOU.
I'LL TAKE THEM.
NICE DAY, ISN'T IT?
YES, IT IS.
...
sigh...
I HATE HOW INARTICULATE I AM.
I WISH I COULD BE LESS AWKWARD...
SHE WAS SUCH A NICE LADY.
SHE DOESN'T HAVE LONG TO LIVE.
HUH?
SHE DIDN'T SMELL VERY APPETIZING.
YOU EAT PEOPLE?
OF COURSE.
I'D BETTER BE CAREFUL.
pit
pat
pit

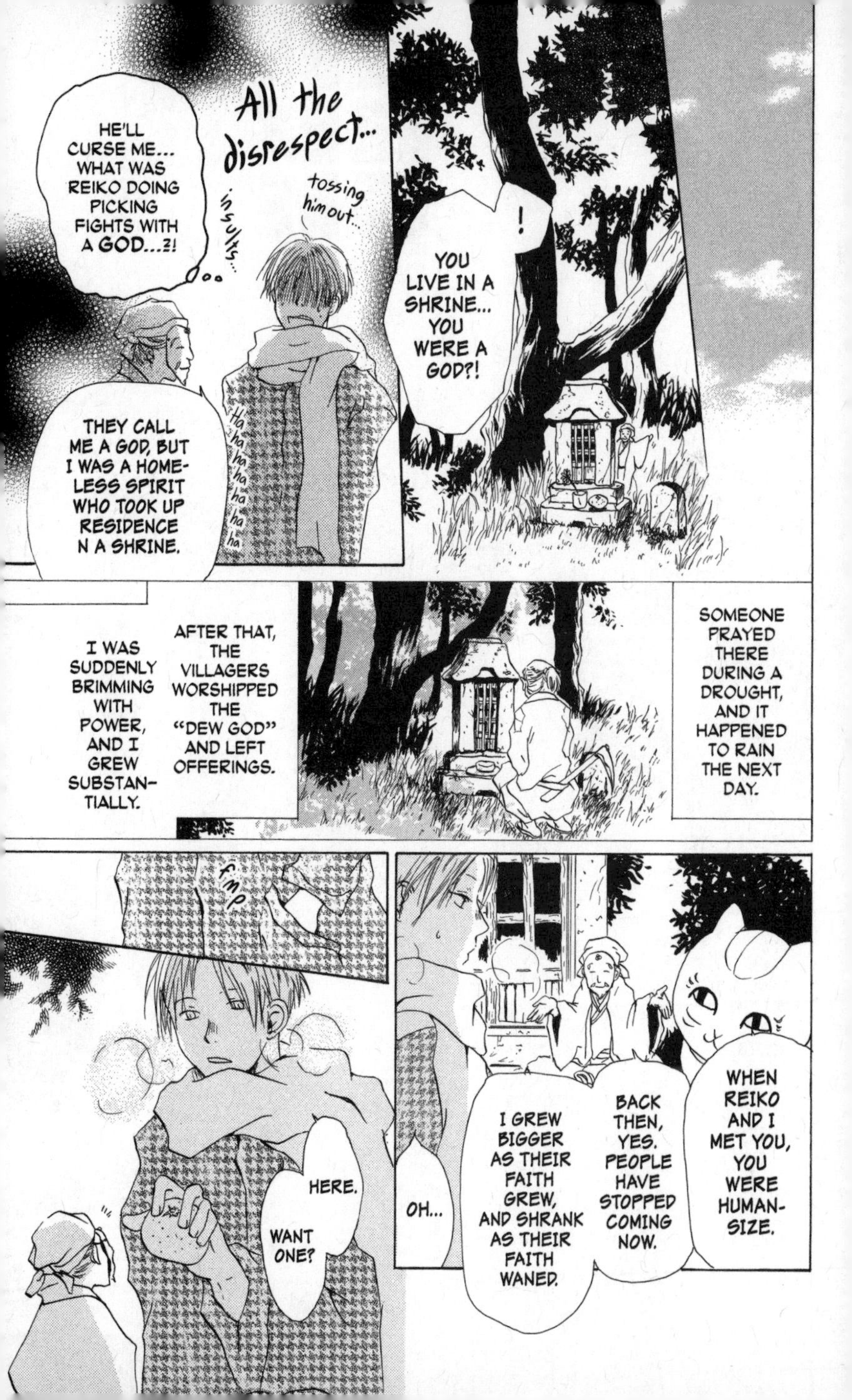
!
YOU LIVE IN A SHRINE... YOU WERE A GOD?!
All the disrespect...
tossing him out...
insults...
HE'LL CURSE ME... WHAT WAS REIKO DOING PICKING FIGHTS WITH A GOD...?!
THEY CALL ME A GOD, BUT I WAS A HOME-LESS SPIRIT WHO TOOK UP RESIDENCE N A SHRINE.
Ha ha ha ha ha ha ha ha
SOMEONE PRAYED THERE DURING A DROUGHT, AND IT HAPPENED TO RAIN THE NEXT DAY.
AFTER THAT, THE VILLAGERS WORSHIPPED THE "DEW GOD" AND LEFT OFFERINGS.
I WAS SUDDENLY BRIMMING WITH POWER, AND I GREW SUBSTANTIALLY.
WHEN REIKO AND I MET YOU, YOU WERE HUMAN-SIZE.
BACK THEN, YES. PEOPLE HAVE STOPPED COMING NOW.
I GREW BIGGER AS THEIR FAITH GREW, AND SHRANK AS THEIR FAITH WANED.
OH...
fmp
HERE.
WANT ONE?

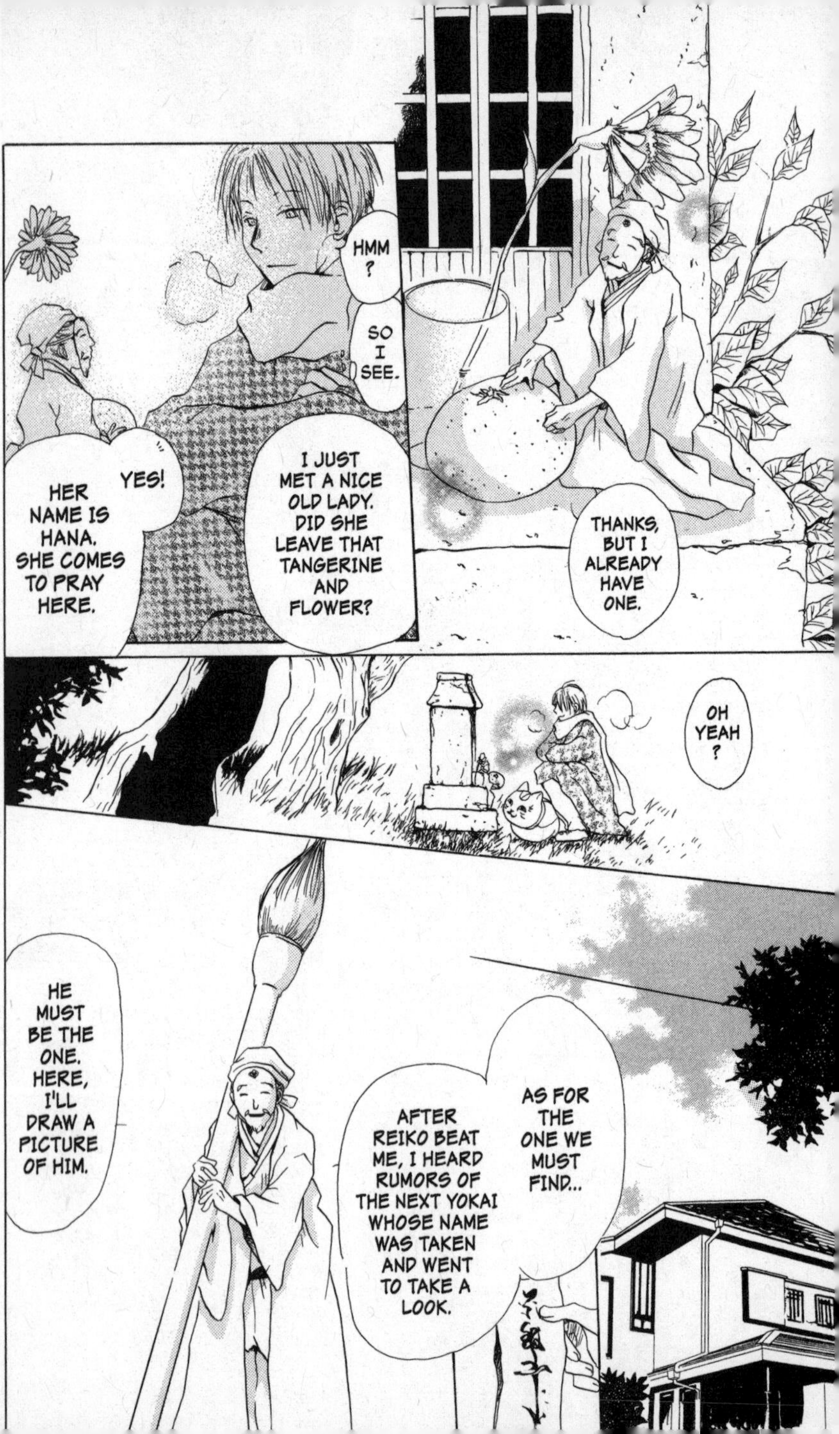
THANKS, BUT I ALREADY HAVE ONE.
HMM?
SO I SEE.
I JUST MET A NICE OLD LADY. DID SHE LEAVE THAT TANGERINE AND FLOWER?
YES! HER NAME IS HANA. SHE COMES TO PRAY HERE.
OH YEAH?
AS FOR THE ONE WE MUST FIND...
AFTER REIKO BEAT ME, I HEARD RUMORS OF THE NEXT YOKAI WHOSE NAME WAS TAKEN AND WENT TO TAKE A LOOK.
HE MUST BE THE ONE. HERE, I'LL DRAW A PICTURE OF HIM.

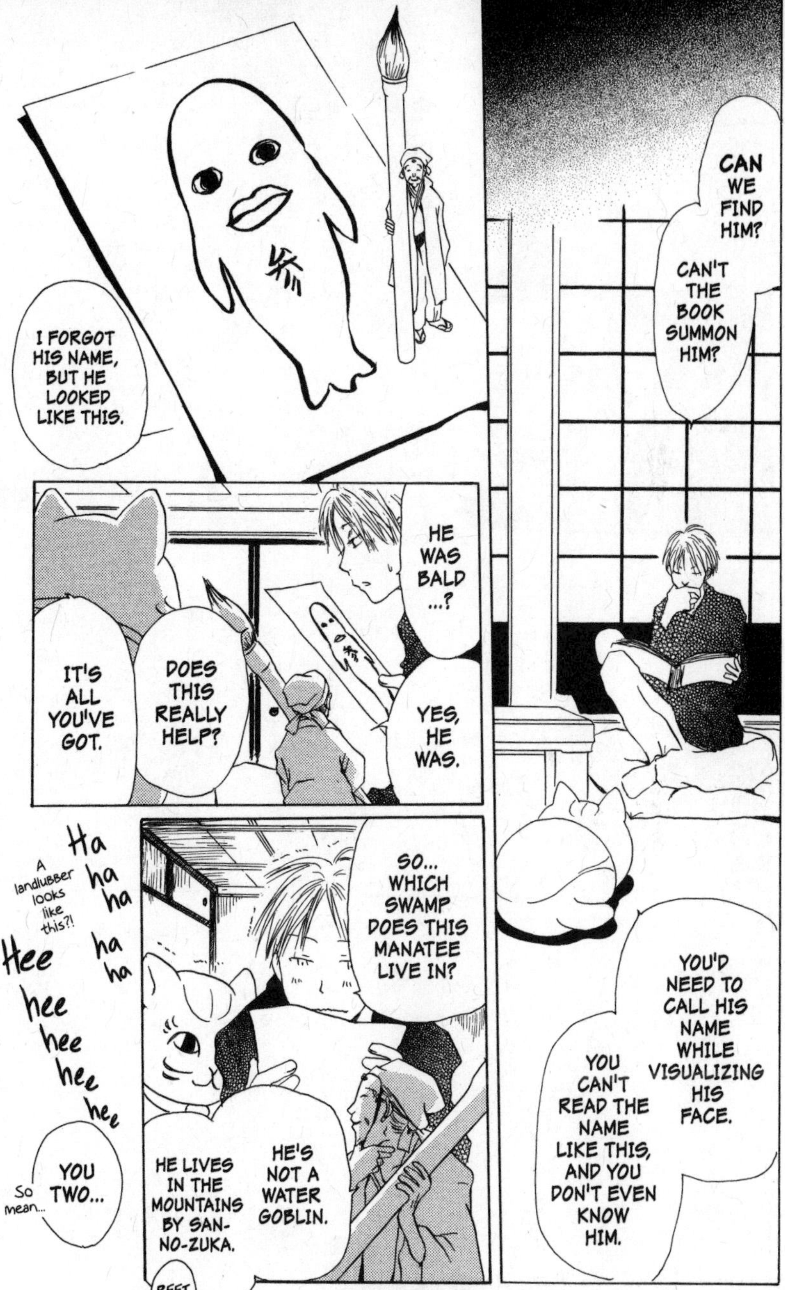
CAN WE FIND HIM?
CAN'T THE BOOK SUMMON HIM?
YOU'D NEED TO CALL HIS NAME WHILE VISUALIZING HIS FACE.
YOU CAN'T READ THE NAME LIKE THIS, AND YOU DON'T EVEN KNOW HIM.
I FORGOT HIS NAME, BUT HE LOOKED LIKE THIS.
HE WAS BALD ...?
YES, HE WAS.
DOES THIS REALLY HELP?
IT'S ALL YOU'VE GOT.
SO... WHICH SWAMP DOES THIS MANATEE LIVE IN?
HE'S NOT A WATER GOBLIN.
HE LIVES IN THE MOUNTAINS BY SAN-NO-ZUKA.
PFFT.
Ha ha ha ha ha
A landlubber looks like this?!
Hee hee hee hee hee
YOU TWO...
So mean...

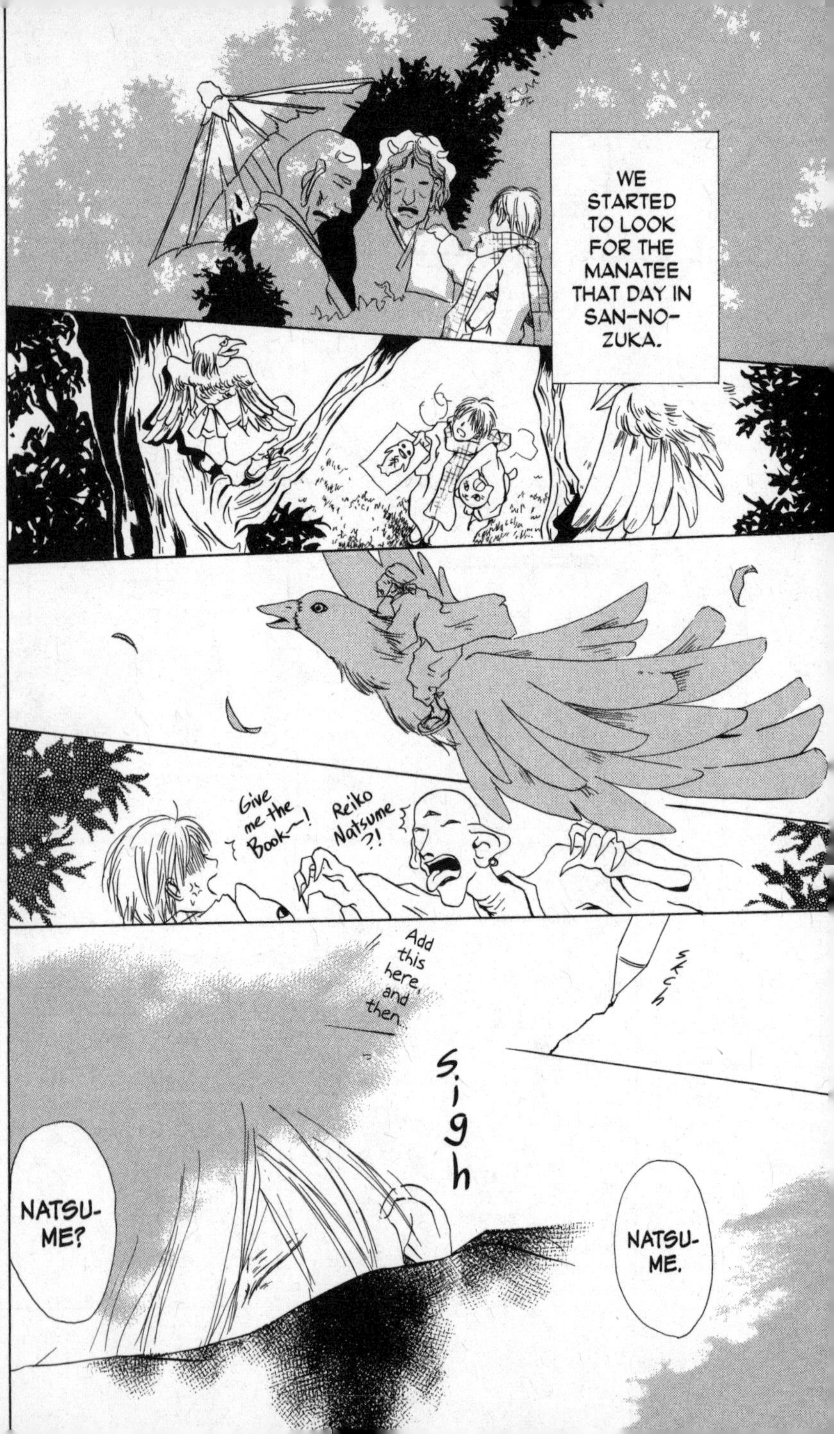
WE STARTED TO LOOK FOR THE MANATEE THAT DAY IN SAN-NO-ZUKA.
Reiko Natsume?!
Give me the Book~!
Add this here, and then...
skch
Sigh
NATSU-ME.
NATSU-ME?

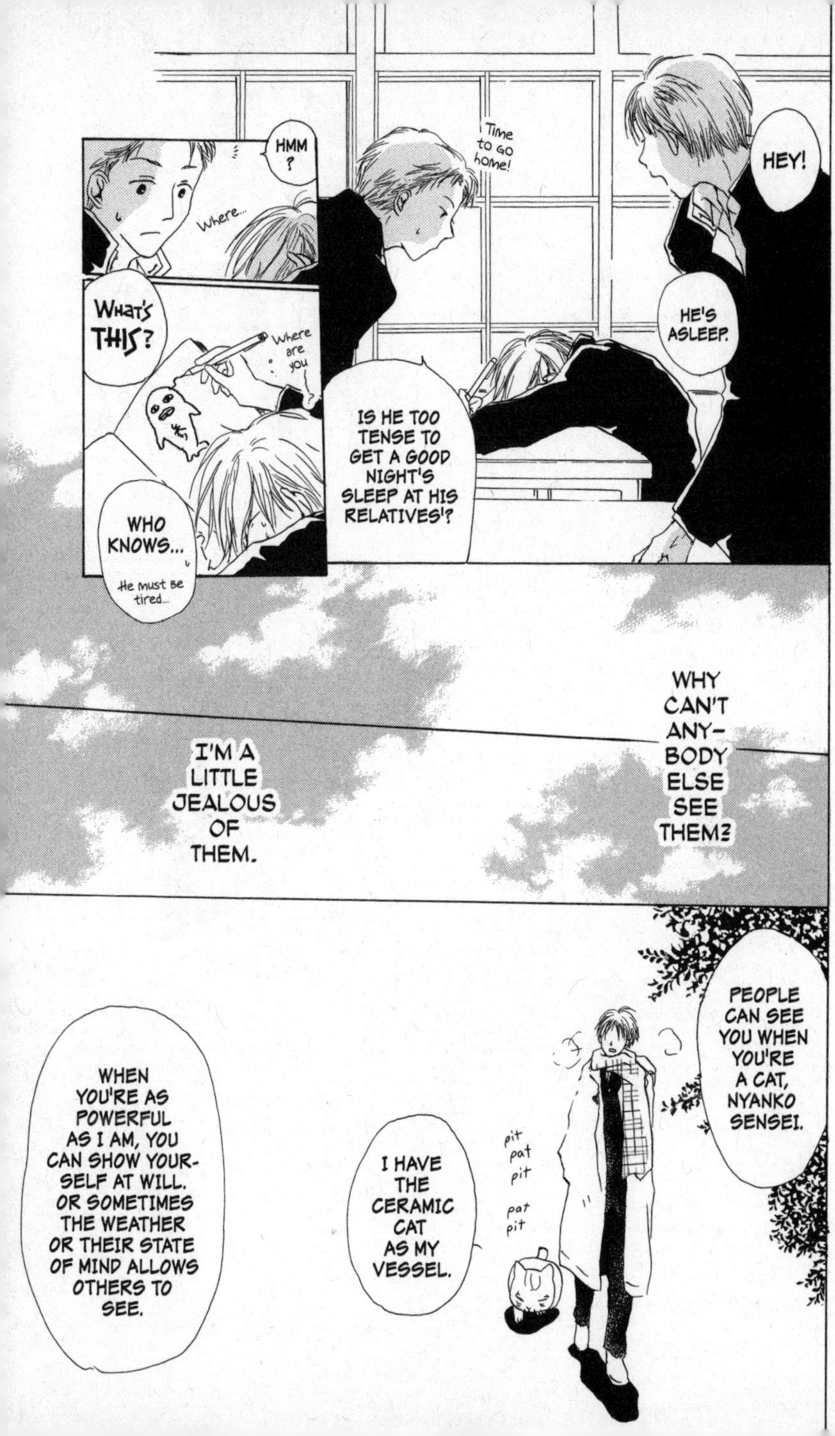
HEY!
HE'S ASLEEP.
Time to go home!
IS HE TOO TENSE TO GET A GOOD NIGHT'S SLEEP AT HIS RELATIVES'?
HMM?
Where...
WHAT'S THIS?
Where are you?
WHO KNOWS...
He must be tired...
WHY CAN'T ANYBODY ELSE SEE THEM?
I'M A LITTLE JEALOUS OF THEM.
PEOPLE CAN SEE YOU WHEN YOU'RE A CAT, NYANKO SENSEI.
pit pat pit
pat pit
I HAVE THE CERAMIC CAT AS MY VESSEL.
WHEN YOU'RE AS POWERFUL AS I AM, YOU CAN SHOW YOURSELF AT WILL. OR SOMETIMES THE WEATHER OR THEIR STATE OF MIND ALLOWS OTHERS TO SEE.

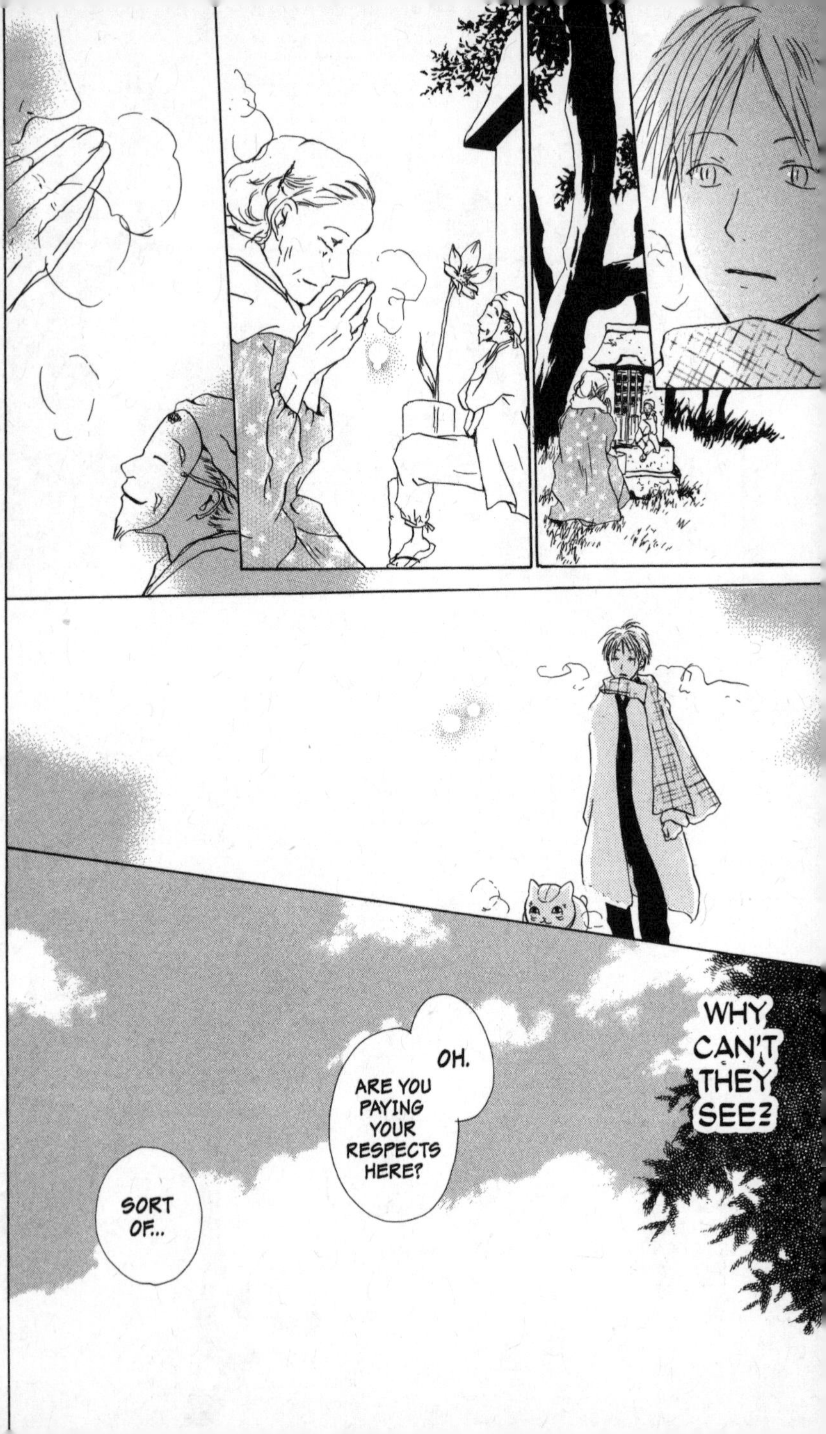
WHY CAN'T THEY SEE?
OH.
ARE YOU PAYING YOUR RESPECTS HERE?
SORT OF...

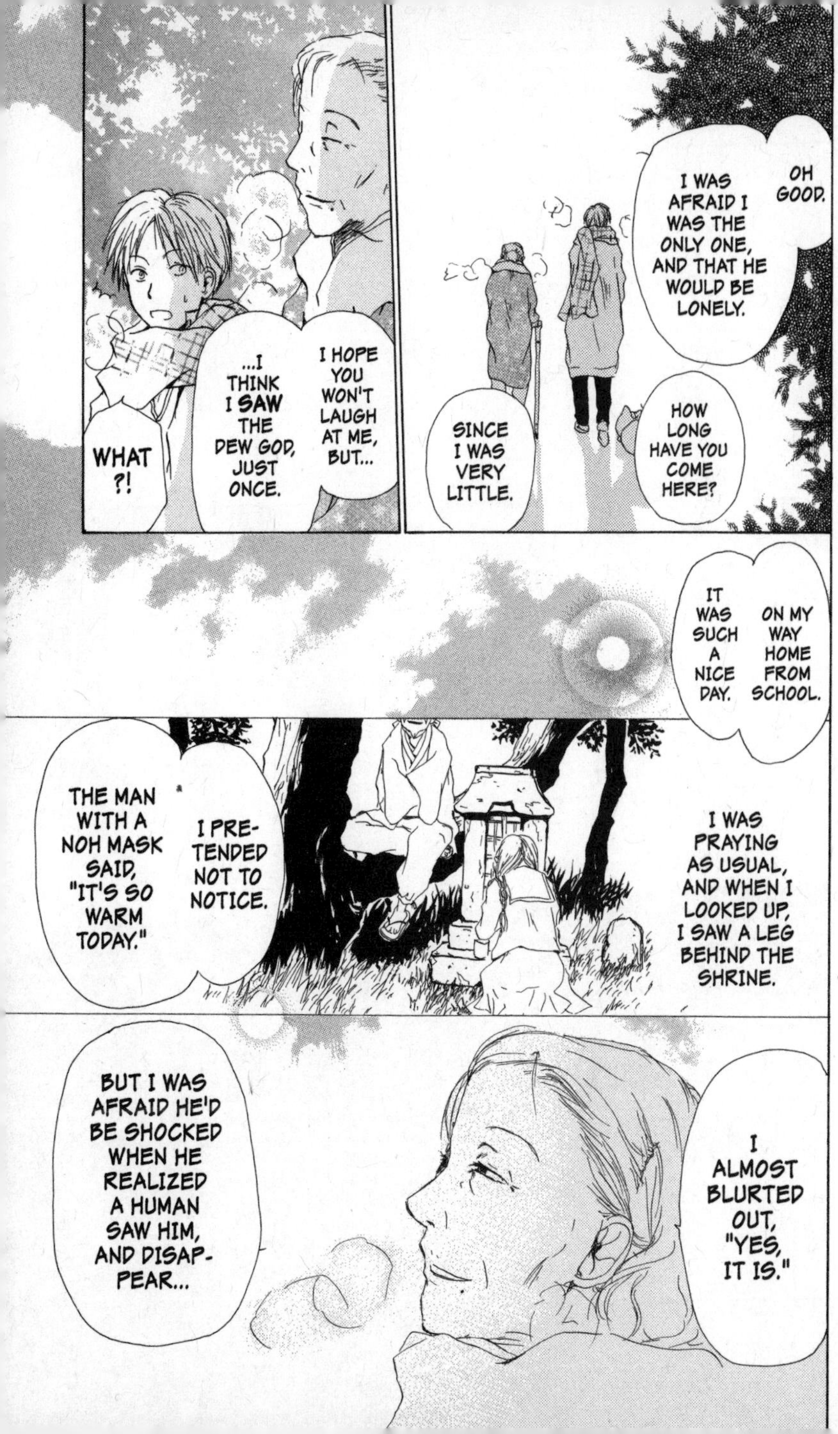
OH GOOD.
I WAS AFRAID I WAS THE ONLY ONE, AND THAT HE WOULD BE LONELY.
HOW LONG HAVE YOU COME HERE?
SINCE I WAS VERY LITTLE.
I HOPE YOU WON'T LAUGH AT ME, BUT...
...I THINK I SAW THE DEW GOD, JUST ONCE.
WHAT?!
ON MY WAY HOME FROM SCHOOL.
IT WAS SUCH A NICE DAY.
I WAS PRAYING AS USUAL, AND WHEN I LOOKED UP, I SAW A LEG BEHIND THE SHRINE.
I PRETENDED NOT TO NOTICE.
THE MAN WITH A NOH MASK SAID, "IT'S SO WARM TODAY."
I ALMOST BLURTED OUT, "YES, IT IS."
BUT I WAS AFRAID HE'D BE SHOCKED WHEN HE REALIZED A HUMAN SAW HIM, AND DISAPPEAR...

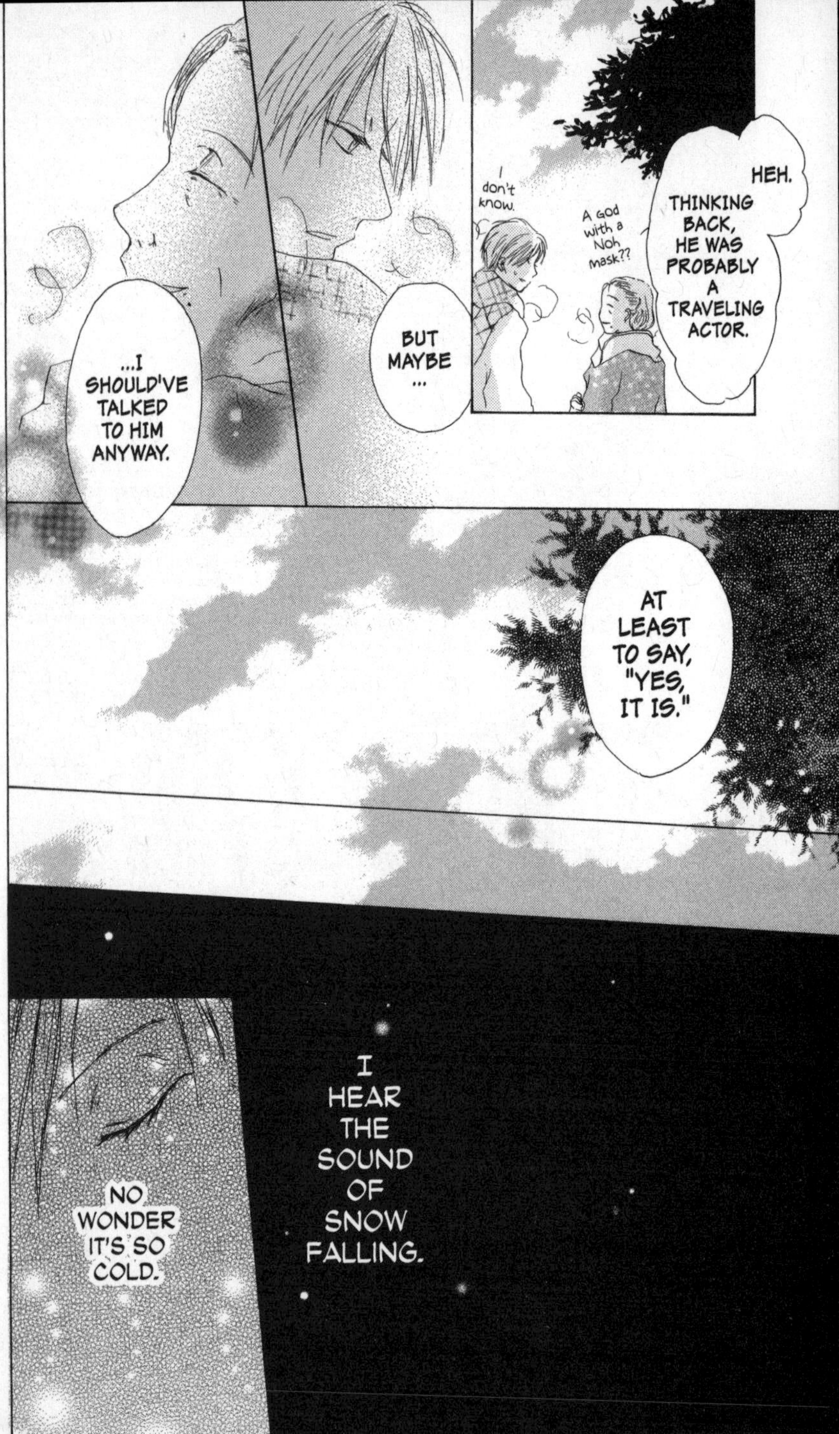
HEH. THINKING BACK, HE WAS PROBABLY A TRAVELING ACTOR.
A God with a Noh mask??
I don't know.
BUT MAYBE ...
...I SHOULD'VE TALKED TO HIM ANYWAY.
AT LEAST TO SAY, "YES, IT IS."
I HEAR THE SOUND OF SNOW FALLING.
NO WONDER IT'S SO COLD.

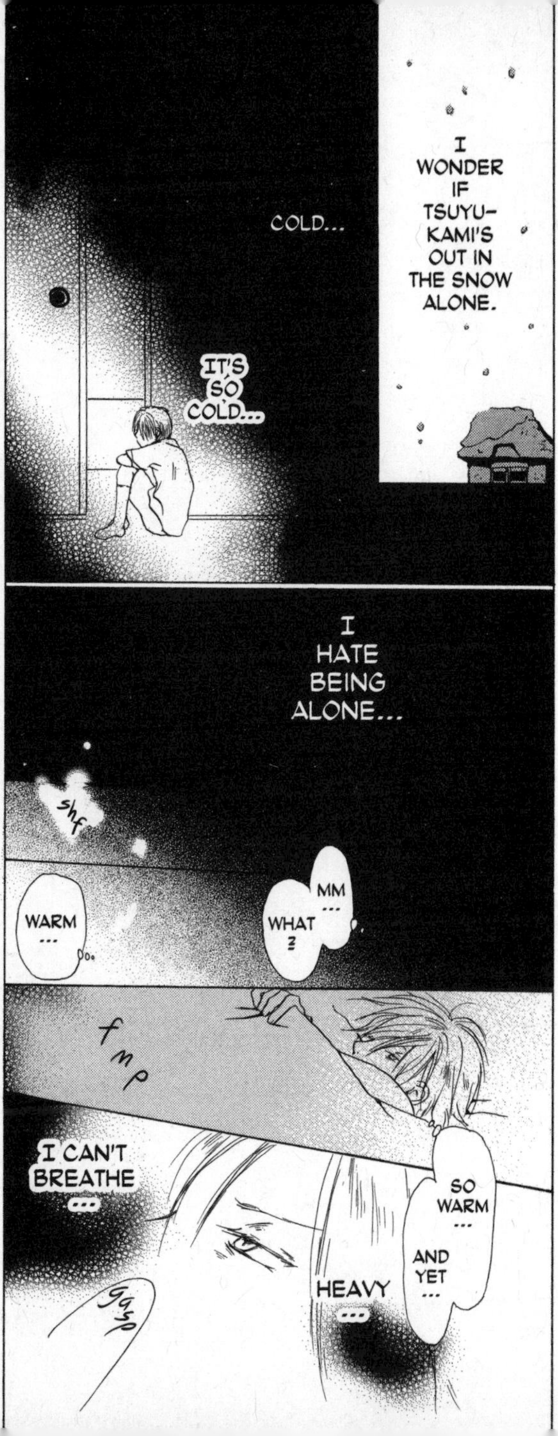
I WONDER IF TSUYUKAMI'S OUT IN THE SNOW ALONE.
COLD...
IT'S SO COLD...
I HATE BEING ALONE...
shf
MM... WHAT?
WARM...
fmp
SO WARM... AND YET...
HEAVY...
I CAN'T BREATHE...
gasp

03

❋~Supernatural stories: part 1~

Back when I was working on *Akaku Saku Koe* (Red Blooming Voices), I got an opportunity to do a one-shot episode in the magazine *LaLa*. It was summer, so I started to work on a ghost story that would give a nice chill down the spine, but we decided it was better to have a bit more of a romantic element. At the time, balancing the two was very difficult, and it was a tough time for me, so I hastily changed the whole thing to something else. (And it ended up exasperating me as well as teaching me things.) After that, it was determined that I needed to practice romantic stories more, so ghost stories were put on the back burner. During that time, I was inspired to do a manga called *Hotaru-bi no Mori e* (To the Forest of Firefly Light). It had been a while since I had done a story like that, with a supernatural element, so I was very happy...but I didn't feel the same satisfaction as working on a ghost story.

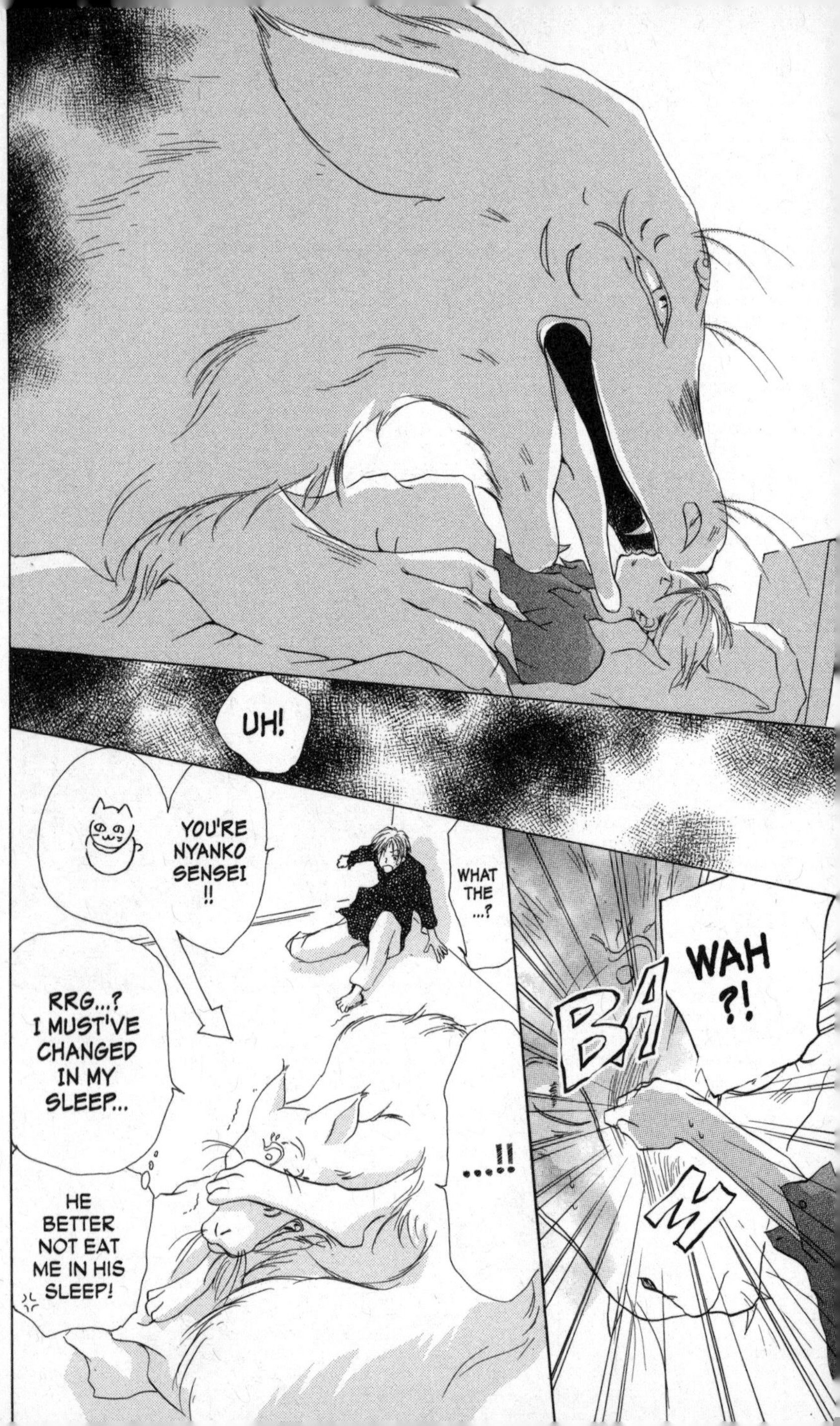
UH!
WAH ?!
BAM
WHAT THE ...?
YOU'RE NYANKO SENSEI !!
...!!
RRG...? I MUST'VE CHANGED IN MY SLEEP...
HE BETTER NOT EAT ME IN HIS SLEEP!

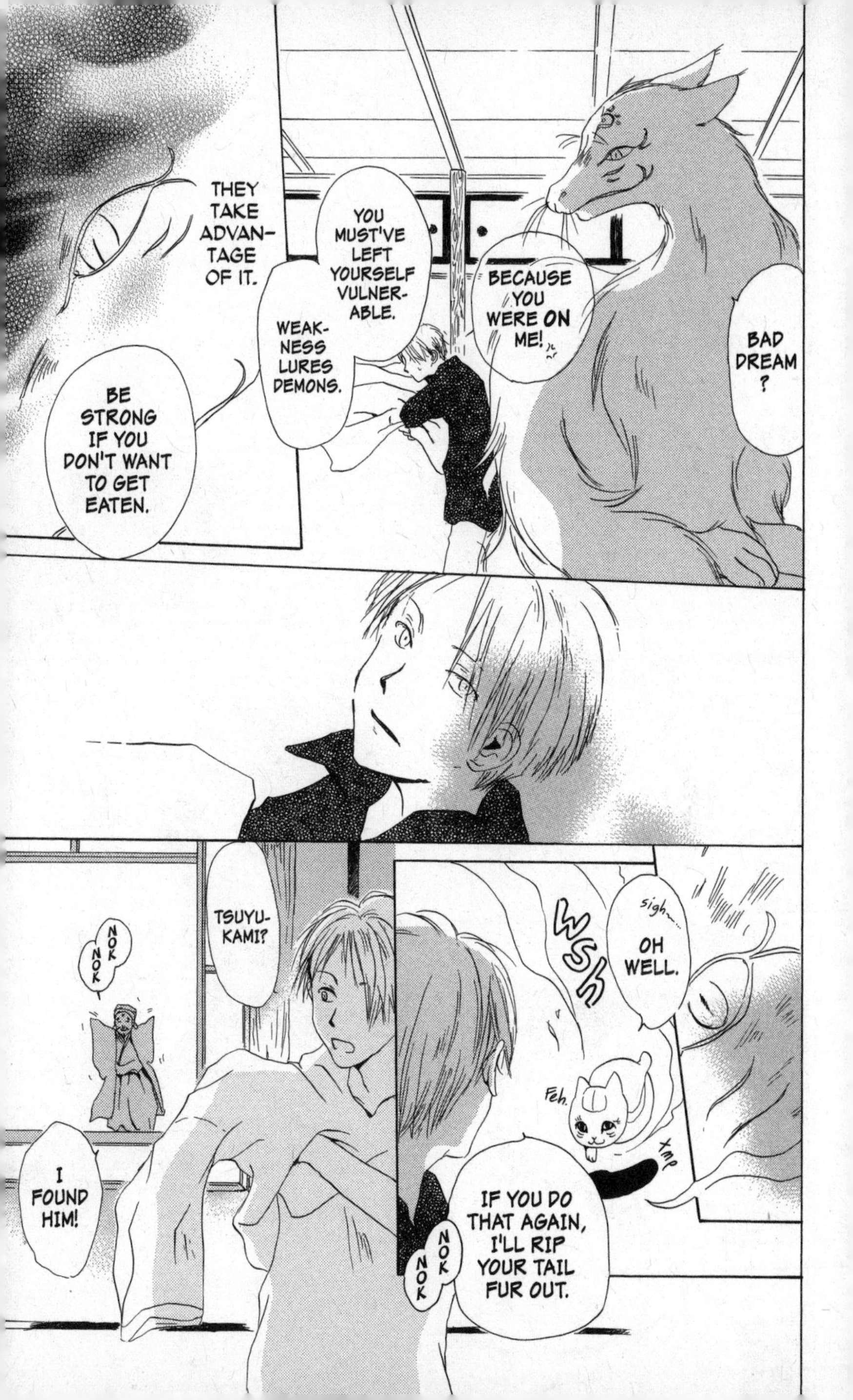
BAD DREAM?
BECAUSE YOU WERE ON ME!
YOU MUST'VE LEFT YOURSELF VULNERABLE.
WEAKNESS LURES DEMONS.
THEY TAKE ADVANTAGE OF IT.
BE STRONG IF YOU DON'T WANT TO GET EATEN.
WSH
sigh... OH WELL.
Feh.
IF YOU DO THAT AGAIN, I'LL RIP YOUR TAIL FUR OUT.
NOK NOK
TSUYU-KAMI?
NOK NOK
I FOUND HIM!

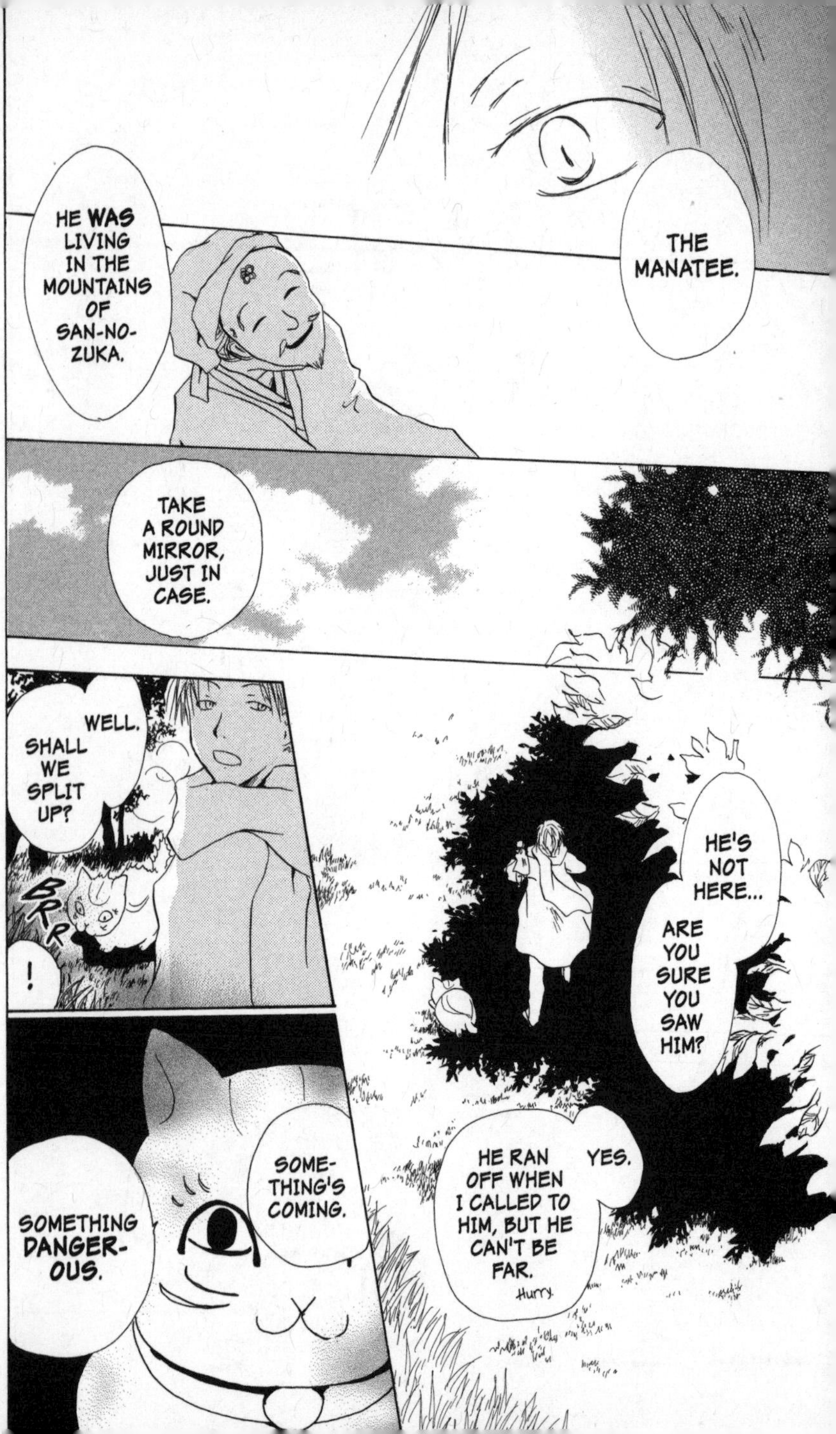
THE MANATEE.
HE WAS LIVING IN THE MOUNTAINS OF SAN-NO-ZUKA.
TAKE A ROUND MIRROR, JUST IN CASE.
HE'S NOT HERE... ARE YOU SURE YOU SAW HIM?
YES.
HE RAN OFF WHEN I CALLED TO HIM, BUT HE CAN'T BE FAR.
Hurry
WELL. SHALL WE SPLIT UP?
BRR
!
SOME-THING'S COMING.
SOMETHING DANGER-OUS.

04

❋ ~My Editor, Mr. S~

My current editor seems to be unemotional about his work, but the more we meet and talk, the more I realize he's really a passionate, hard working person with lots of ambition. I used to be so caught up in being conservative and refining my work, but he's made me remember how nice it feels to work with someone with such fire. The challenge used to be to see if I was capable of doing something. But now we have the joys and tribulations of engineering a manga to make people think, and he works and suffers alongside me. I keep worrying that I'm going to derail between the direction I've always wanted to go and the direction they want me to go, but he's very patient with me. And he strives hard to improve himself so that he can, in turn, help develop many good manga artists. So he makes me want to try even harder, for his sake.

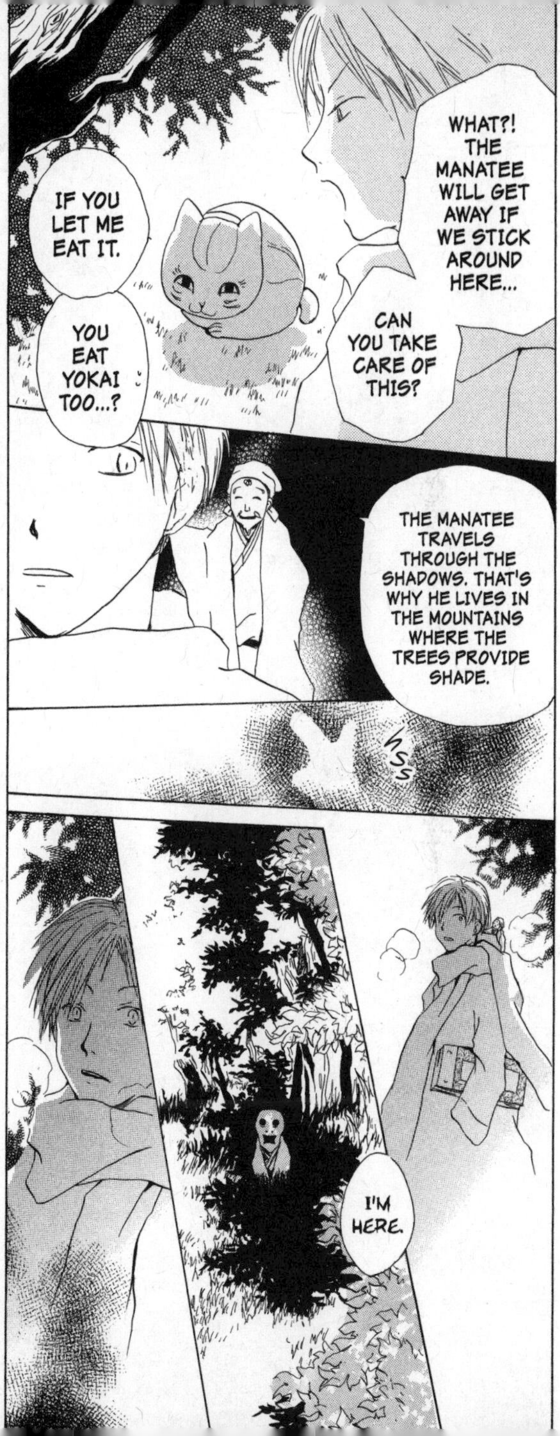
WHAT?! THE MANATEE WILL GET AWAY IF WE STICK AROUND HERE...
CAN YOU TAKE CARE OF THIS?
IF YOU LET ME EAT IT.
YOU EAT YOKAI TOO...?
THE MANATEE TRAVELS THROUGH THE SHADOWS. THAT'S WHY HE LIVES IN THE MOUNTAINS WHERE THE TREES PROVIDE SHADE.
HSS
I'M HERE.

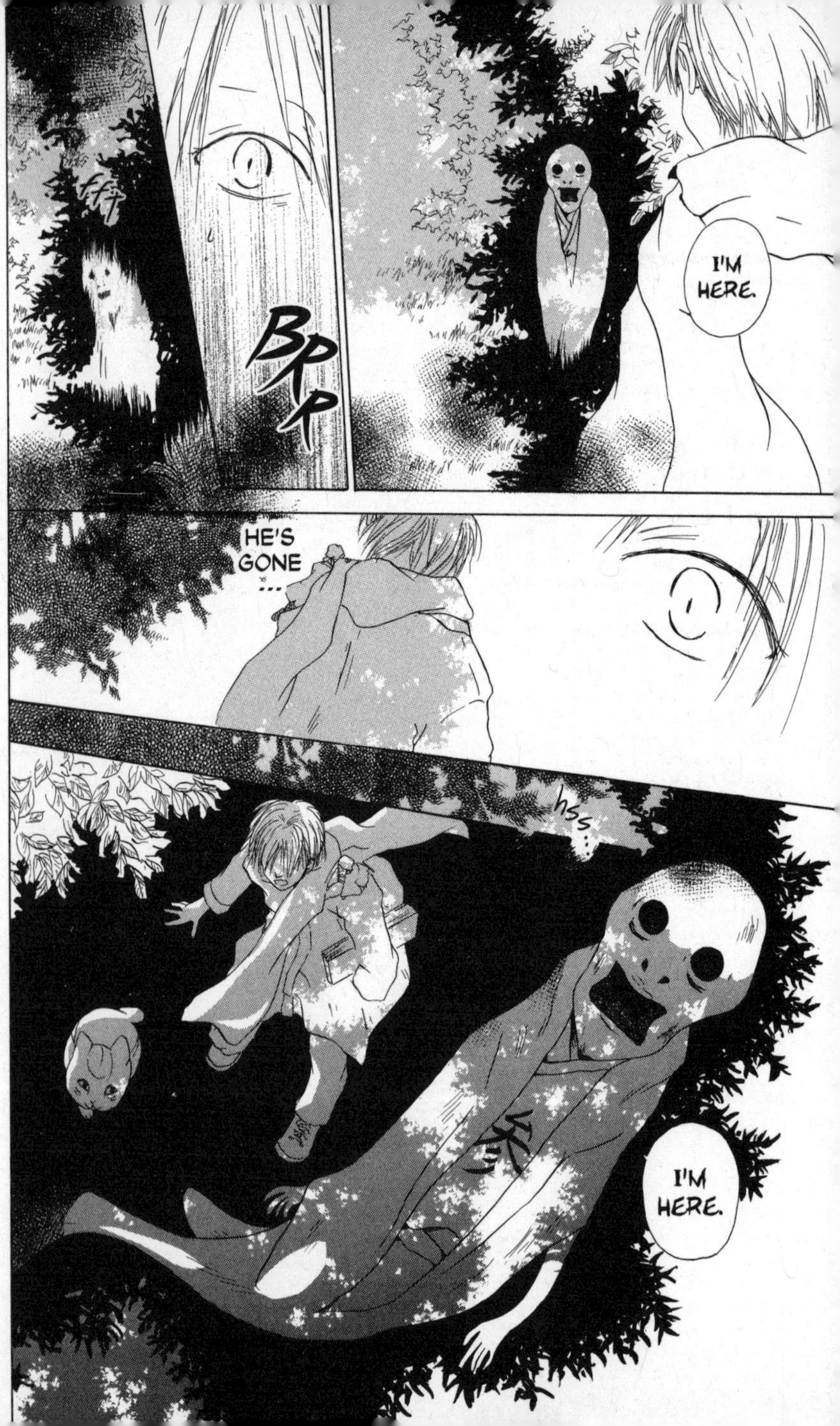
I'M HERE.
BRR
HE'S GONE...
hss...
I'M HERE.

05

❋~Supernatural stories: part 2~

So when I was teamed up with my editor, my repressed desire to make a supernatural manga without much of a romantic element was suddenly incited. That's how I came to work on this manga.

I grew up close to the mountains and forests, where it always seemed like something was lurking. I was exposed to many anecdotes about the supernatural, yokai and local gods that stirred my imagination. There were stories behind weird place names and most mountains and rivers. I would get excited about all of them. I hope to create that kind of everyday excitement.

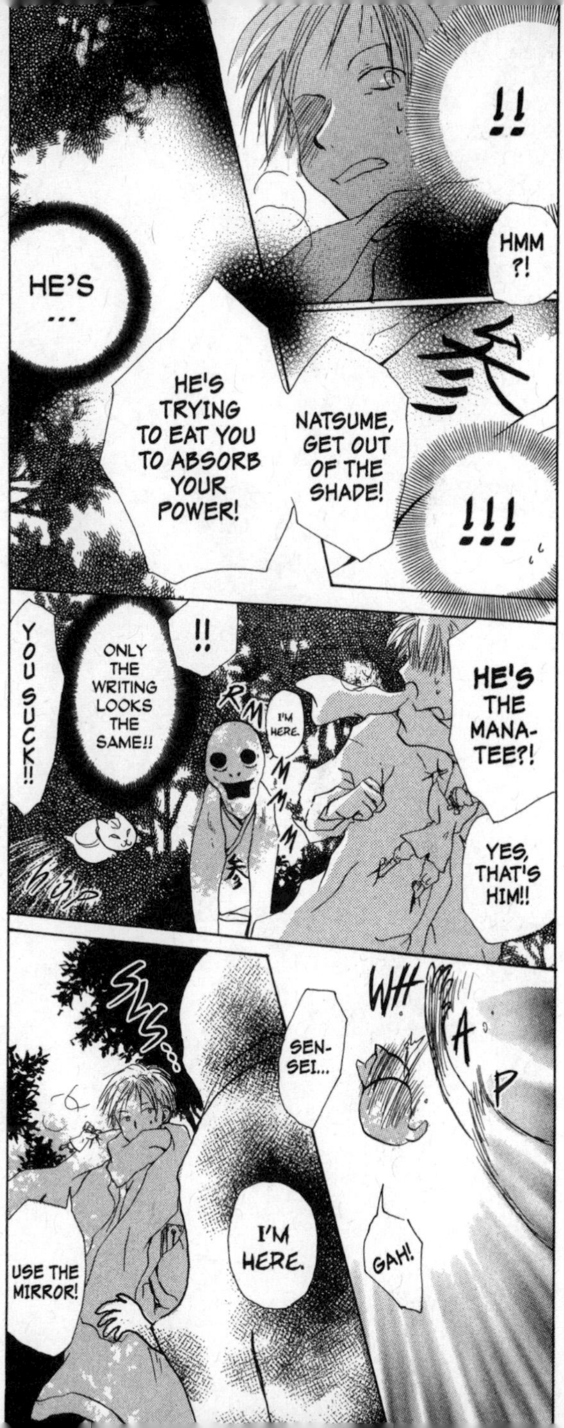
!!
HMM ?!
HE'S ...
!!!
NATSUME, GET OUT OF THE SHADE!
HE'S TRYING TO EAT YOU TO ABSORB YOUR POWER!
HE'S THE MANATEE?!
YES, THAT'S HIM!!
I'M HERE.
RMMMMMM
!!
ONLY THE WRITING LOOKS THE SAME!!
YOU SUCK!!
WHAP
GAH!
SEN-SEI...
I'M HERE.
USE THE MIRROR!

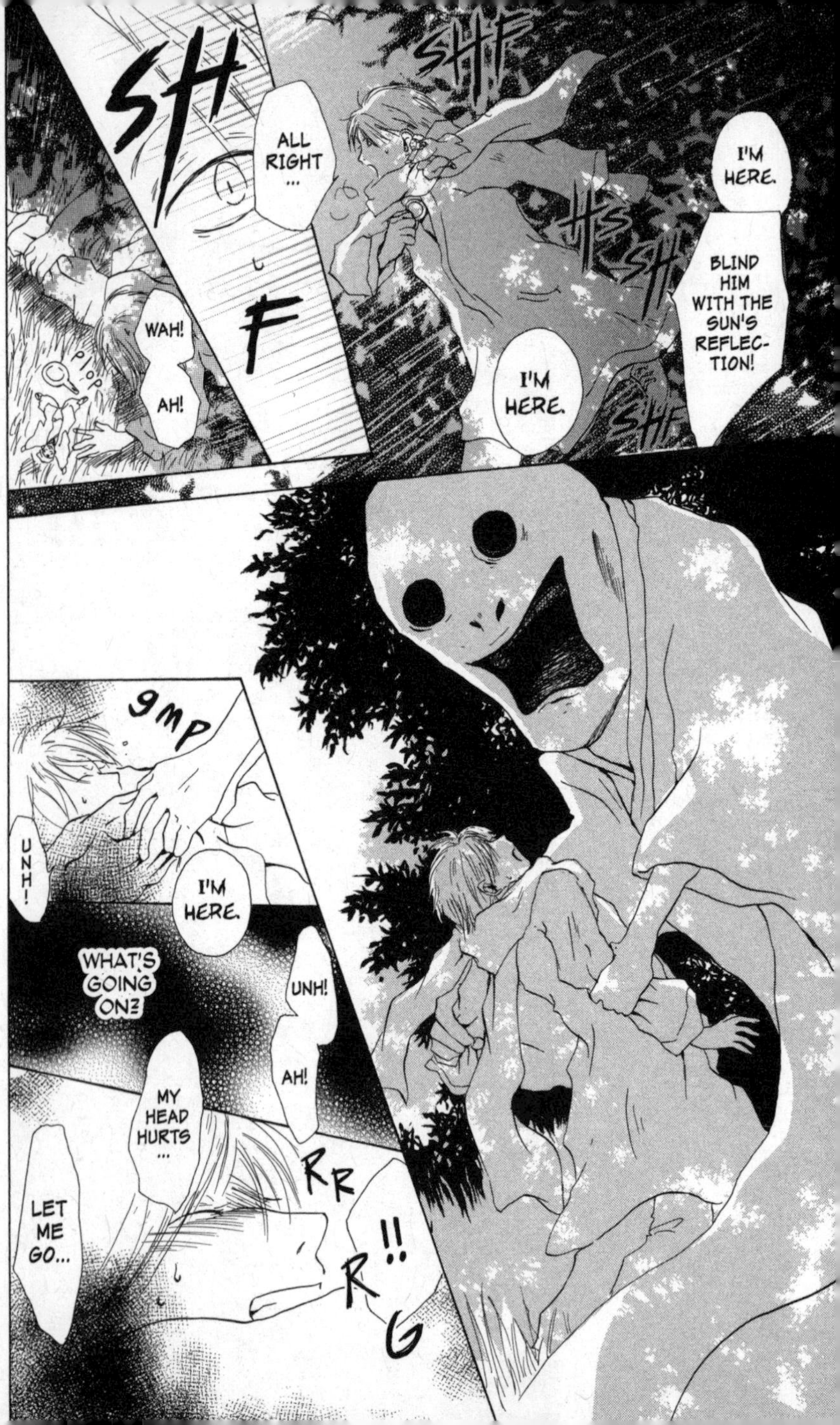
SHF
I'M HERE.
HSS
SH
BLIND HIM WITH THE SUN'S REFLECTION!
I'M HERE.
SHF
ALL RIGHT ...
F
SH
WAH!
PLOP
AH!
gmp
UNH!
I'M HERE.
WHAT'S GOING ON?
UNH!
AH!
MY HEAD HURTS ...
LET ME GO...
RRRG!!

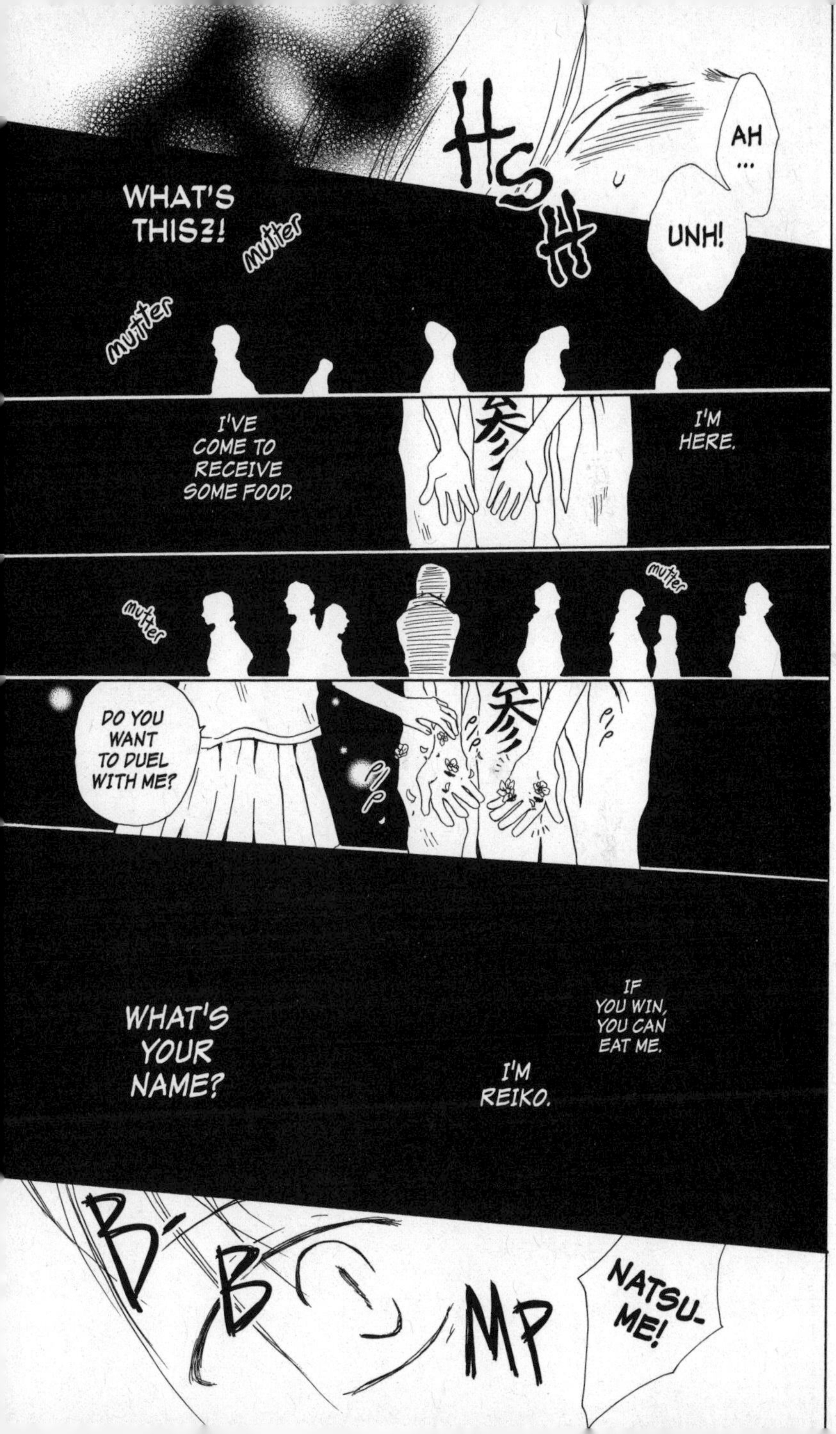
HSH
AH...
UNH!
WHAT'S THIS?!
mutter
mutter
参
I'M HERE.
I'VE COME TO RECEIVE SOME FOOD.
mutter
mutter
参
DO YOU WANT TO DUEL WITH ME?
IF YOU WIN, YOU CAN EAT ME.
I'M REIKO.
WHAT'S YOUR NAME?
NATSU-ME!
B-BOMP

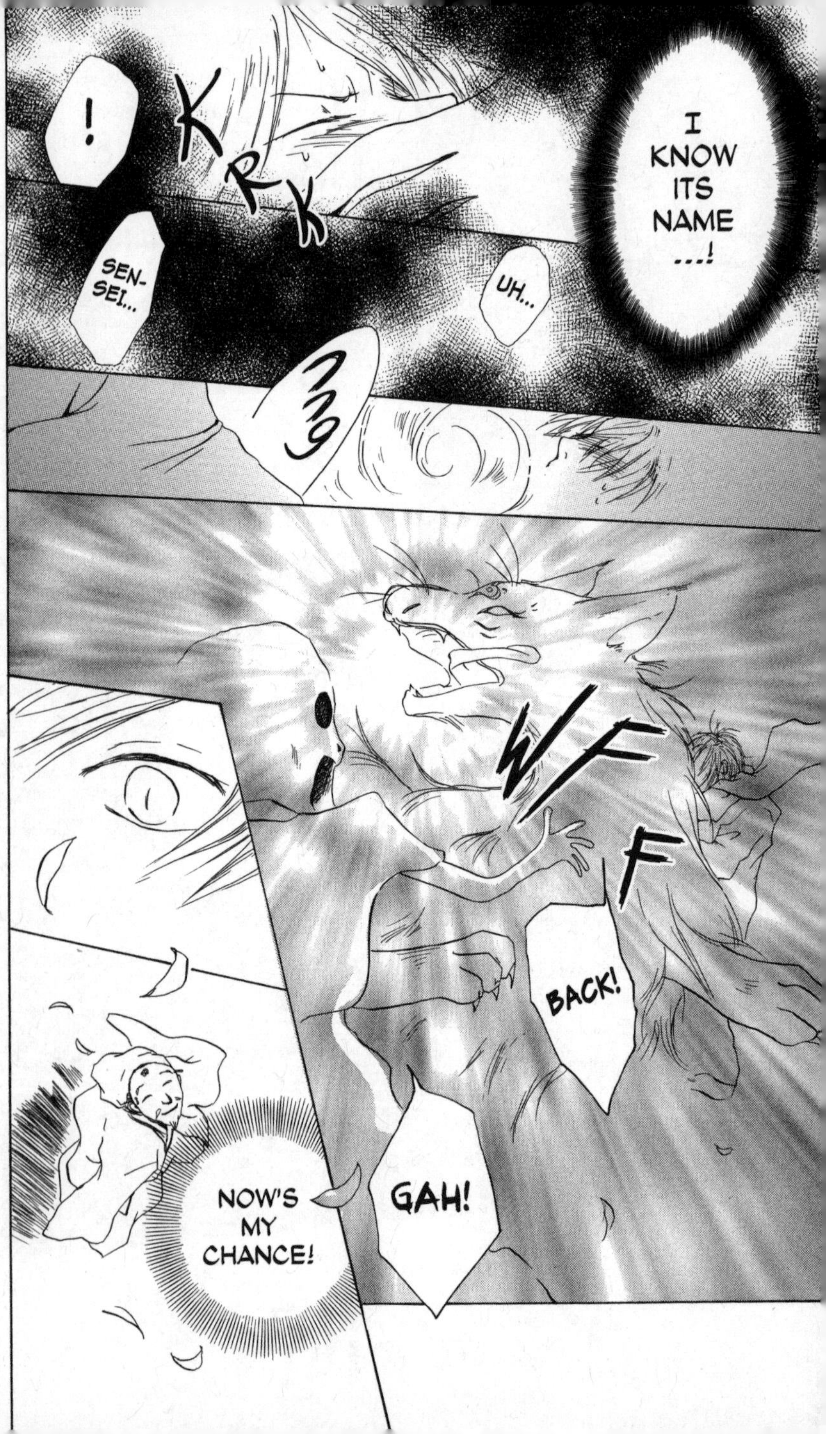

!
KRK
I KNOW ITS NAME ...!
UH...
SEN-SEI...
WFF
BACK!
GAH!
NOW'S MY CHANCE!

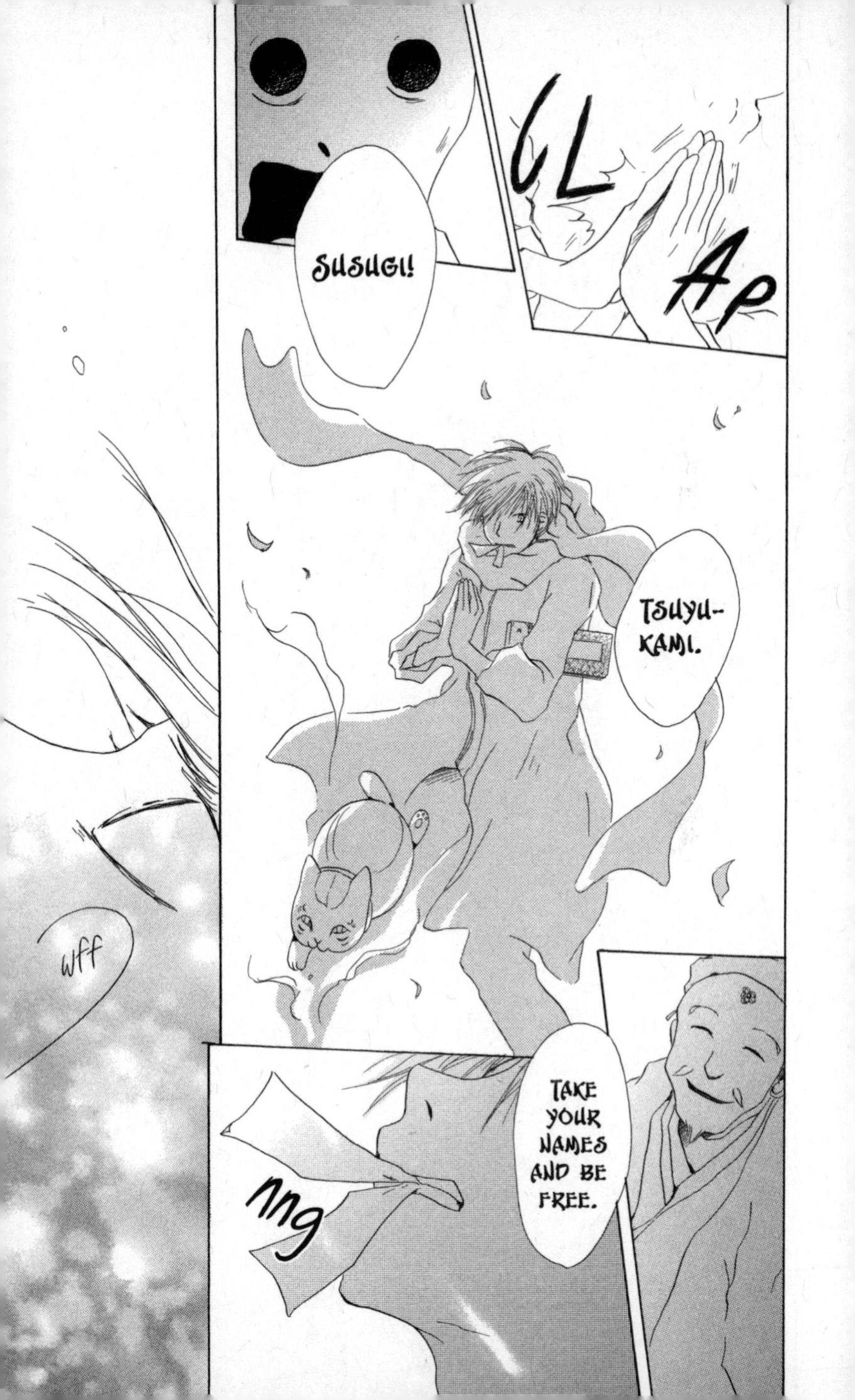
CLAP
SUSUGI!
TSUYU-KAMI.
TAKE YOUR NAMES AND BE FREE.
nng
wff

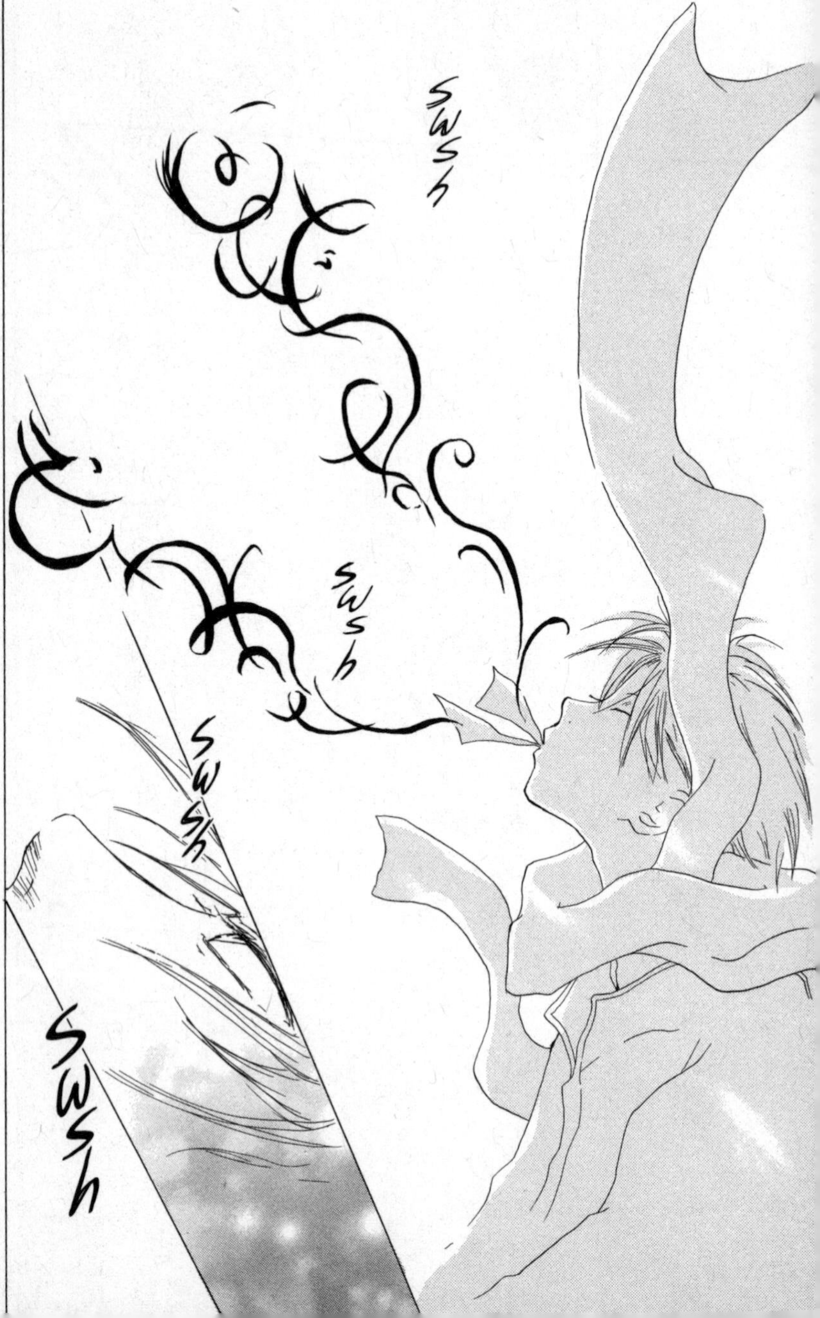
swsh
swsh
swsh
swsh

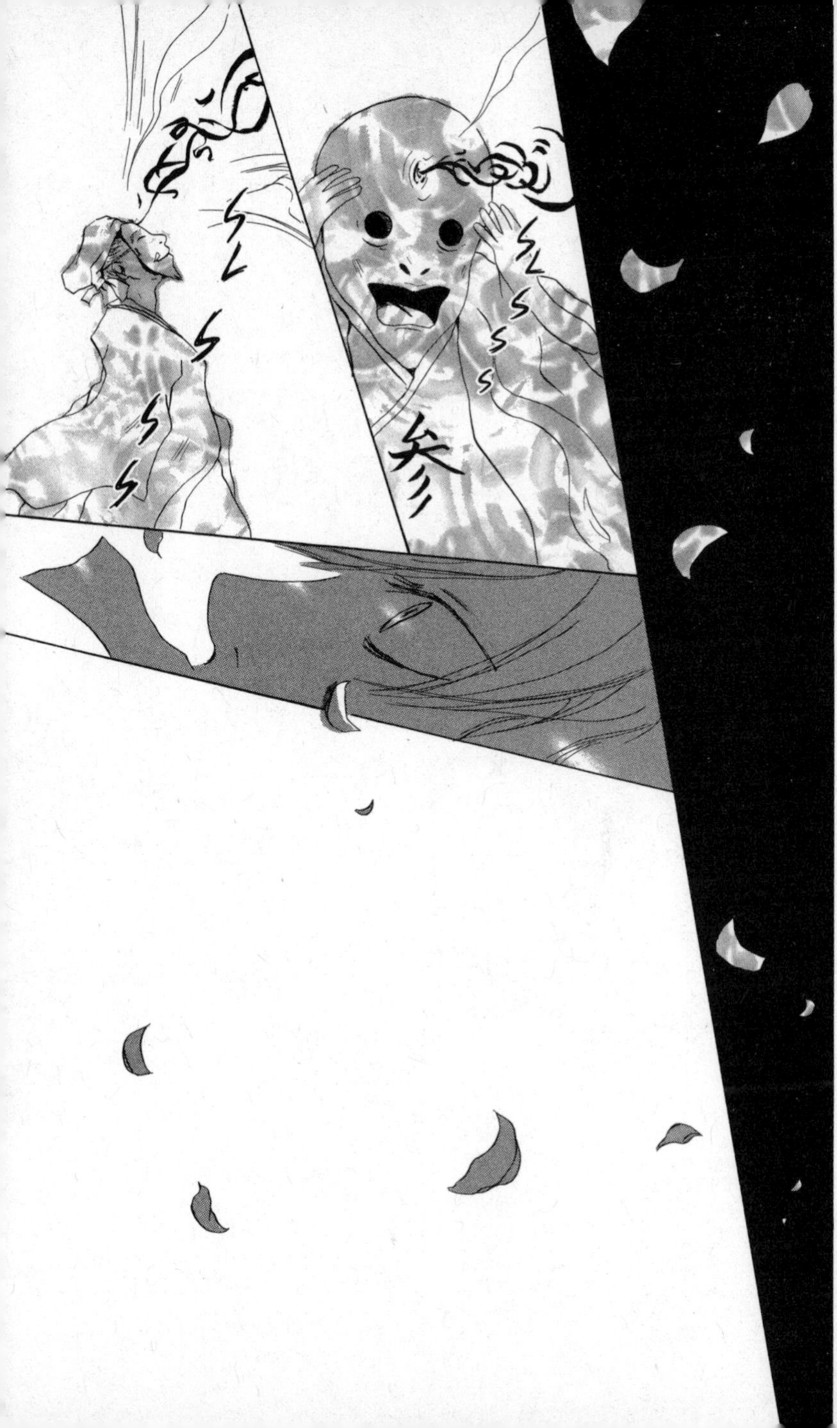

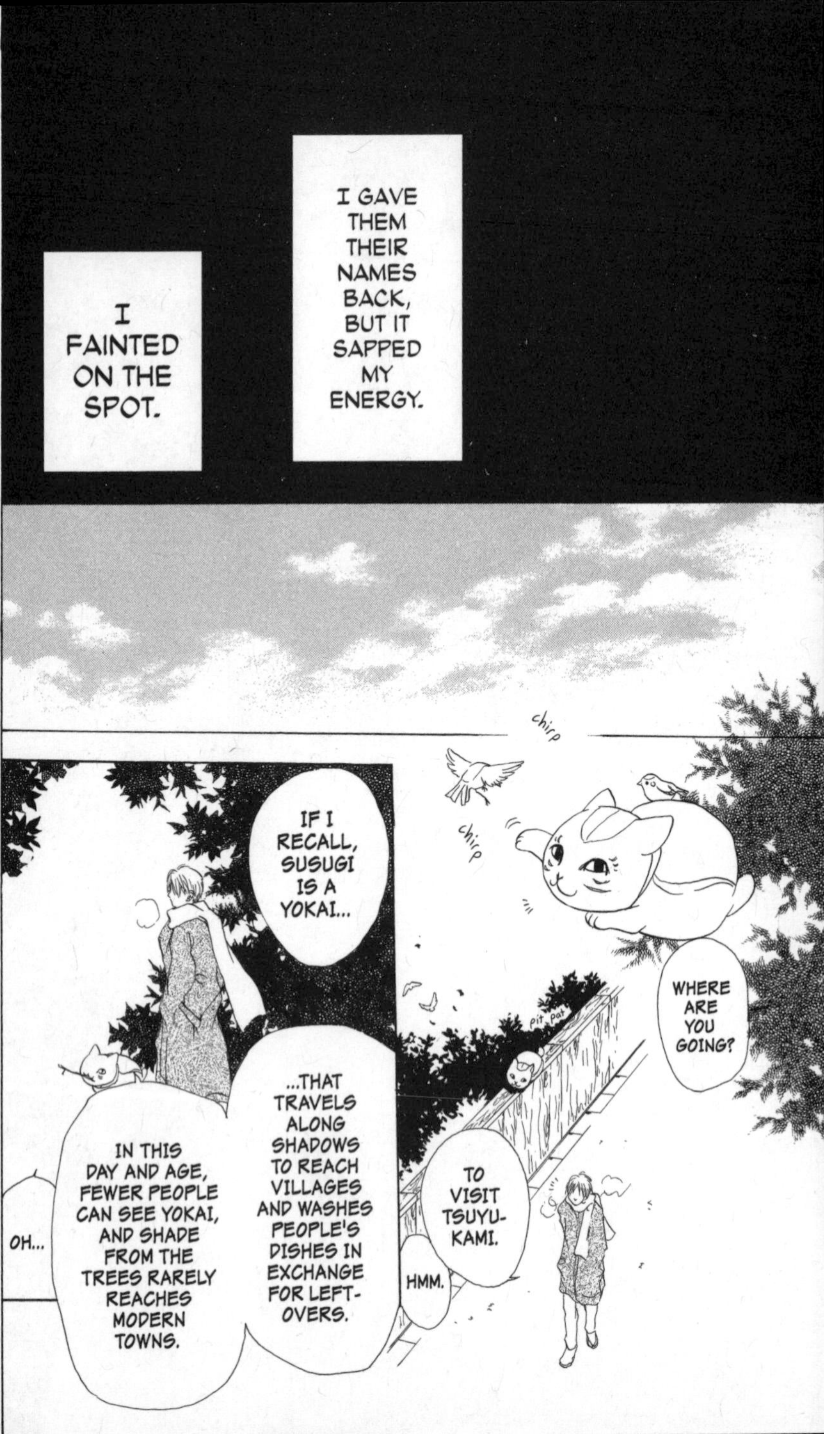
I GAVE THEM THEIR NAMES BACK, BUT IT SAPPED MY ENERGY.
I FAINTED ON THE SPOT.
chirp
chirp
WHERE ARE YOU GOING?
pit pat
TO VISIT TSUYU-KAMI.
HMM.
IF I RECALL, SUSUGI IS A YOKAI...
...THAT TRAVELS ALONG SHADOWS TO REACH VILLAGES AND WASHES PEOPLE'S DISHES IN EXCHANGE FOR LEFT-OVERS.
IN THIS DAY AND AGE, FEWER PEOPLE CAN SEE YOKAI, AND SHADE FROM THE TREES RARELY REACHES MODERN TOWNS.
OH...

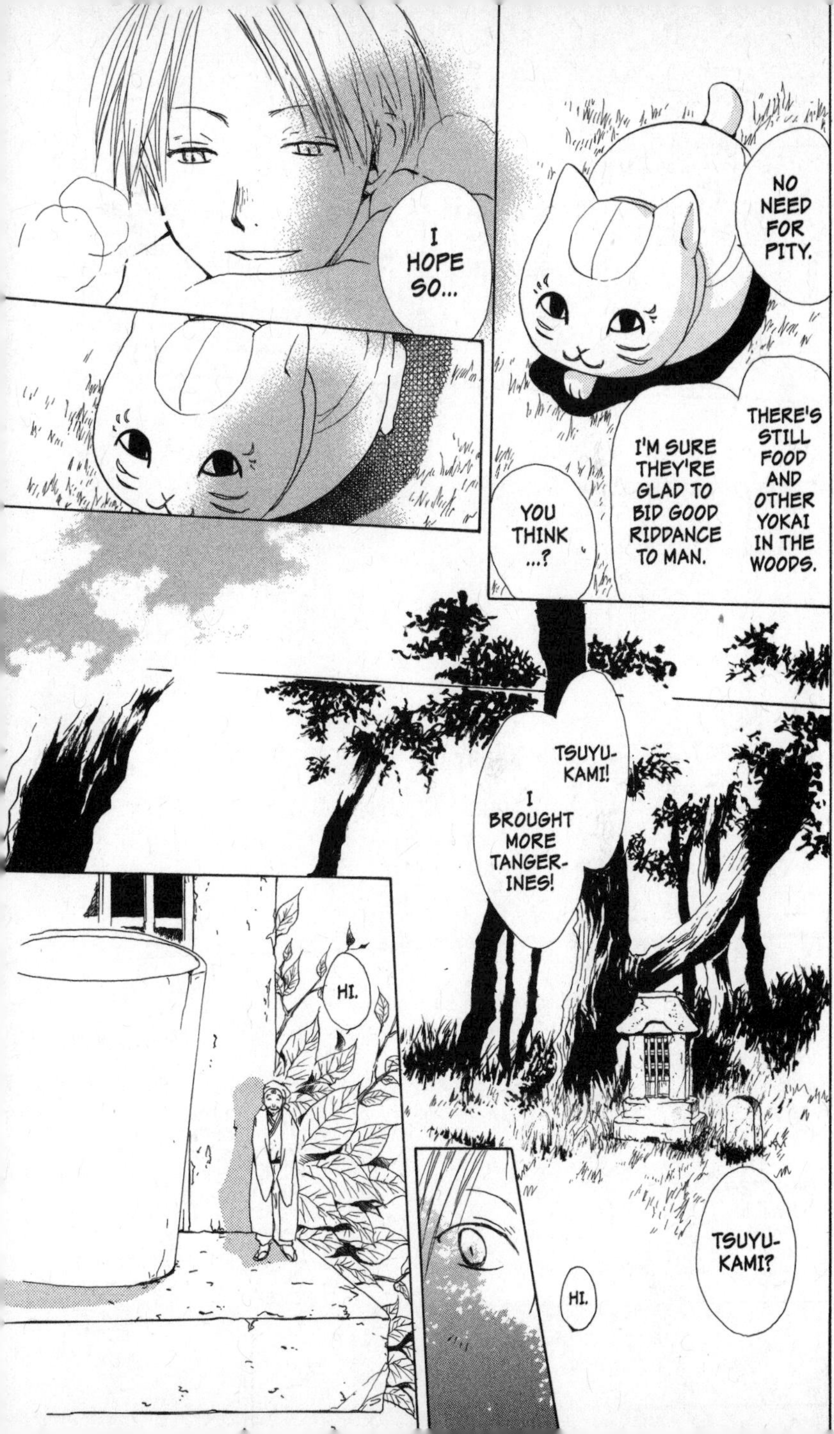
NO NEED FOR PITY.
THERE'S STILL FOOD AND OTHER YOKAI IN THE WOODS.
I'M SURE THEY'RE GLAD TO BID GOOD RIDDANCE TO MAN.
YOU THINK ...?
I HOPE SO...
TSUYU-KAMI!
I BROUGHT MORE TANGER-INES!
TSUYU-KAMI?
HI.
HI.

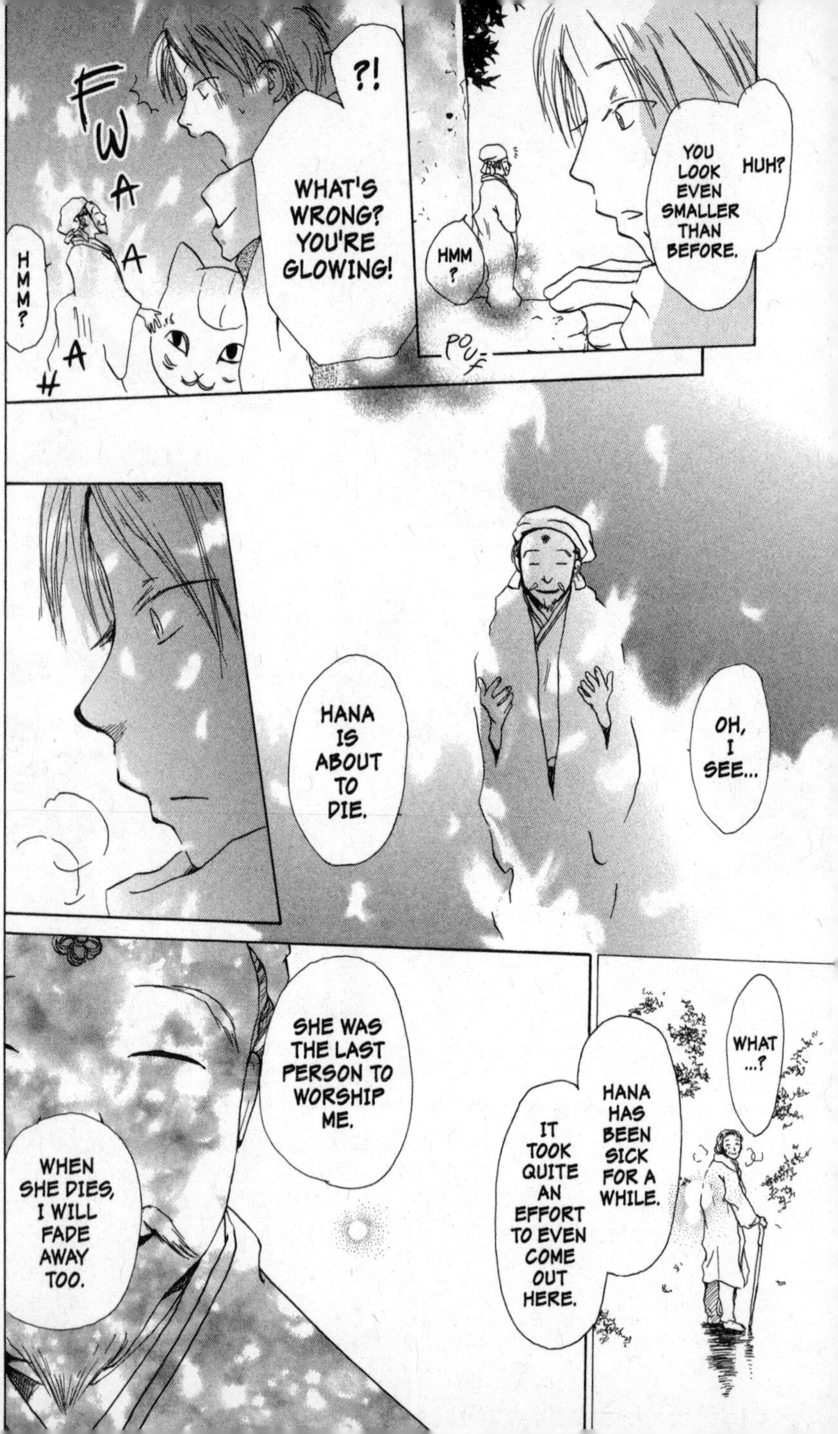
HUH?
YOU LOOK EVEN SMALLER THAN BEFORE.
HMM ?
POUF
?!
WHAT'S WRONG? YOU'RE GLOWING!
FWAAAH
HMM?
OH, I SEE...
HANA IS ABOUT TO DIE.
WHAT ...?
HANA HAS BEEN SICK FOR A WHILE.
IT TOOK QUITE AN EFFORT TO EVEN COME OUT HERE.
SHE WAS THE LAST PERSON TO WORSHIP ME.
WHEN SHE DIES, I WILL FADE AWAY TOO.

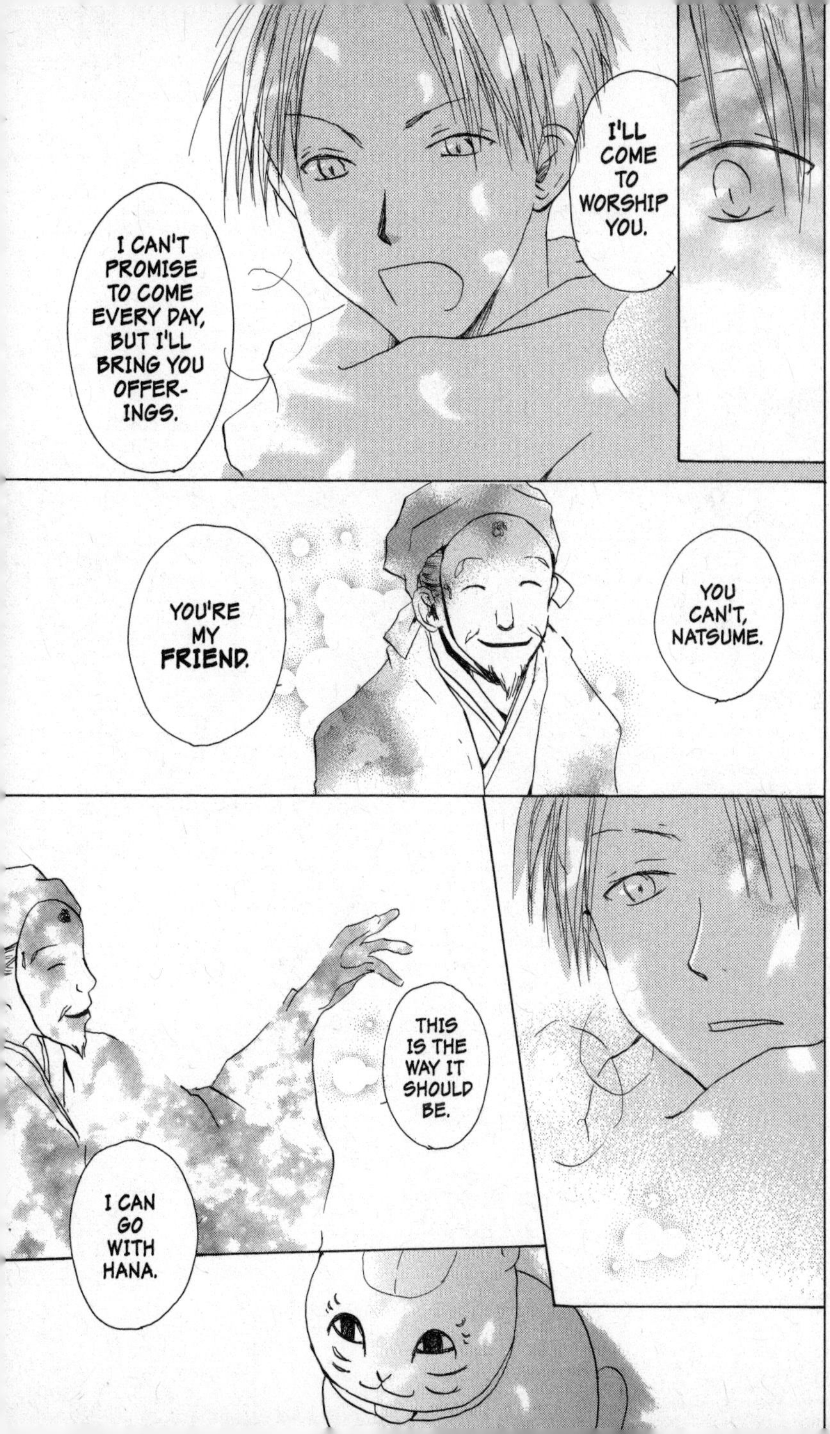
I'LL COME TO WORSHIP YOU.
I CAN'T PROMISE TO COME EVERY DAY, BUT I'LL BRING YOU OFFER-INGS.
YOU CAN'T, NATSUME.
YOU'RE MY FRIEND.
THIS IS THE WAY IT SHOULD BE.
I CAN GO WITH HANA.

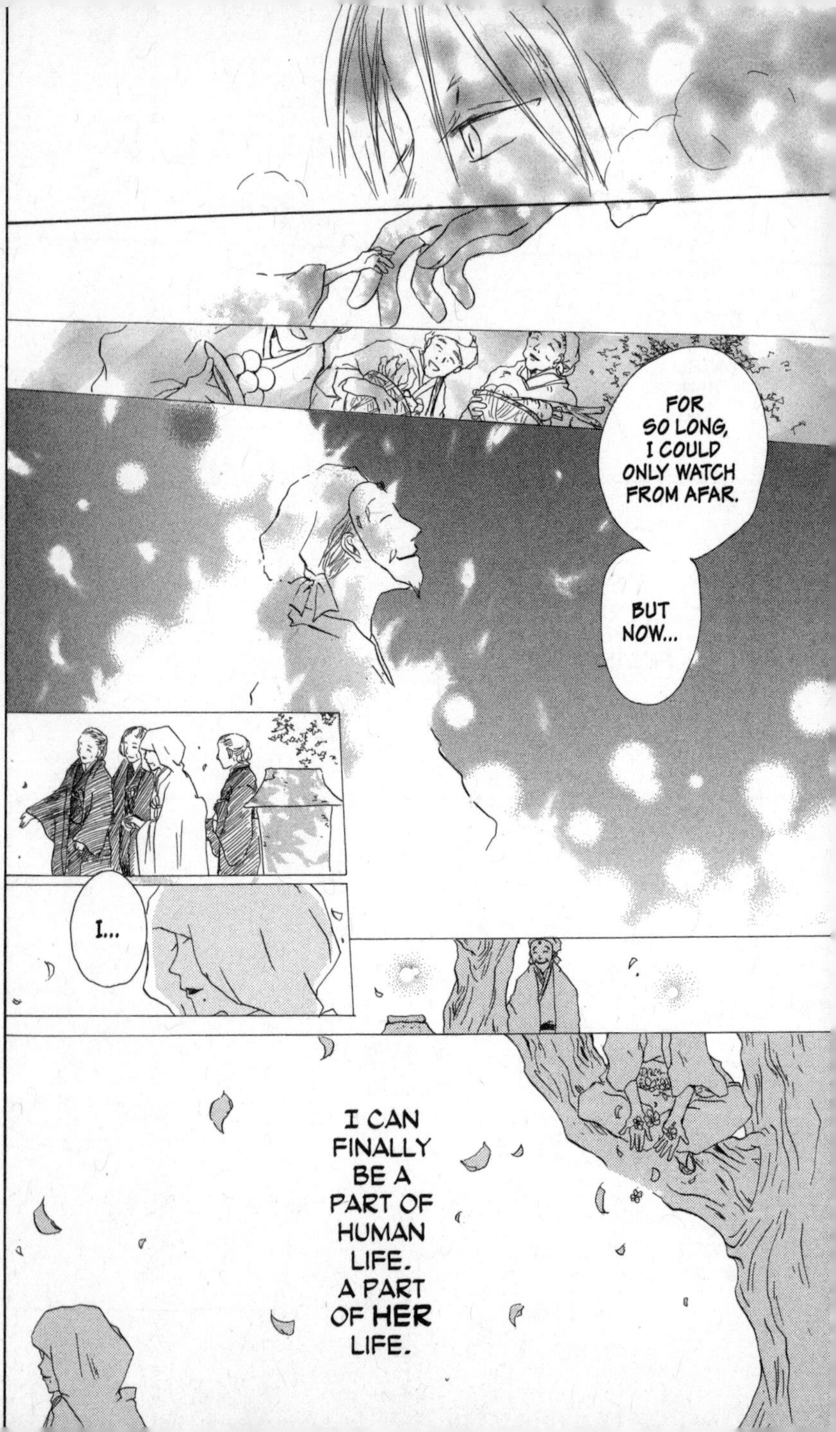
FOR SO LONG, I COULD ONLY WATCH FROM AFAR.
BUT NOW...
I...
I CAN FINALLY BE A PART OF HUMAN LIFE. A PART OF HER LIFE.

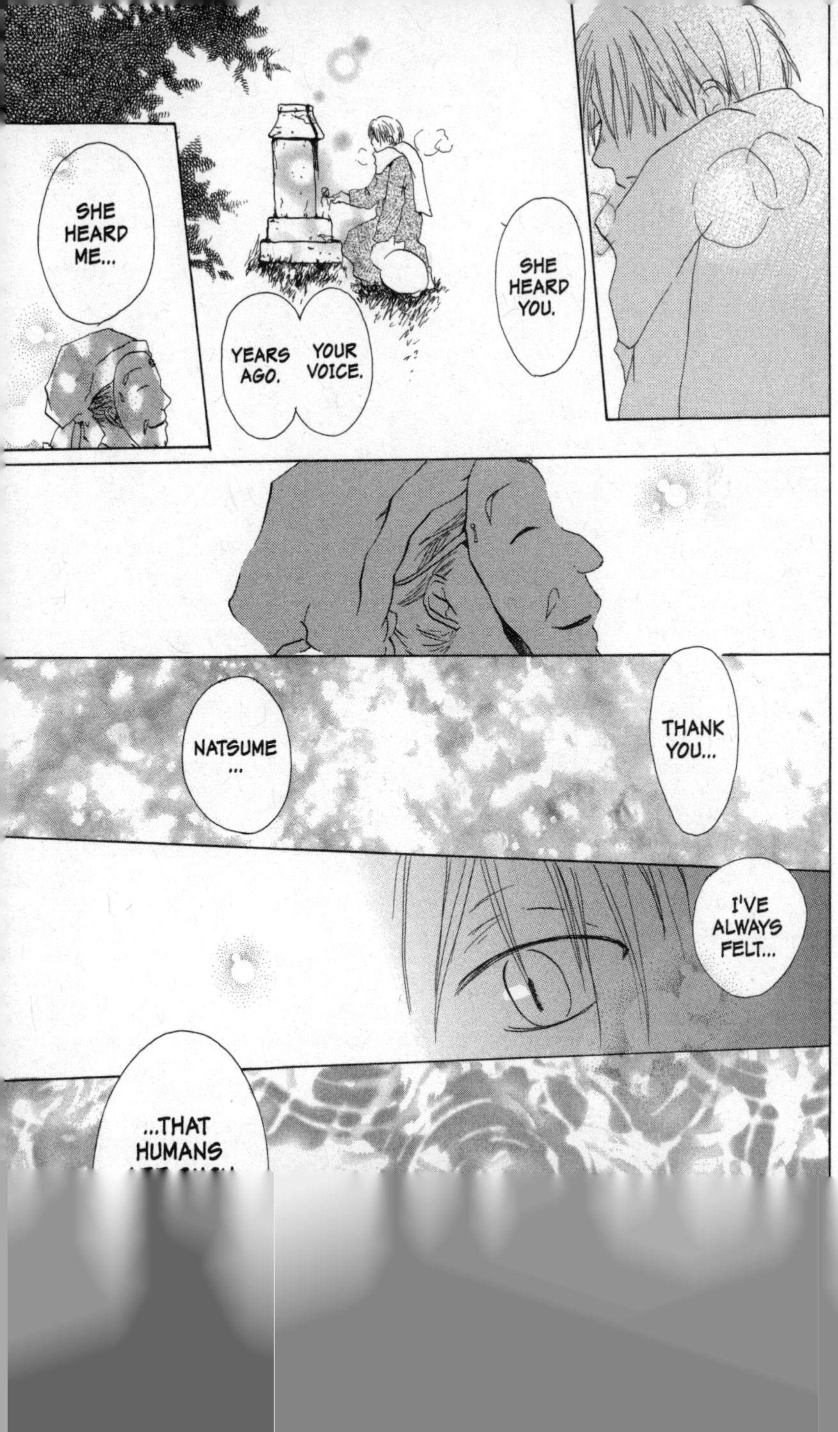
SHE HEARD YOU.
YOUR VOICE.
YEARS AGO.
SHE HEARD ME...
THANK YOU...
NATSUME ...
I'VE ALWAYS FELT...
...THAT HUMANS

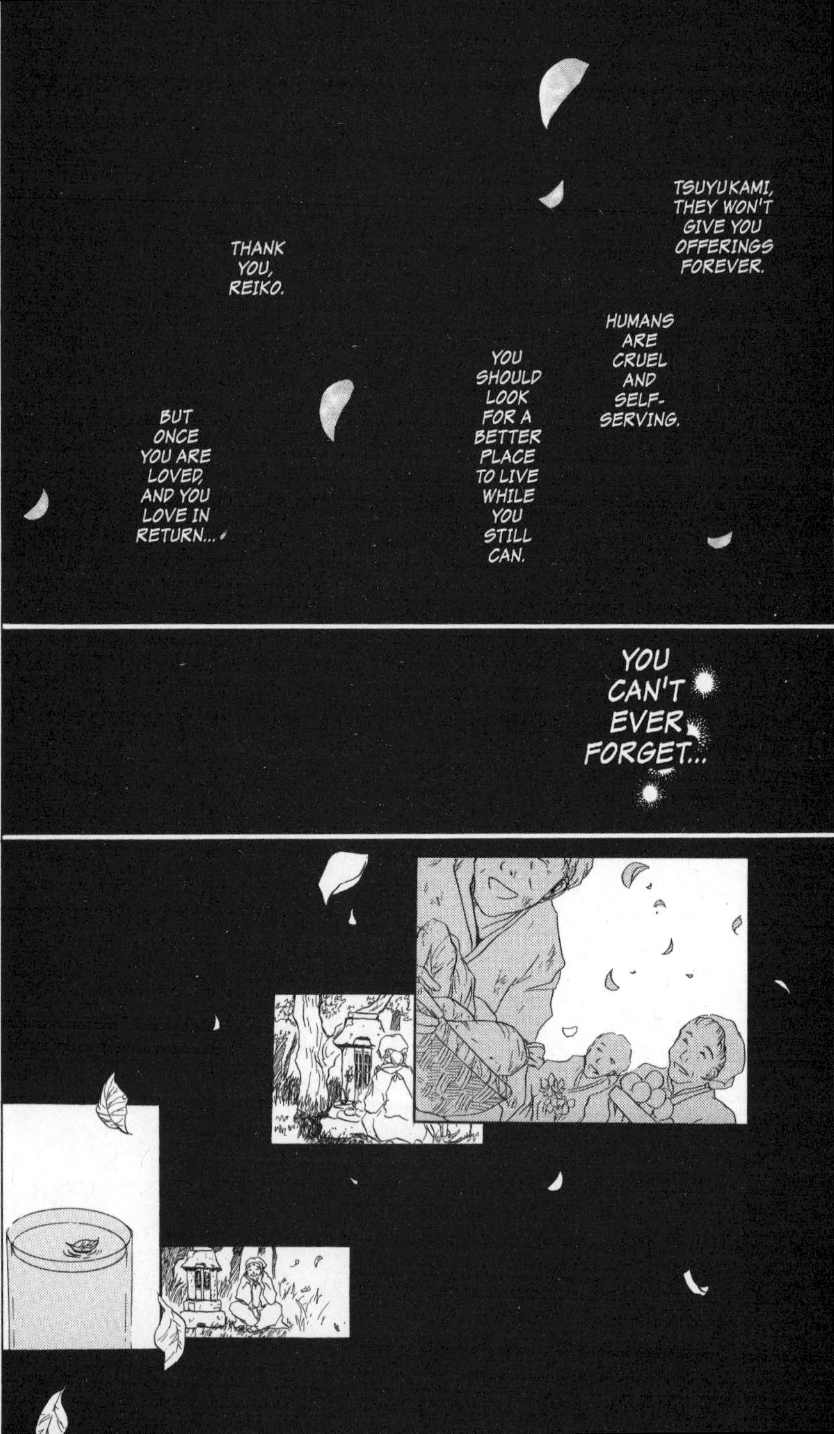
TSUYUKAMI, THEY WON'T GIVE YOU OFFERINGS FOREVER.
HUMANS ARE CRUEL AND SELF-SERVING.
YOU SHOULD LOOK FOR A BETTER PLACE TO LIVE WHILE YOU STILL CAN.
THANK YOU, REIKO.
BUT ONCE YOU ARE LOVED, AND YOU LOVE IN RETURN...
YOU CAN'T EVER FORGET...

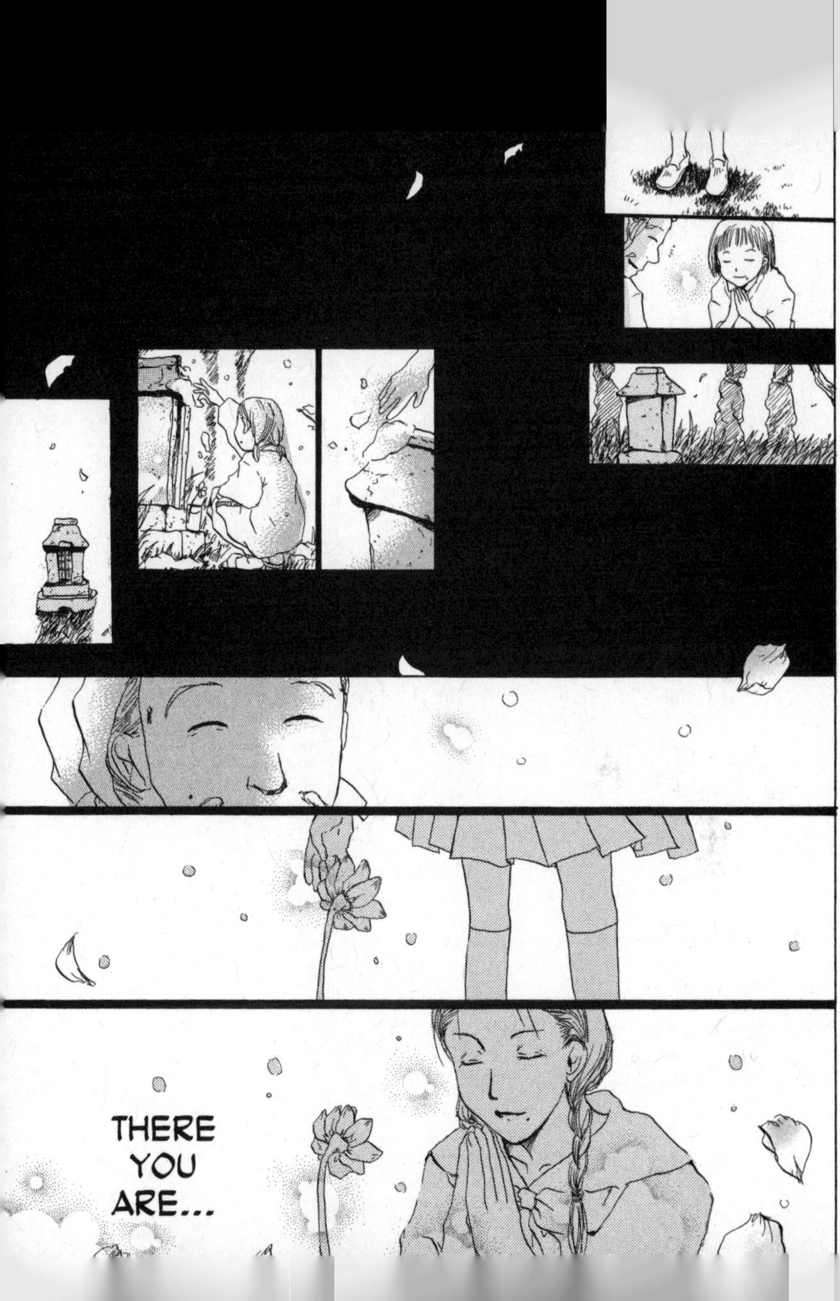
THERE YOU ARE...

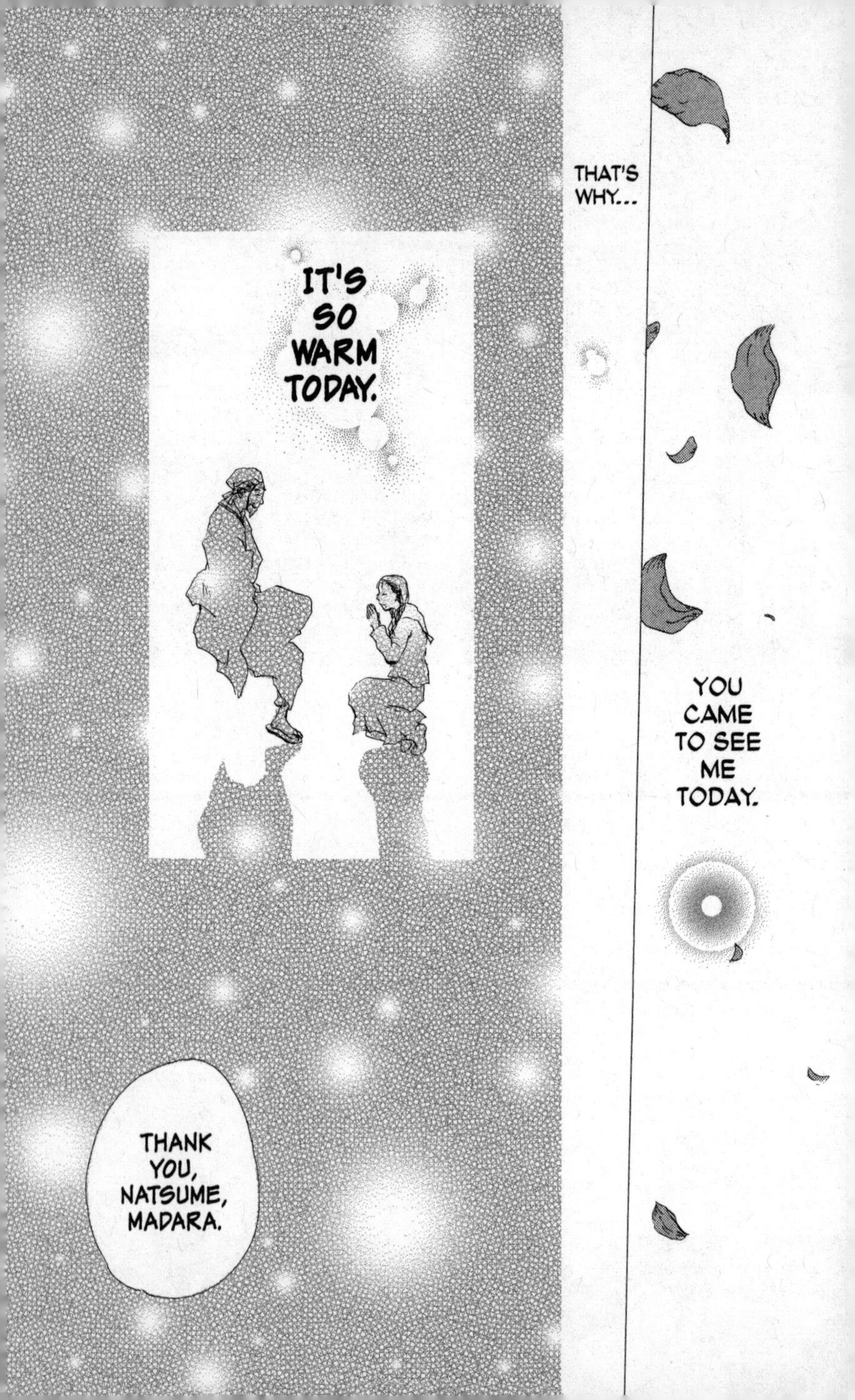
YOU CAME TO SEE ME TODAY.
THAT'S WHY...
IT'S SO WARM TODAY.
THANK YOU, NATSUME, MADARA.

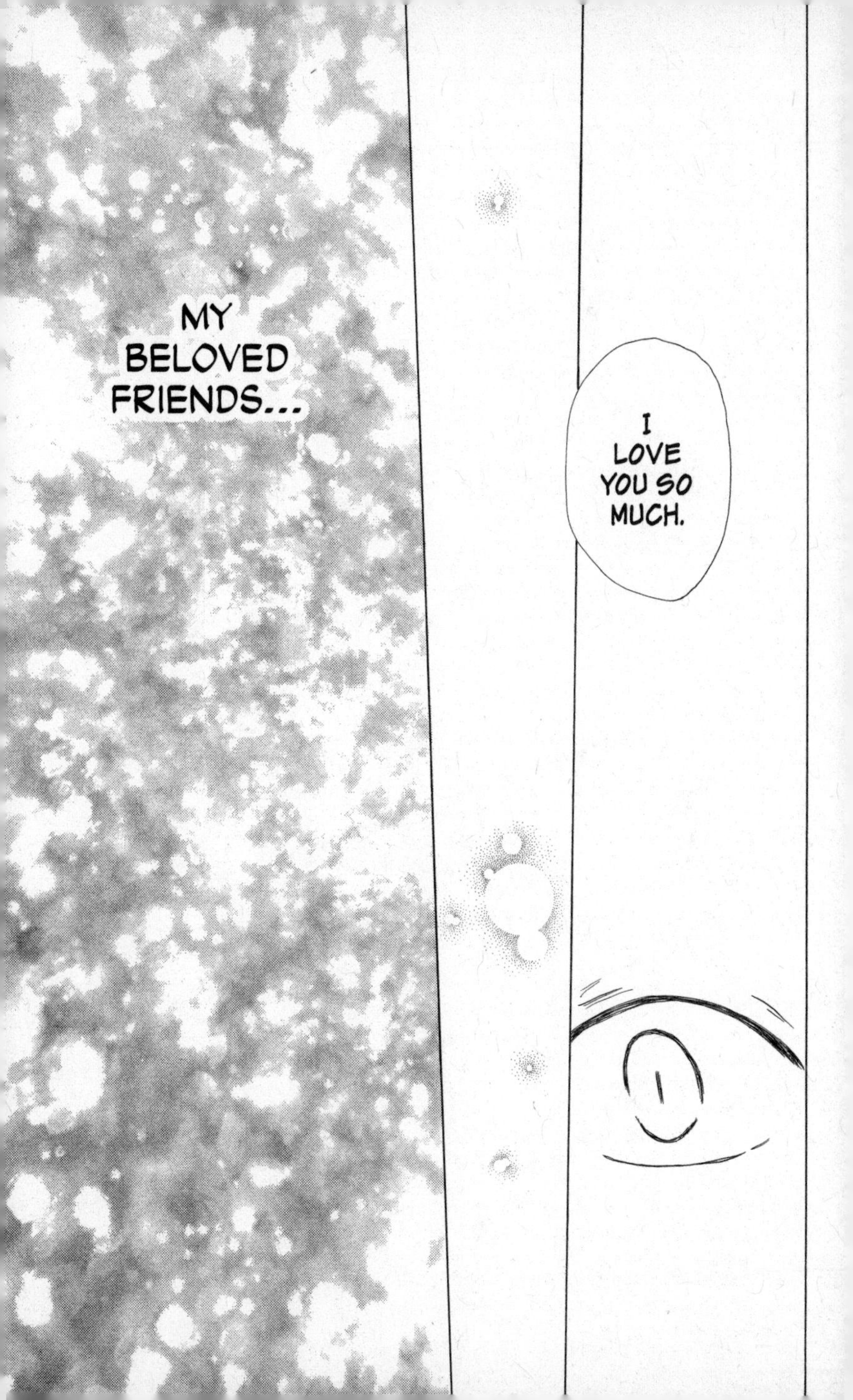
I LOVE YOU SO MUCH.
MY BELOVED FRIENDS...

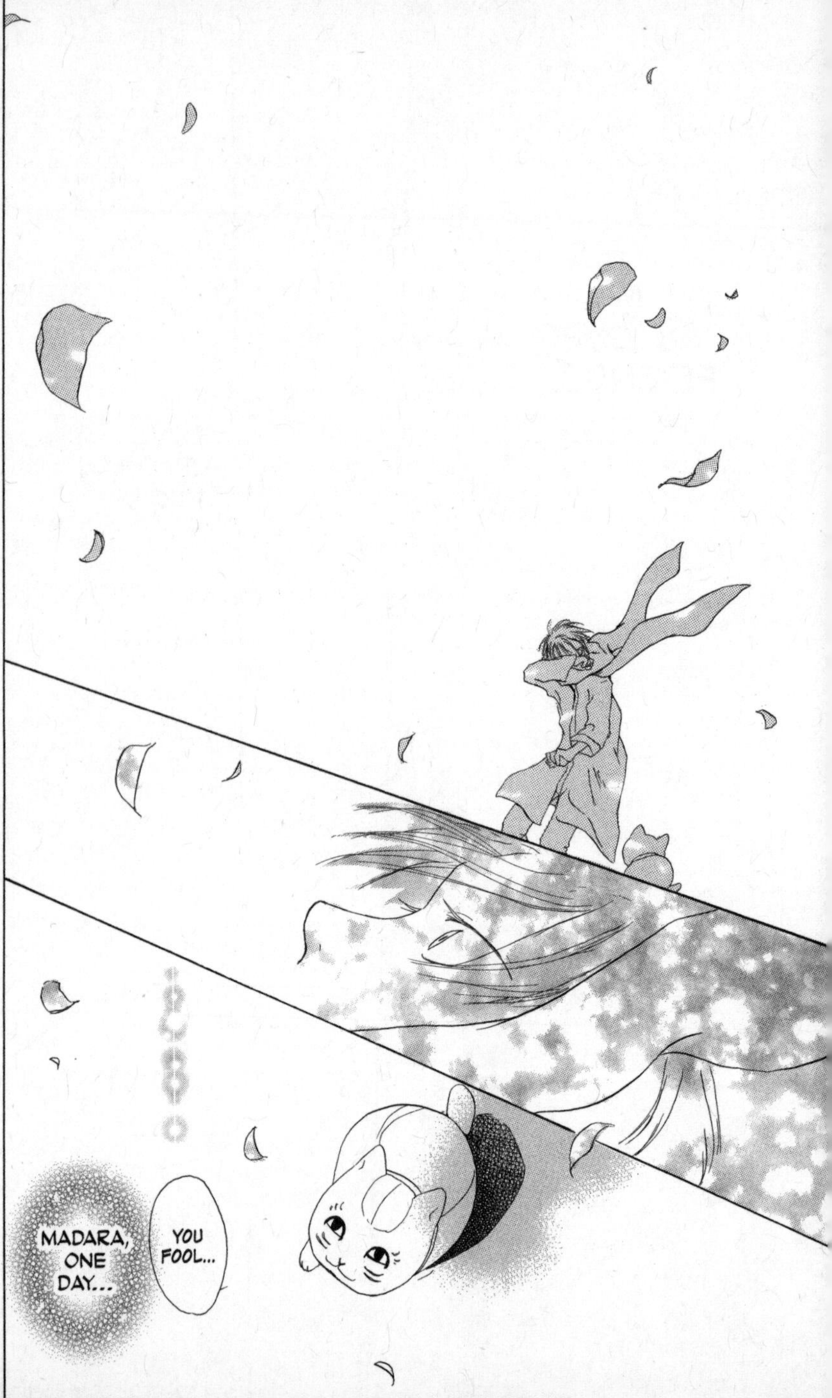
YOU FOOL...
MADARA, ONE DAY...

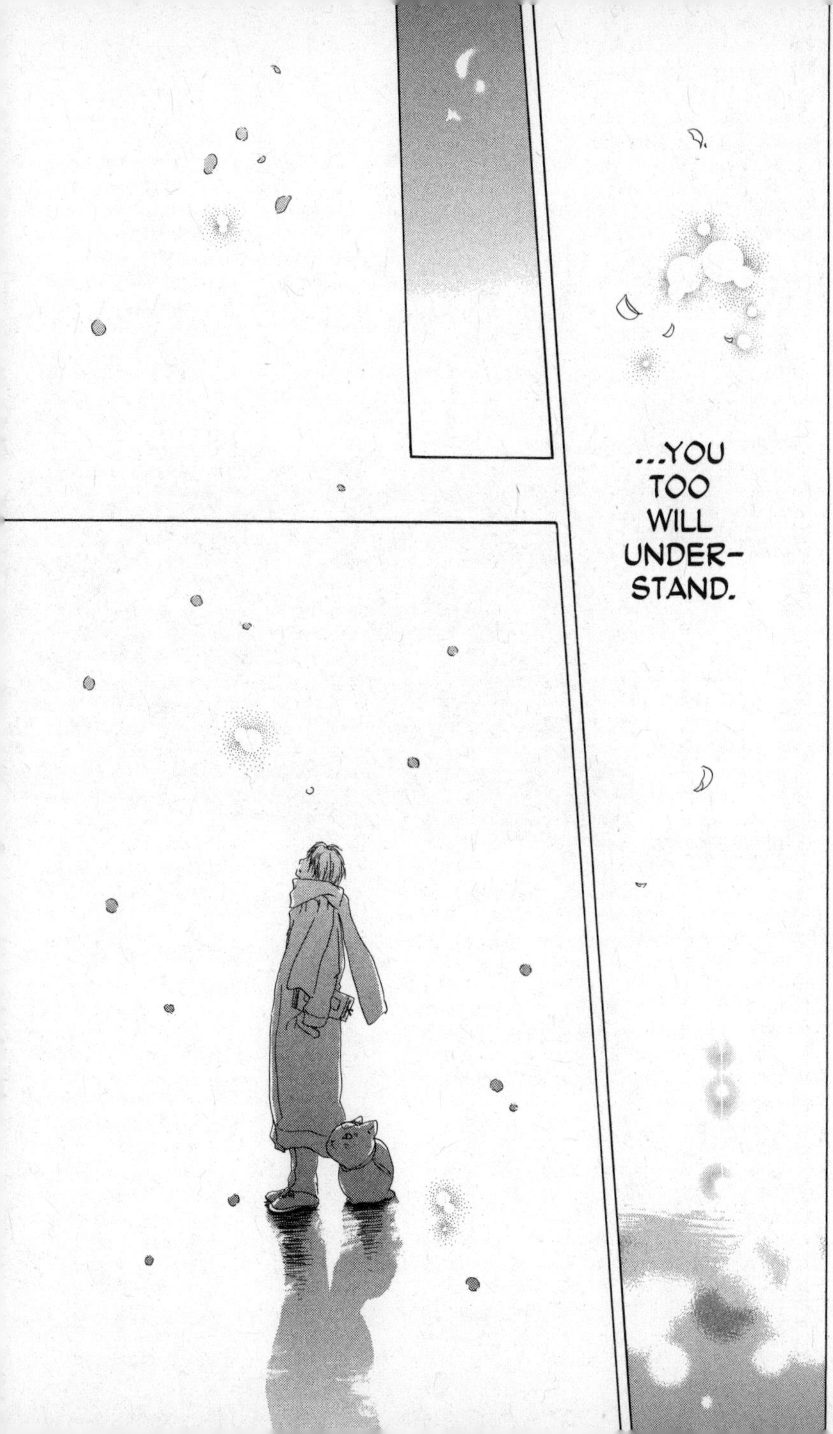
...YOU TOO WILL UNDER-STAND.

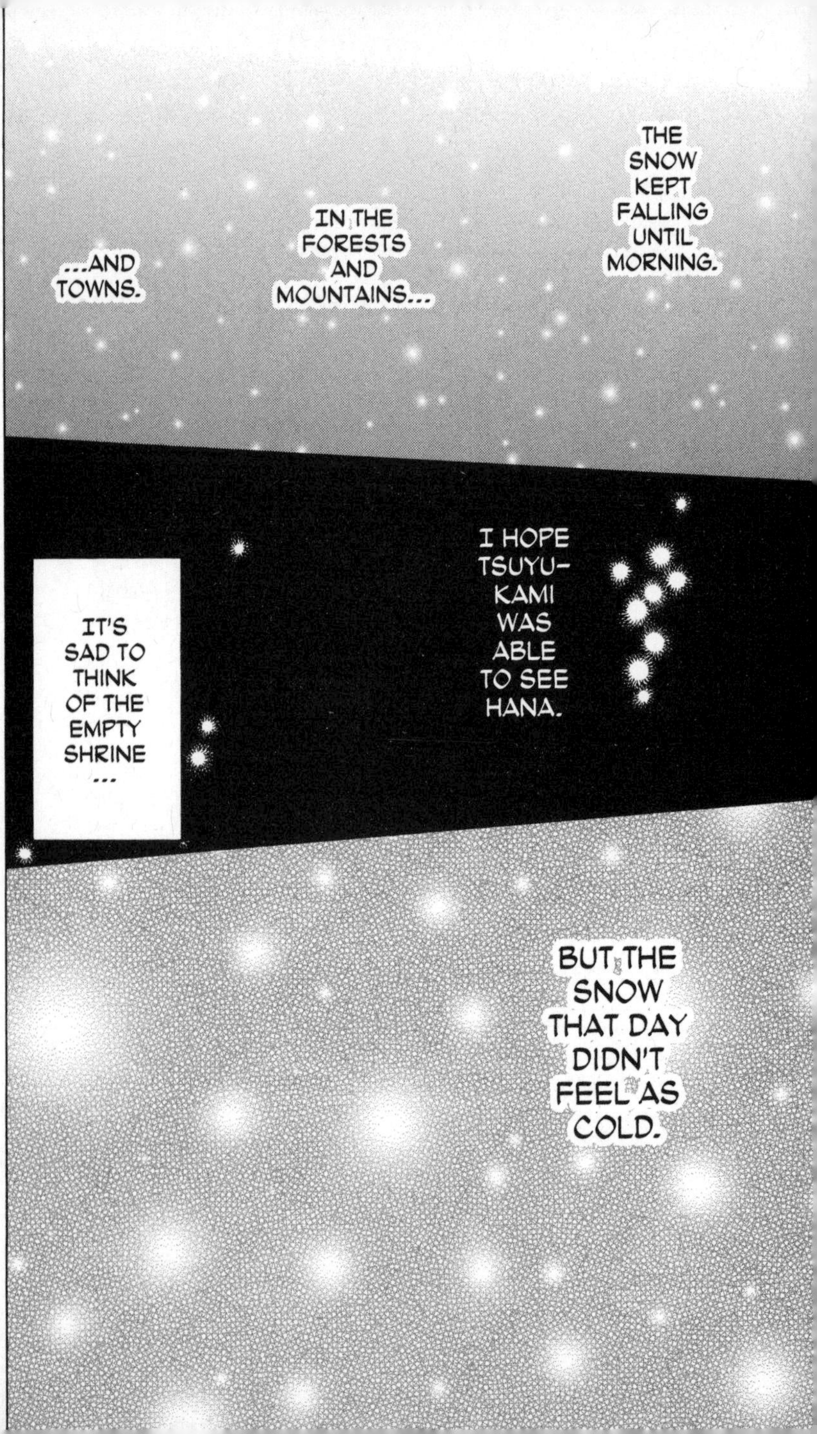
THE SNOW KEPT FALLING UNTIL MORNING.
IN THE FORESTS AND MOUNTAINS...
...AND TOWNS.
I HOPE TSUYU-KAMI WAS ABLE TO SEE HANA.
IT'S SAD TO THINK OF THE EMPTY SHRINE...
BUT THE SNOW THAT DAY DIDN'T FEEL AS COLD.

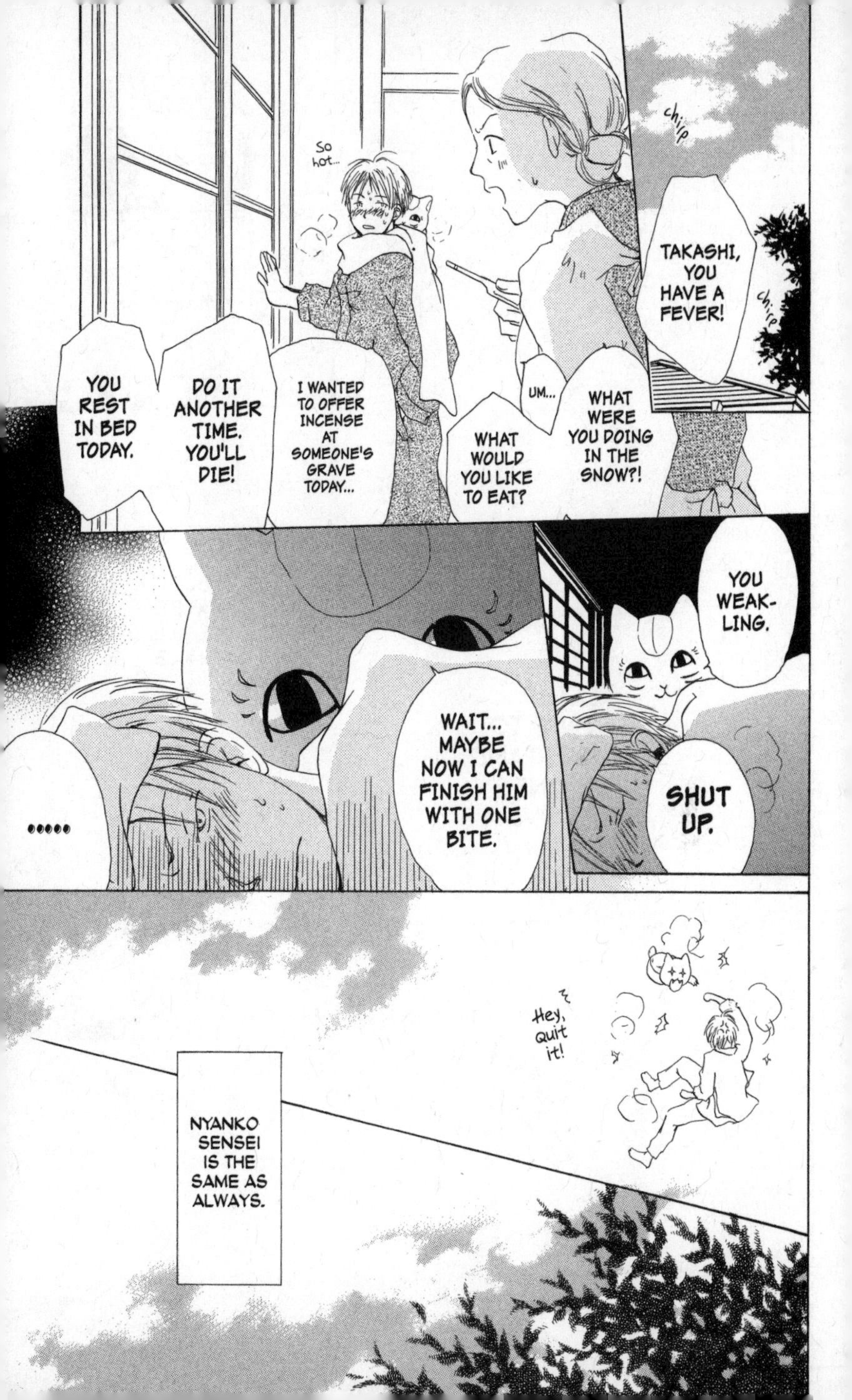
chirp
TAKASHI, YOU HAVE A FEVER!
chirp
WHAT WERE YOU DOING IN THE SNOW?!
UM...
WHAT WOULD YOU LIKE TO EAT?
So hot...
I WANTED TO OFFER INCENSE AT SOMEONE'S GRAVE TODAY...
DO IT ANOTHER TIME. YOU'LL DIE!
YOU REST IN BED TODAY.
YOU WEAK-LING.
SHUT UP.
WAIT... MAYBE NOW I CAN FINISH HIM WITH ONE BITE.
.....
Hey, Quit it!
NYANKO SENSEI IS THE SAME AS ALWAYS.

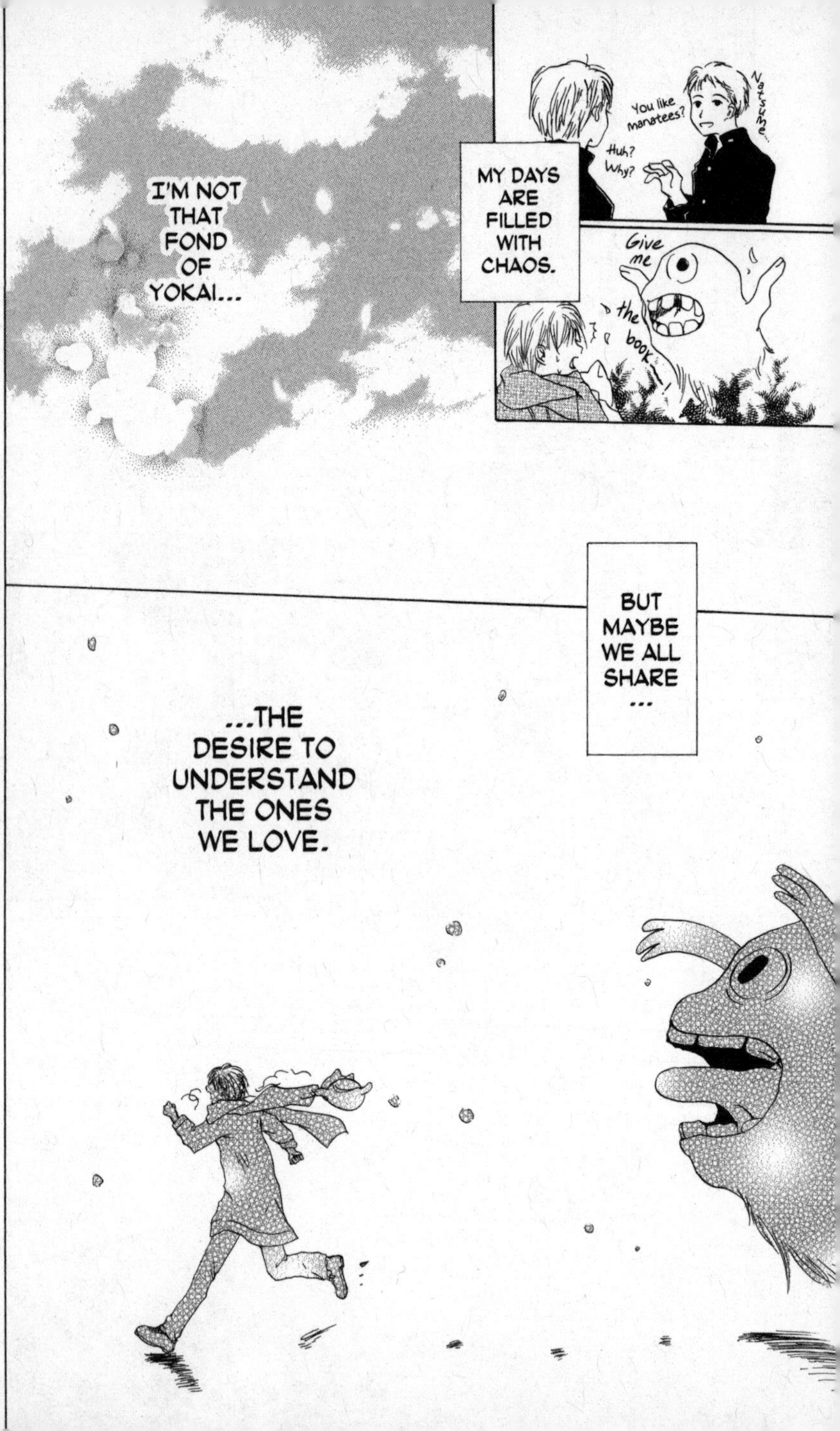
Natsume...
You like manatees?
Huh? Why?
MY DAYS ARE FILLED WITH CHAOS.
Give me the book...!
I'M NOT THAT FOND OF YOKAI...
BUT MAYBE WE ALL SHARE...
...THE DESIRE TO UNDERSTAND THE ONES WE LOVE.

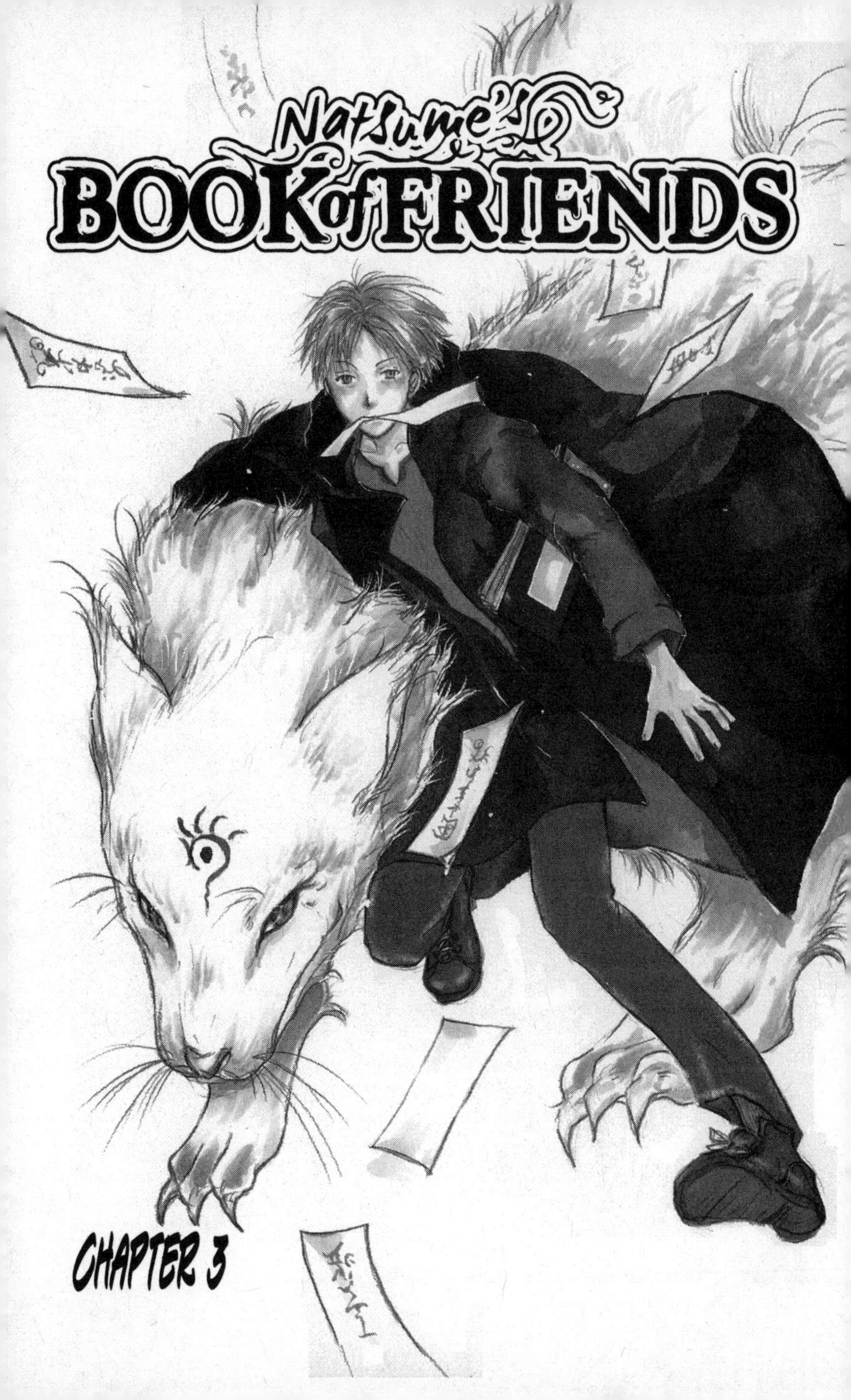
Natsume's
BOOK of FRIENDS
CHAPTER 3

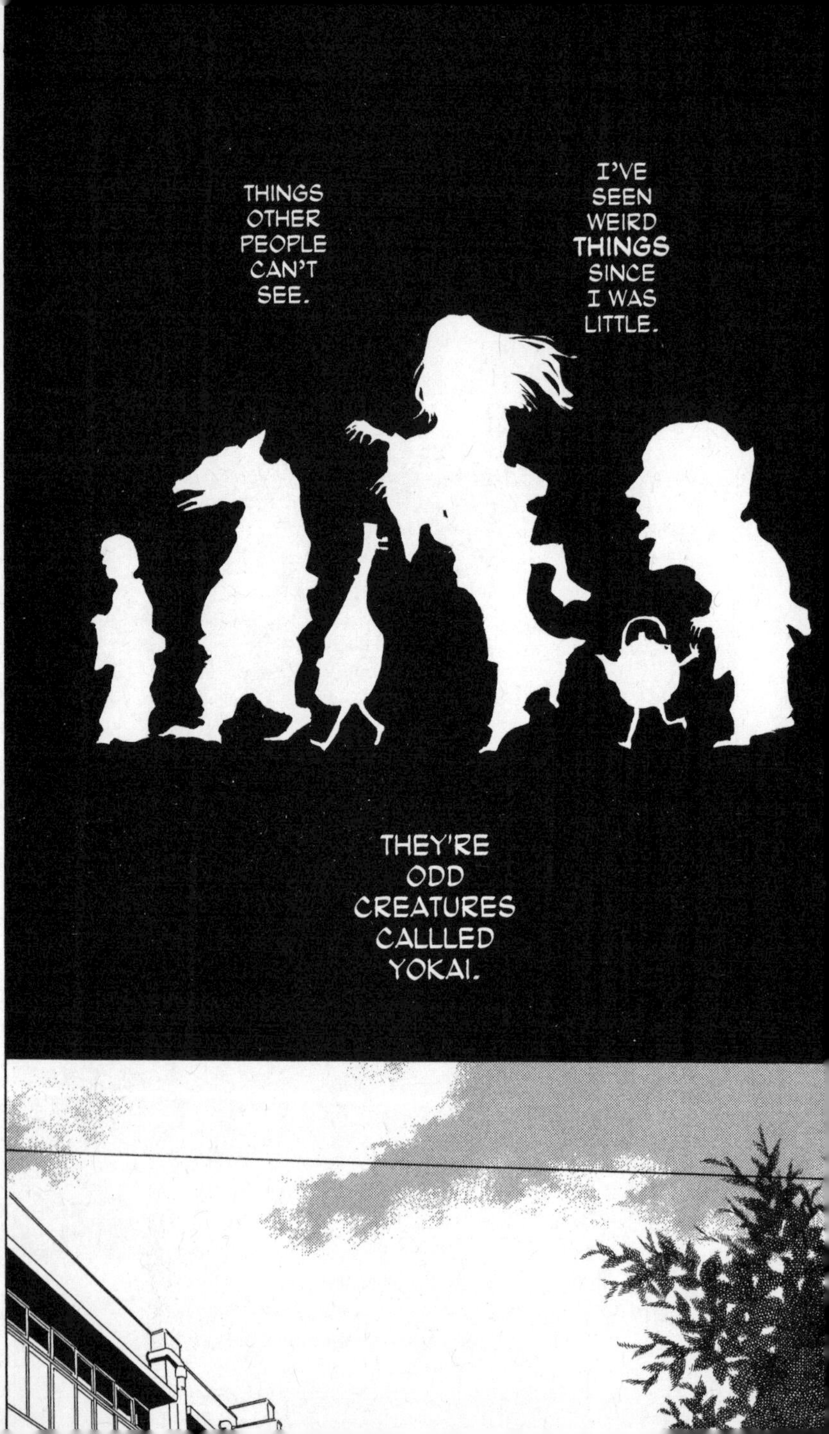
I'VE SEEN WEIRD THINGS SINCE I WAS LITTLE.
THINGS OTHER PEOPLE CAN'T SEE.
THEY'RE ODD CREATURES CALLLED YOKAI.

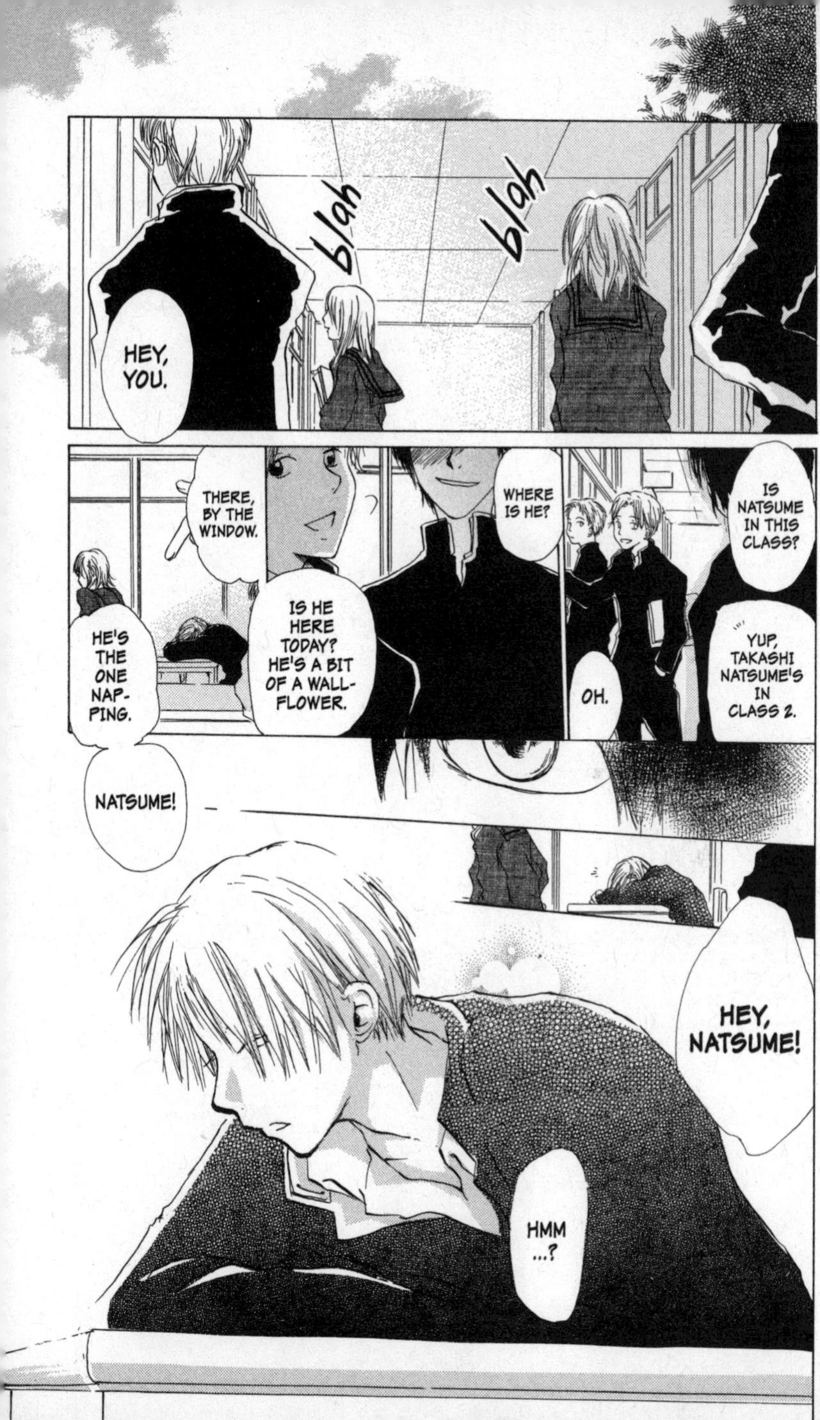
blah
blah
HEY, YOU.
IS NATSUME IN THIS CLASS?
YUP, TAKASHI NATSUME'S IN CLASS 2.
OH.
WHERE IS HE?
IS HE HERE TODAY? HE'S A BIT OF A WALL-FLOWER.
THERE, BY THE WINDOW.
HE'S THE ONE NAP-PING.
NATSUME!
HEY, NATSUME!
HMM ...?

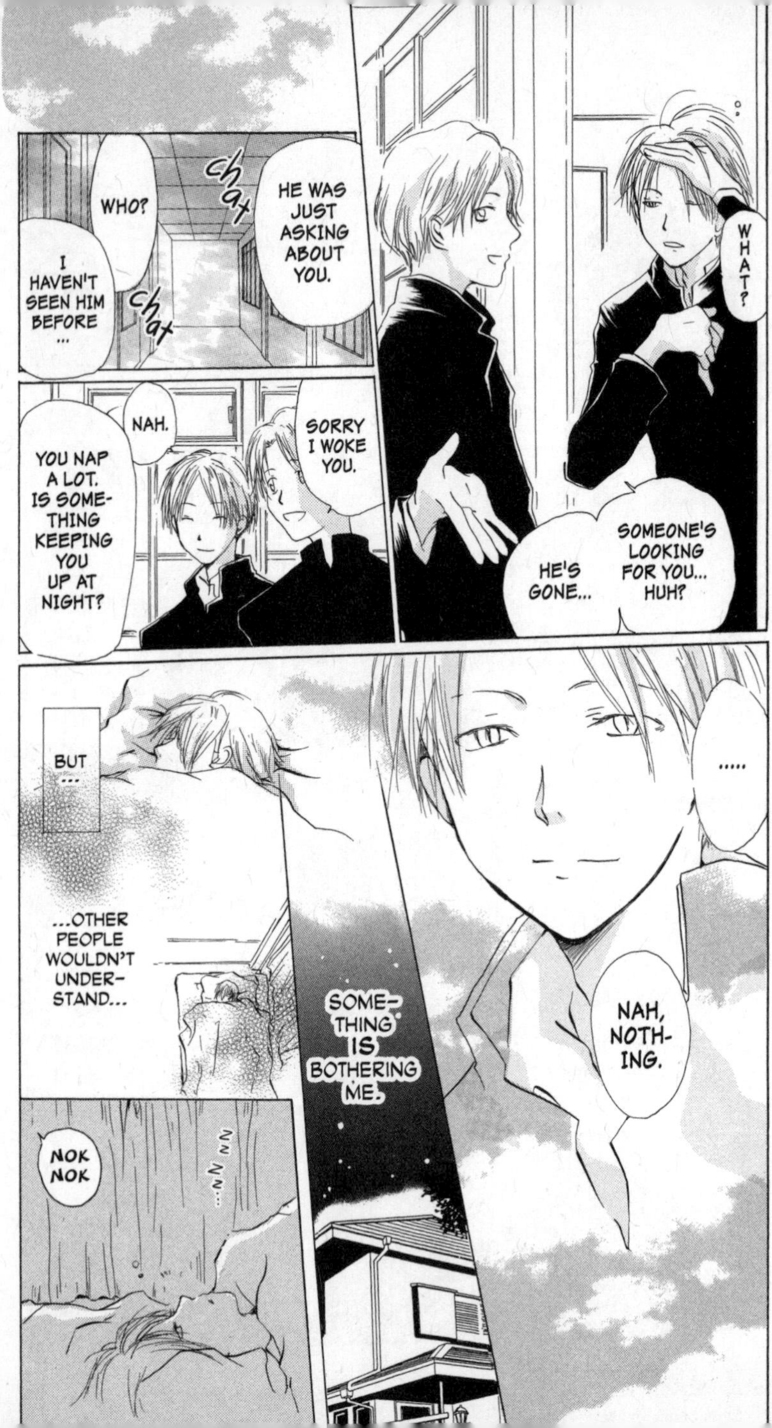

WHAT?
SOMEONE'S LOOKING FOR YOU... HUH?
HE'S GONE...
HE WAS JUST ASKING ABOUT YOU.
chat
WHO?
chat
I HAVEN'T SEEN HIM BEFORE...
SORRY I WOKE YOU.
NAH.
YOU NAP A LOT. IS SOMETHING KEEPING YOU UP AT NIGHT?
.....
NAH, NOTHING.
SOMETHING IS BOTHERING ME.
BUT...
...OTHER PEOPLE WOULDN'T UNDERSTAND...
NOK NOK
Z Z Z Z...

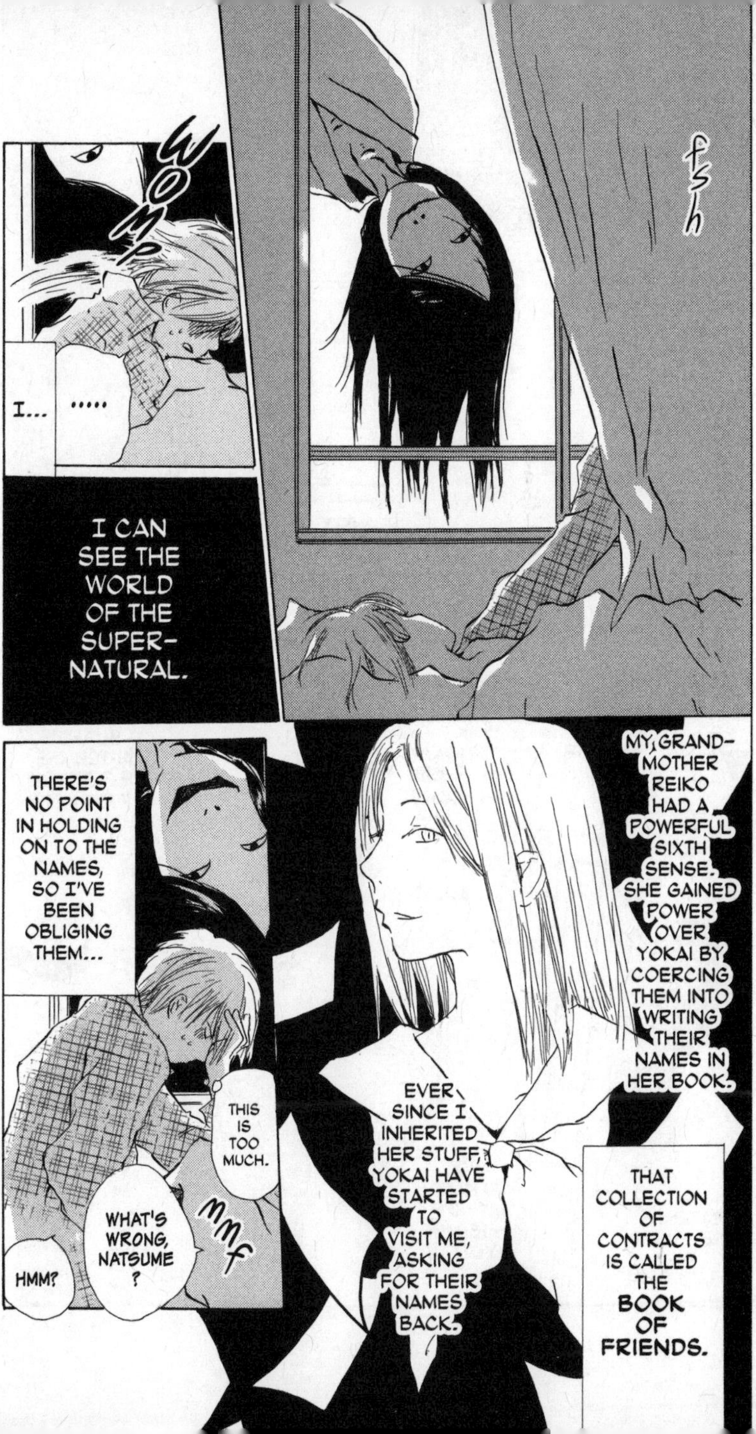
fsh
WOMP
I...
.....
I CAN SEE THE WORLD OF THE SUPER-NATURAL.
MY GRAND-MOTHER REIKO HAD A POWERFUL SIXTH SENSE. SHE GAINED POWER OVER YOKAI BY COERCING THEM INTO WRITING THEIR NAMES IN HER BOOK.
EVER SINCE I INHERITED HER STUFF, YOKAI HAVE STARTED TO VISIT ME, ASKING FOR THEIR NAMES BACK.
THAT COLLECTION OF CONTRACTS IS CALLED THE BOOK OF FRIENDS.
THERE'S NO POINT IN HOLDING ON TO THE NAMES, SO I'VE BEEN OBLIGING THEM...
THIS IS TOO MUCH.
mmf
WHAT'S WRONG, NATSUME?
HMM?

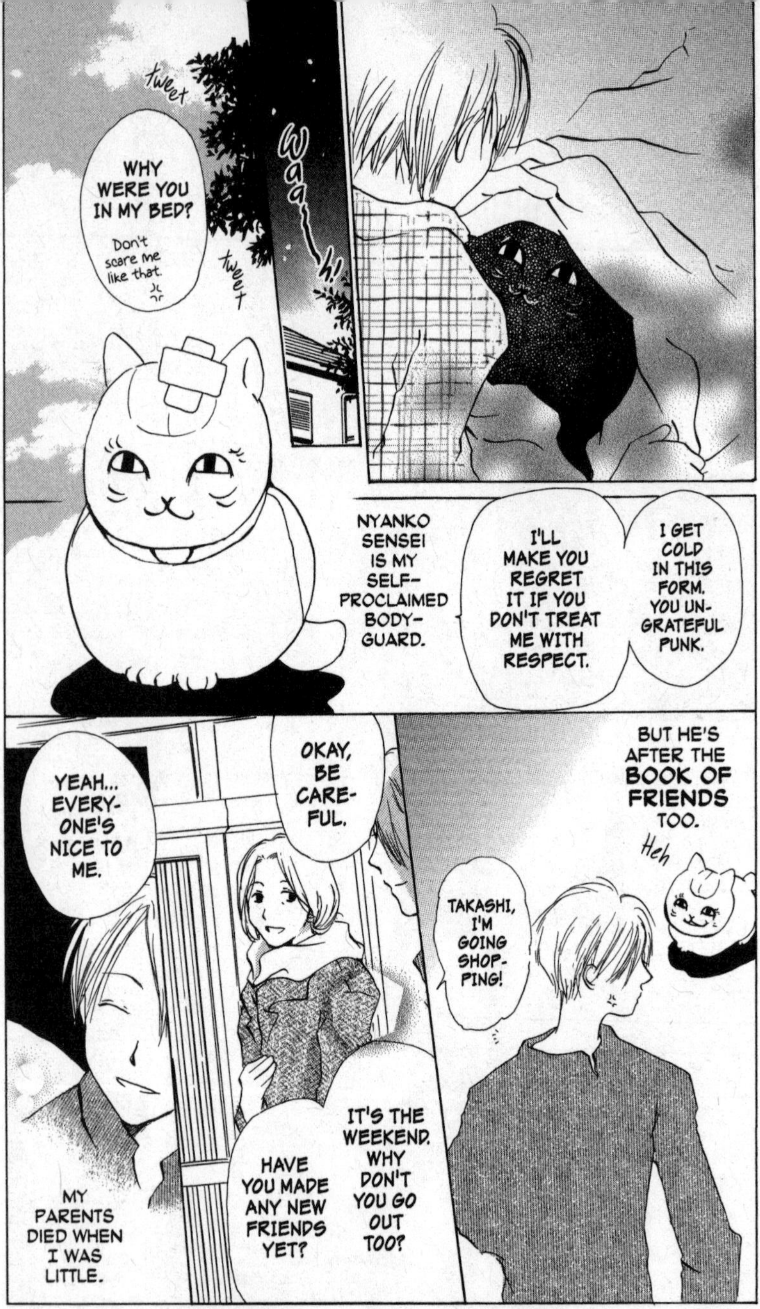
Waaa—h!
tweet
WHY WERE YOU IN MY BED?
Don't scare me like that.
tweet
I GET COLD IN THIS FORM. YOU UNGRATEFUL PUNK.
I'LL MAKE YOU REGRET IT IF YOU DON'T TREAT ME WITH RESPECT.
NYANKO SENSEI IS MY SELF-PROCLAIMED BODYGUARD.
BUT HE'S AFTER THE BOOK OF FRIENDS TOO.
Heh
TAKASHI, I'M GOING SHOPPING!
OKAY, BE CAREFUL.
IT'S THE WEEKEND. WHY DON'T YOU GO OUT TOO?
HAVE YOU MADE ANY NEW FRIENDS YET?
YEAH... EVERYONE'S NICE TO ME.
MY PARENTS DIED WHEN I WAS LITTLE.

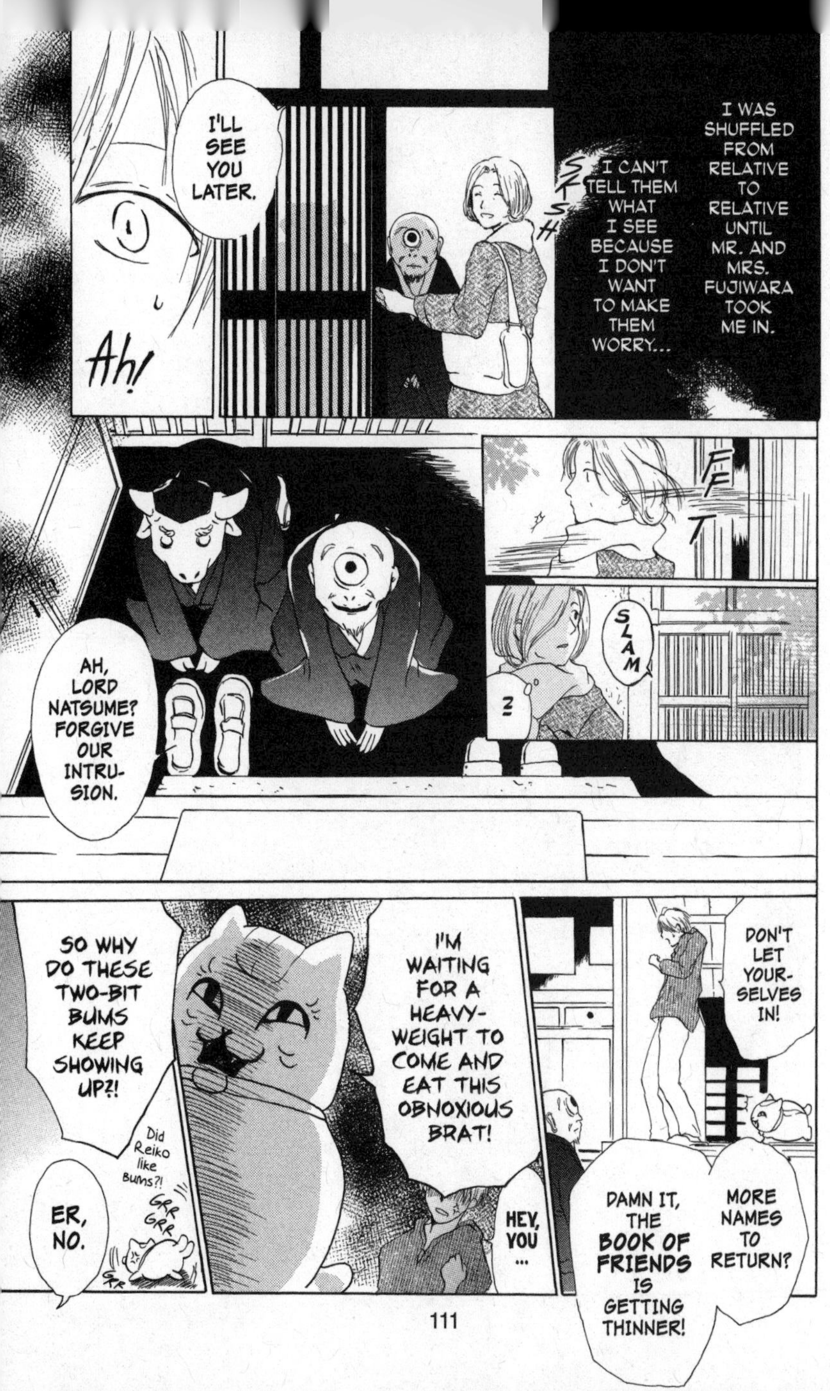

I WAS SHUFFLED FROM RELATIVE TO RELATIVE UNTIL MR. AND MRS. FUJIWARA TOOK ME IN.
I CAN'T TELL THEM WHAT I SEE BECAUSE I DON'T WANT TO MAKE THEM WORRY...
SKSH
I'LL SEE YOU LATER.
Ah!
FFT
SLAM
AH, LORD NATSUME? FORGIVE OUR INTRUSION.
DON'T LET YOURSELVES IN!
MORE NAMES TO RETURN?
DAMN IT, THE BOOK OF FRIENDS IS GETTING THINNER!
I'M WAITING FOR A HEAVYWEIGHT TO COME AND EAT THIS OBNOXIOUS BRAT!
HEY, YOU...
SO WHY DO THESE TWO-BIT BUMS KEEP SHOWING UP?!
Did Reiko like Bums?!
GRR GRR GRR
ER, NO.

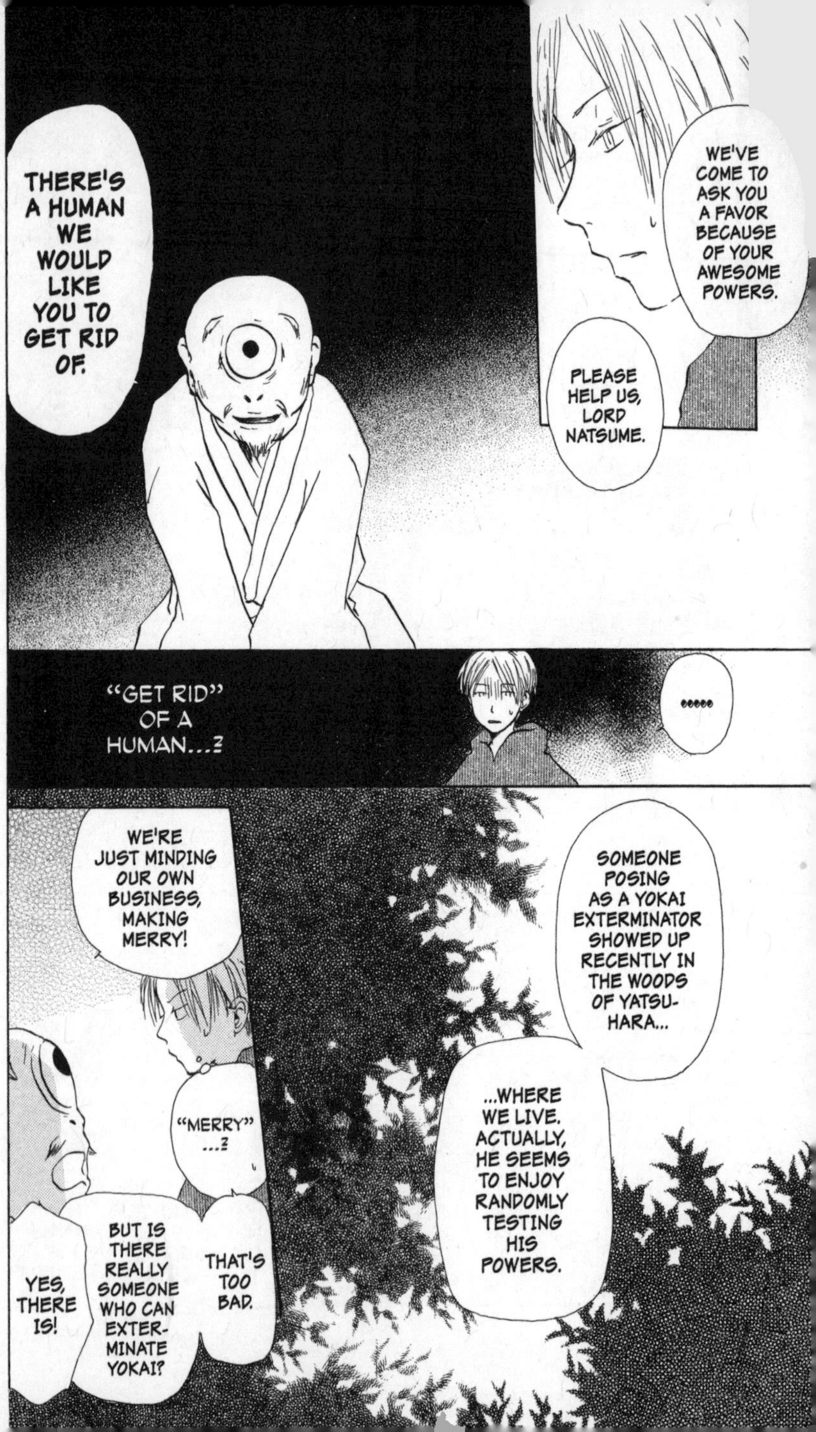
WE'VE COME TO ASK YOU A FAVOR BECAUSE OF YOUR AWESOME POWERS.
PLEASE HELP US, LORD NATSUME.
THERE'S A HUMAN WE WOULD LIKE YOU TO GET RID OF.
.....
"GET RID" OF A HUMAN...?
SOMEONE POSING AS A YOKAI EXTERMINATOR SHOWED UP RECENTLY IN THE WOODS OF YATSU-HARA...
...WHERE WE LIVE. ACTUALLY, HE SEEMS TO ENJOY RANDOMLY TESTING HIS POWERS.
WE'RE JUST MINDING OUR OWN BUSINESS, MAKING MERRY!
"MERRY" ...?
THAT'S TOO BAD.
BUT IS THERE REALLY SOMEONE WHO CAN EXTER-MINATE YOKAI?
YES, THERE IS!

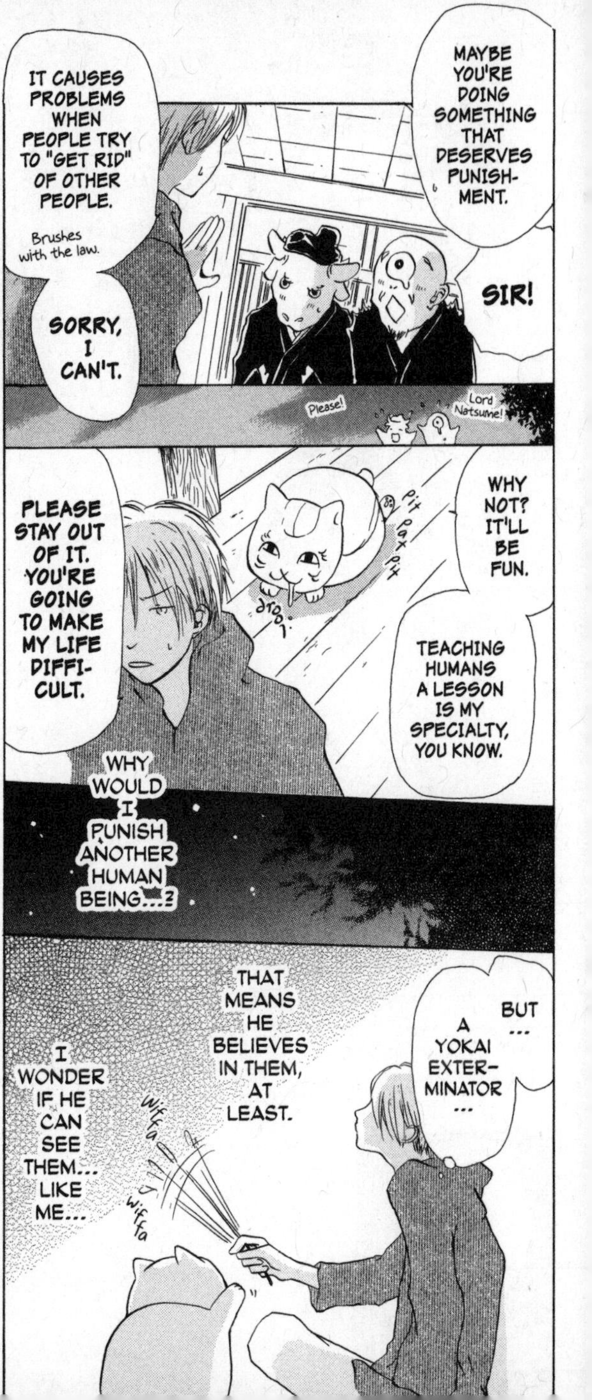
MAYBE YOU'RE DOING SOMETHING THAT DESERVES PUNISHMENT.
SIR!
IT CAUSES PROBLEMS WHEN PEOPLE TRY TO "GET RID" OF OTHER PEOPLE.
Brushes with the law.
SORRY, I CAN'T.
Lord Natsume!
Please!
WHY NOT? IT'LL BE FUN.
TEACHING HUMANS A LESSON IS MY SPECIALTY, YOU KNOW.
pit pat pit
drool
PLEASE STAY OUT OF IT. YOU'RE GOING TO MAKE MY LIFE DIFFICULT.
WHY WOULD I PUNISH ANOTHER HUMAN BEING...?
BUT...
A YOKAI EXTERMINATOR...
THAT MEANS HE BELIEVES IN THEM, AT LEAST.
I WONDER IF HE CAN SEE THEM... LIKE ME...
wiffa
wiffa

06

❋~Things I like~

People write me letters asking what kinds of things I like. I'm touched. There are many things I'd love to talk passionately about, but I think some people will lose interest in the manga when they find out the creator's real interests. I'll eventually bring them up bit by bit.

❋~The way I draw~

When I want to draw a story with certain scenes that flow a certain way, I pick a character who's a good match, throw him in and have him act it out. I feel like I'm chasing characters around, sketchbook in one hand, with a megaphone in the other. Especially when the stories are about students. I tell them where to go, but I leave the dialogue and actions up to them. So composing the rough draft gets very tiring, but it's also very fun.

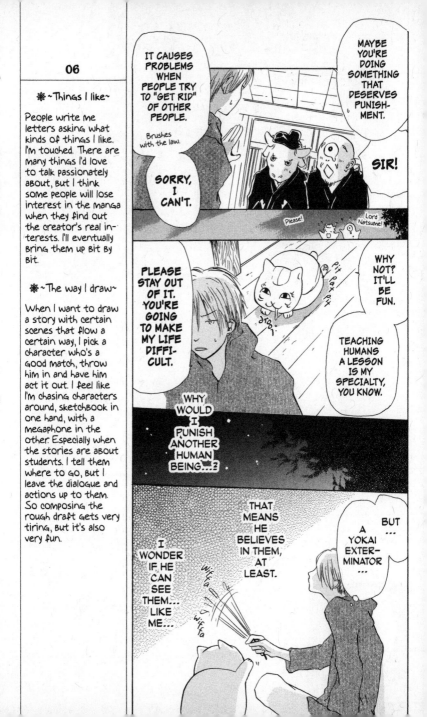

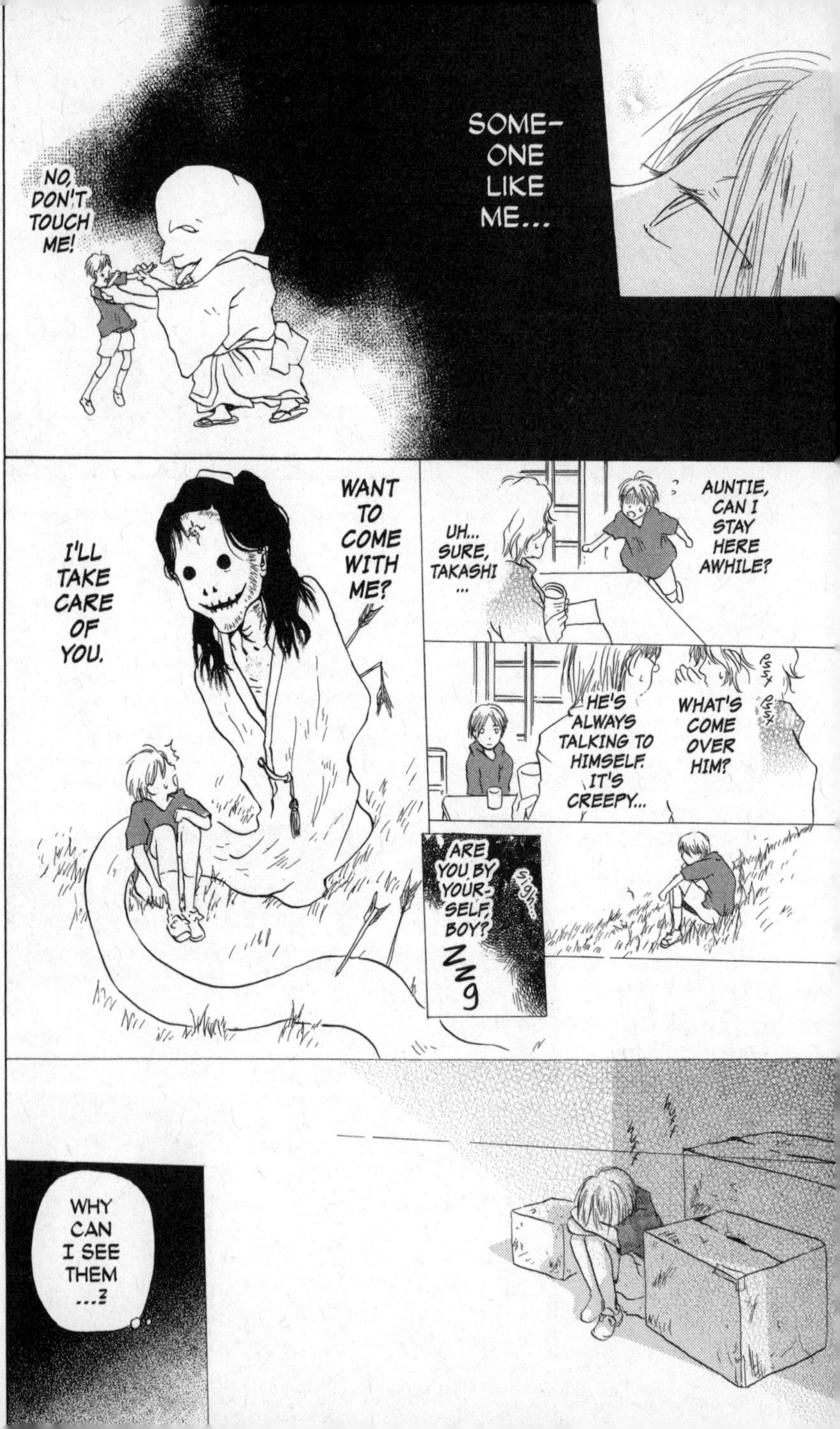
SOME-ONE LIKE ME...
NO, DON'T TOUCH ME!
AUNTIE, CAN I STAY HERE AWHILE?
UH... SURE, TAKASHI ...
WHAT'S COME OVER HIM?
HE'S ALWAYS TALKING TO HIMSELF. IT'S CREEPY...
sigh...
ARE YOU BY YOURSELF, BOY?
ZZG
WANT TO COME WITH ME?
I'LL TAKE CARE OF YOU.
WHY CAN I SEE THEM ...?

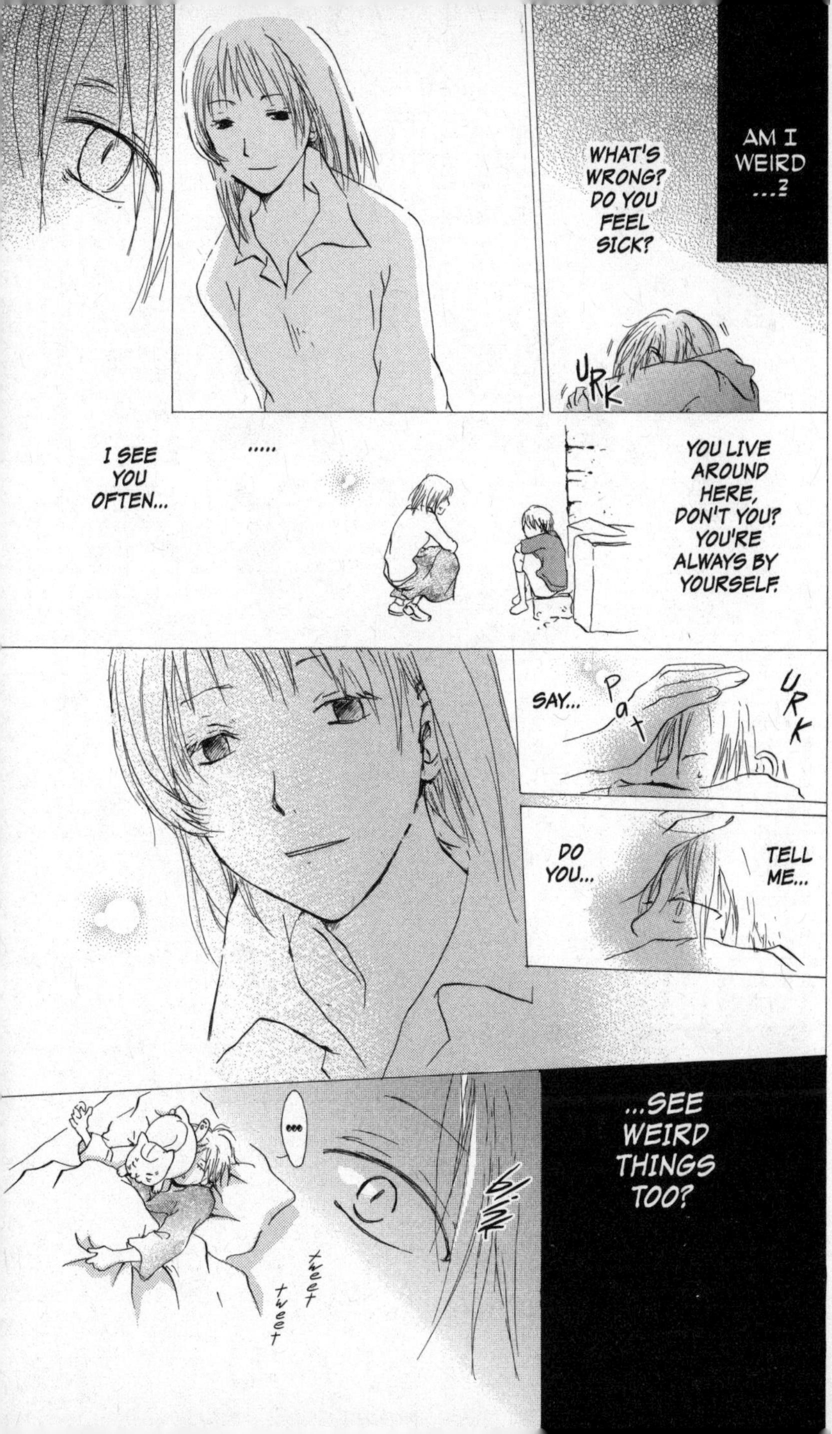

AM I WEIRD ...?
WHAT'S WRONG? DO YOU FEEL SICK?
URK
YOU LIVE AROUND HERE, DON'T YOU? YOU'RE ALWAYS BY YOURSELF.
.....
I SEE YOU OFTEN...
URK
SAY...
Pat
TELL ME...
DO YOU...
...SEE WEIRD THINGS TOO?
blink
...
tweet tweet

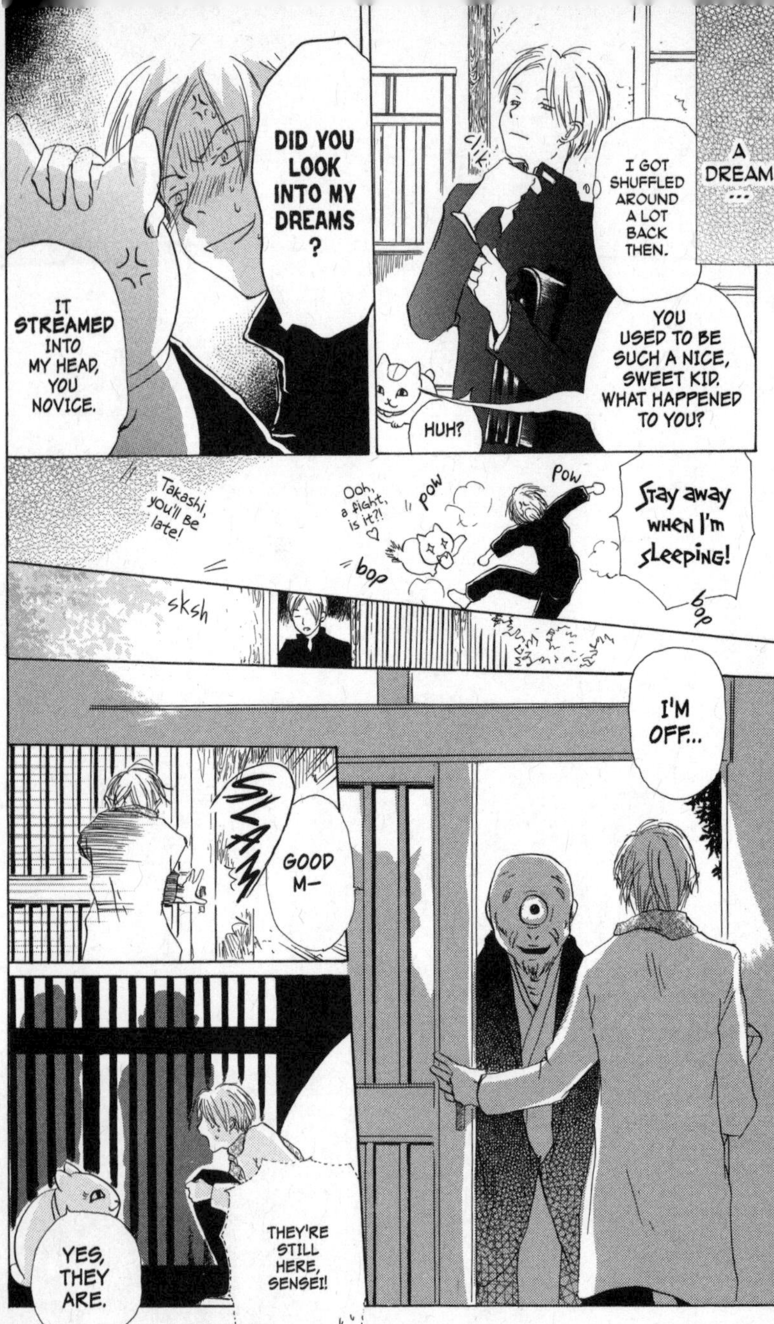
A DREAM...
clik
I GOT SHUFFLED AROUND A LOT BACK THEN.
YOU USED TO BE SUCH A NICE, SWEET KID. WHAT HAPPENED TO YOU?
HUH?
DID YOU LOOK INTO MY DREAMS?
IT STREAMED INTO MY HEAD, YOU NOVICE.
Stay away when I'm sleeping!
pow
pow
Ooh, a fight, is it?! ♡
Takashi, you'll be late!
bop
bop
sksh
I'M OFF...
GOOD M—
SLAM
THEY'RE STILL HERE, SENSEI!
YES, THEY ARE.

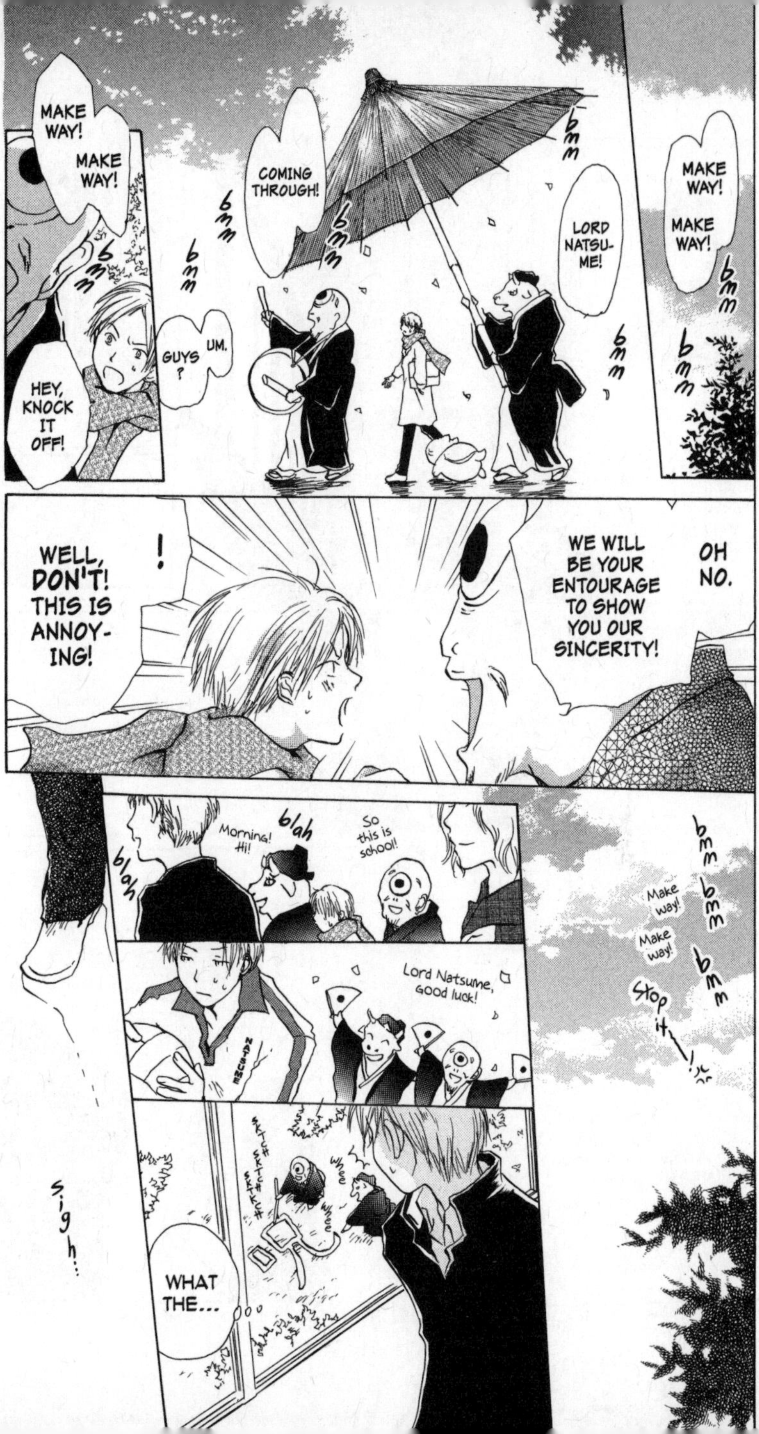
MAKE WAY! MAKE WAY!
bmm bmm bmm
LORD NATSUME!
bmm
COMING THROUGH!
bmm bmm bmm
UM, GUYS?
MAKE WAY! MAKE WAY!
bmm
HEY, KNOCK IT OFF!
OH NO.
WE WILL BE YOUR ENTOURAGE TO SHOW YOU OUR SINCERITY!
!
WELL, DON'T! THIS IS ANNOY-ING!
bmm bmm bmm
Make way! Make way!
Stop it—!
So this is school!
blah
Morning! Hi!
blah
Lord Natsume, good luck!
NATSUME
whee
SKTCH SKTCH SKTCH
WHAT THE...
Sigh...

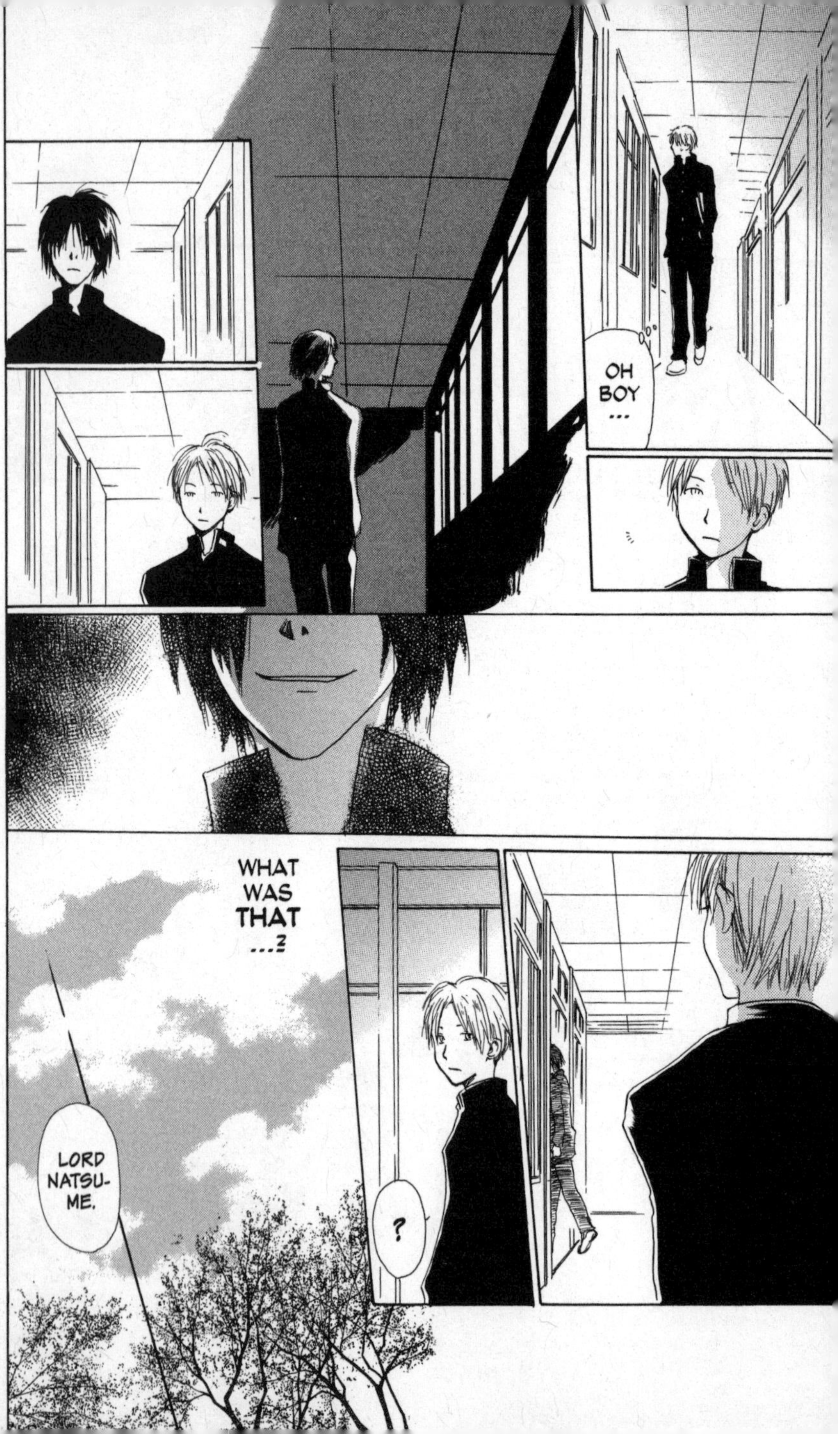
OH BOY ...
WHAT WAS THAT ...?
LORD NATSU-ME.
?

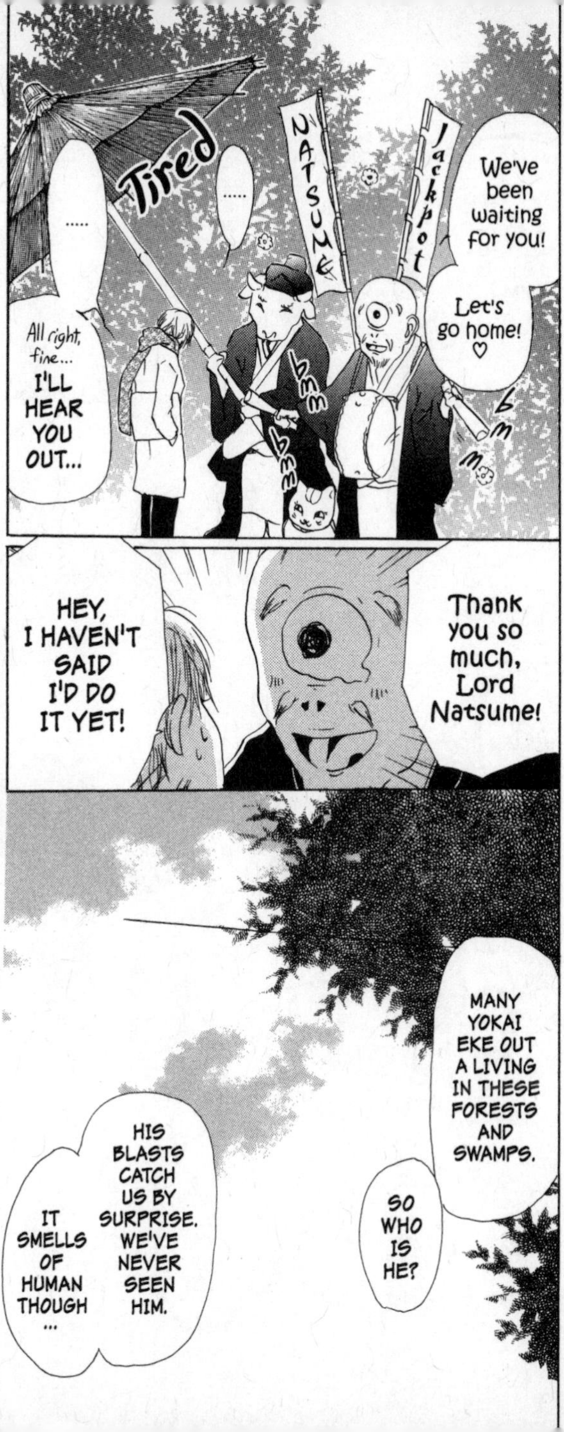
We've been waiting for you!
Let's go home! ♡
Jackpot
NATSUME
Tired
.....
.....
All right, fine... I'LL HEAR YOU OUT...
bmm
bmm
bmm
Thank you so much, Lord Natsume!
HEY, I HAVEN'T SAID I'D DO IT YET!
MANY YOKAI EKE OUT A LIVING IN THESE FORESTS AND SWAMPS.
SO WHO IS HE?
HIS BLASTS CATCH US BY SURPRISE. WE'VE NEVER SEEN HIM.
IT SMELLS OF HUMAN THOUGH ...

07

❋~People to whom I owe everything~

It takes me a while to do rough drafts, and I'm slow in general, so there are people who help me out. They lend their talents to make my manuscripts the best they can be. Except for my earlier titles such as *Akaku Saku Koe* (Voices Blooming Red), *Atsui Hibi* (Hot Days), *Hana no Ato* (Flower Prints) and *Hotaru-bi no Mori e* (Woods of Firefly Light), I usually receive help from assistants. So I took this opportunity to have my assistants in Natsume, Tamao Ohki and Chika, draw something! I'm sorry the columns are so small. I'm such a lucky person. Whenever I get depressed or start panicking about making deadlines, they always say, "It's all right, leave it to me"—even when they're busy themselves. They're so cool and wonderful. I have a lot of respect for them.

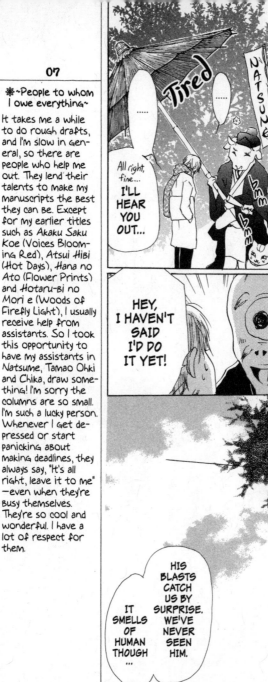

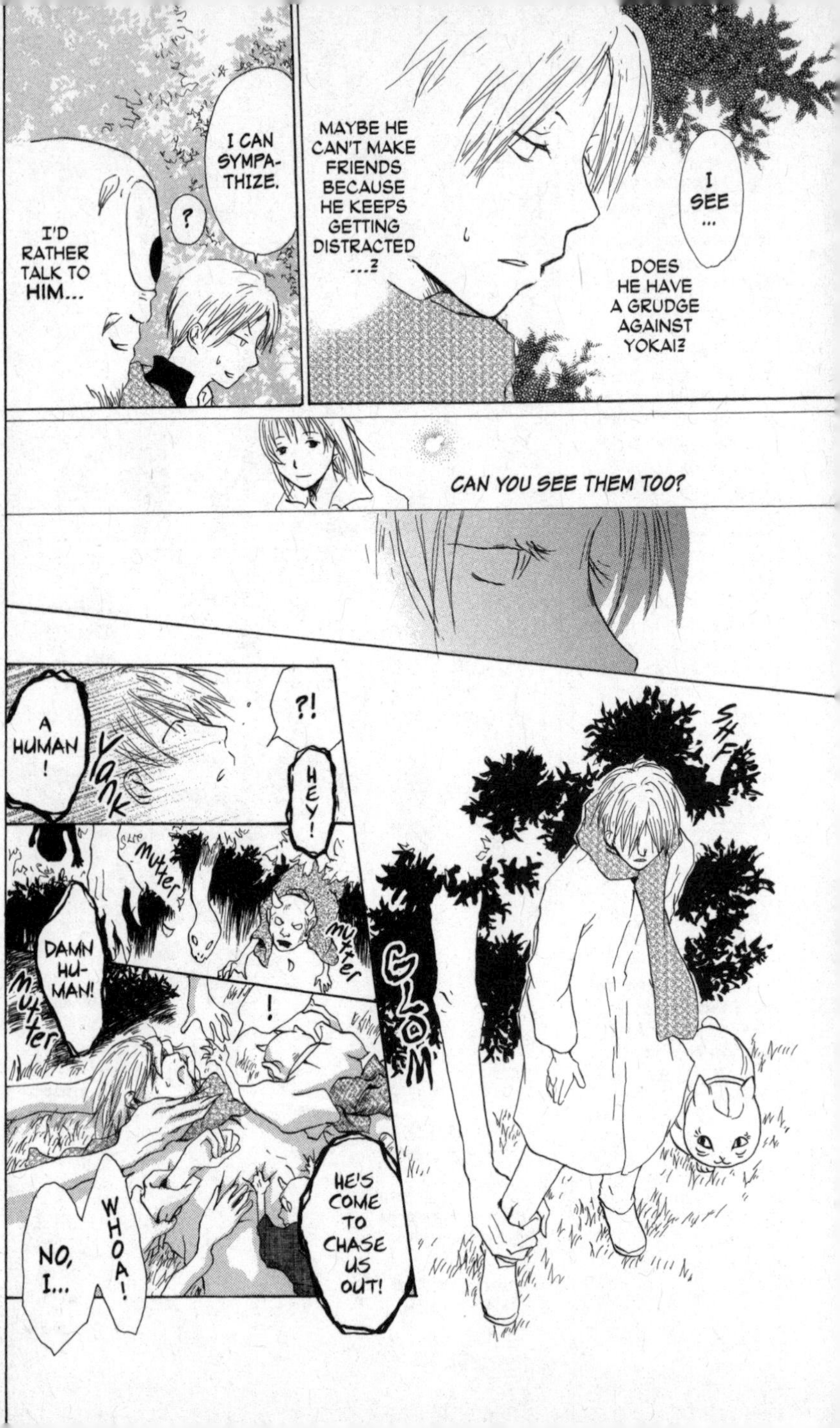
I SEE...
DOES HE HAVE A GRUDGE AGAINST YOKAI?
MAYBE HE CAN'T MAKE FRIENDS BECAUSE HE KEEPS GETTING DISTRACTED...?
I CAN SYMPATHIZE.
?
I'D RATHER TALK TO HIM...
CAN YOU SEE THEM TOO?
SHF
GLOM
?!
A HUMAN!
Yank
HEY!
mutter
mutter
DAMN HUMAN!
mutter
!
HE'S COME TO CHASE US OUT!
WHOA!
NO, I...

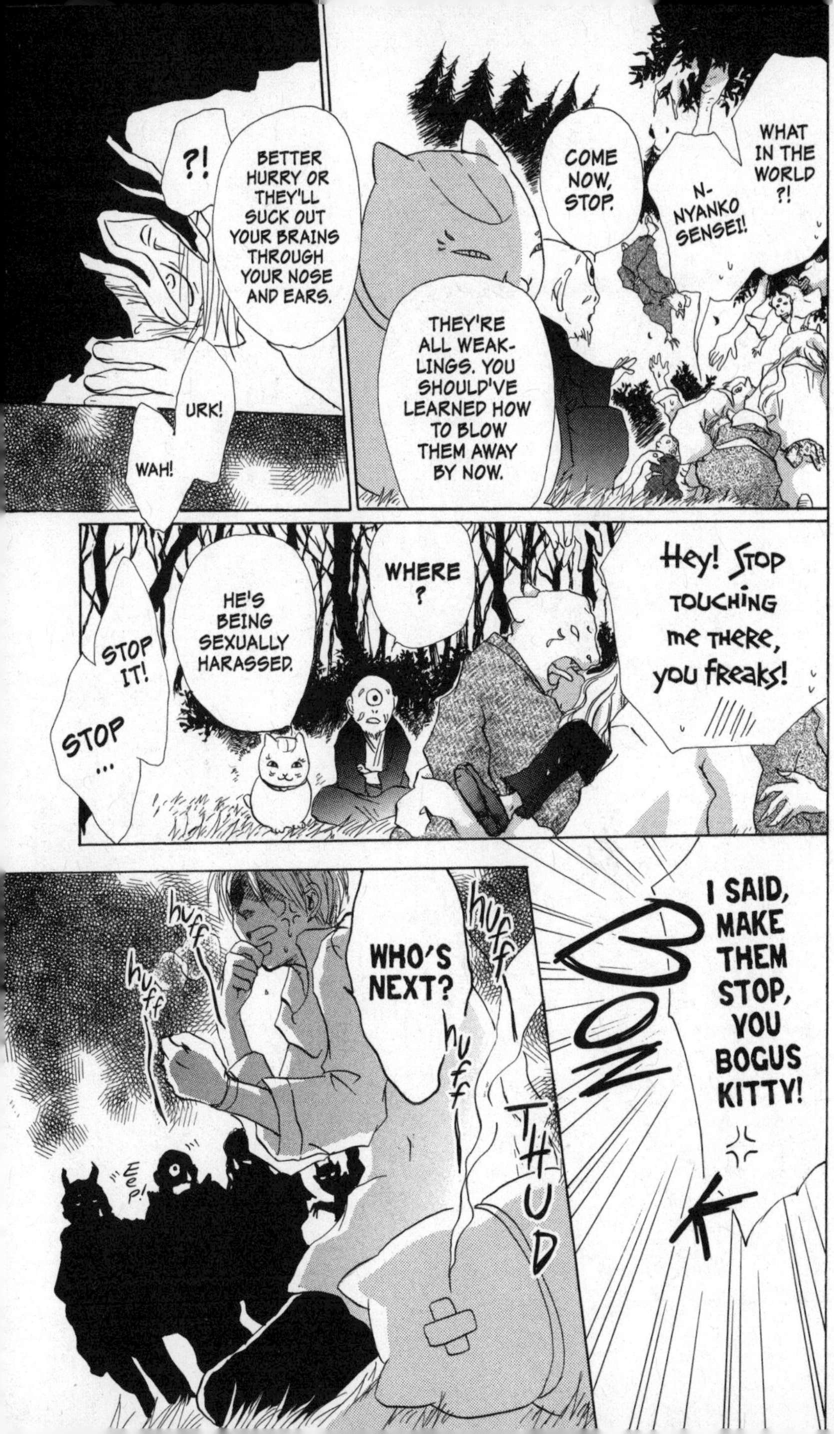
WHAT IN THE WORLD ?!
N-NYANKO SENSEI!
COME NOW, STOP.
THEY'RE ALL WEAK-LINGS. YOU SHOULD'VE LEARNED HOW TO BLOW THEM AWAY BY NOW.
BETTER HURRY OR THEY'LL SUCK OUT YOUR BRAINS THROUGH YOUR NOSE AND EARS.
?!
URK!
WAH!
Hey! Stop TOUCHING me THERE, you freaks!
WHERE ?
HE'S BEING SEXUALLY HARASSED.
STOP IT!
STOP ...
I SAID, MAKE THEM STOP, YOU BOGUS KITTY!
BONK
THUD
huff
huff
WHO'S NEXT?
huff
huff
Eep!

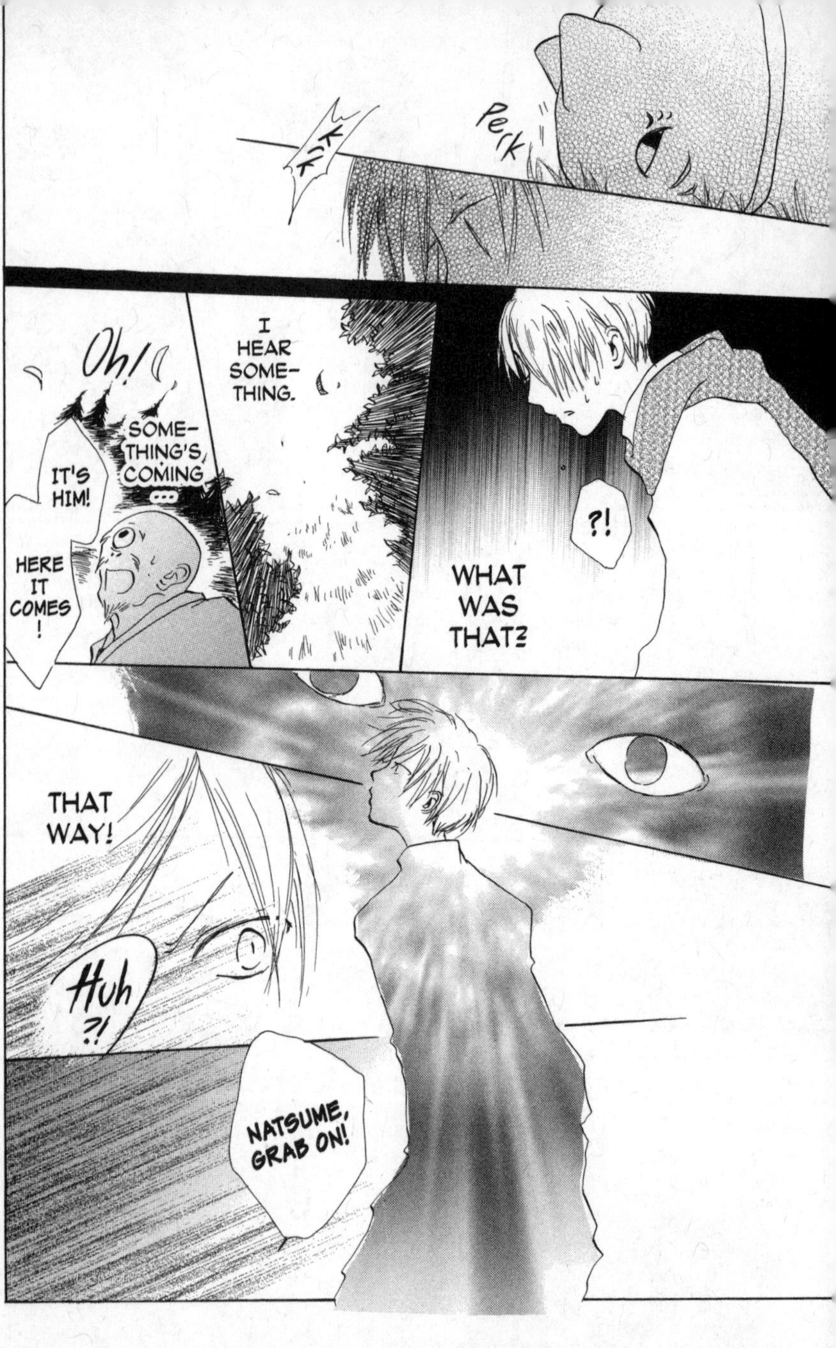
Perk
Kik
?!
WHAT WAS THAT?
I HEAR SOME-THING.
Oh!
SOME-THING'S COMING...
IT'S HIM!
HERE IT COMES!
THAT WAY!
Huh ?!
NATSUME, GRAB ON!

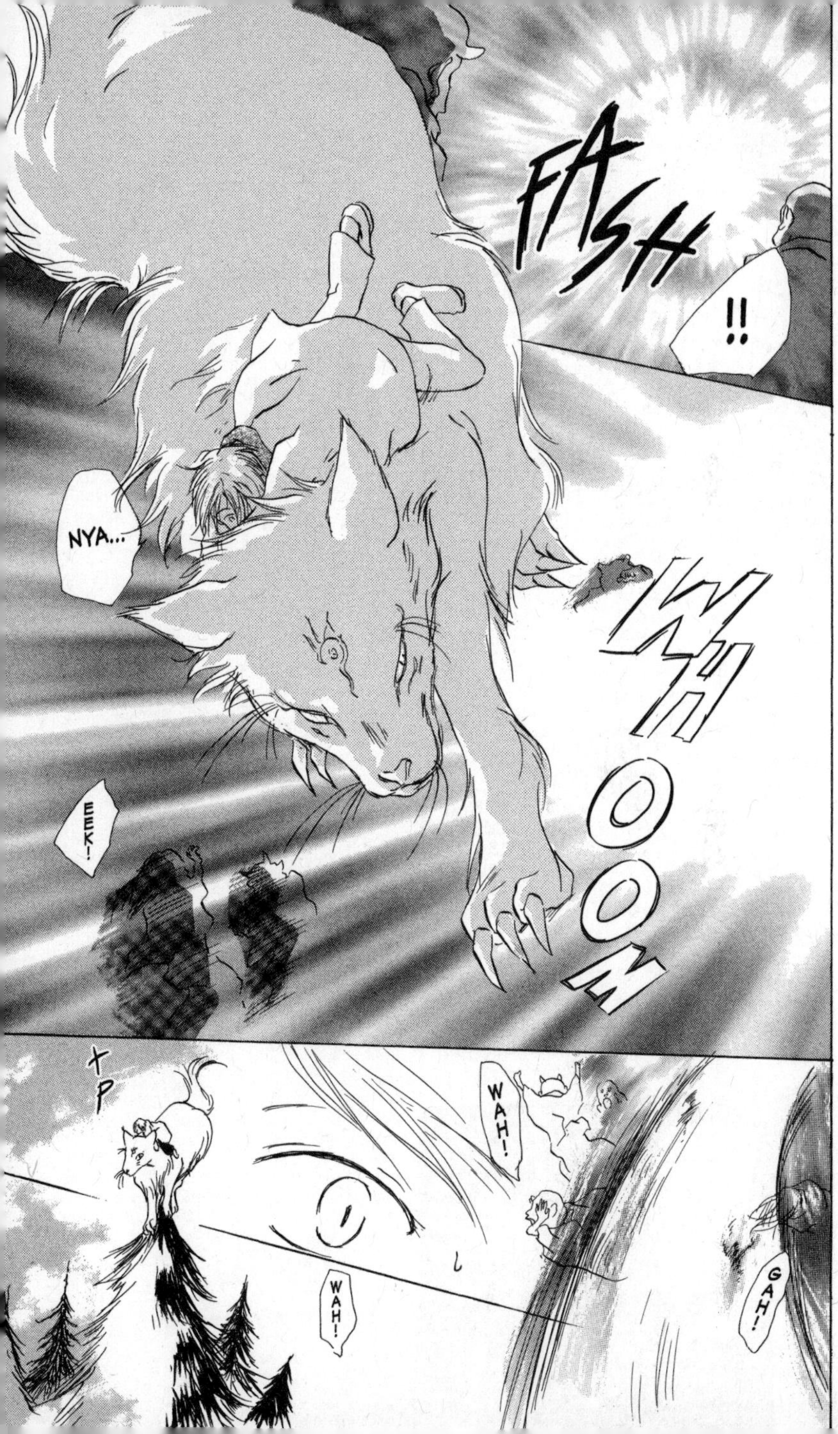
FASH
!!
WHOOOM
NYA...
EEK!
GAH!
WAH!
WAH!
TP

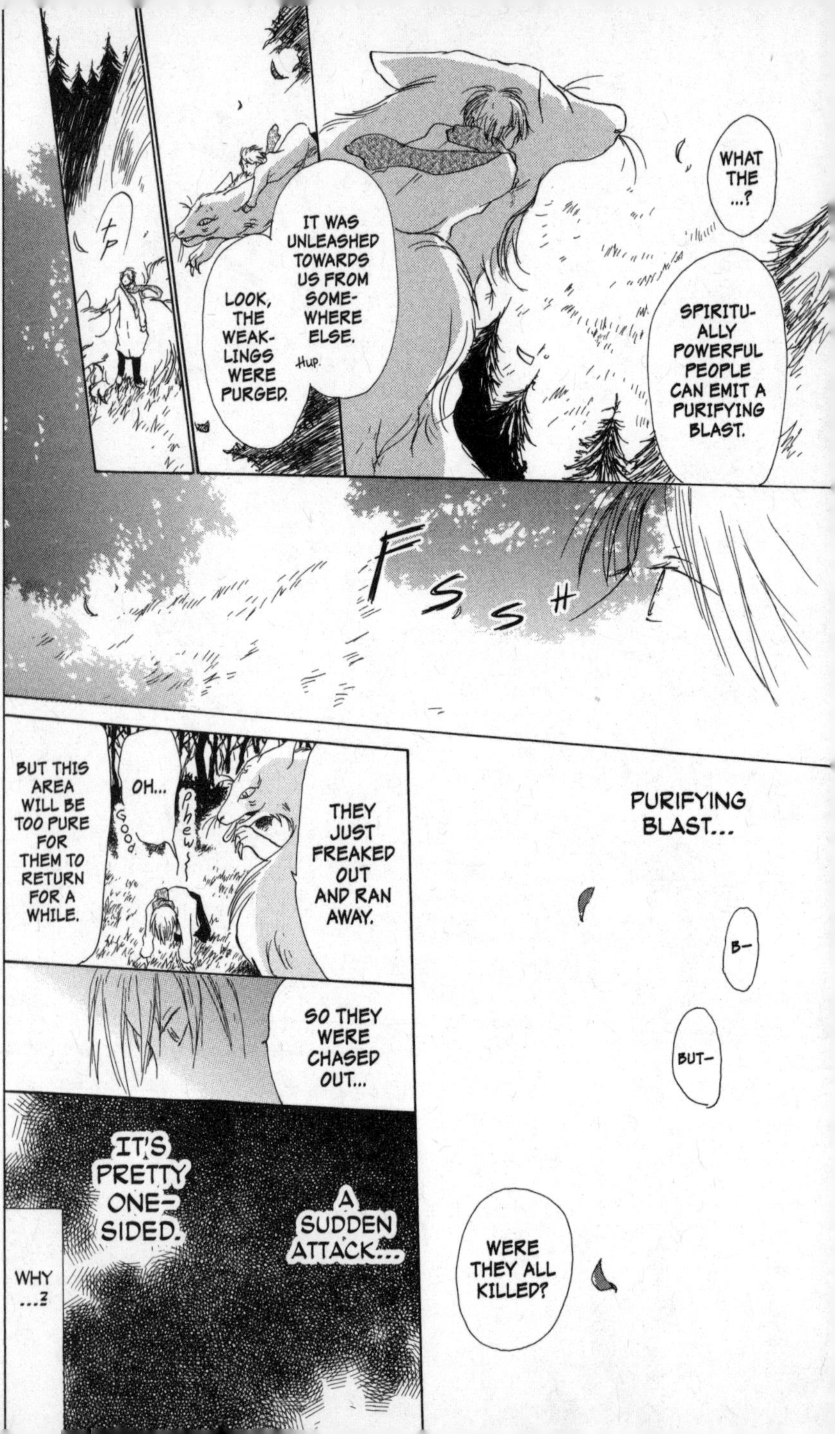
WHAT THE ...?
SPIRITUALLY POWERFUL PEOPLE CAN EMIT A PURIFYING BLAST.
IT WAS UNLEASHED TOWARDS US FROM SOMEWHERE ELSE.
Hup.
LOOK, THE WEAKLINGS WERE PURGED.
FSSSH
PURIFYING BLAST...
B—
BUT—
WERE THEY ALL KILLED?
THEY JUST FREAKED OUT AND RAN AWAY.
OH...
Phew
Good
BUT THIS AREA WILL BE TOO PURE FOR THEM TO RETURN FOR A WHILE.
SO THEY WERE CHASED OUT...
A SUDDEN ATTACK...
IT'S PRETTY ONE-SIDED.
WHY...?

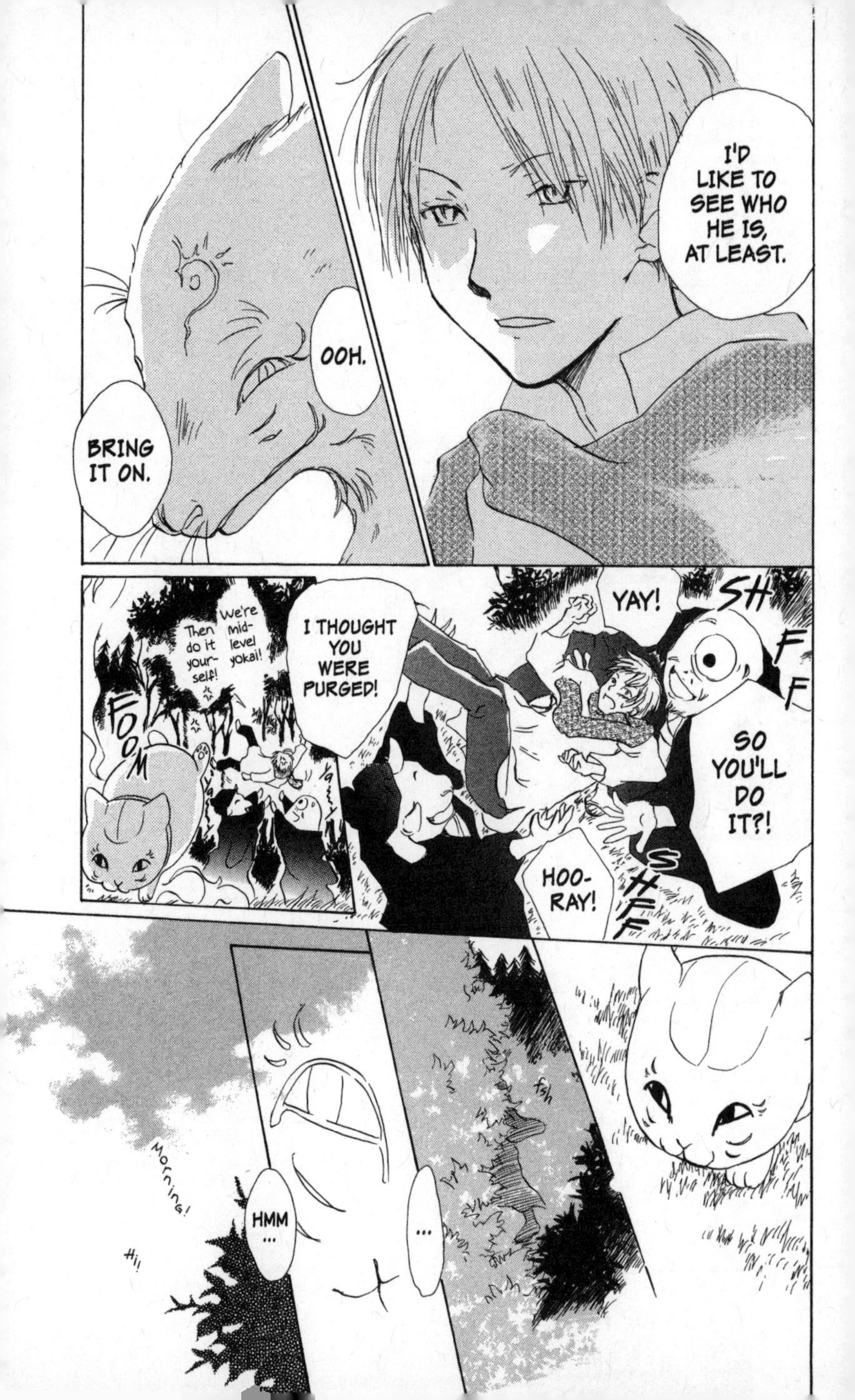
I'D LIKE TO SEE WHO HE IS, AT LEAST.
OOH.
BRING IT ON.
YAY!
SHFF
SO YOU'LL DO IT?!
HOO-RAY!
SHFF
I THOUGHT YOU WERE PURGED!
We're mid-level yokai!
Then do it your-self!
FOOM
fsh
...
HMM ...
Morning!
Hi!

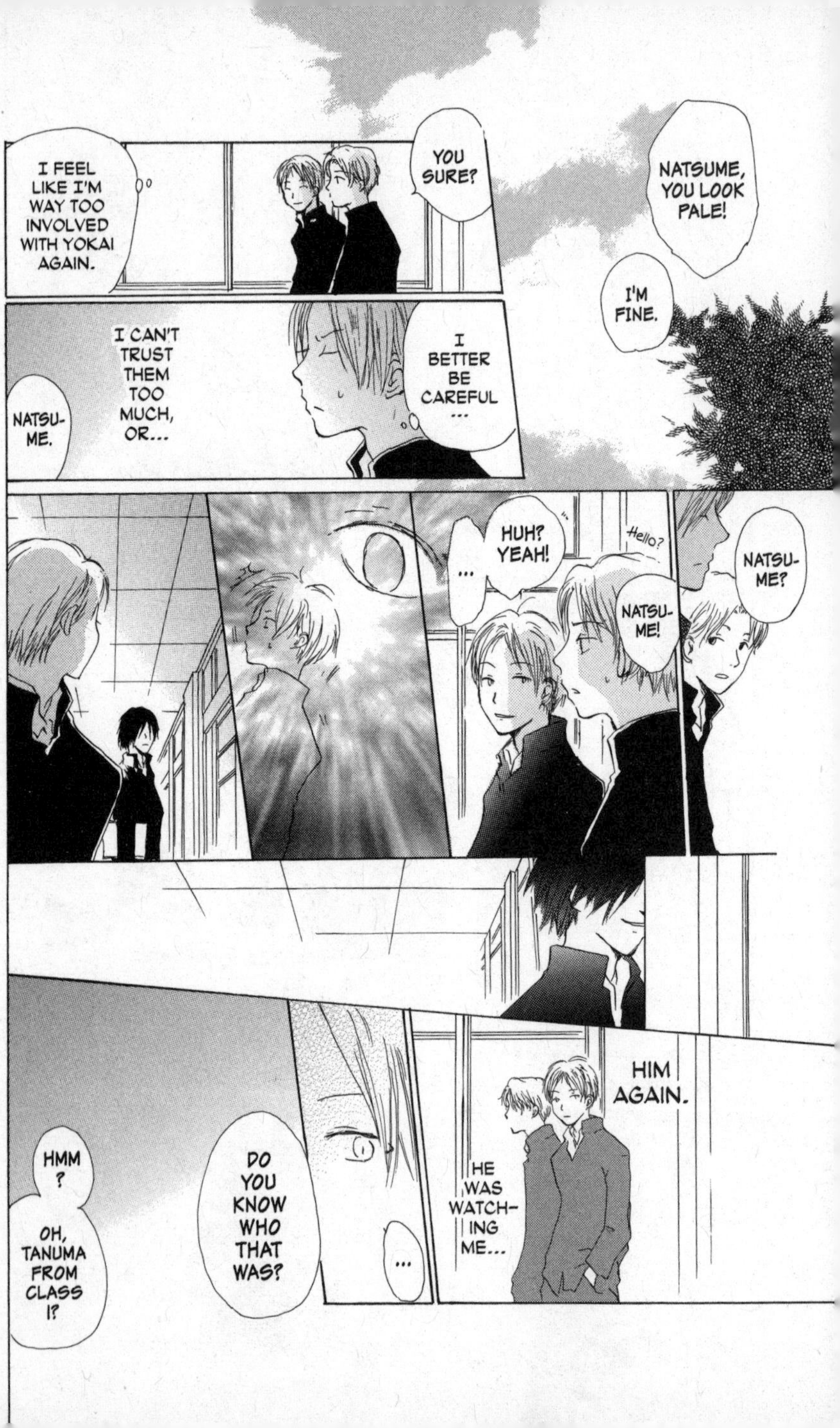
NATSUME, YOU LOOK PALE!
I'M FINE.
YOU SURE?
I FEEL LIKE I'M WAY TOO INVOLVED WITH YOKAI AGAIN.
I BETTER BE CAREFUL ...
I CAN'T TRUST THEM TOO MUCH, OR...
NATSUME.
NATSUME?
Hello?
NATSUME!
HUH? YEAH!
...
HIM AGAIN.
HE WAS WATCHING ME...
...
DO YOU KNOW WHO THAT WAS?
HMM?
OH, TANUMA FROM CLASS 1?

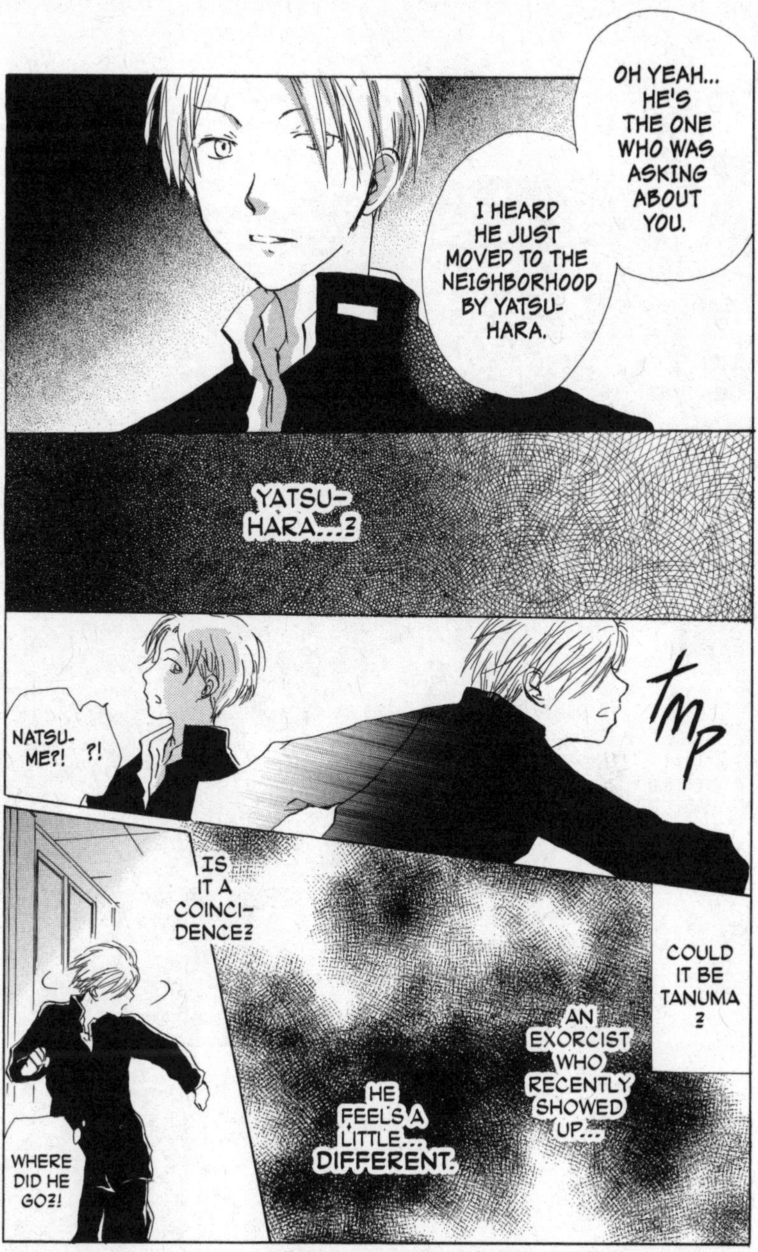
OH YEAH... HE'S THE ONE WHO WAS ASKING ABOUT YOU.
I HEARD HE JUST MOVED TO THE NEIGHBORHOOD BY YATSU-HARA.
YATSU-HARA...?
tmp
?!
NATSU-ME?!
COULD IT BE TANUMA?
AN EXORCIST WHO RECENTLY SHOWED UP...
HE FEELS A LITTLE... DIFFERENT.
IS IT A COINCI-DENCE?
WHERE DID HE GO?!

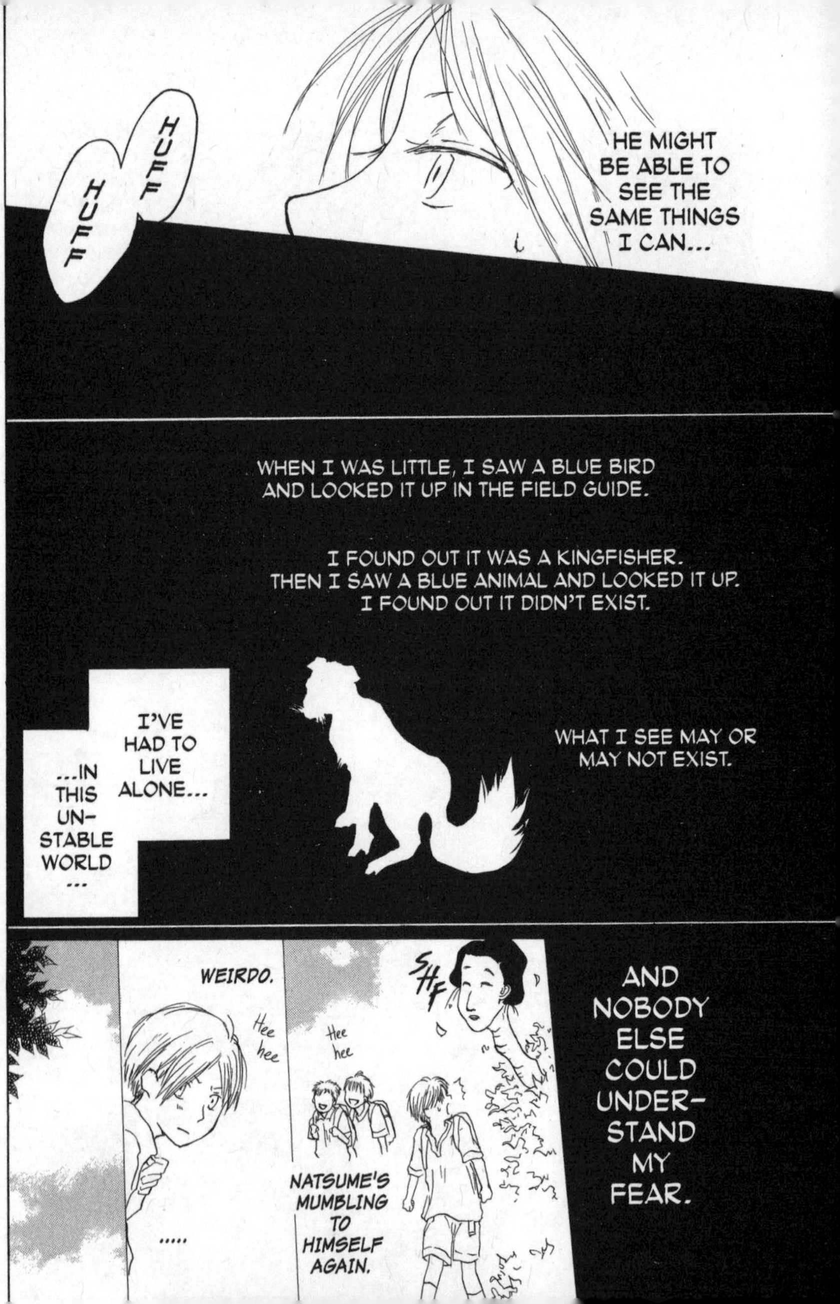
HE MIGHT BE ABLE TO SEE THE SAME THINGS I CAN...
HUFF
HUFF
WHEN I WAS LITTLE, I SAW A BLUE BIRD AND LOOKED IT UP IN THE FIELD GUIDE.
I FOUND OUT IT WAS A KINGFISHER. THEN I SAW A BLUE ANIMAL AND LOOKED IT UP. I FOUND OUT IT DIDN'T EXIST.
WHAT I SEE MAY OR MAY NOT EXIST.
I'VE HAD TO LIVE ALONE...
...IN THIS UN-STABLE WORLD...
AND NOBODY ELSE COULD UNDER-STAND MY FEAR.
SHF
Hee hee
NATSUME'S MUMBLING TO HIMSELF AGAIN.
WEIRDO.
Hee hee
.....

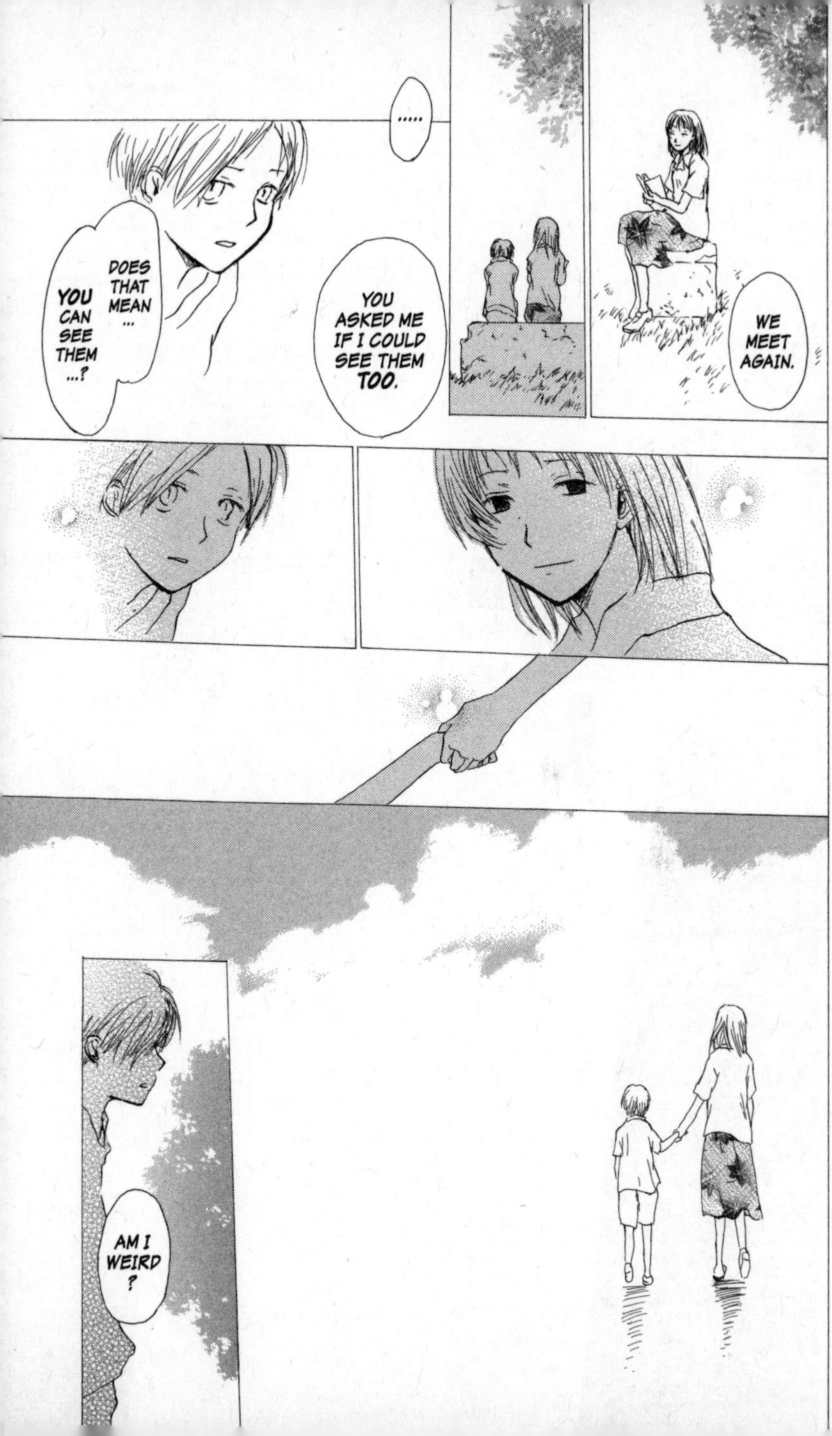
WE MEET AGAIN.
.....
YOU ASKED ME IF I COULD SEE THEM TOO.
DOES THAT MEAN ... YOU CAN SEE THEM ...?
AM I WEIRD ?

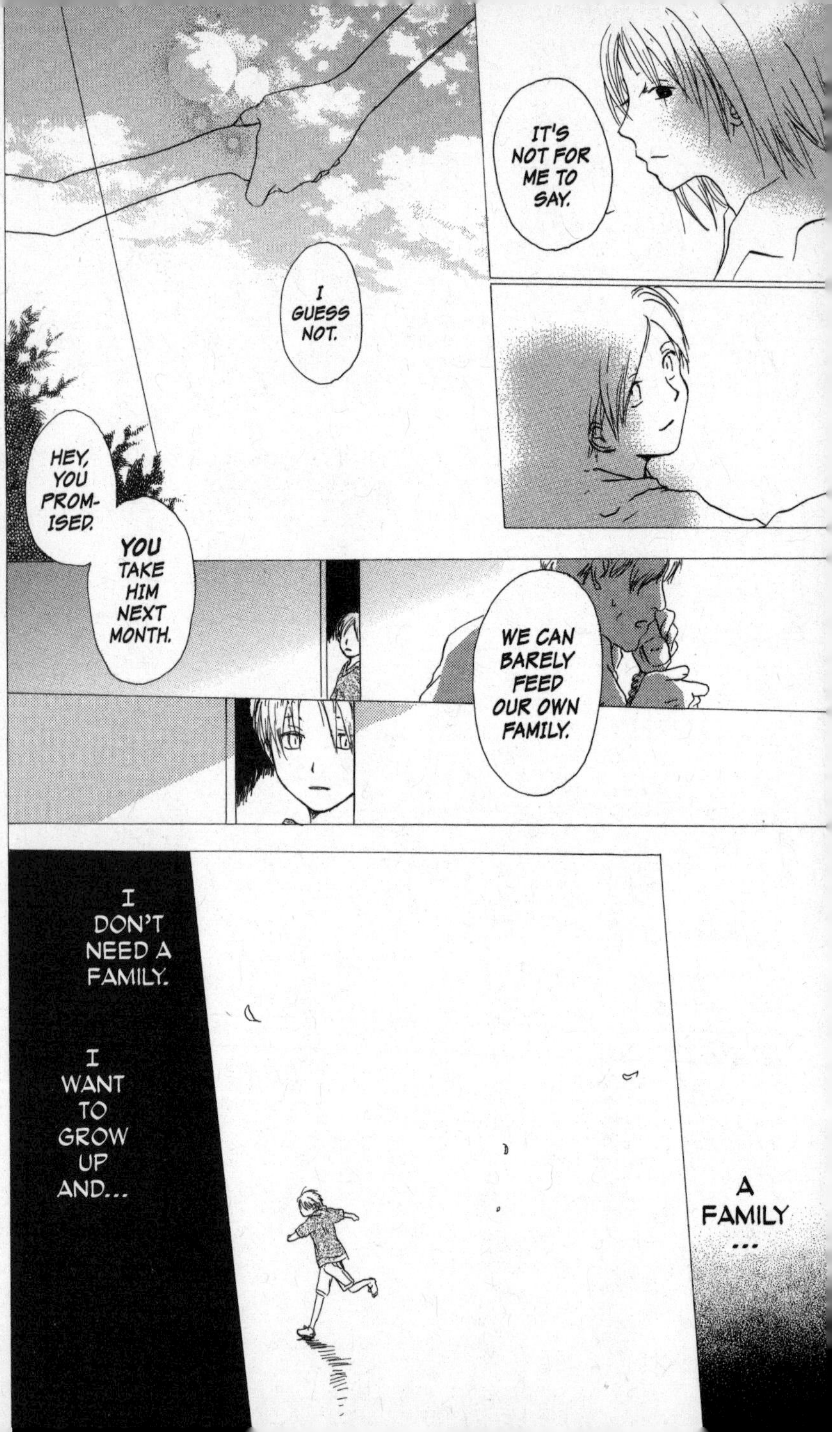
IT'S NOT FOR ME TO SAY.
I GUESS NOT.
HEY, YOU PROMISED.
YOU TAKE HIM NEXT MONTH.
WE CAN BARELY FEED OUR OWN FAMILY.
A FAMILY...
I DON'T NEED A FAMILY.
I WANT TO GROW UP AND...

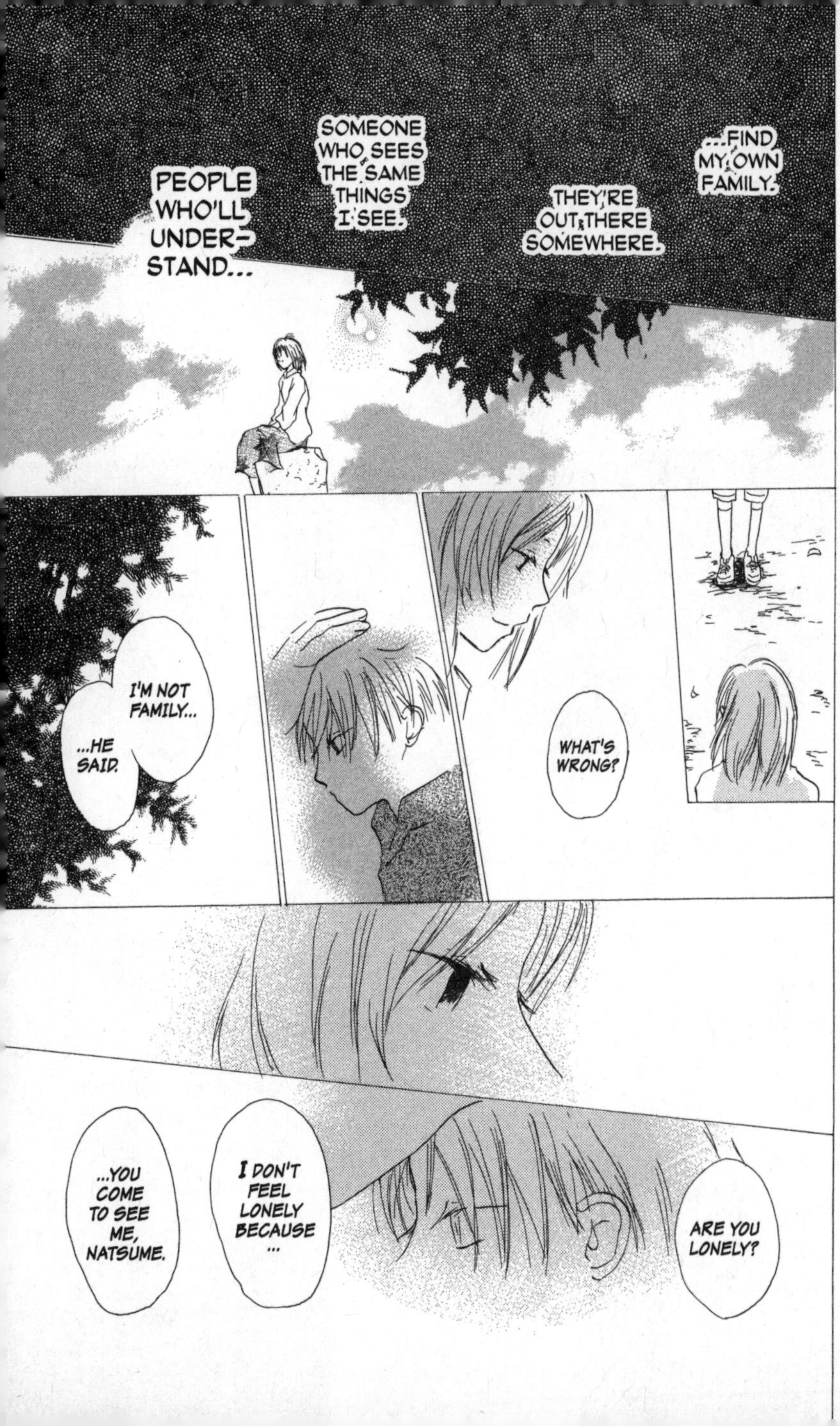
...FIND MY OWN FAMILY.
THEY'RE OUT THERE SOMEWHERE.
SOMEONE WHO SEES THE SAME THINGS I SEE.
PEOPLE WHO'LL UNDER-STAND...
WHAT'S WRONG?
I'M NOT FAMILY...
...HE SAID.
ARE YOU LONELY?
I DON'T FEEL LONELY BECAUSE ...
...YOU COME TO SEE ME, NATSUME.

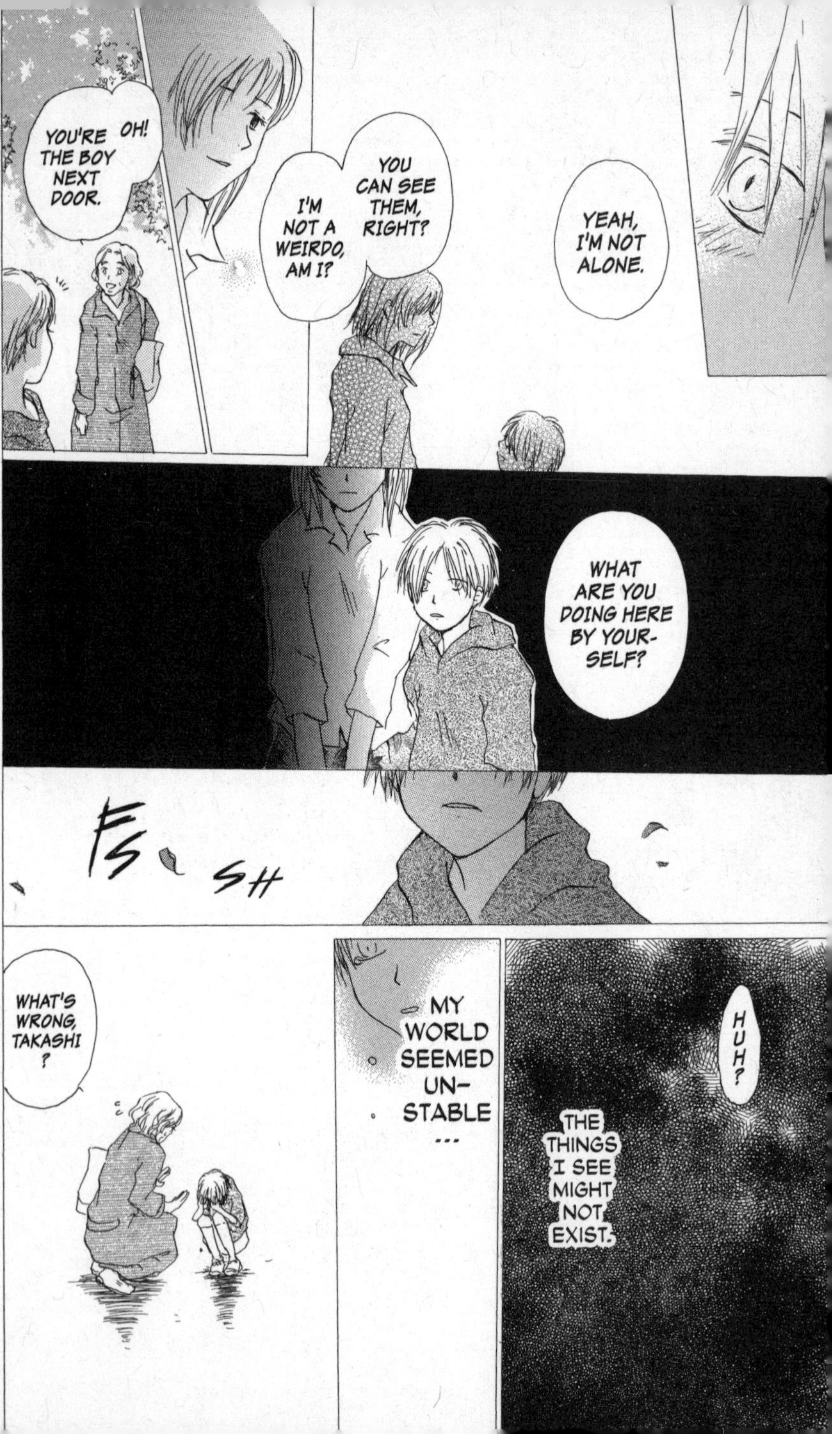

YEAH, I'M NOT ALONE.
YOU CAN SEE THEM, RIGHT?
I'M NOT A WEIRDO, AM I?
OH!
YOU'RE THE BOY NEXT DOOR.
WHAT ARE YOU DOING HERE BY YOUR-SELF?
FS
SH
HUH?
THE THINGS I SEE MIGHT NOT EXIST.
MY WORLD SEEMED UN-STABLE...
WHAT'S WRONG, TAKASHI?

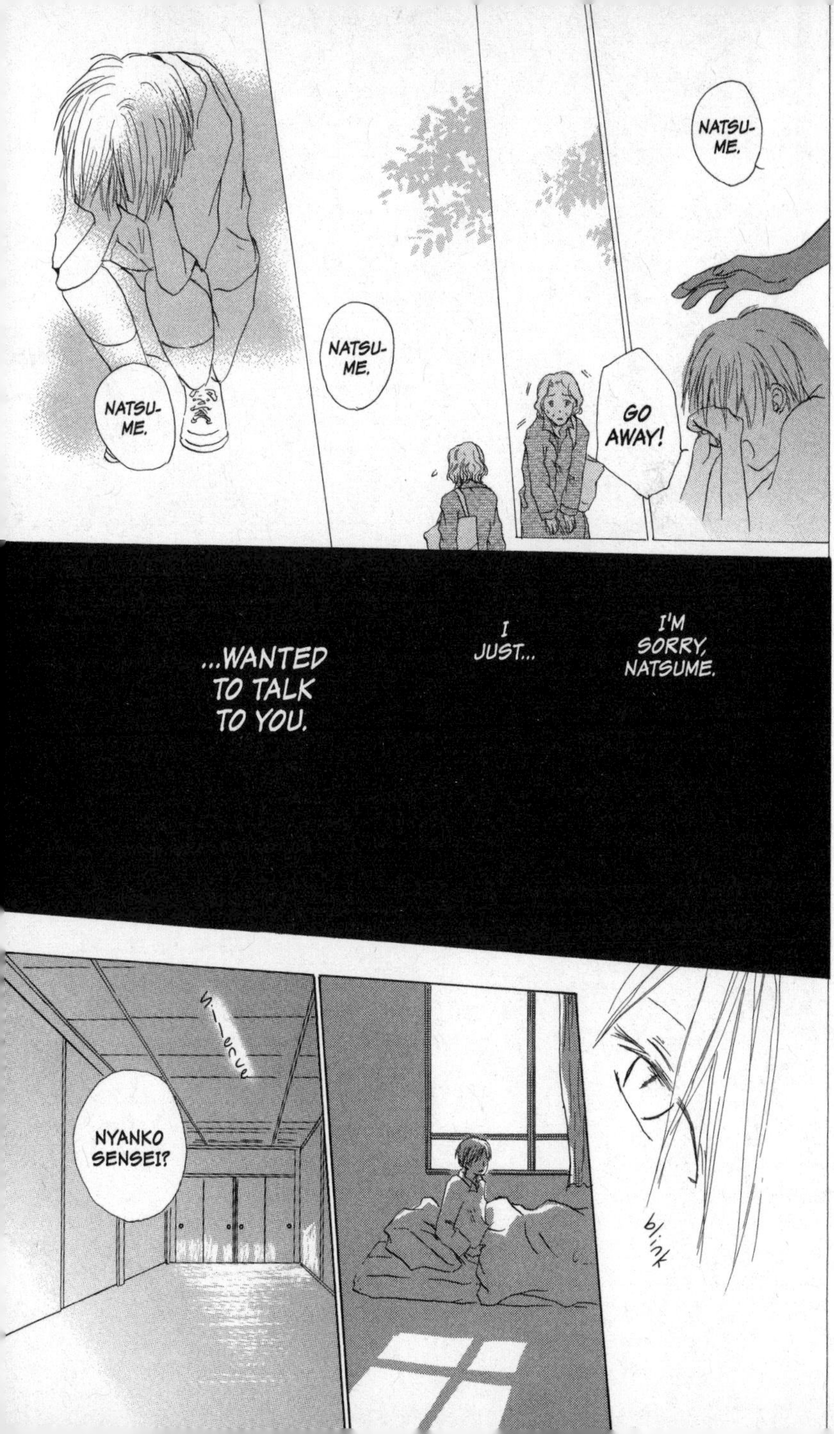
NATSU-ME.
GO AWAY!
NATSU-ME.
NATSU-ME.
I'M SORRY, NATSUME.
I JUST...
...WANTED TO TALK TO YOU.
blink
silence
NYANKO SENSEI?

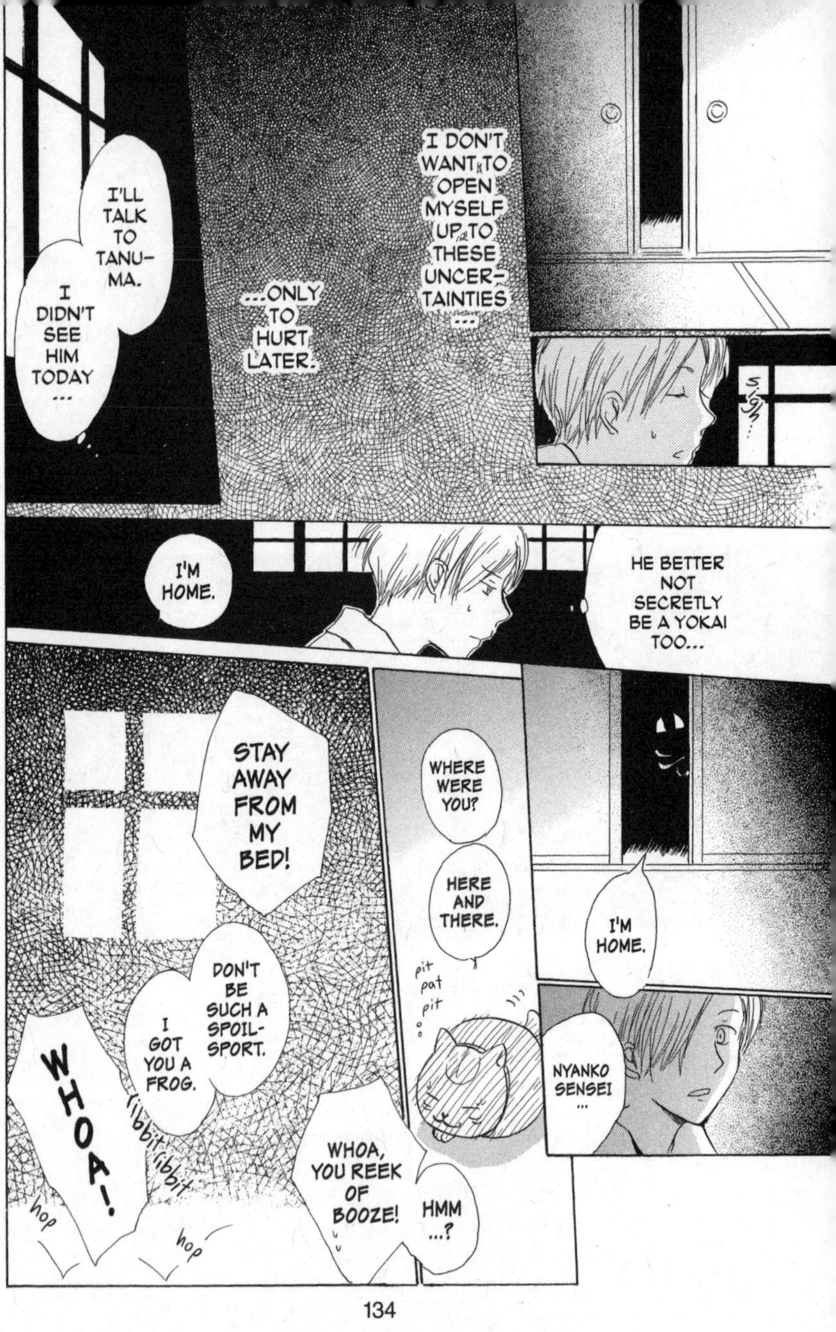
I DON'T WANT TO OPEN MYSELF UP TO THESE UNCERTAINTIES...
...ONLY TO HURT LATER.
sigh...
I'LL TALK TO TANU-MA.
I DIDN'T SEE HIM TODAY...
HE BETTER NOT SECRETLY BE A YOKAI TOO...
I'M HOME.
I'M HOME.
NYANKO SENSEI...
WHERE WERE YOU?
HERE AND THERE.
pit pat pit
HMM...?
WHOA, YOU REEK OF BOOZE!
STAY AWAY FROM MY BED!
DON'T BE SUCH A SPOIL-SPORT.
I GOT YOU A FROG.
ribbit ribbit
WHOA!
hop
hop

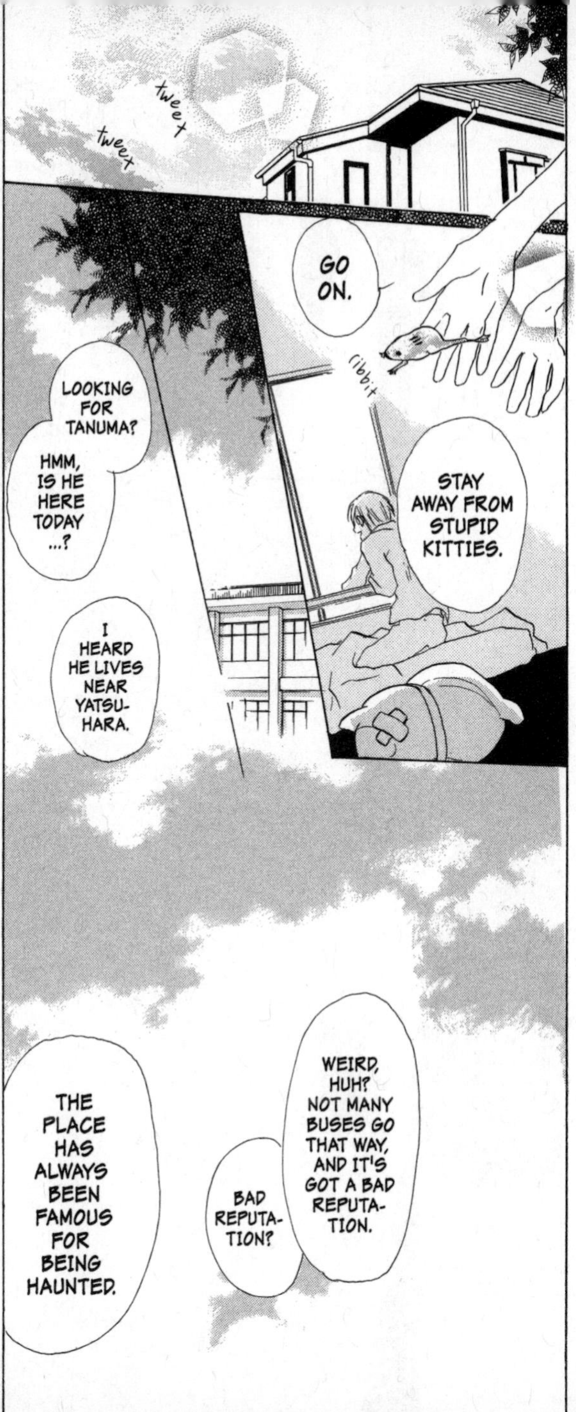
tweet
tweet
GO ON.
ribbit
STAY AWAY FROM STUPID KITTIES.
LOOKING FOR TANUMA?
HMM, IS HE HERE TODAY ...?
I HEARD HE LIVES NEAR YATSU-HARA.
WEIRD, HUH? NOT MANY BUSES GO THAT WAY, AND IT'S GOT A BAD REPUTA-TION.
BAD REPUTA-TION?
THE PLACE HAS ALWAYS BEEN FAMOUS FOR BEING HAUNTED.

08

First, Tamao Ohki

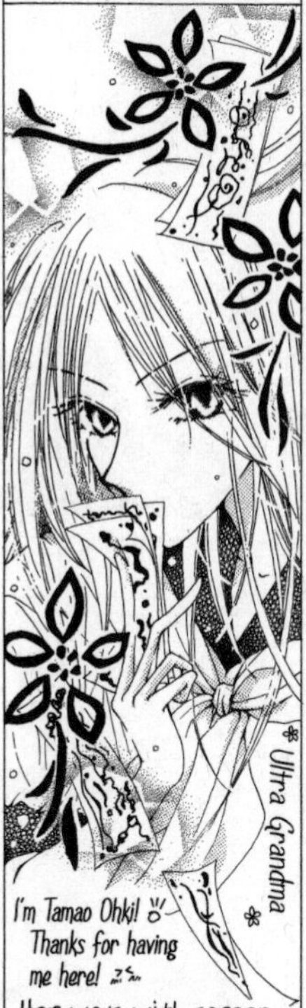
Ultra Grandma
I'm Tamao Ohki!
Thanks for having me here!

Her ways with screen-tone lend such subtle beauty and depth to facial expressions. She's so meticulous yet works quickly, and her delicate skills really show in her designs. I get excited every time we meet.

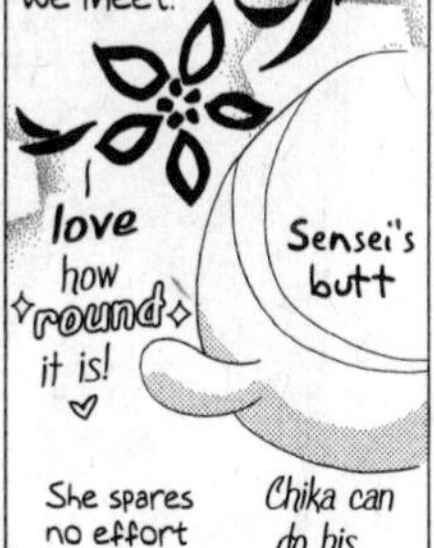
I **love** how ✧**round**✧ it is! ♡
Sensei's butt
She spares no effort on research.
Chika can do his face!

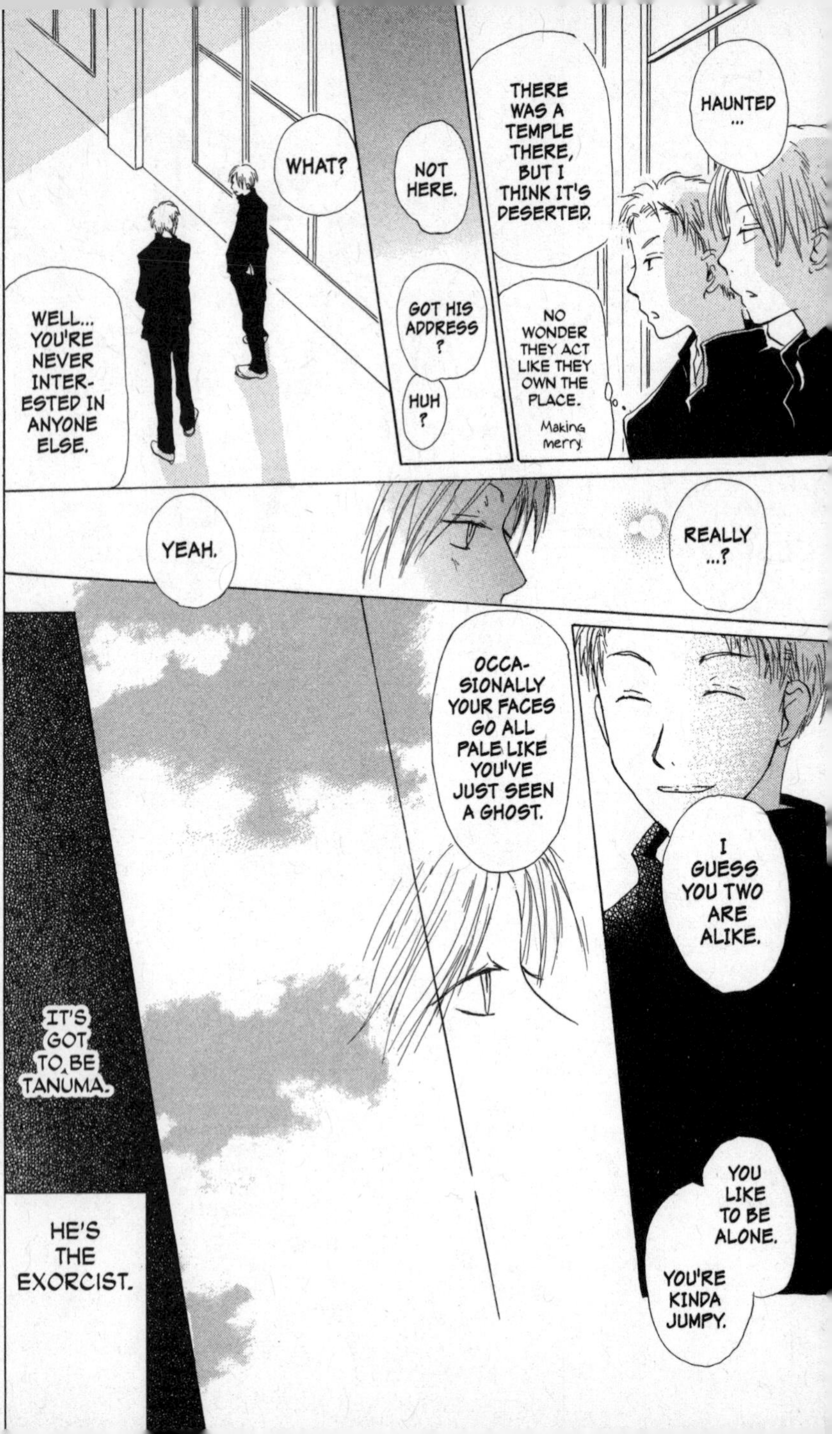

HAUNTED ...
THERE WAS A TEMPLE THERE, BUT I THINK IT'S DESERTED.
NO WONDER THEY ACT LIKE THEY OWN THE PLACE.
Making merry.
NOT HERE.
GOT HIS ADDRESS ?
HUH ?
WHAT?
WELL... YOU'RE NEVER INTER-ESTED IN ANYONE ELSE.
REALLY ...?
YEAH.
OCCA-SIONALLY YOUR FACES GO ALL PALE LIKE YOU'VE JUST SEEN A GHOST.
I GUESS YOU TWO ARE ALIKE.
YOU LIKE TO BE ALONE.
YOU'RE KINDA JUMPY.
IT'S GOT TO BE TANUMA.
HE'S THE EXORCIST.

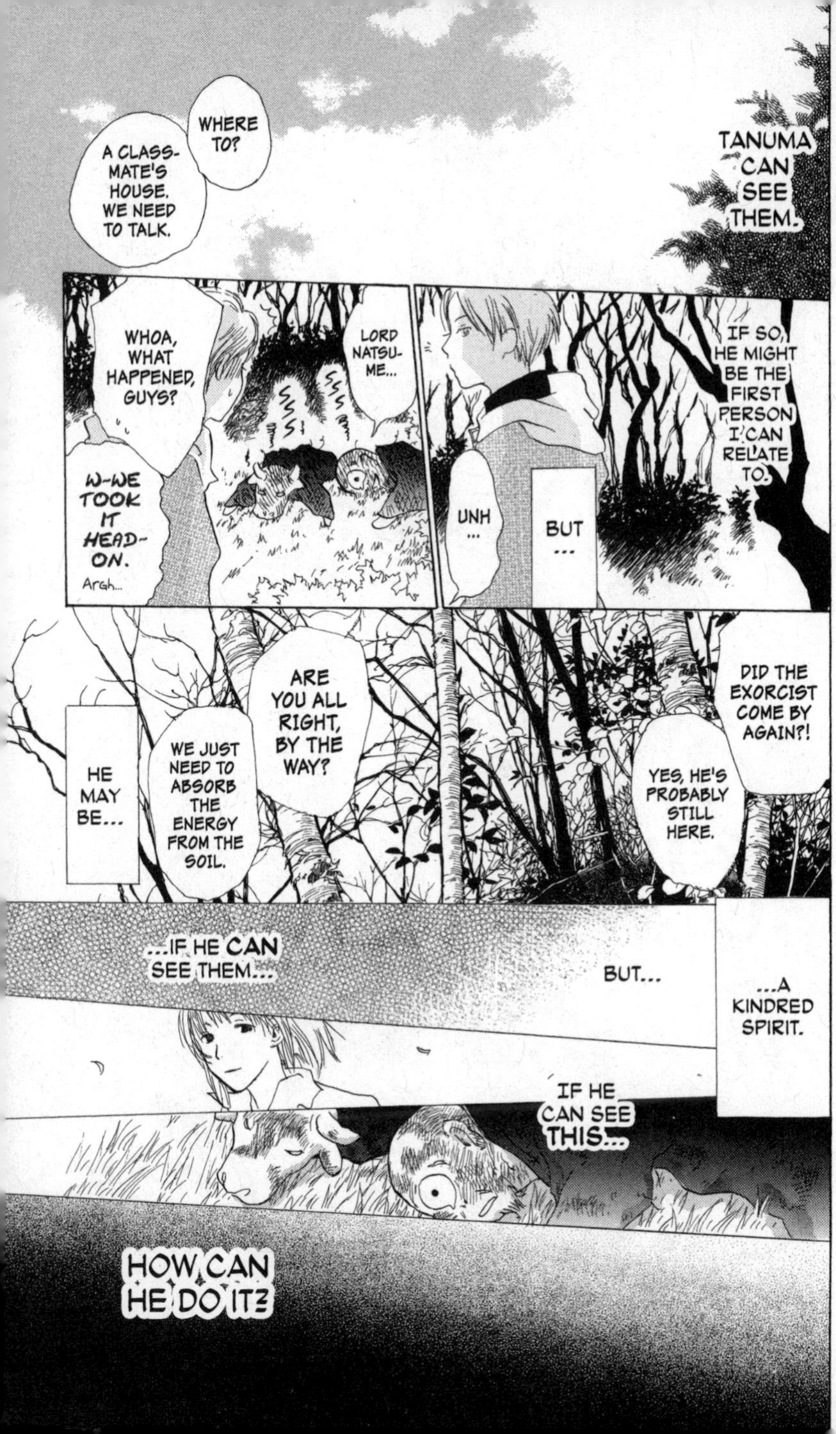
TANUMA CAN SEE THEM.
WHERE TO?
A CLASS-MATE'S HOUSE. WE NEED TO TALK.
IF SO, HE MIGHT BE THE FIRST PERSON I CAN RELATE TO.
BUT...
UNH...
LORD NATSU-ME...
WHOA, WHAT HAPPENED, GUYS?
W-WE TOOK IT HEAD-ON.
Argh...
DID THE EXORCIST COME BY AGAIN?!
YES, HE'S PROBABLY STILL HERE.
ARE YOU ALL RIGHT, BY THE WAY?
WE JUST NEED TO ABSORB THE ENERGY FROM THE SOIL.
HE MAY BE...
...A KINDRED SPIRIT.
BUT...
...IF HE CAN SEE THEM...
IF HE CAN SEE THIS...
HOW CAN HE DO IT?

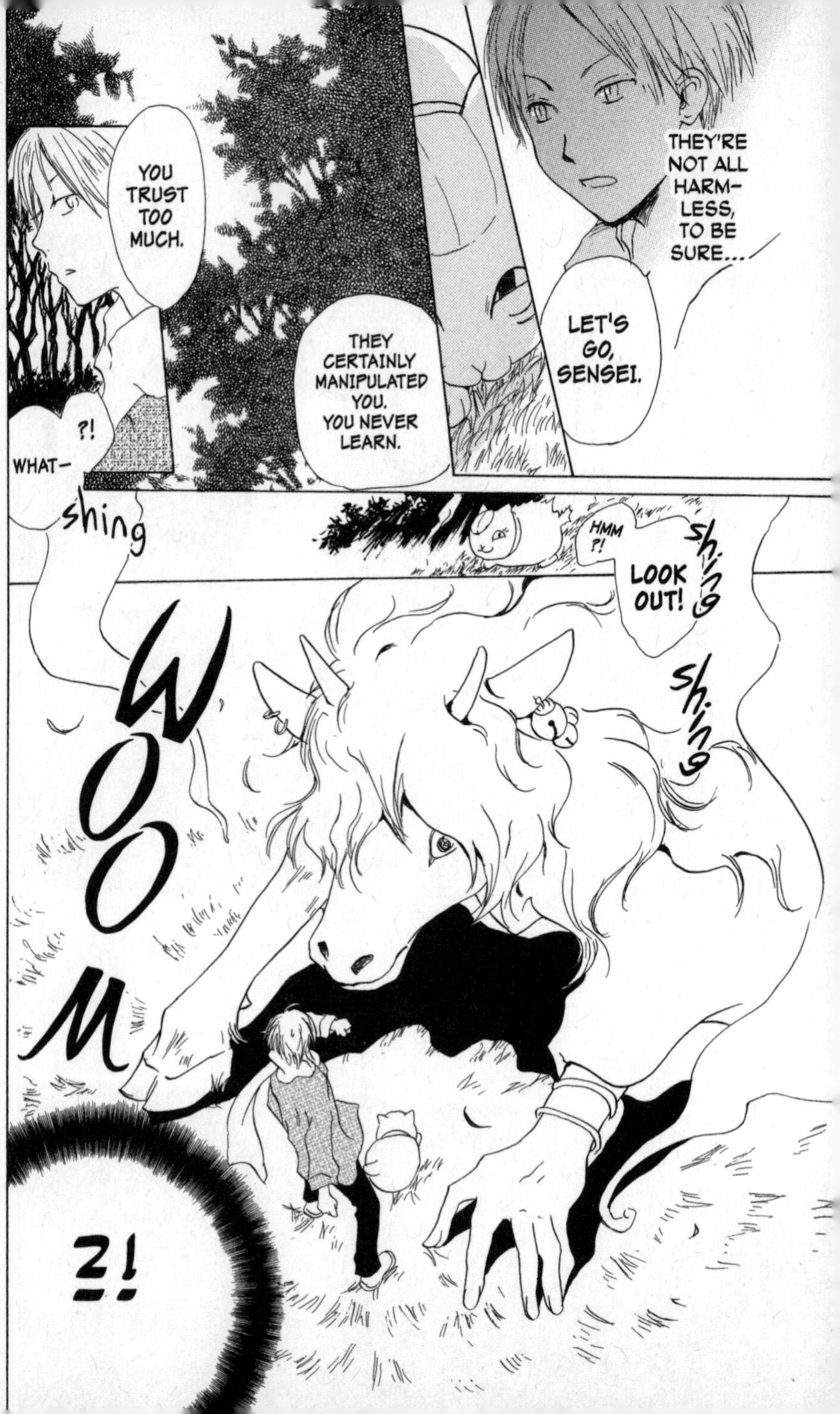
THEY'RE NOT ALL HARMLESS, TO BE SURE...
LET'S GO, SENSEI.
THEY CERTAINLY MANIPULATED YOU. YOU NEVER LEARN.
YOU TRUST TOO MUCH.
?!
WHAT-
HMM ?!
shing
shing
LOOK OUT!
shing
WOOOM
Z!

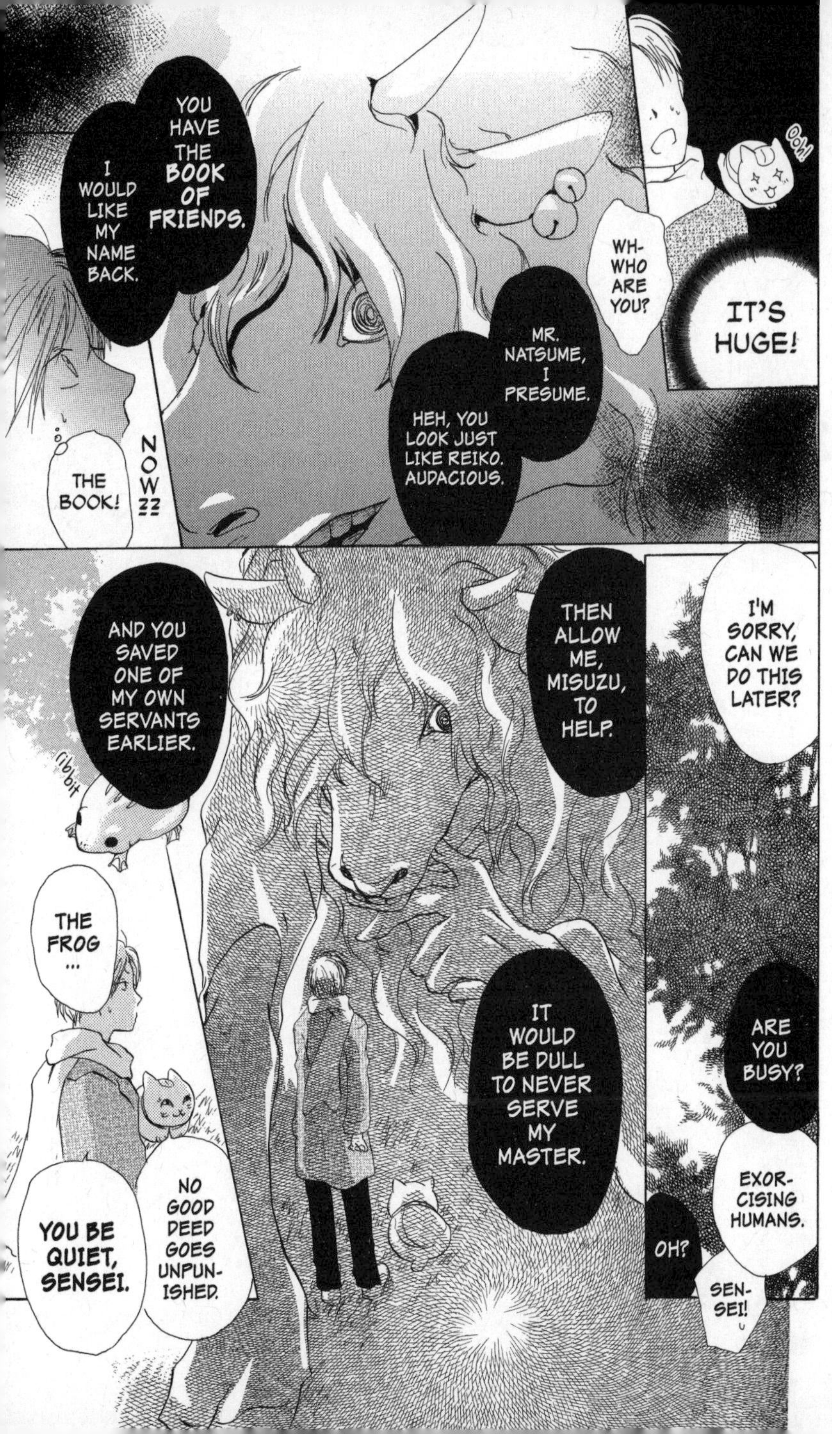
OOH!
WH-WHO ARE YOU?
IT'S HUGE!
MR. NATSUME, I PRESUME.
HEH, YOU LOOK JUST LIKE REIKO. AUDACIOUS.
YOU HAVE THE BOOK OF FRIENDS.
I WOULD LIKE MY NAME BACK.
NOW
THE BOOK!
I'M SORRY, CAN WE DO THIS LATER?
ARE YOU BUSY?
EXORCISING HUMANS.
OH?
SENSEI!
THEN ALLOW ME, MISUZU, TO HELP.
IT WOULD BE DULL TO NEVER SERVE MY MASTER.
AND YOU SAVED ONE OF MY OWN SERVANTS EARLIER.
ribbit
THE FROG...
NO GOOD DEED GOES UNPUNISHED.
YOU BE QUIET, SENSEI.

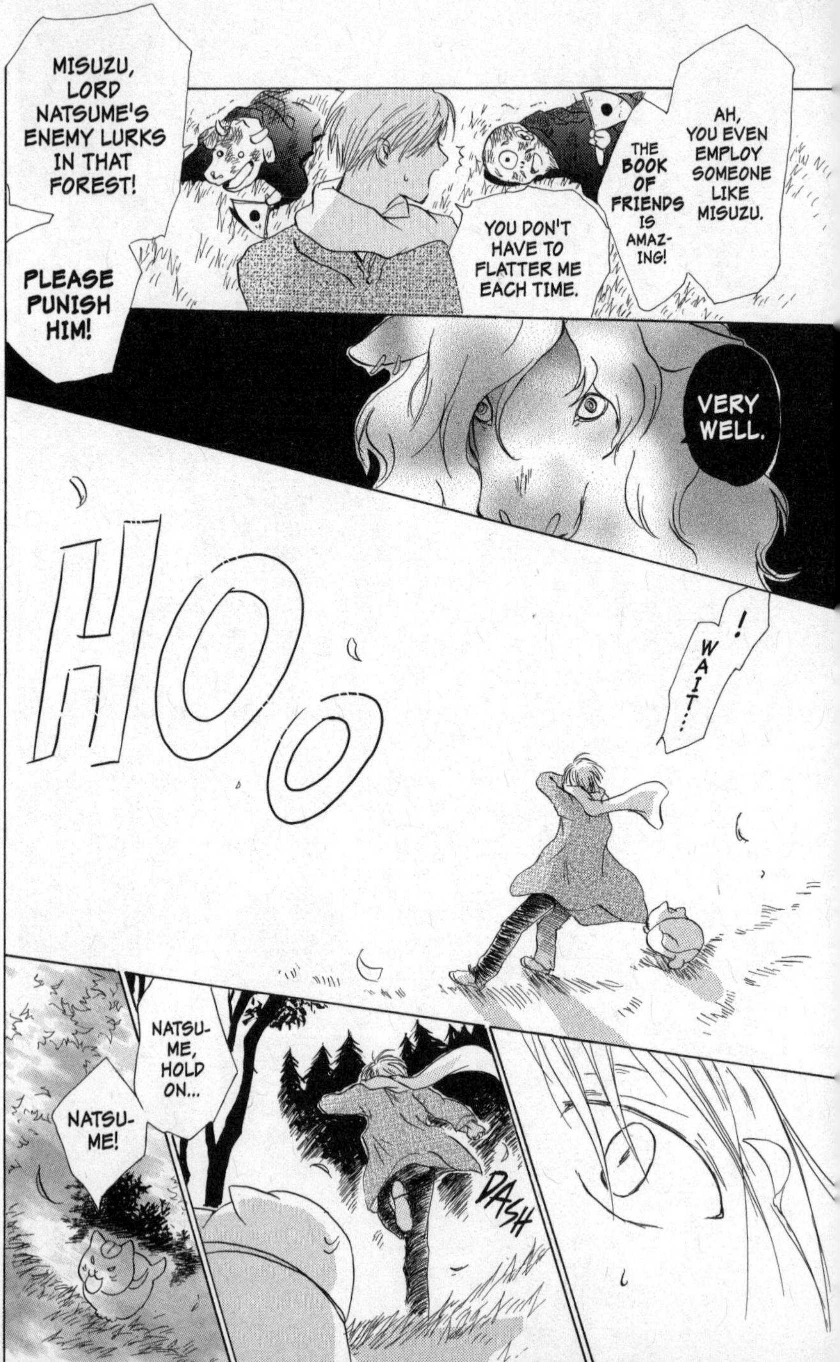
AH, YOU EVEN EMPLOY SOMEONE LIKE MISUZU.
THE BOOK OF FRIENDS IS AMAZ-ING!
YOU DON'T HAVE TO FLATTER ME EACH TIME.
MISUZU, LORD NATSUME'S ENEMY LURKS IN THAT FOREST!
PLEASE PUNISH HIM!
VERY WELL.
!
WAIT...
HOOO
DASH
NATSU-ME, HOLD ON...
NATSU-ME!

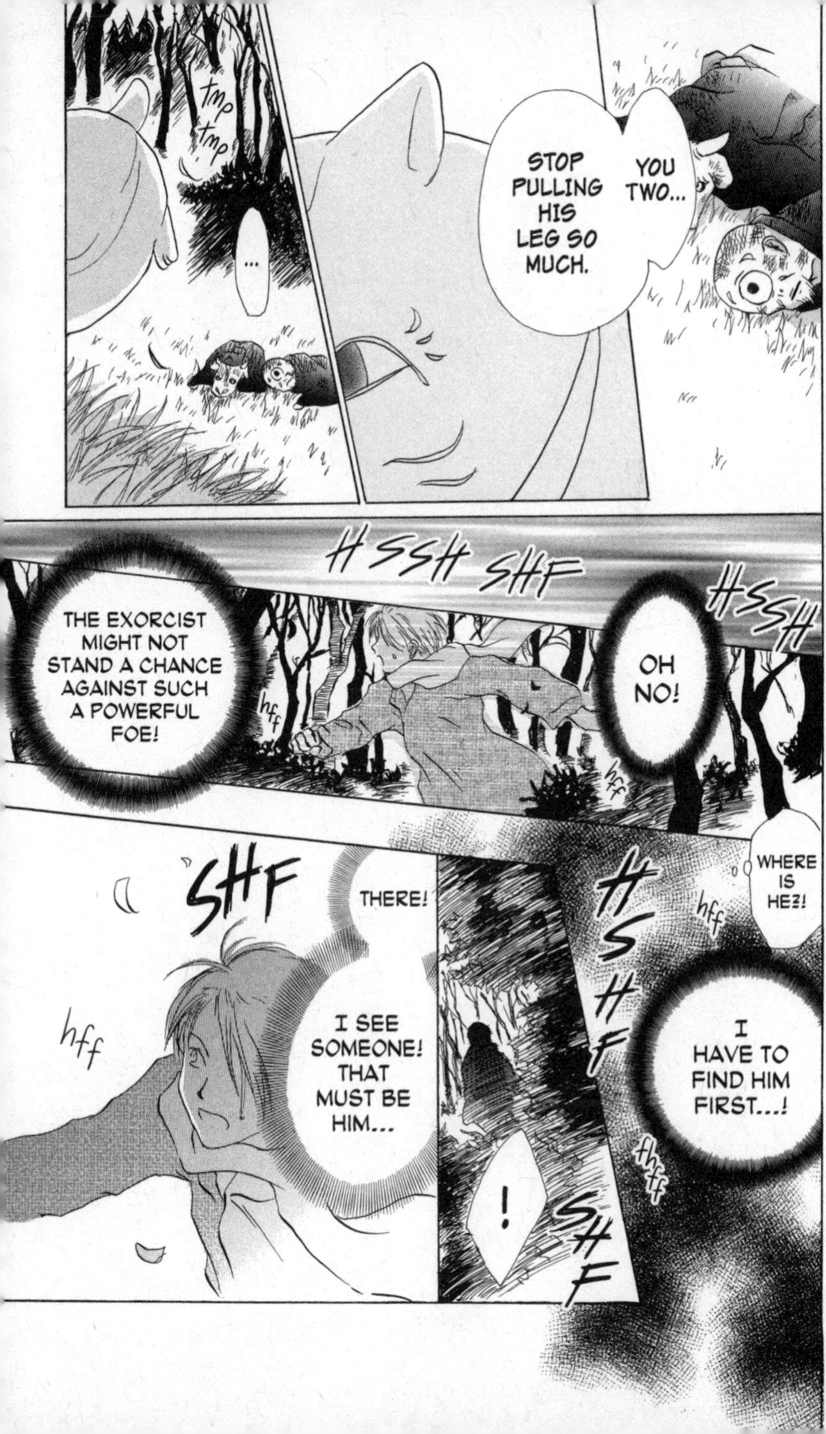
YOU TWO...
STOP PULLING HIS LEG SO MUCH.
tmp tmp
...
HSSH
OH NO!
HSSH SHF
THE EXORCIST MIGHT NOT STAND A CHANCE AGAINST SUCH A POWERFUL FOE!
hff
hff
WHERE IS HE?!
HSHF
hff
I HAVE TO FIND HIM FIRST...!
thff
SHF
!
SHF
THERE!
I SEE SOMEONE! THAT MUST BE HIM...
hff

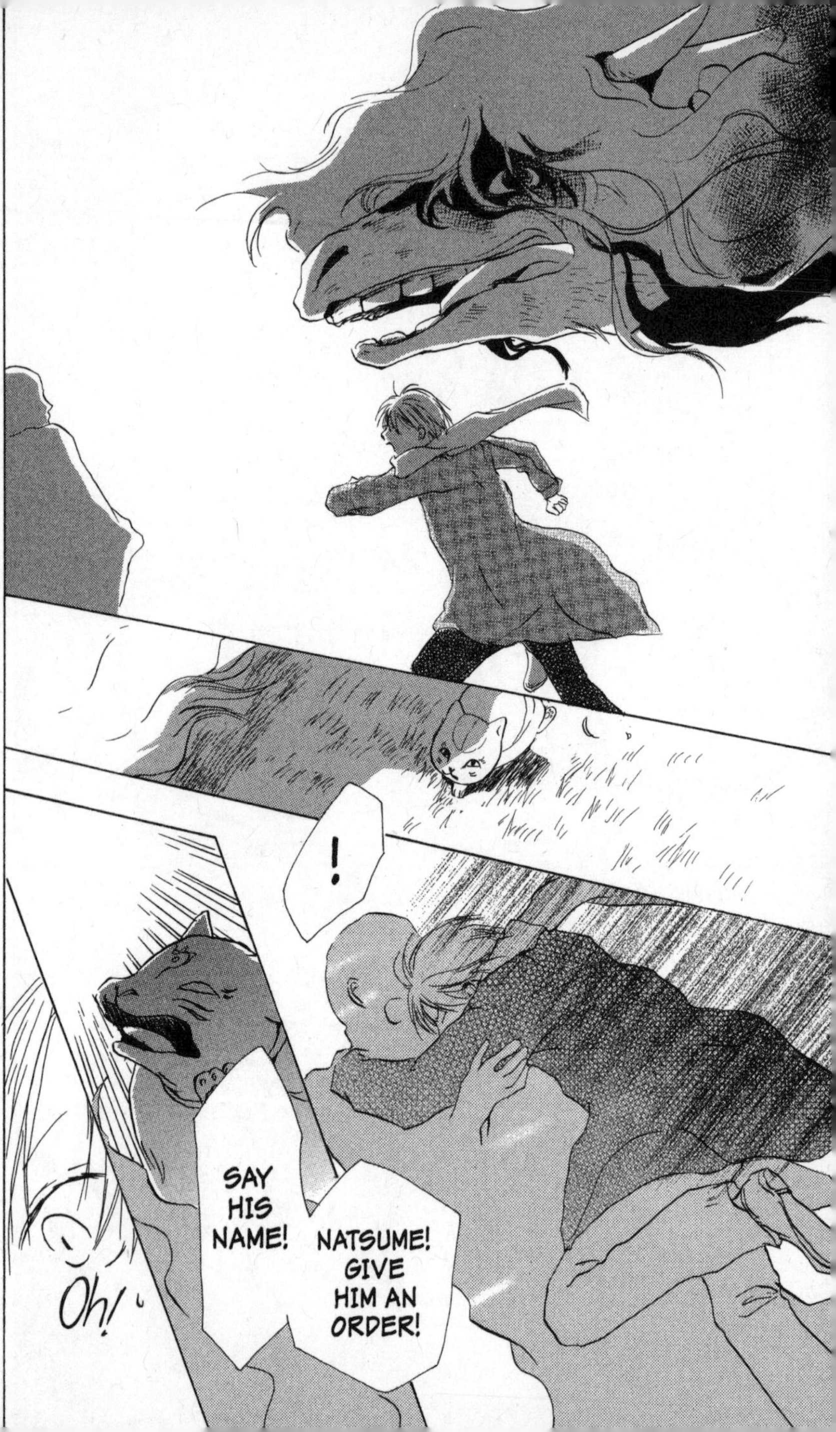
!
NATSUME! GIVE HIM AN ORDER!
SAY HIS NAME!
Oh!

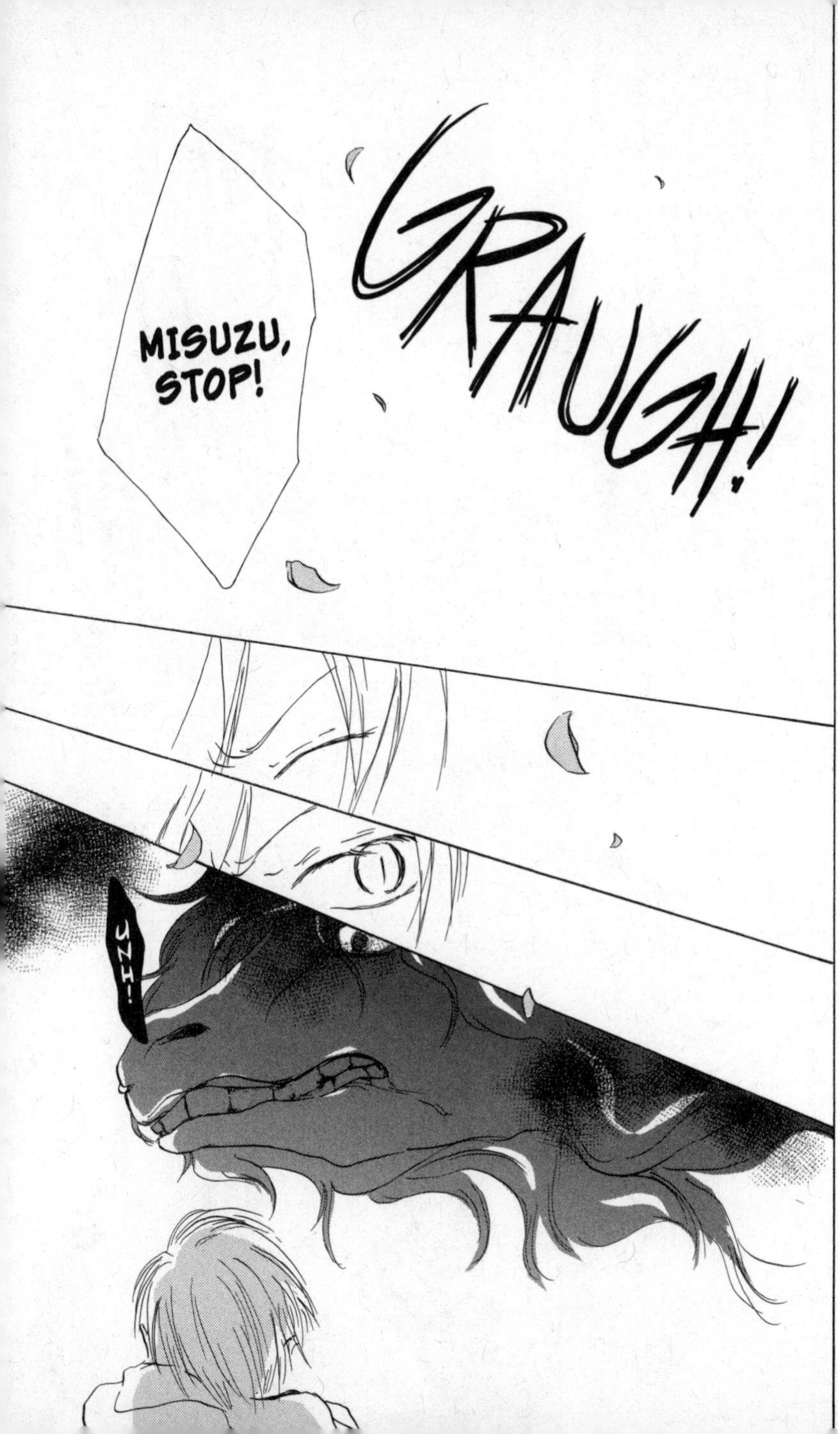
GRAUGH!
MISUZU, STOP!
UNH!

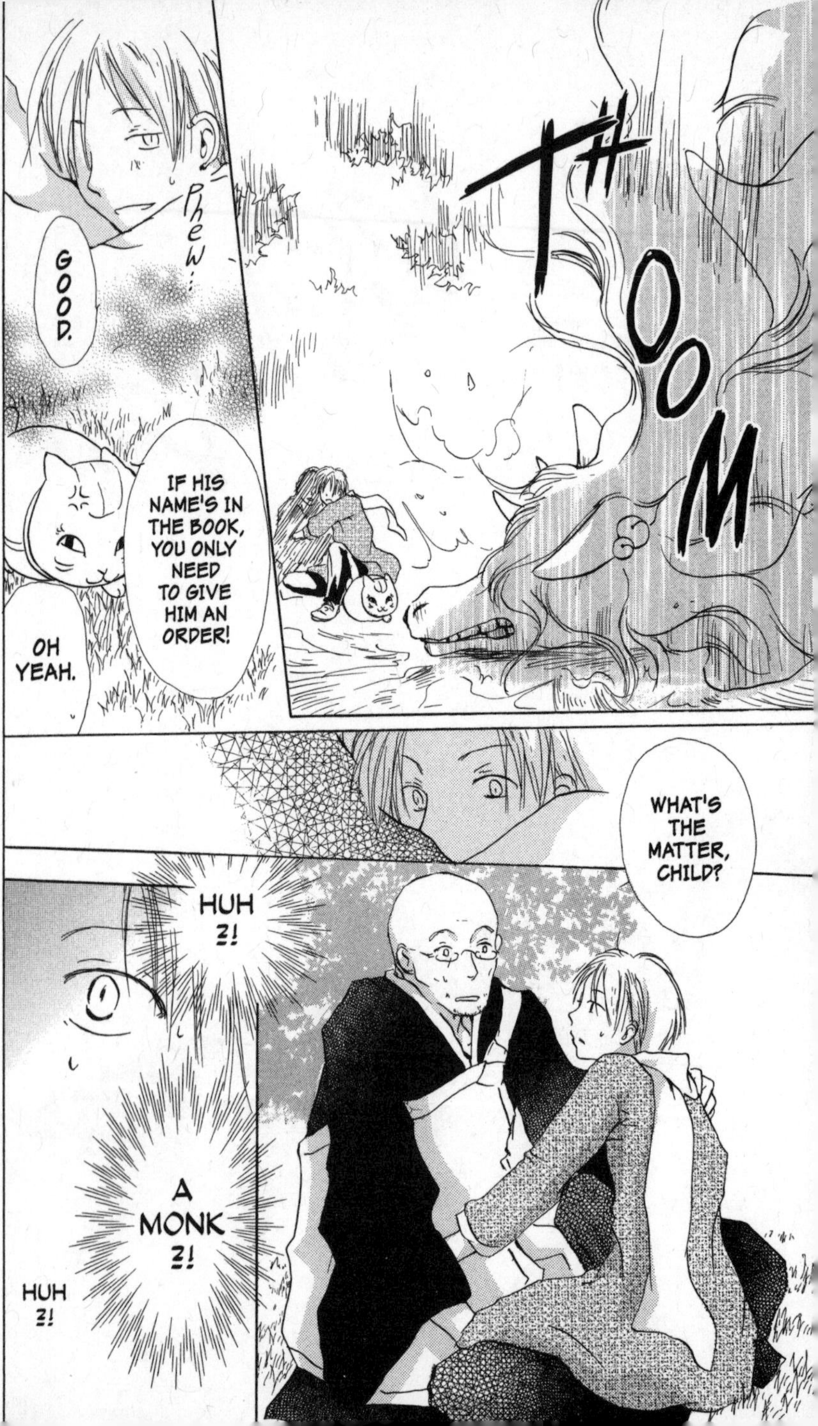
THOOOM
Phew...
GOOD.
IF HIS NAME'S IN THE BOOK, YOU ONLY NEED TO GIVE HIM AN ORDER!
OH YEAH.
WHAT'S THE MATTER, CHILD?
HUH?!
A MONK?!
HUH?!

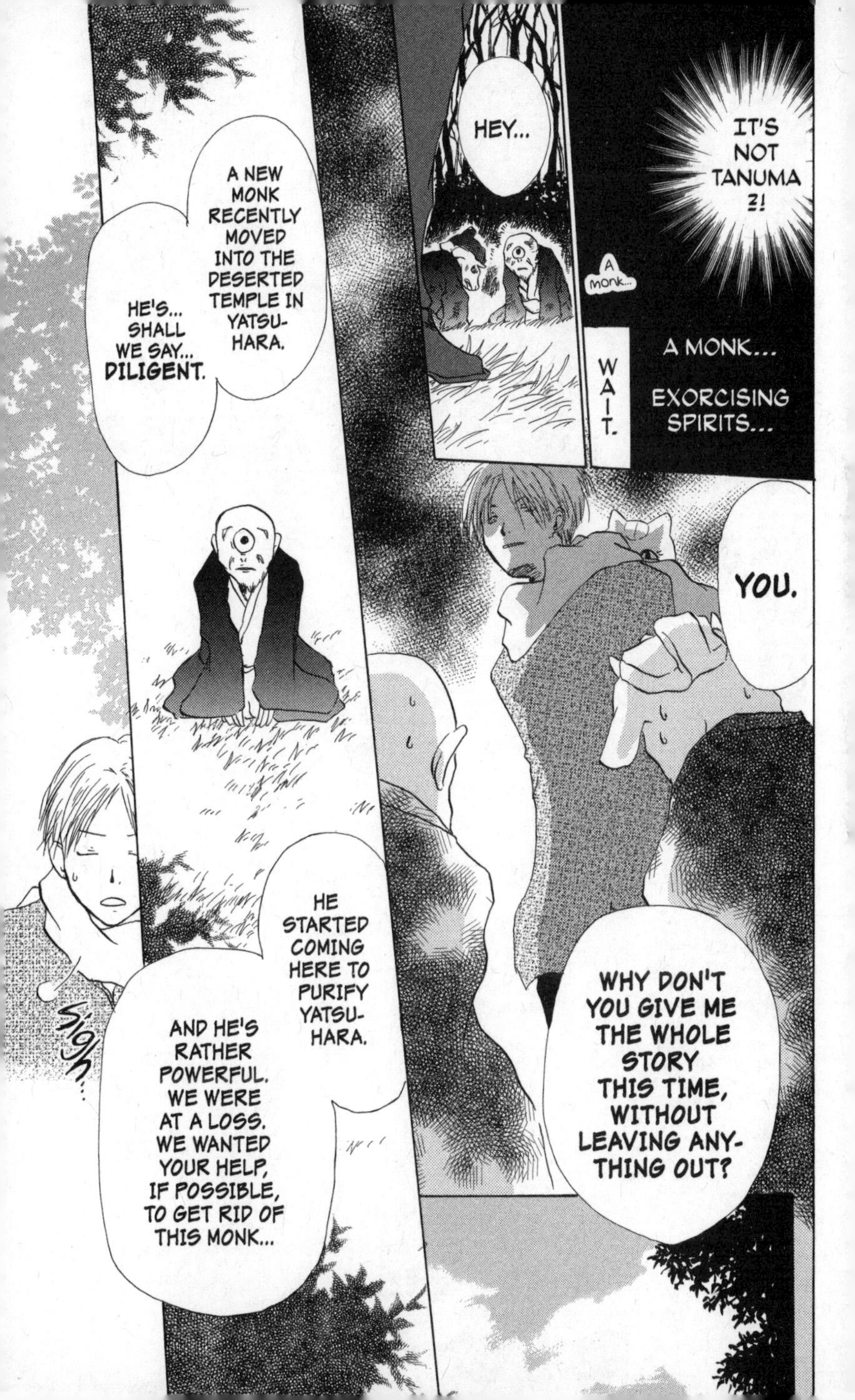
IT'S NOT TANUMA?!
A MONK...
EXORCISING SPIRITS...
WAIT.
HEY...
A monk...
YOU.
WHY DON'T YOU GIVE ME THE WHOLE STORY THIS TIME, WITHOUT LEAVING ANY-THING OUT?
A NEW MONK RECENTLY MOVED INTO THE DESERTED TEMPLE IN YATSU-HARA.
HE'S... SHALL WE SAY... DILIGENT.
HE STARTED COMING HERE TO PURIFY YATSU-HARA.
AND HE'S RATHER POWERFUL. WE WERE AT A LOSS. WE WANTED YOUR HELP, IF POSSIBLE, TO GET RID OF THIS MONK...
Sigh...

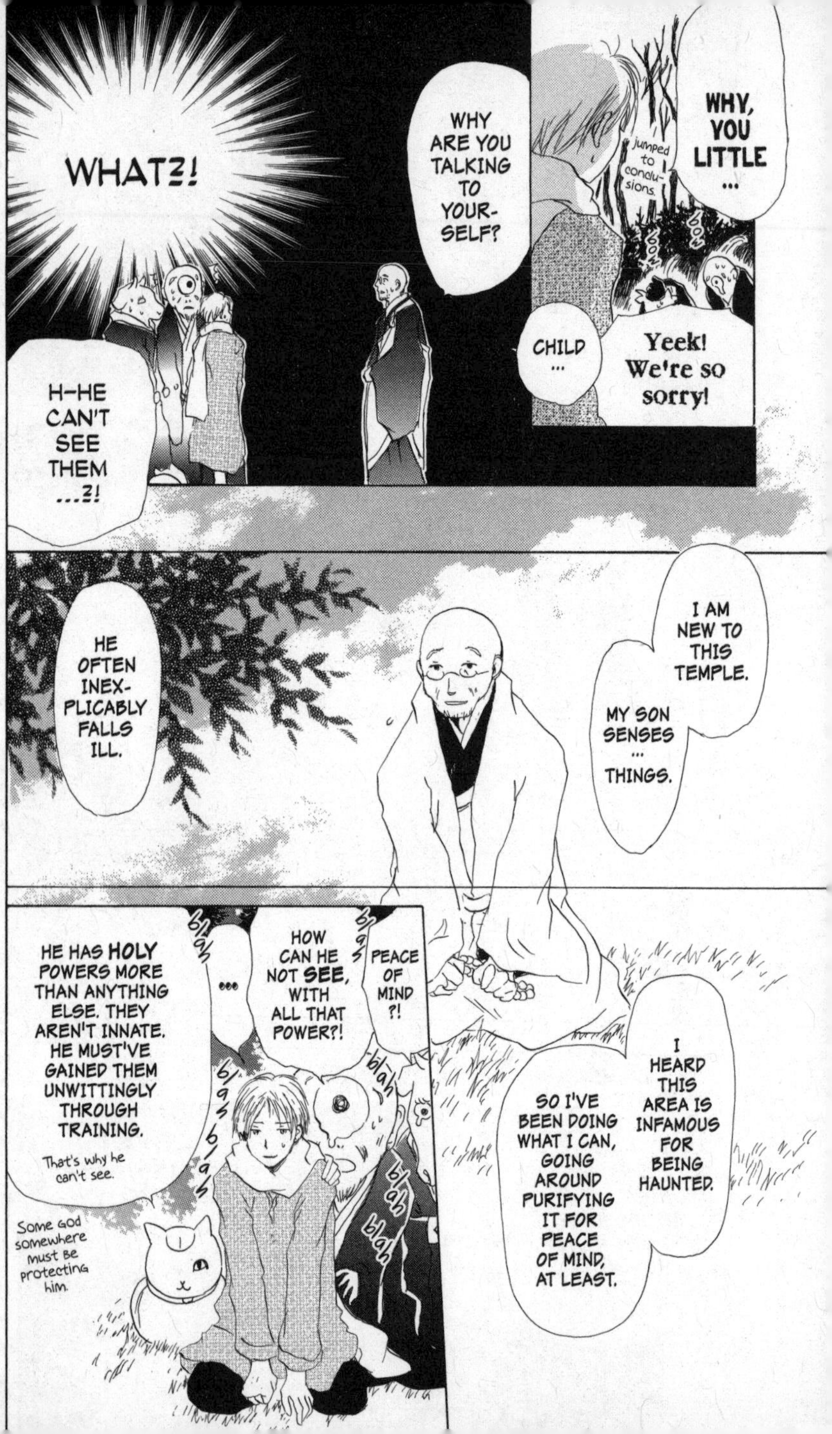
WHY, YOU LITTLE ...
jumped to conclusions.
bow bow
Yeek! We're so sorry!
CHILD ...
WHY ARE YOU TALKING TO YOURSELF?
WHAT?!
H-HE CAN'T SEE THEM ...?!
I AM NEW TO THIS TEMPLE.
MY SON SENSES ... THINGS.
HE OFTEN INEXPLICABLY FALLS ILL.
I HEARD THIS AREA IS INFAMOUS FOR BEING HAUNTED.
SO I'VE BEEN DOING WHAT I CAN, GOING AROUND PURIFYING IT FOR PEACE OF MIND, AT LEAST.
PEACE OF MIND?!
HOW CAN HE NOT SEE, WITH ALL THAT POWER?!
...
HE HAS HOLY POWERS MORE THAN ANYTHING ELSE. THEY AREN'T INNATE. HE MUST'VE GAINED THEM UNWITTINGLY THROUGH TRAINING.
That's why he can't see.
blah blah blah blah
blah blah blah
Some God somewhere must be protecting him.

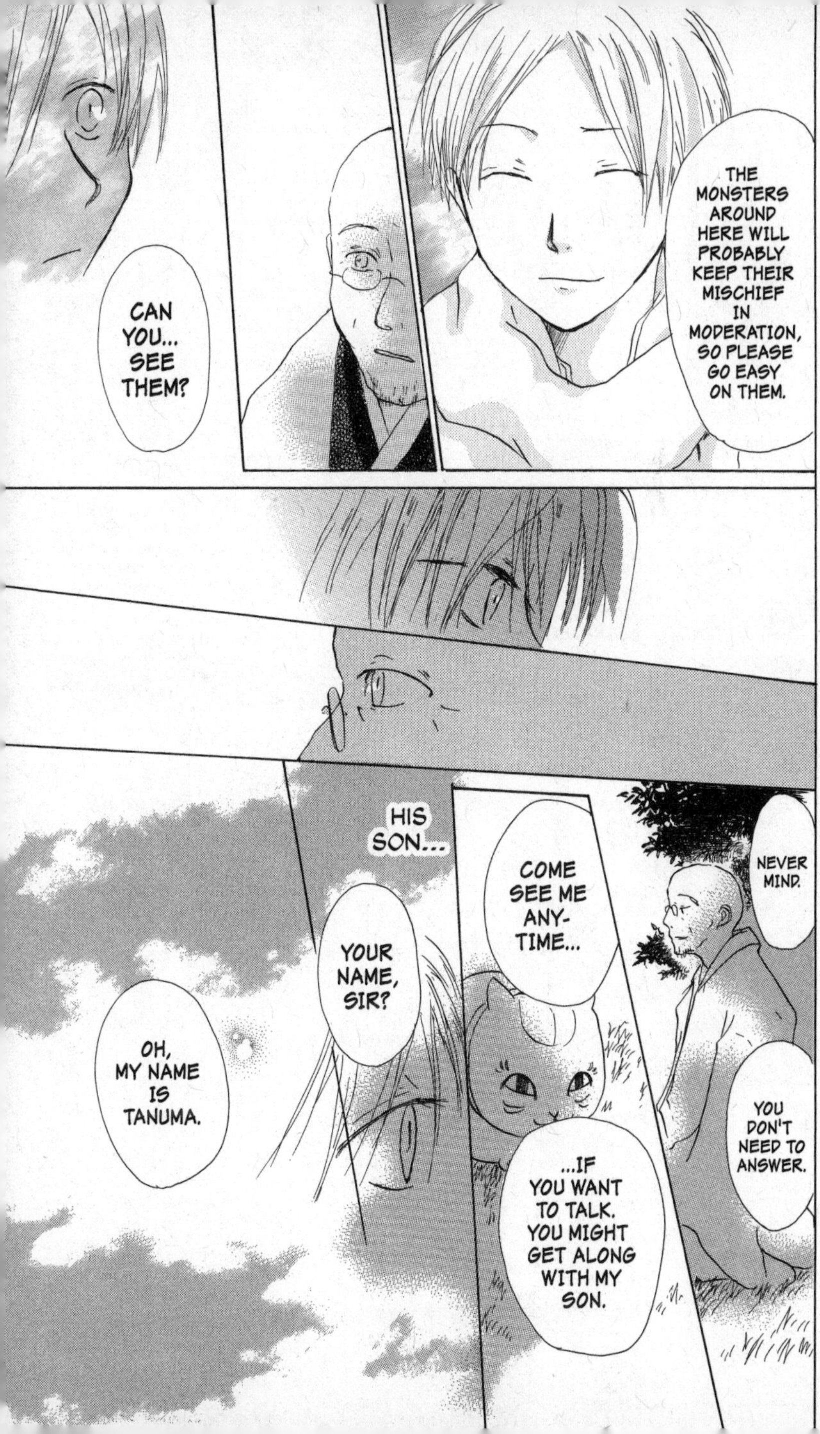
THE MONSTERS AROUND HERE WILL PROBABLY KEEP THEIR MISCHIEF IN MODERATION, SO PLEASE GO EASY ON THEM.
CAN YOU... SEE THEM?
NEVER MIND.
YOU DON'T NEED TO ANSWER.
COME SEE ME ANY-TIME...
...IF YOU WANT TO TALK. YOU MIGHT GET ALONG WITH MY SON.
HIS SON...
YOUR NAME, SIR?
OH, MY NAME IS TANUMA.

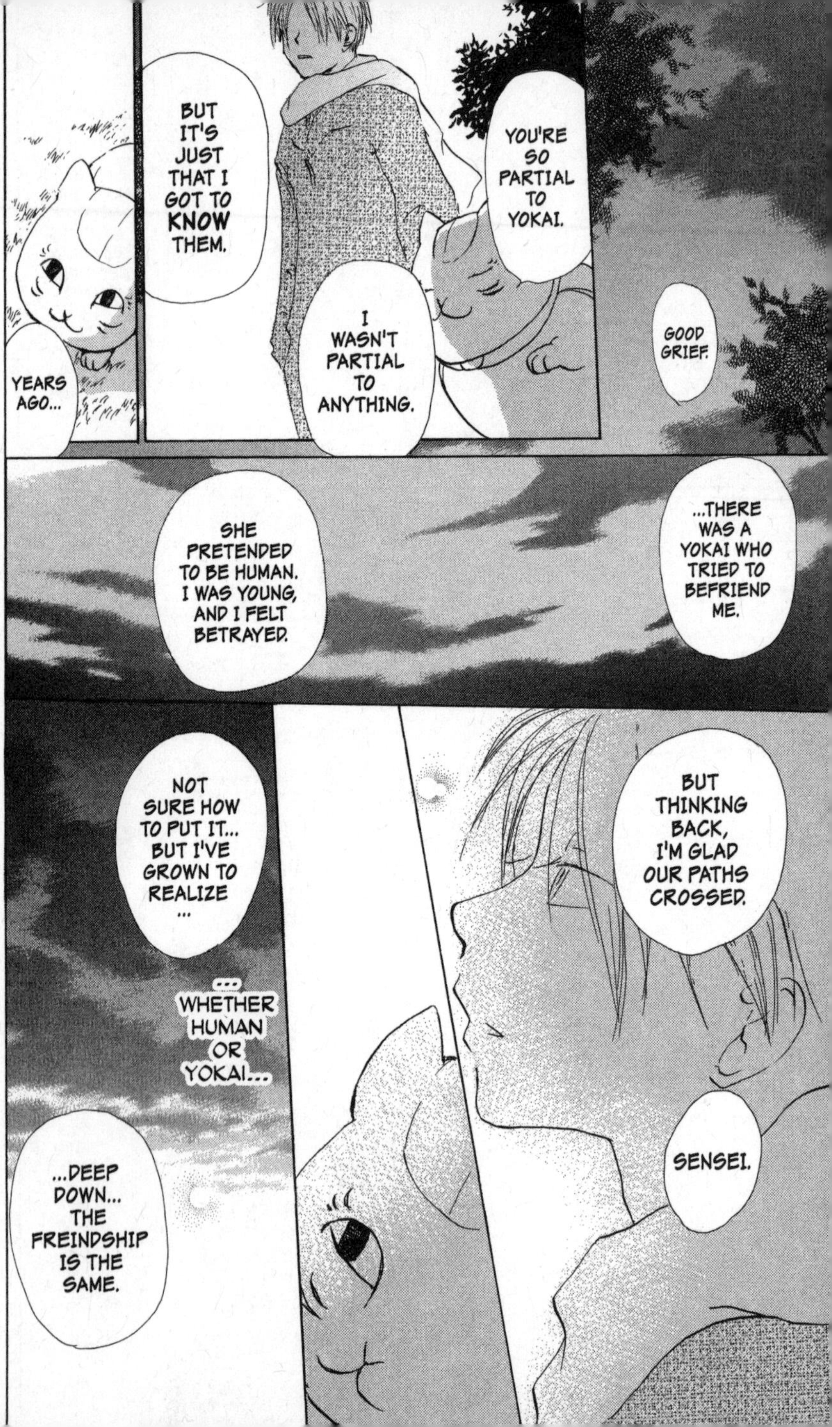
YOU'RE SO PARTIAL TO YOKAI.
GOOD GRIEF.
I WASN'T PARTIAL TO ANYTHING.
BUT IT'S JUST THAT I GOT TO KNOW THEM.
YEARS AGO...
...THERE WAS A YOKAI WHO TRIED TO BEFRIEND ME.
SHE PRETENDED TO BE HUMAN. I WAS YOUNG, AND I FELT BETRAYED.
BUT THINKING BACK, I'M GLAD OUR PATHS CROSSED.
SENSEI.
NOT SURE HOW TO PUT IT... BUT I'VE GROWN TO REALIZE ...
... WHETHER HUMAN OR YOKAI...
...DEEP DOWN... THE FREINDSHIP IS THE SAME.

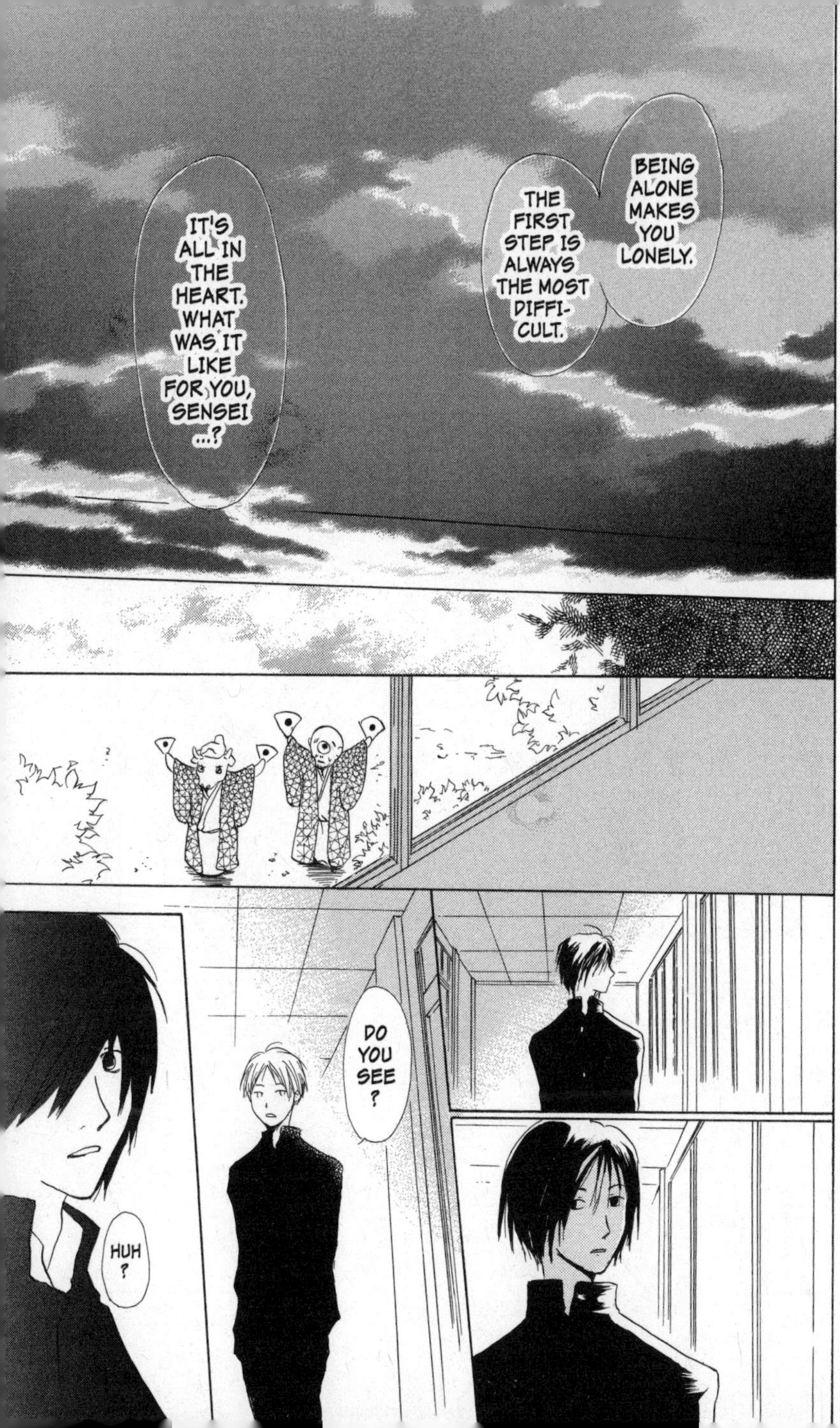
BEING ALONE MAKES YOU LONELY.
THE FIRST STEP IS ALWAYS THE MOST DIFFI- CULT.
IT'S ALL IN THE HEART. WHAT WAS IT LIKE FOR YOU, SENSEI ...?
DO YOU SEE ?
HUH ?

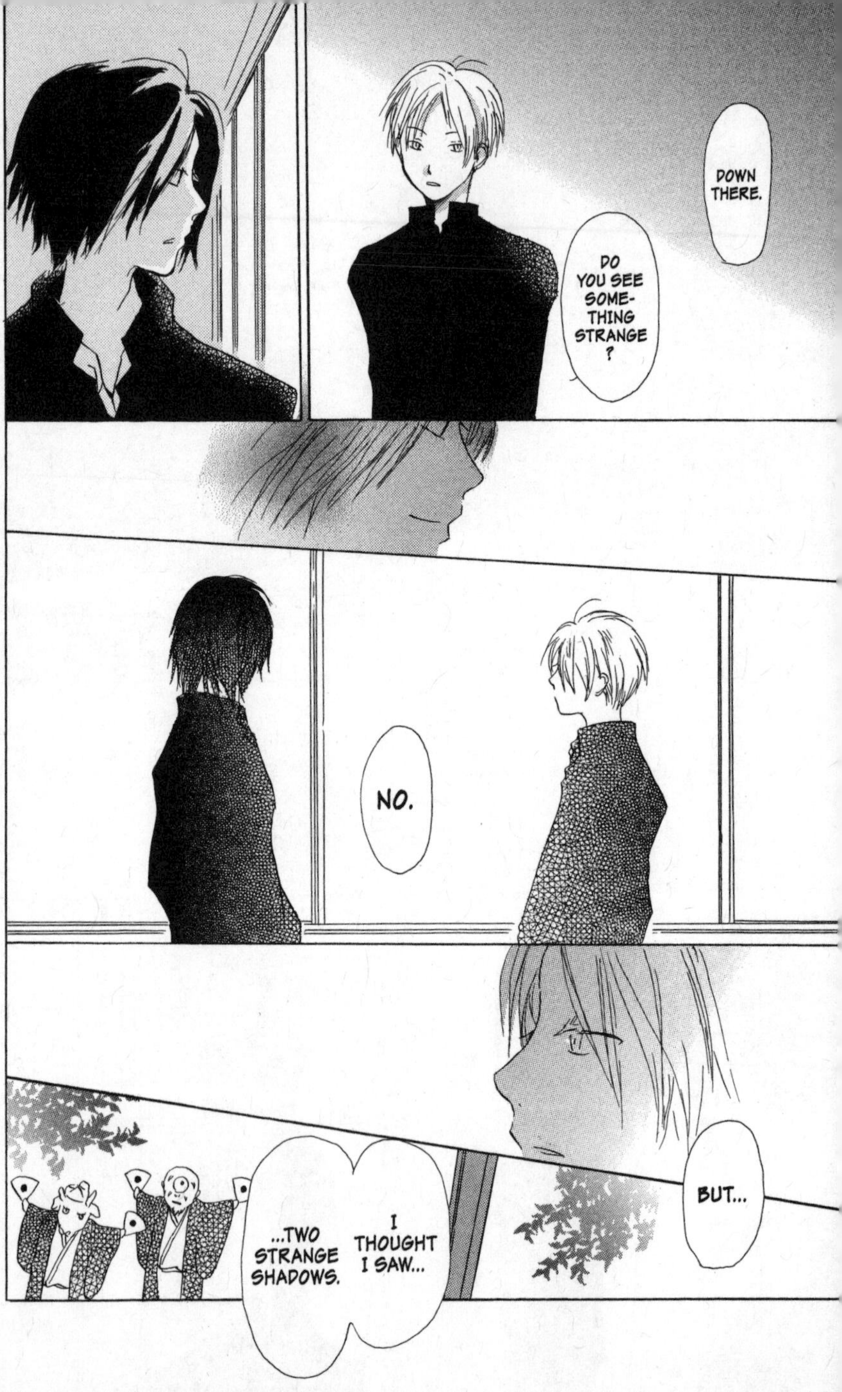
DOWN THERE.
DO YOU SEE SOME-THING STRANGE?
NO.
BUT...
I THOUGHT I SAW...
...TWO STRANGE SHADOWS.

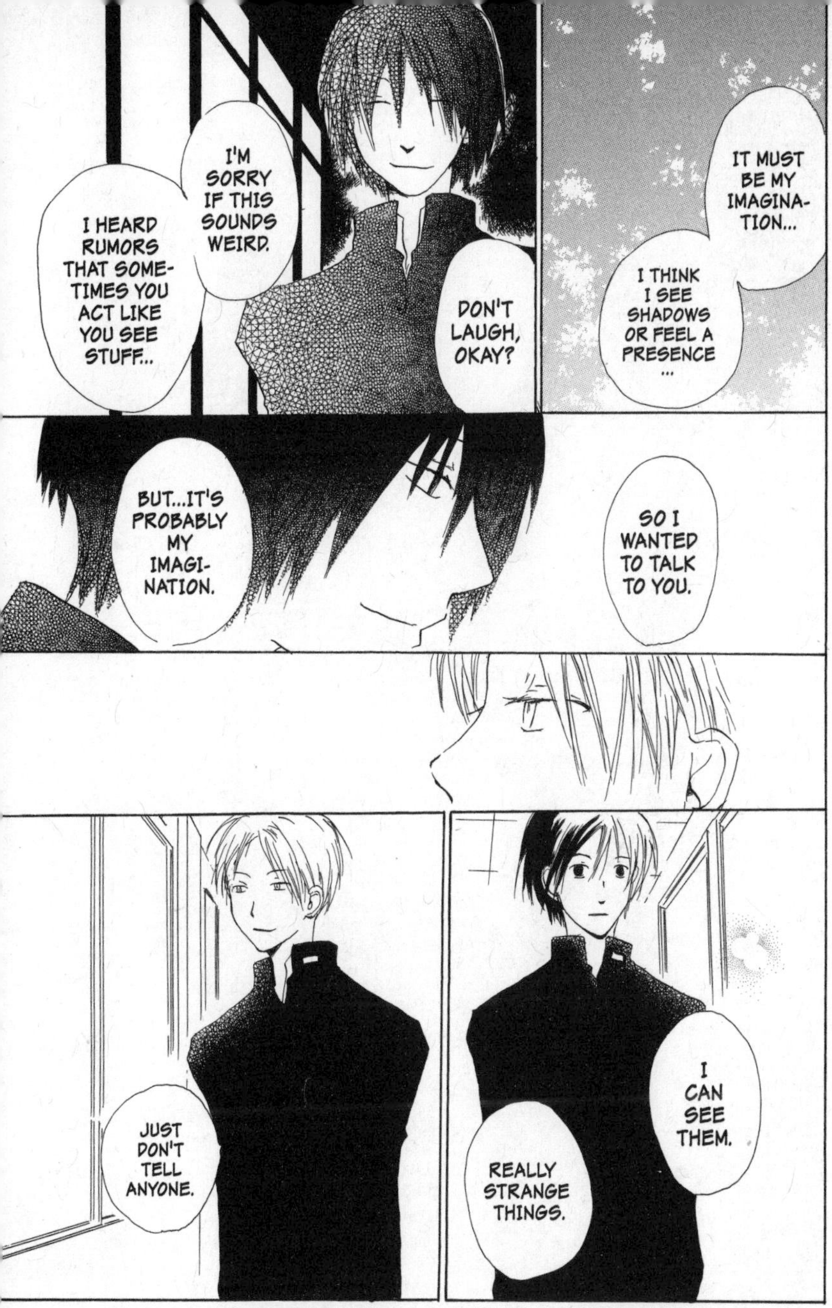
IT MUST BE MY IMAGINATION...
I THINK I SEE SHADOWS OR FEEL A PRESENCE ...
DON'T LAUGH, OKAY?
I'M SORRY IF THIS SOUNDS WEIRD.
I HEARD RUMORS THAT SOME-TIMES YOU ACT LIKE YOU SEE STUFF...
SO I WANTED TO TALK TO YOU.
BUT...IT'S PROBABLY MY IMAGI-NATION.
I CAN SEE THEM.
REALLY STRANGE THINGS.
JUST DON'T TELL ANYONE.

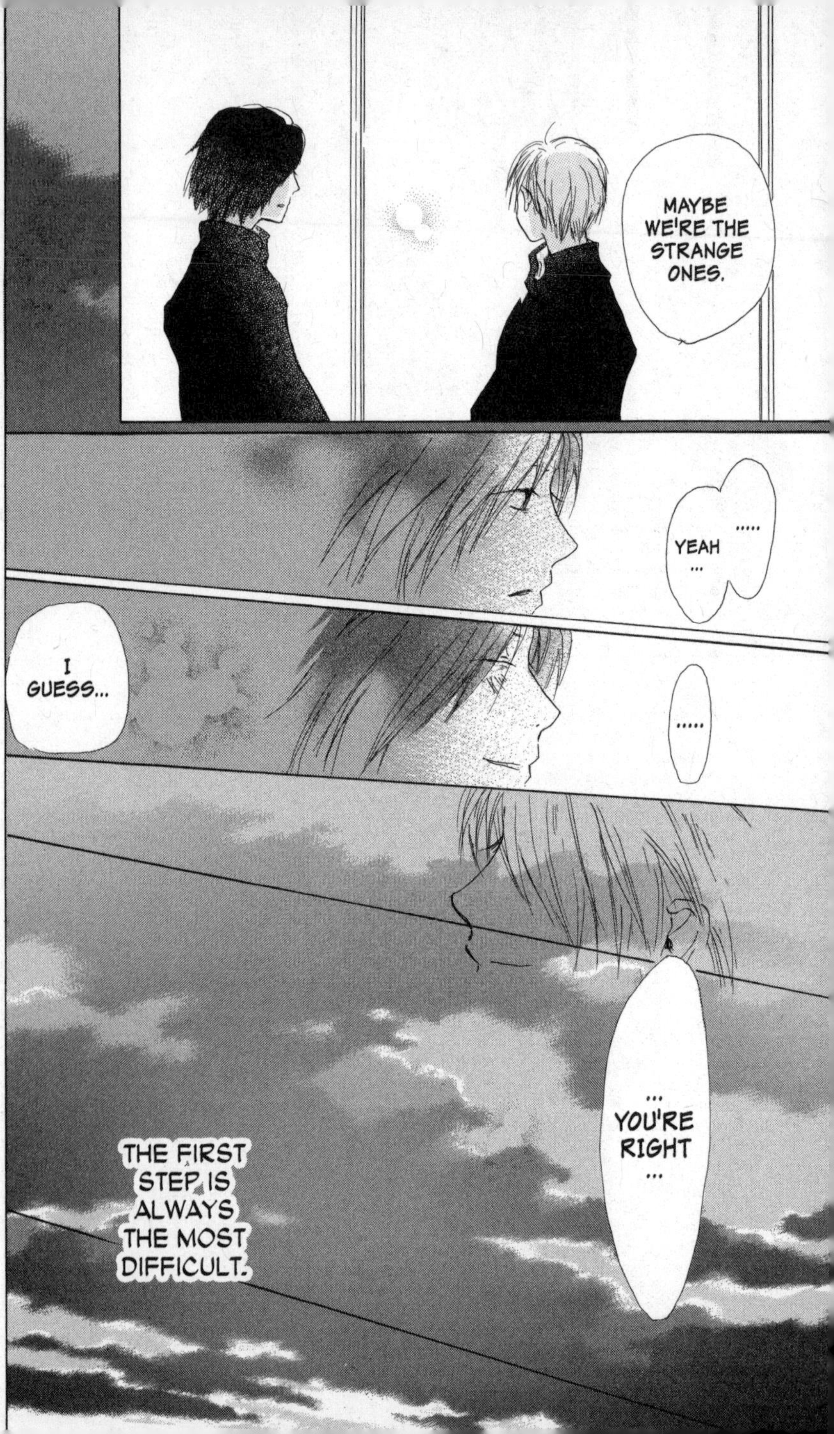
MAYBE WE'RE THE STRANGE ONES.
.....
YEAH ...
.....
I GUESS...
... YOU'RE RIGHT ...
THE FIRST STEP IS ALWAYS THE MOST DIFFICULT.

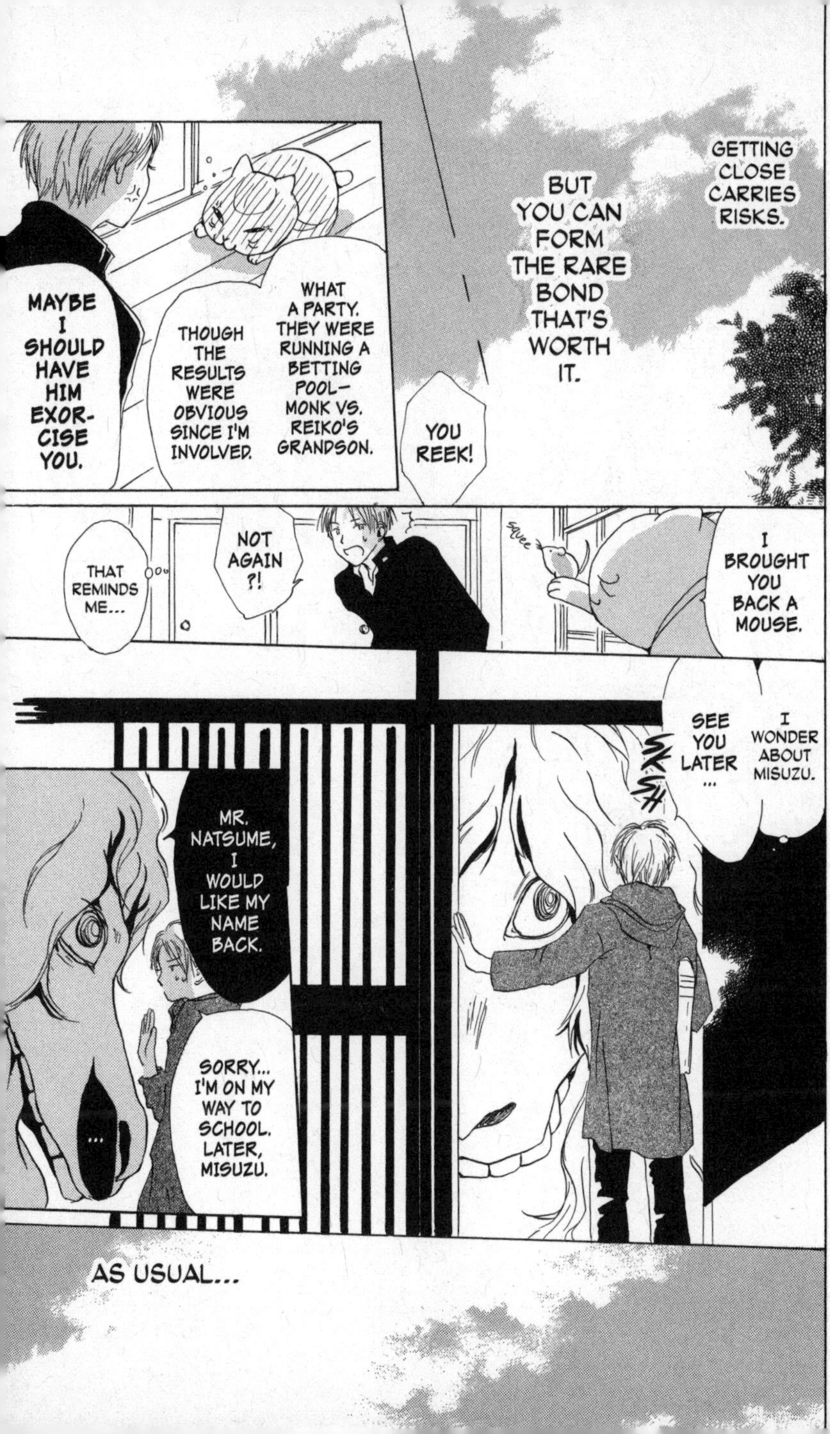
GETTING CLOSE CARRIES RISKS.
BUT YOU CAN FORM THE RARE BOND THAT'S WORTH IT.
YOU REEK!
WHAT A PARTY. THEY WERE RUNNING A BETTING POOL— MONK VS. REIKO'S GRANDSON.
THOUGH THE RESULTS WERE OBVIOUS SINCE I'M INVOLVED.
MAYBE I SHOULD HAVE HIM EXORCISE YOU.
I BROUGHT YOU BACK A MOUSE.
squee
NOT AGAIN ?!
THAT REMINDS ME...
I WONDER ABOUT MISUZU.
SEE YOU LATER ...
SKSH
MR. NATSUME, I WOULD LIKE MY NAME BACK.
SORRY... I'M ON MY WAY TO SCHOOL. LATER, MISUZU.
...
AS USUAL...

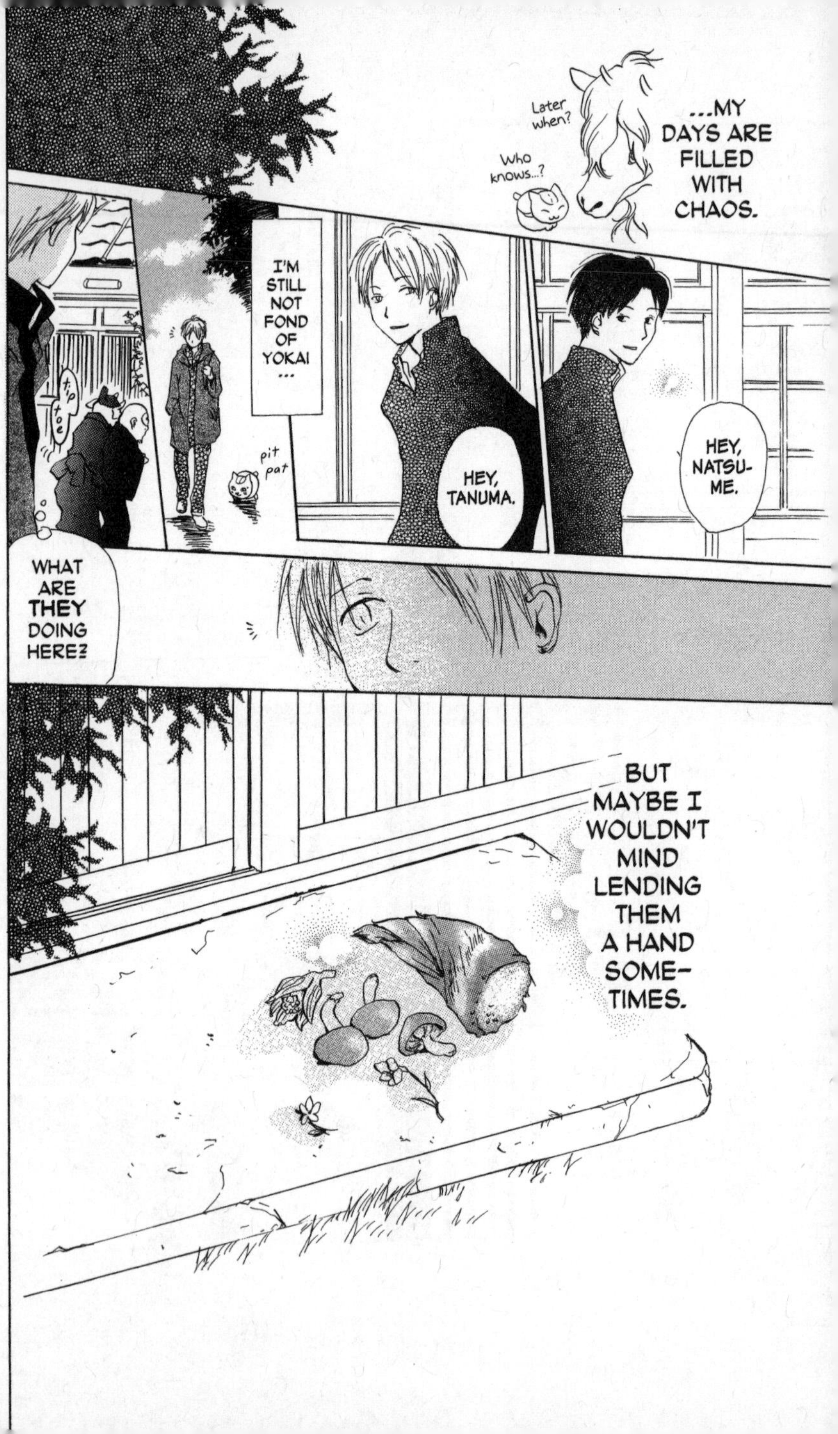
...MY DAYS ARE FILLED WITH CHAOS.
Later when?
Who knows...?
HEY, NATSU-ME.
I'M STILL NOT FOND OF YOKAI...
HEY, TANUMA.
pit pat
tip toe
WHAT ARE THEY DOING HERE?
BUT MAYBE I WOULDN'T MIND LENDING THEM A HAND SOME-TIMES.

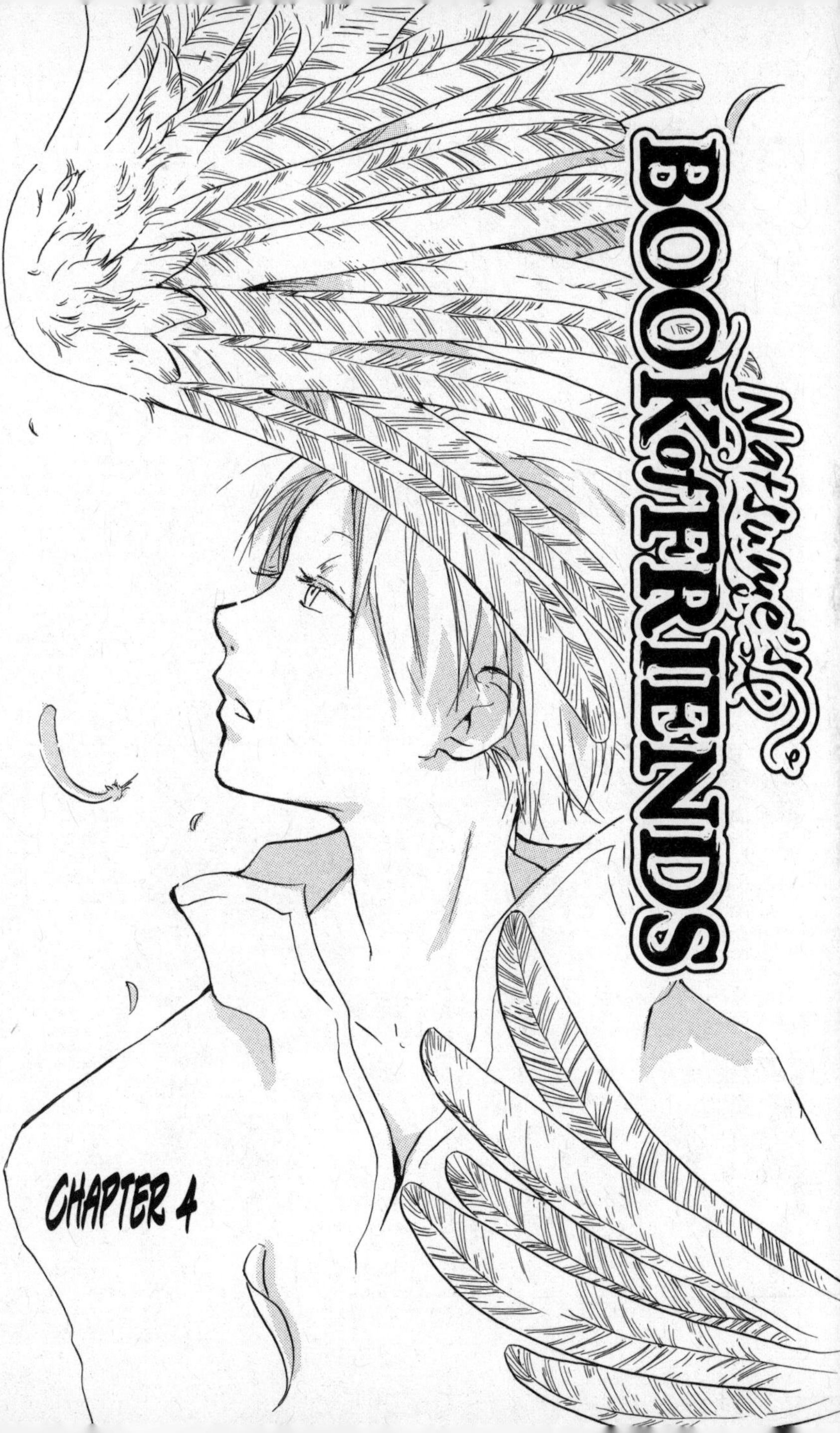
Natsume's BOOK of FRIENDS
CHAPTER 4

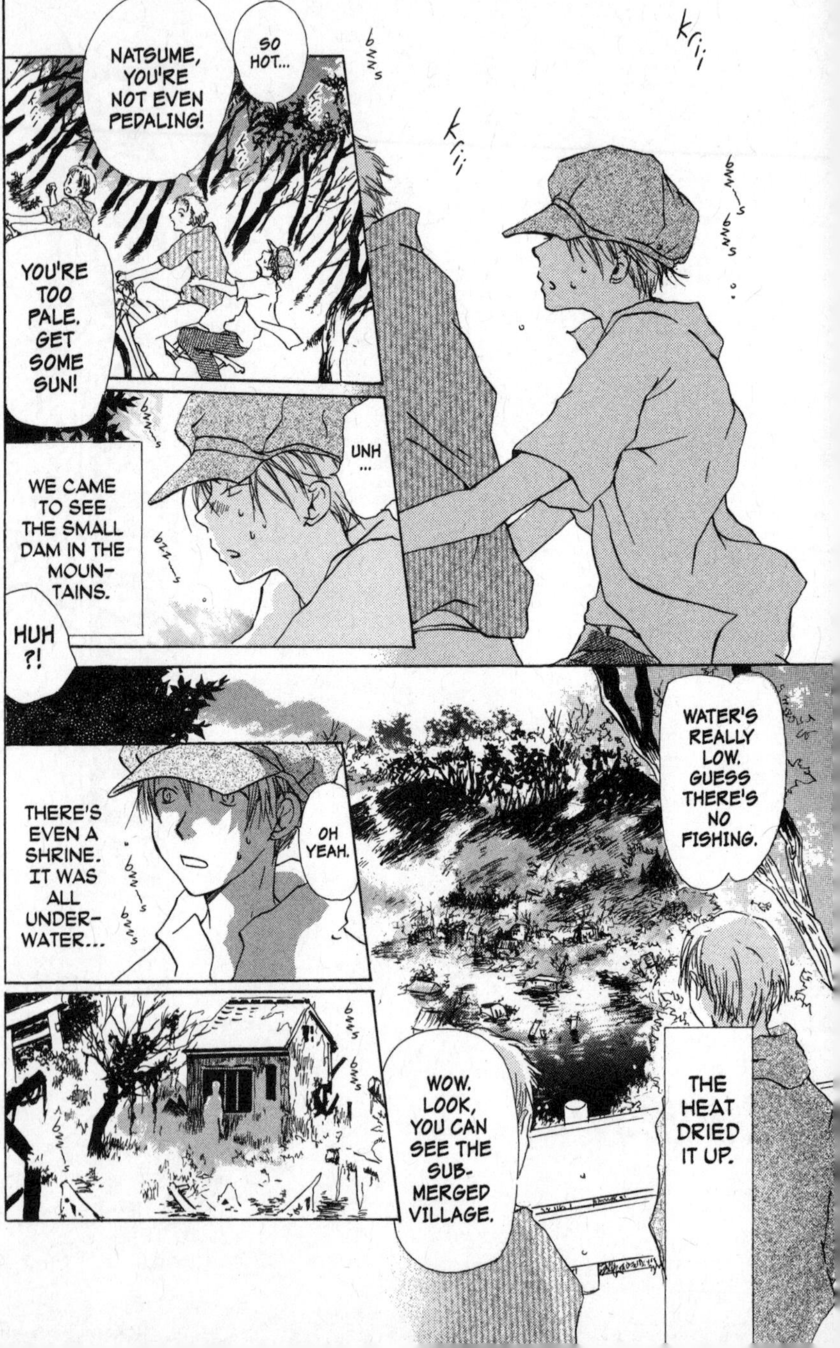
kriii
kriii
SO HOT...
NATSUME, YOU'RE NOT EVEN PEDALING!
YOU'RE TOO PALE. GET SOME SUN!
UNH...
WE CAME TO SEE THE SMALL DAM IN THE MOUN-TAINS.
HUH?!
WATER'S REALLY LOW. GUESS THERE'S NO FISHING.
THE HEAT DRIED IT UP.
WOW. LOOK, YOU CAN SEE THE SUB-MERGED VILLAGE.
OH YEAH.
THERE'S EVEN A SHRINE. IT WAS ALL UNDER-WATER...

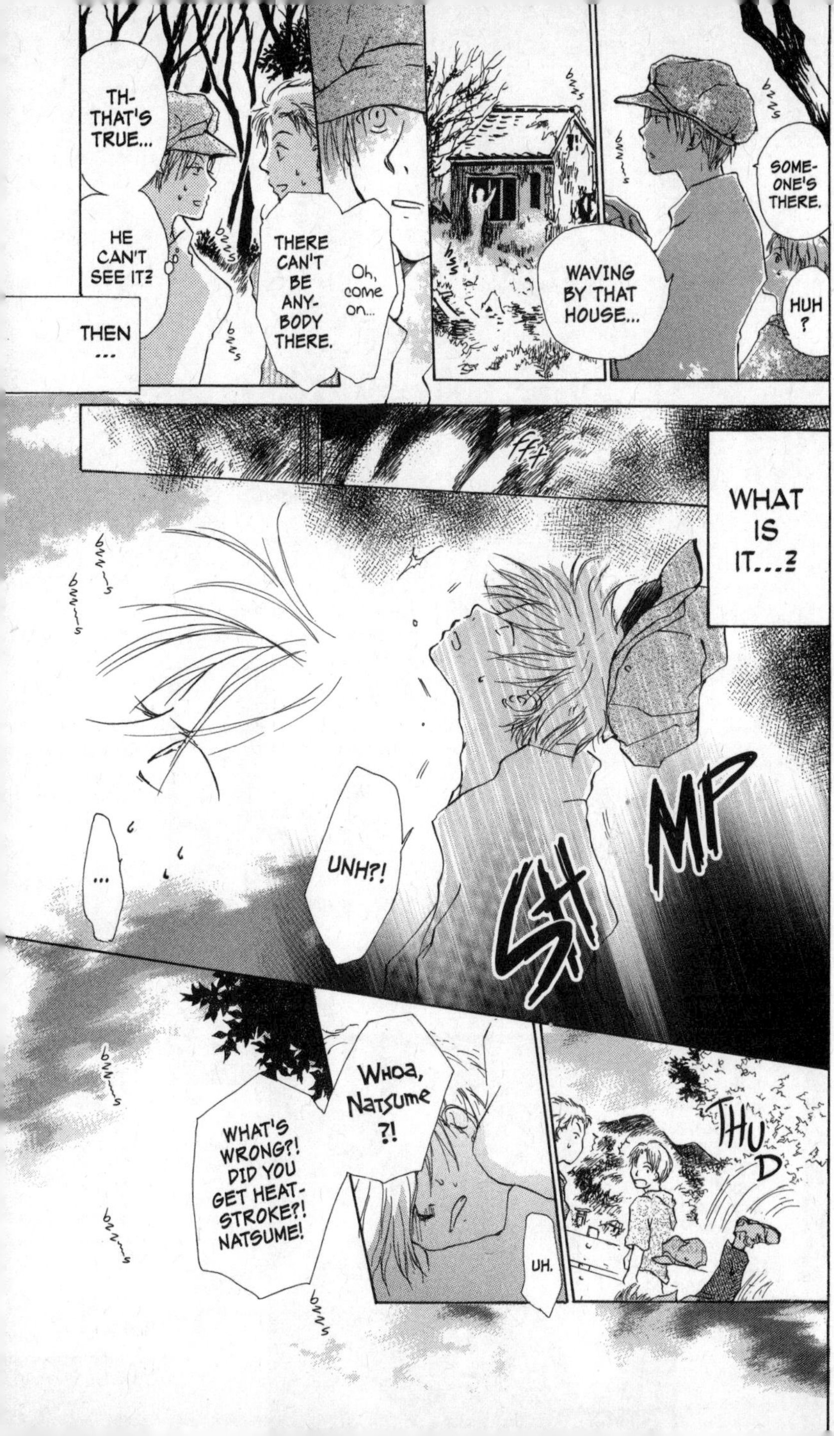
SOME-ONE'S THERE.
HUH?
WAVING BY THAT HOUSE...
Oh, come on...
THERE CAN'T BE ANY-BODY THERE.
TH-THAT'S TRUE...
HE CAN'T SEE IT?
THEN...
WHAT IS IT...?
SHMP
UNH?!
...
THUD
Whoa, Natsume?!
WHAT'S WRONG?! DID YOU GET HEAT-STROKE?! NATSUME!
UH.

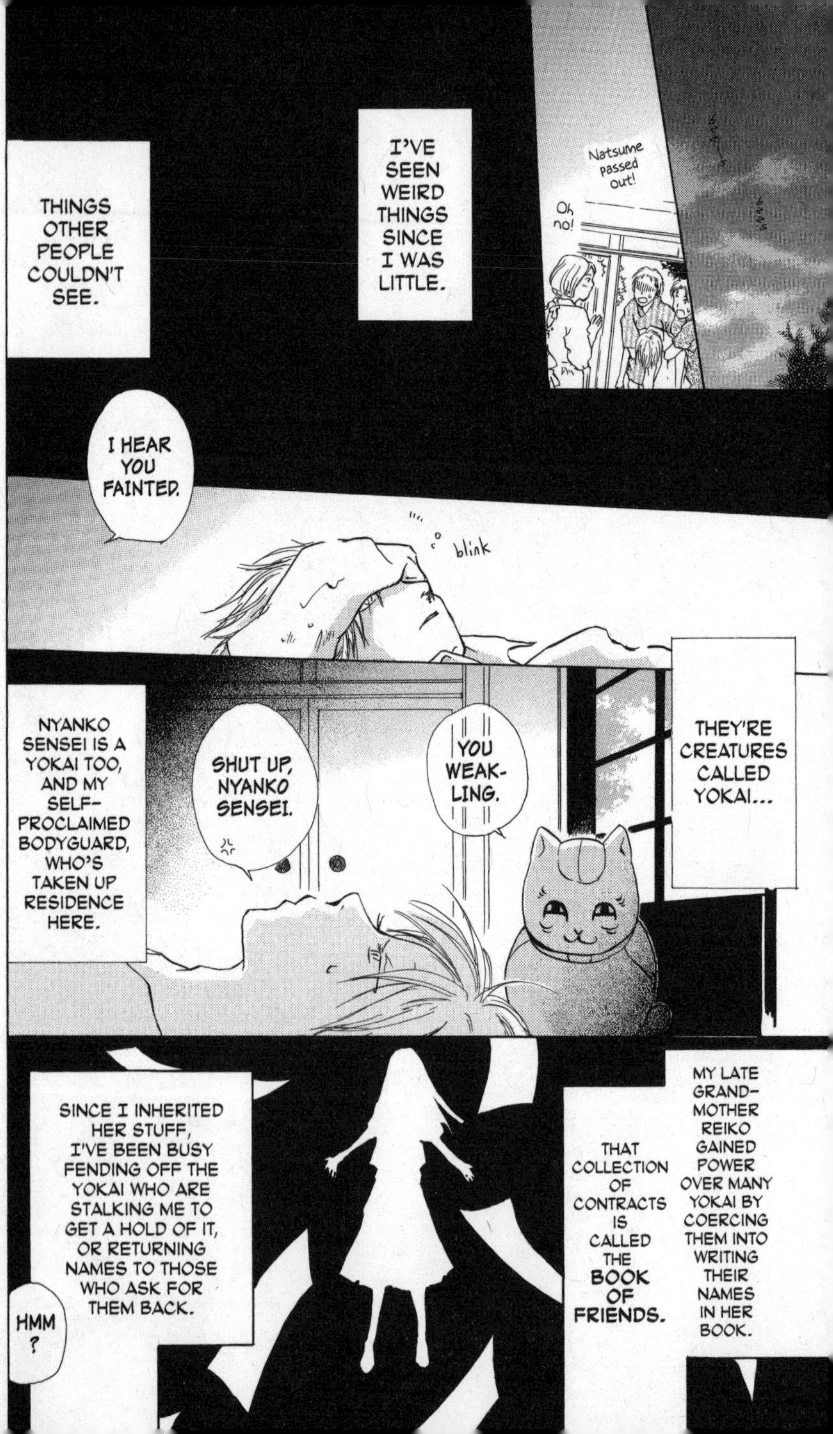
Natsume passed out!
Oh no!
I'VE SEEN WEIRD THINGS SINCE I WAS LITTLE.
THINGS OTHER PEOPLE COULDN'T SEE.
I HEAR YOU FAINTED.
blink
THEY'RE CREATURES CALLED YOKAI...
YOU WEAK-LING.
SHUT UP, NYANKO SENSEI.
NYANKO SENSEI IS A YOKAI TOO, AND MY SELF-PROCLAIMED BODYGUARD, WHO'S TAKEN UP RESIDENCE HERE.
MY LATE GRAND-MOTHER REIKO GAINED POWER OVER MANY YOKAI BY COERCING THEM INTO WRITING THEIR NAMES IN HER BOOK.
THAT COLLECTION OF CONTRACTS IS CALLED THE BOOK OF FRIENDS.
SINCE I INHERITED HER STUFF, I'VE BEEN BUSY FENDING OFF THE YOKAI WHO ARE STALKING ME TO GET A HOLD OF IT, OR RETURNING NAMES TO THOSE WHO ASK FOR THEM BACK.
HMM?

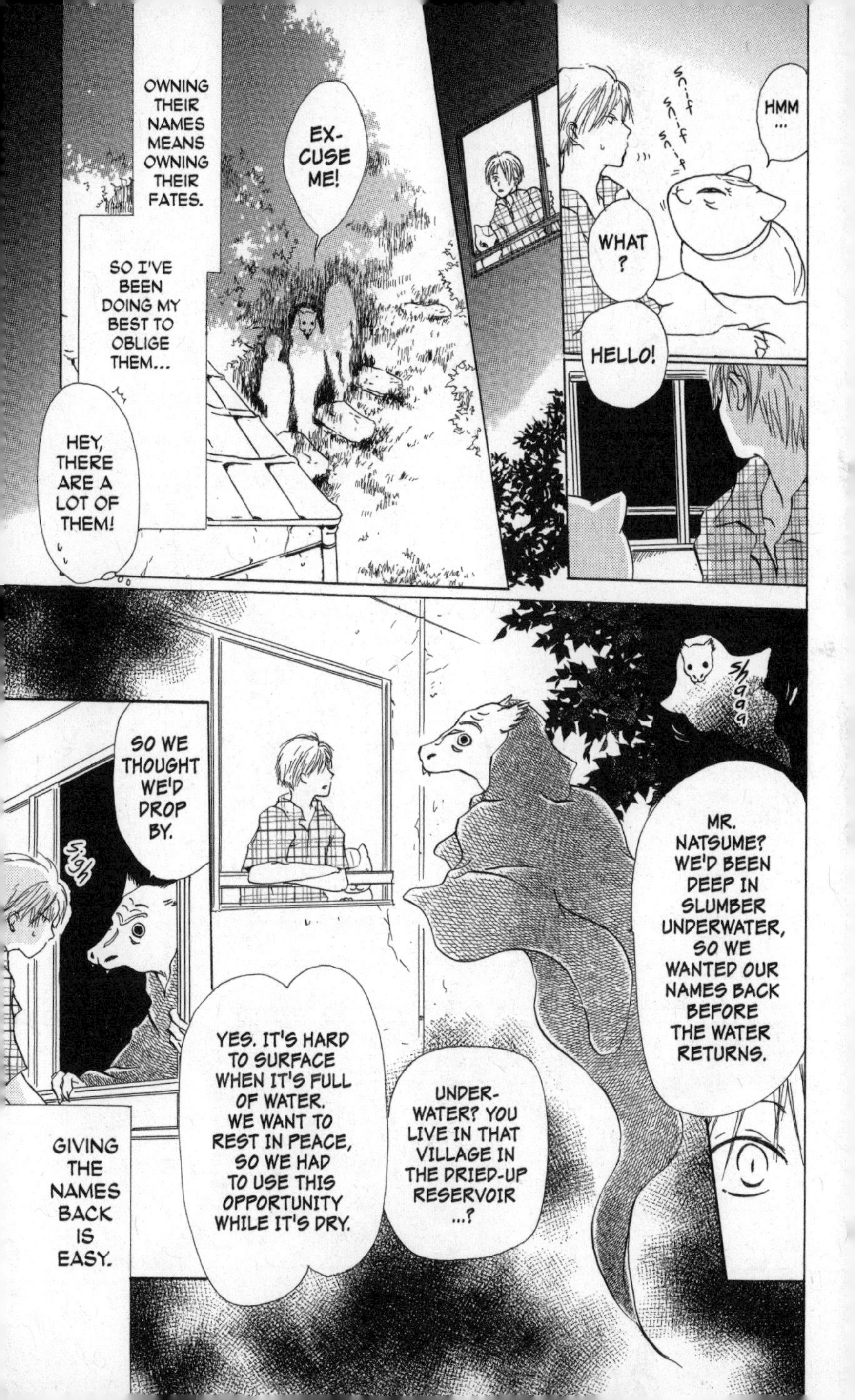
HMM...
sniff sniff sniff
WHAT?
HELLO!
EX-CUSE ME!
OWNING THEIR NAMES MEANS OWNING THEIR FATES.
SO I'VE BEEN DOING MY BEST TO OBLIGE THEM...
HEY, THERE ARE A LOT OF THEM!
shaaa
MR. NATSUME? WE'D BEEN DEEP IN SLUMBER UNDERWATER, SO WE WANTED OUR NAMES BACK BEFORE THE WATER RETURNS.
SO WE THOUGHT WE'D DROP BY.
sigh
UNDER-WATER? YOU LIVE IN THAT VILLAGE IN THE DRIED-UP RESERVOIR ...?
YES. IT'S HARD TO SURFACE WHEN IT'S FULL OF WATER. WE WANT TO REST IN PEACE, SO WE HAD TO USE THIS OPPORTUNITY WHILE IT'S DRY.
GIVING THE NAMES BACK IS EASY.

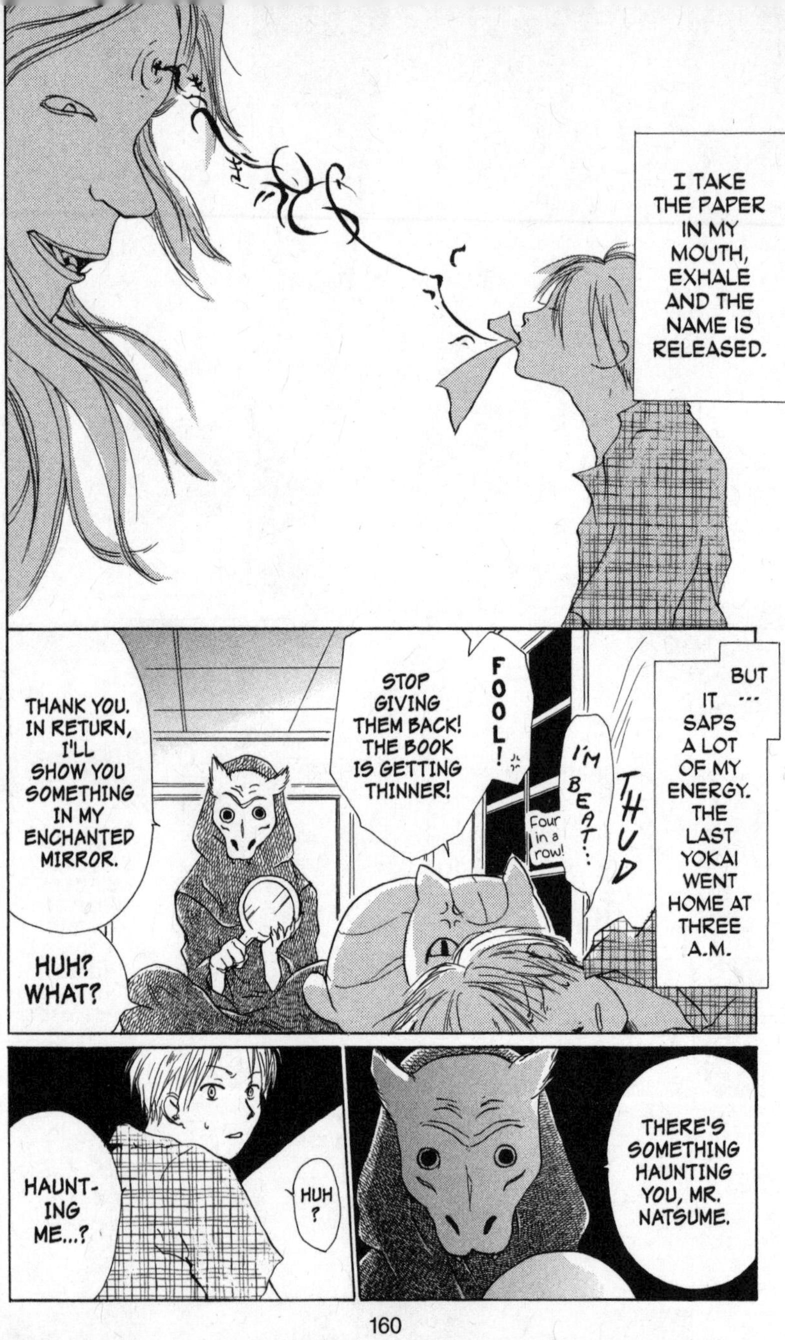

I TAKE THE PAPER IN MY MOUTH, EXHALE AND THE NAME IS RELEASED.
BUT ... IT SAPS A LOT OF MY ENERGY. THE LAST YOKAI WENT HOME AT THREE A.M.
I'M BEAT...
THUD
Four in a row!
FOOL!
STOP GIVING THEM BACK! THE BOOK IS GETTING THINNER!
THANK YOU. IN RETURN, I'LL SHOW YOU SOMETHING IN MY ENCHANTED MIRROR.
HUH? WHAT?
THERE'S SOMETHING HAUNTING YOU, MR. NATSUME.
HUH?
HAUNT-ING ME...?

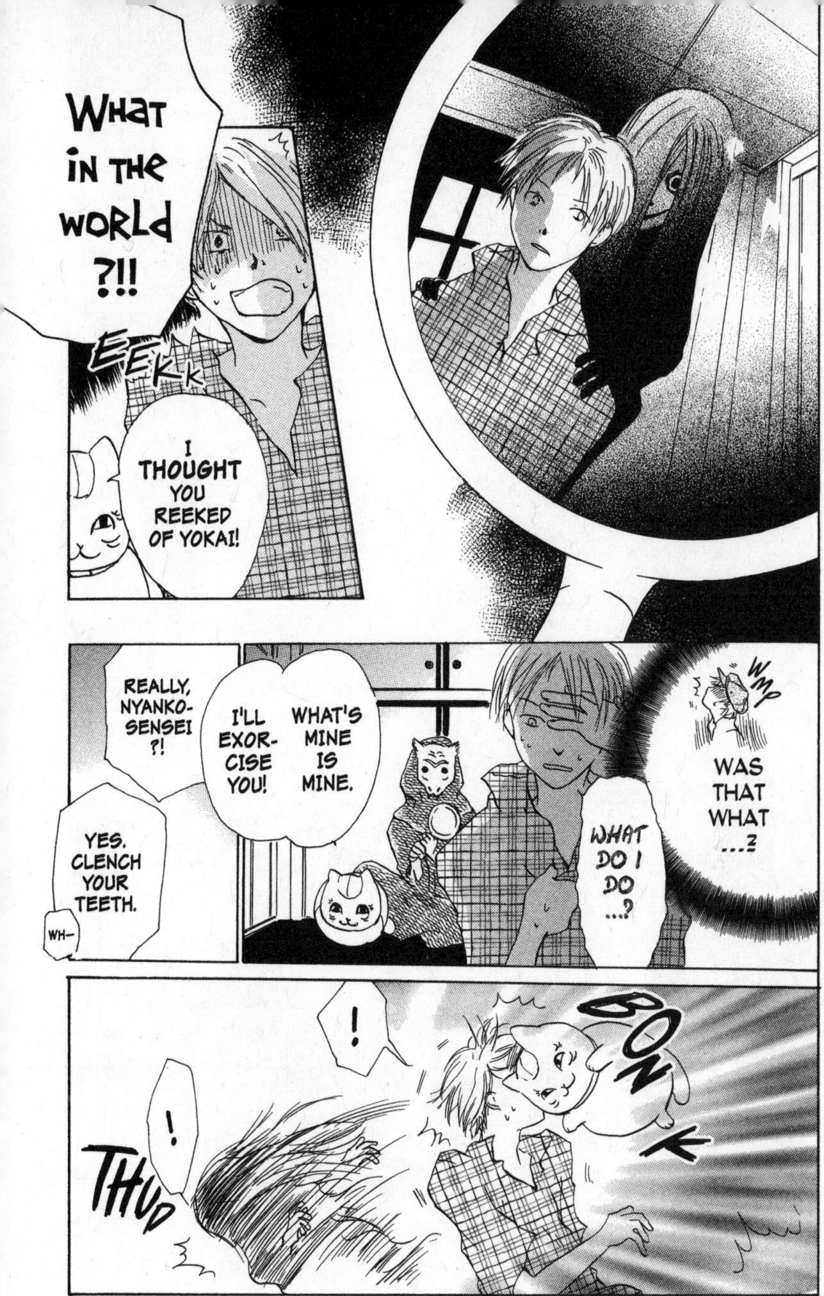
WHAT IN THE WORLD ?!!
EEKK
I THOUGHT YOU REEKED OF YOKAI!
WMP
WAS THAT WHAT ...?
WHAT DO I DO ...?
WHAT'S MINE IS MINE.
I'LL EXORCISE YOU!
REALLY, NYANKO-SENSEI ?!
YES. CLENCH YOUR TEETH.
WH–
BONK
!
!
THUD

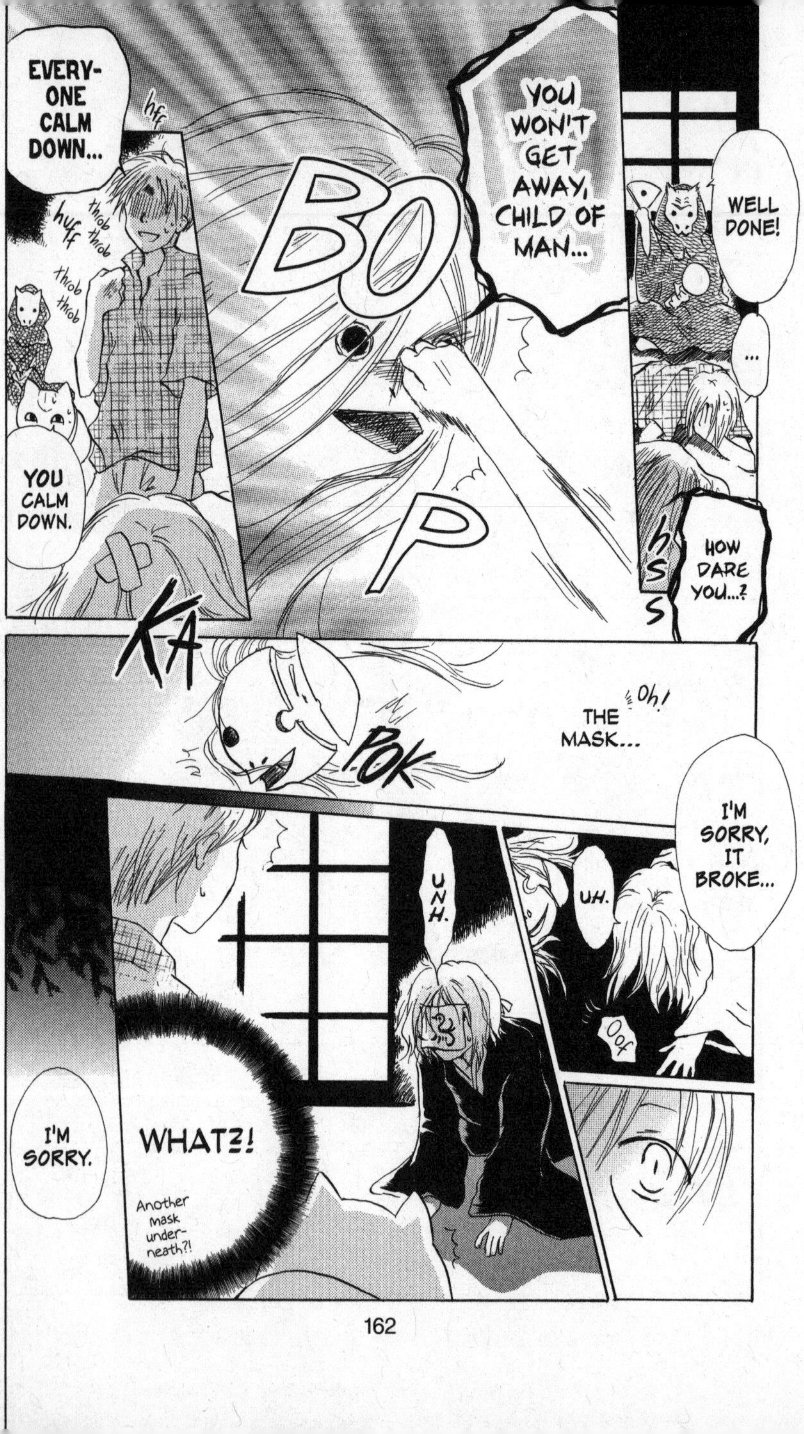
WELL DONE!
...
HOW DARE YOU...?
hiss
YOU WON'T GET AWAY, CHILD OF MAN...
BOP
EVERY-ONE CALM DOWN...
hff
huff
throb throb
throb throb
YOU CALM DOWN.
KA
POK
Oh!
THE MASK...
I'M SORRY, IT BROKE...
UH.
Oof
UNH.
WHAT?!
Another mask under-neath?!
I'M SORRY.

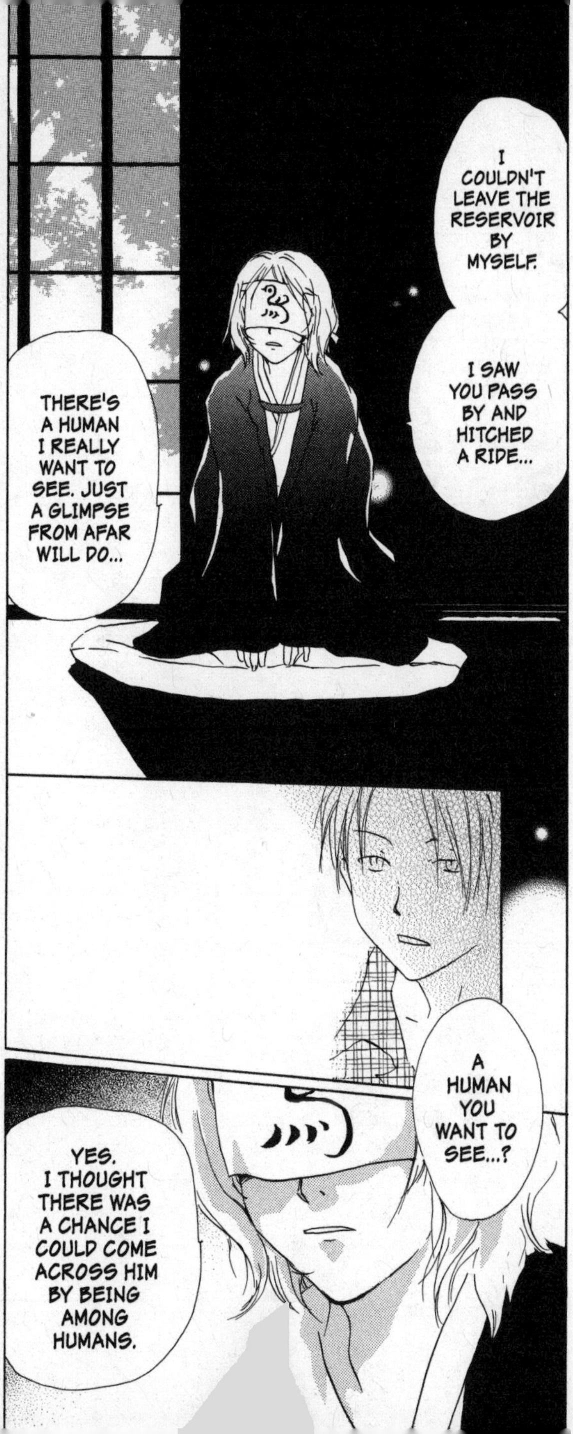
I COULDN'T LEAVE THE RESERVOIR BY MYSELF.
I SAW YOU PASS BY AND HITCHED A RIDE...
THERE'S A HUMAN I REALLY WANT TO SEE. JUST A GLIMPSE FROM AFAR WILL DO...
A HUMAN YOU WANT TO SEE...?
YES. I THOUGHT THERE WAS A CHANCE I COULD COME ACROSS HIM BY BEING AMONG HUMANS.

09

Next, Chika

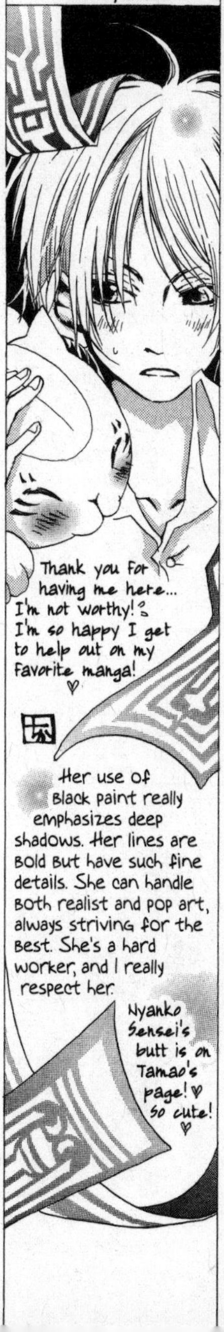
Thank you for having me here... I'm not worthy! I'm so happy I get to help out on my favorite manga!
Her use of black paint really emphasizes deep shadows. Her lines are bold but have such fine details. She can handle both realist and pop art, always striving for the best. She's a hard worker, and I really respect her.
Nyanko Sensei's butt is on Tamao's page! So cute!

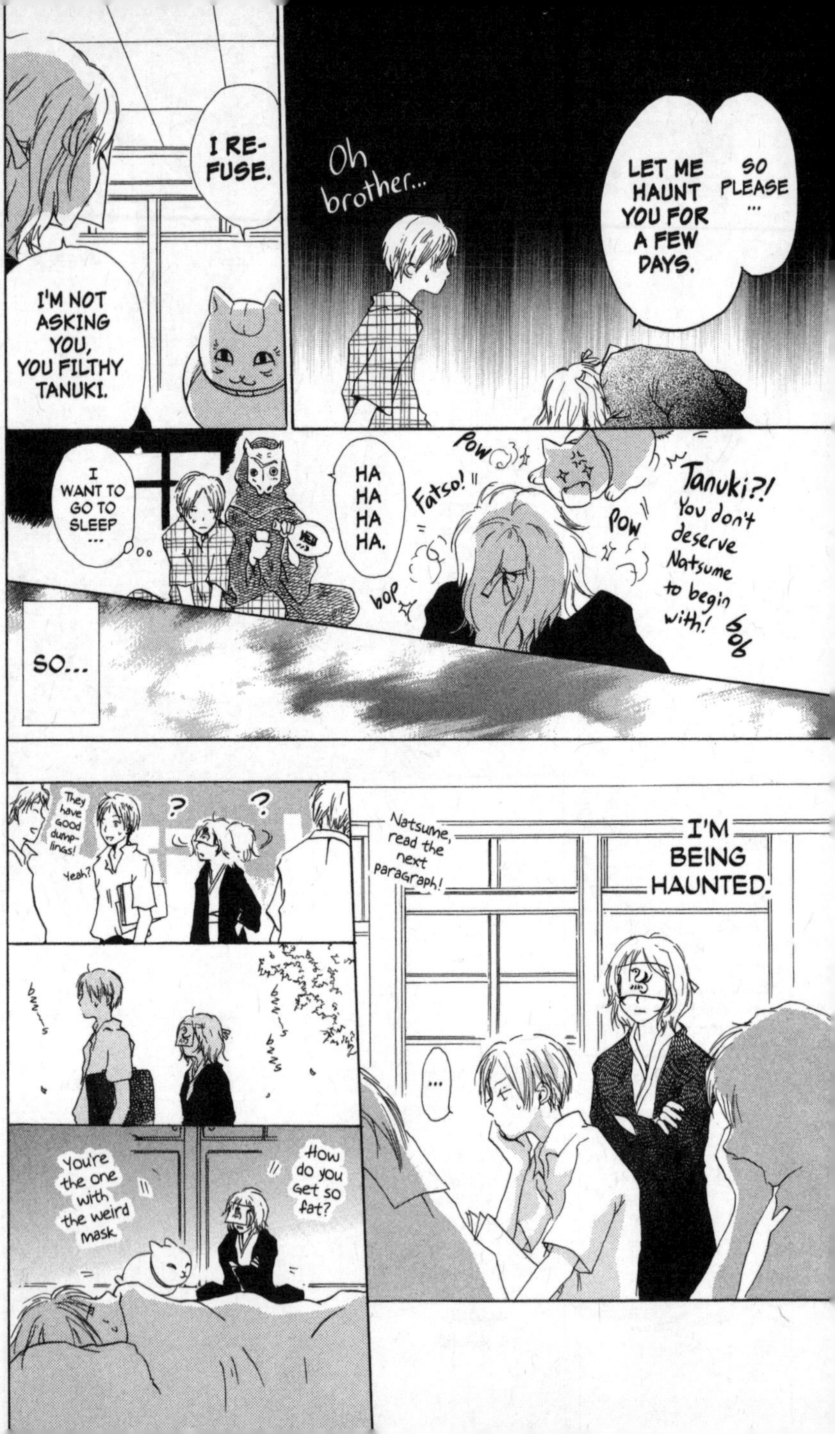

SO PLEASE...
LET ME HAUNT YOU FOR A FEW DAYS.
Oh brother...
I RE-FUSE.
I'M NOT ASKING YOU, YOU FILTHY TANUKI.
Tanuki?! You don't deserve Natsume to begin with!
POW
POW
Fatso!
bop
bob
HA HA HA HA.
I WANT TO GO TO SLEEP...
SO...
I'M BEING HAUNTED.
Natsume, read the next paragraph!
...
They have good dump-lings!
Yeah?
?
?
bzz
bzz
bzz
How do you get so fat?
You're the one with the weird mask.

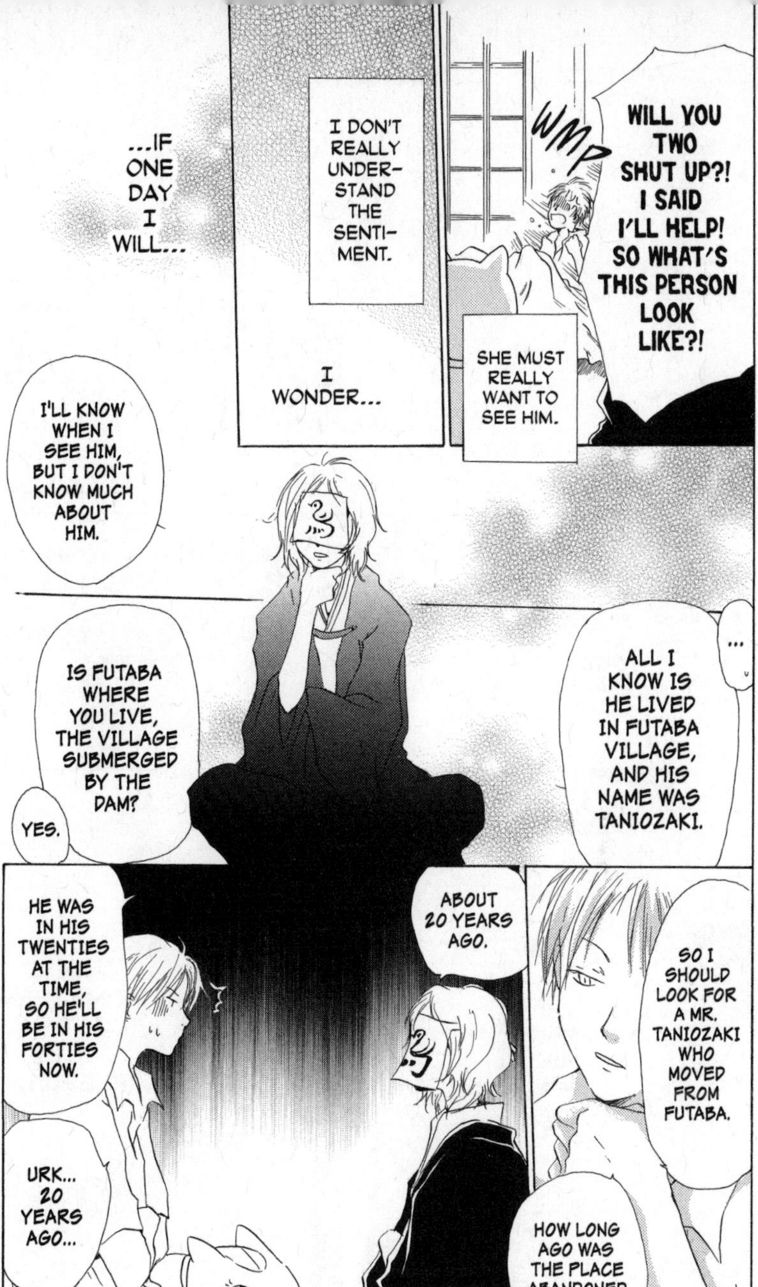
WILL YOU TWO SHUT UP?! I SAID I'LL HELP! SO WHAT'S THIS PERSON LOOK LIKE?!
WMP
SHE MUST REALLY WANT TO SEE HIM.
I DON'T REALLY UNDERSTAND THE SENTIMENT.
I WONDER...
...IF ONE DAY I WILL...
I'LL KNOW WHEN I SEE HIM, BUT I DON'T KNOW MUCH ABOUT HIM.
...
ALL I KNOW IS HE LIVED IN FUTABA VILLAGE, AND HIS NAME WAS TANIOZAKI.
IS FUTABA WHERE YOU LIVE, THE VILLAGE SUBMERGED BY THE DAM?
YES.
SO I SHOULD LOOK FOR A MR. TANIOZAKI WHO MOVED FROM FUTABA.
HOW LONG AGO WAS THE PLACE ABANDONED?
ABOUT 20 YEARS AGO.
HE WAS IN HIS TWENTIES AT THE TIME, SO HE'LL BE IN HIS FORTIES NOW.
URK... 20 YEARS AGO...

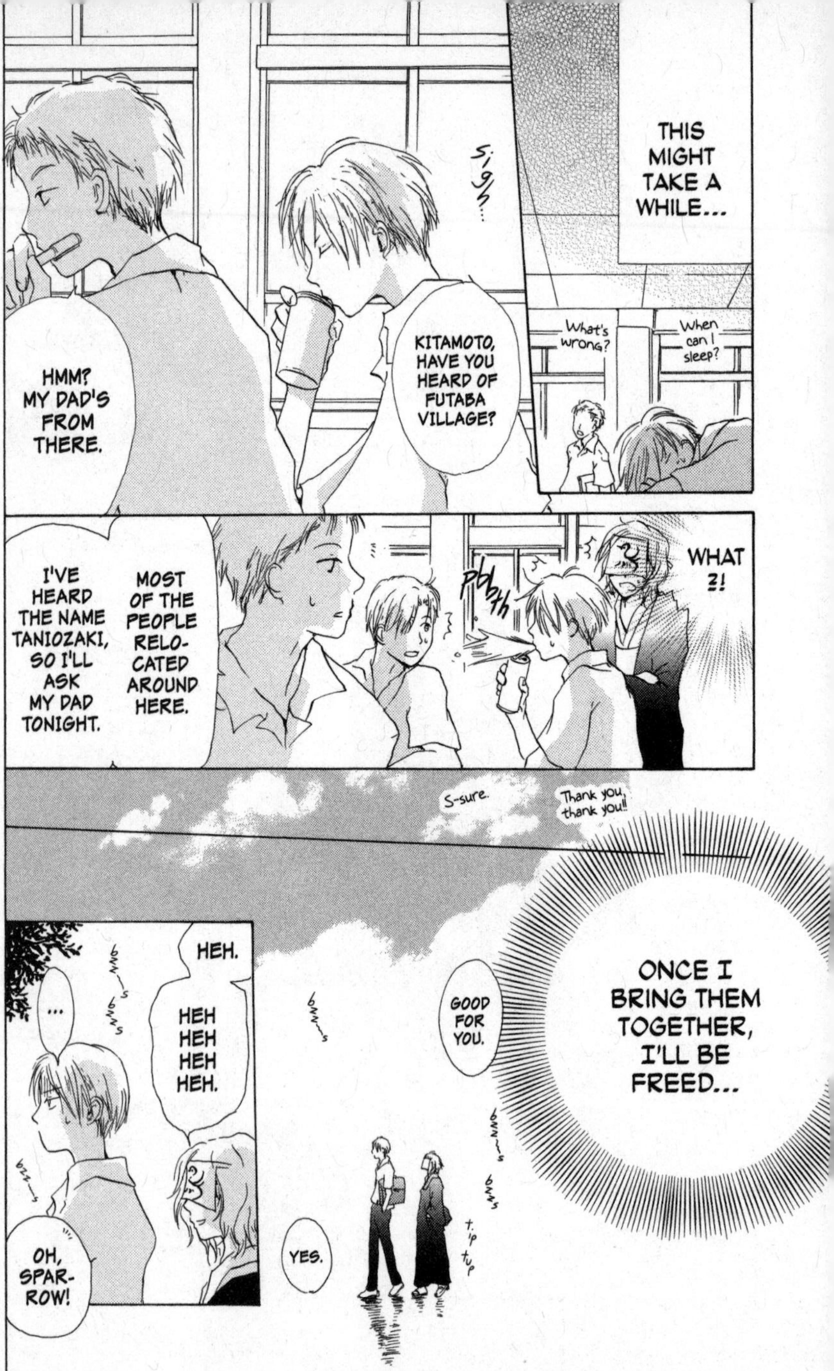
THIS MIGHT TAKE A WHILE...
When can I sleep?
What's wrong?
sigh...
KITAMOTO, HAVE YOU HEARD OF FUTABA VILLAGE?
HMM? MY DAD'S FROM THERE.
WHAT?!
pbbth
MOST OF THE PEOPLE RELOCATED AROUND HERE.
I'VE HEARD THE NAME TANIOZAKI, SO I'LL ASK MY DAD TONIGHT.
Thank you, thank you!!
S-sure.
ONCE I BRING THEM TOGETHER, I'LL BE FREED...
bzzz
tip tup
GOOD FOR YOU.
YES.
HEH.
HEH HEH HEH HEH.
...
OH, SPARROW!

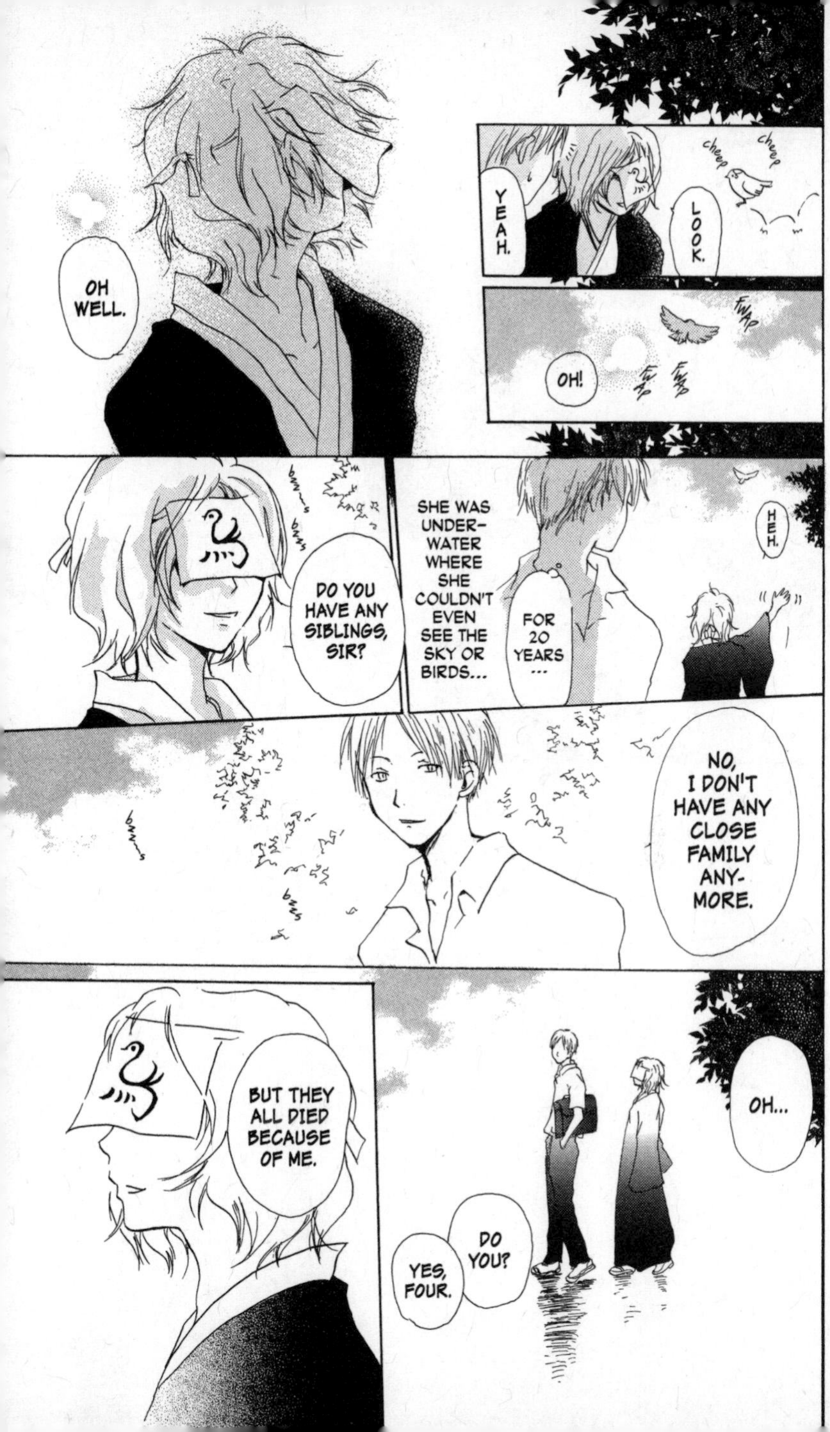

cheep
cheep
LOOK.
YEAH.
FWAP
OH!
FWAP
FWAP
OH WELL.
HEH.
FOR 20 YEARS...
SHE WAS UNDERWATER WHERE SHE COULDN'T EVEN SEE THE SKY OR BIRDS...
DO YOU HAVE ANY SIBLINGS, SIR?
NO, I DON'T HAVE ANY CLOSE FAMILY ANYMORE.
OH...
DO YOU?
YES, FOUR.
BUT THEY ALL DIED BECAUSE OF ME.

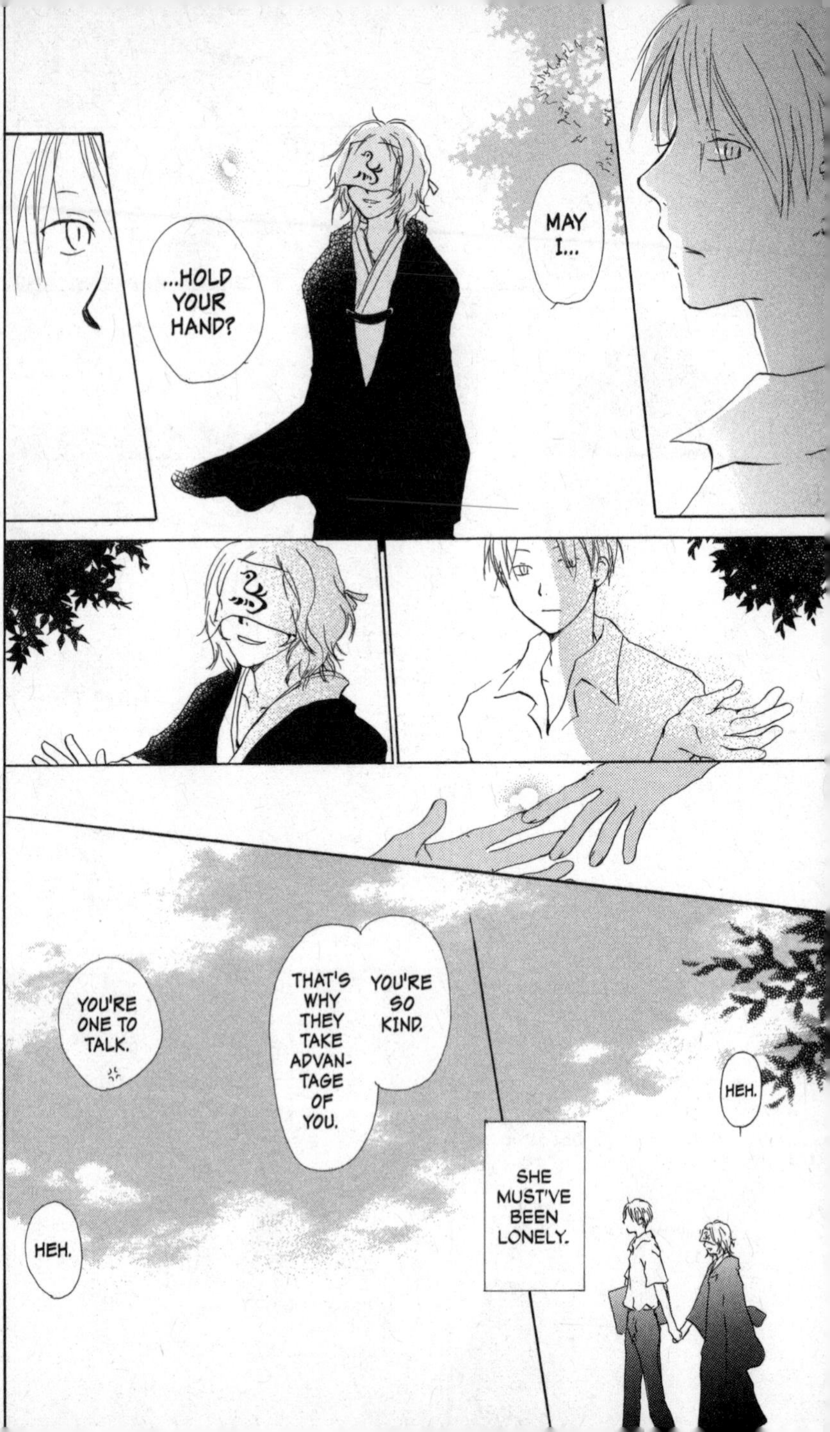
MAY I...
...HOLD YOUR HAND?
HEH.
SHE MUST'VE BEEN LONELY.
YOU'RE SO KIND.
THAT'S WHY THEY TAKE ADVANTAGE OF YOU.
YOU'RE ONE TO TALK.
HEH.

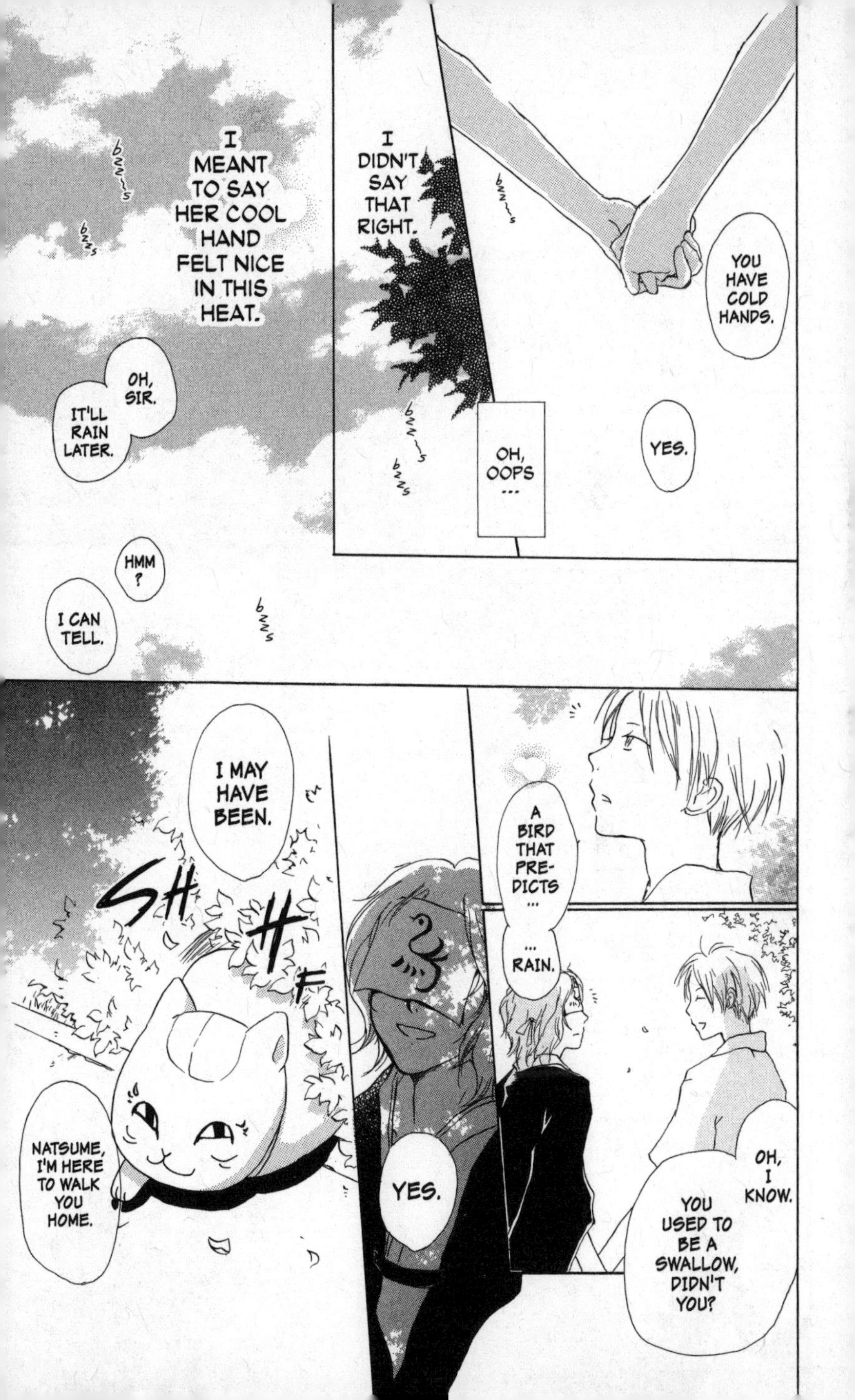

YOU HAVE COLD HANDS.
YES.
I DIDN'T SAY THAT RIGHT.
OH, OOPS...
I MEANT TO SAY HER COOL HAND FELT NICE IN THIS HEAT.
OH, SIR.
IT'LL RAIN LATER.
HMM?
I CAN TELL.
A BIRD THAT PREDICTS...
...RAIN.
OH, I KNOW.
YOU USED TO BE A SWALLOW, DIDN'T YOU?
YES.
I MAY HAVE BEEN.
SHHF
NATSUME, I'M HERE TO WALK YOU HOME.

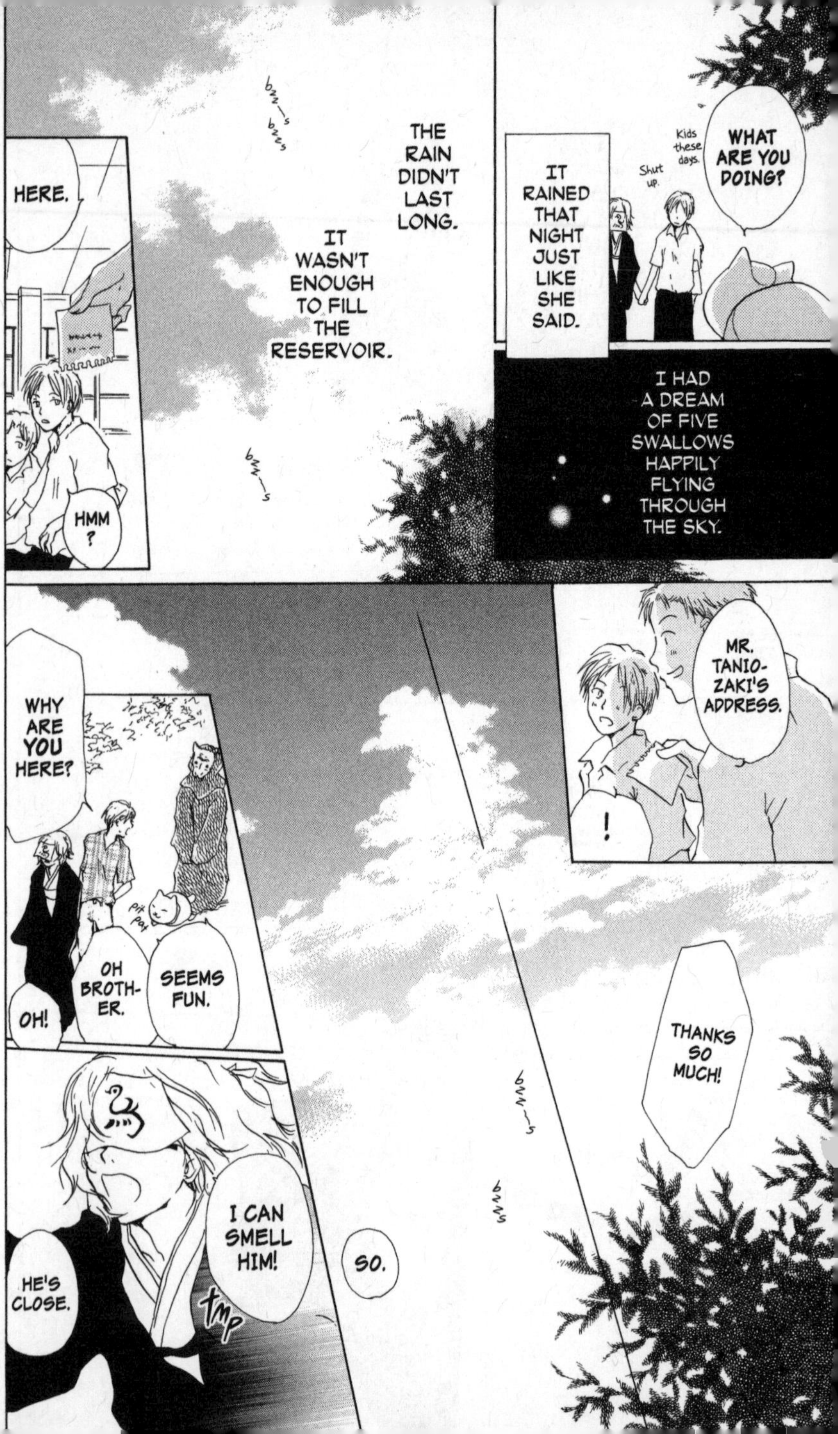
WHAT ARE YOU DOING?
Kids these days.
Shut up.
IT RAINED THAT NIGHT JUST LIKE SHE SAID.
I HAD A DREAM OF FIVE SWALLOWS HAPPILY FLYING THROUGH THE SKY.
THE RAIN DIDN'T LAST LONG.
IT WASN'T ENOUGH TO FILL THE RESERVOIR.
bzz-s bzzs
bzz-s
HERE.
HMM?
MR. TANIO-ZAKI'S ADDRESS.
!
THANKS SO MUCH!
bzz-s
bzzs
WHY ARE YOU HERE?
SEEMS FUN.
pit pat
OH BROTHER.
OH!
I CAN SMELL HIM!
SO.
HE'S CLOSE.
tmp

10

And when I'm swamped with manga, my sister helps me out with tidying up, meals, the screentones and blacking-in solids. I'm really grateful.

I'm able to keep writing manga through the help of so many people.

I'm working hard to get better with each title, and I want to learn new things. I hope I get to earn your continued support.

End of $\frac{1}{4}$ columns.

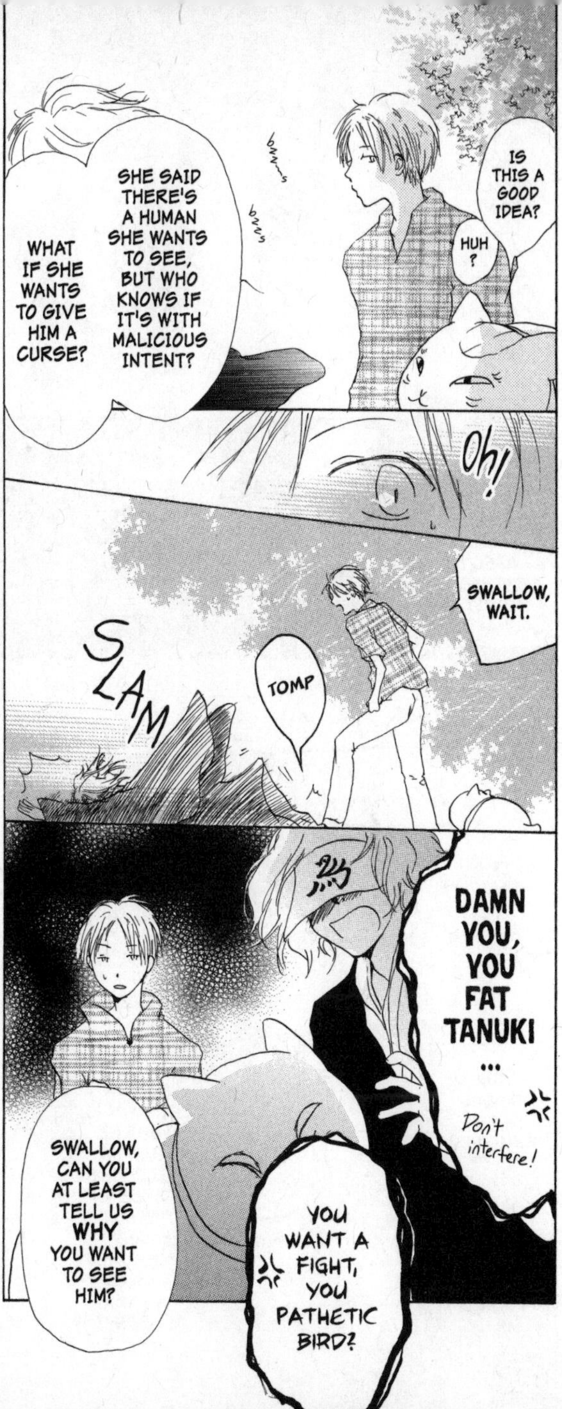
IS THIS A GOOD IDEA?
HUH?
SHE SAID THERE'S A HUMAN SHE WANTS TO SEE, BUT WHO KNOWS IF IT'S WITH MALICIOUS INTENT?
WHAT IF SHE WANTS TO GIVE HIM A CURSE?
Oh!
SWALLOW, WAIT.
TOMP
SLAM
DAMN YOU, YOU FAT TANUKI...
Don't interfere!
YOU WANT A FIGHT, YOU PATHETIC BIRD?
SWALLOW, CAN YOU AT LEAST TELL US WHY YOU WANT TO SEE HIM?

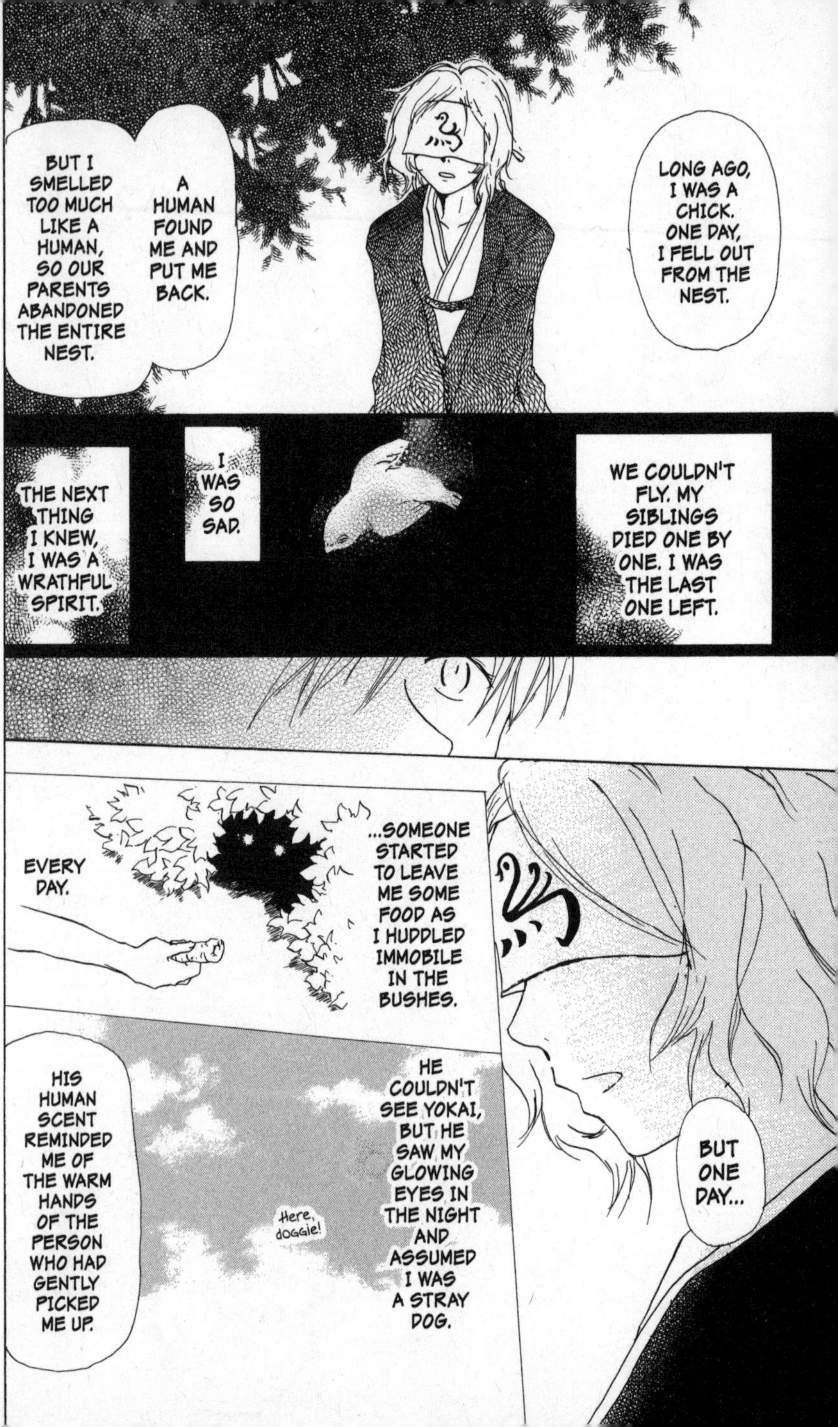
LONG AGO, I WAS A CHICK. ONE DAY, I FELL OUT FROM THE NEST.
A HUMAN FOUND ME AND PUT ME BACK.
BUT I SMELLED TOO MUCH LIKE A HUMAN, SO OUR PARENTS ABANDONED THE ENTIRE NEST.
WE COULDN'T FLY. MY SIBLINGS DIED ONE BY ONE. I WAS THE LAST ONE LEFT.
I WAS SO SAD.
THE NEXT THING I KNEW, I WAS A WRATHFUL SPIRIT.
BUT ONE DAY...
...SOMEONE STARTED TO LEAVE ME SOME FOOD AS I HUDDLED IMMOBILE IN THE BUSHES.
EVERY DAY.
HE COULDN'T SEE YOKAI, BUT HE SAW MY GLOWING EYES IN THE NIGHT AND ASSUMED I WAS A STRAY DOG.
Here, doggie!
HIS HUMAN SCENT REMINDED ME OF THE WARM HANDS OF THE PERSON WHO HAD GENTLY PICKED ME UP.

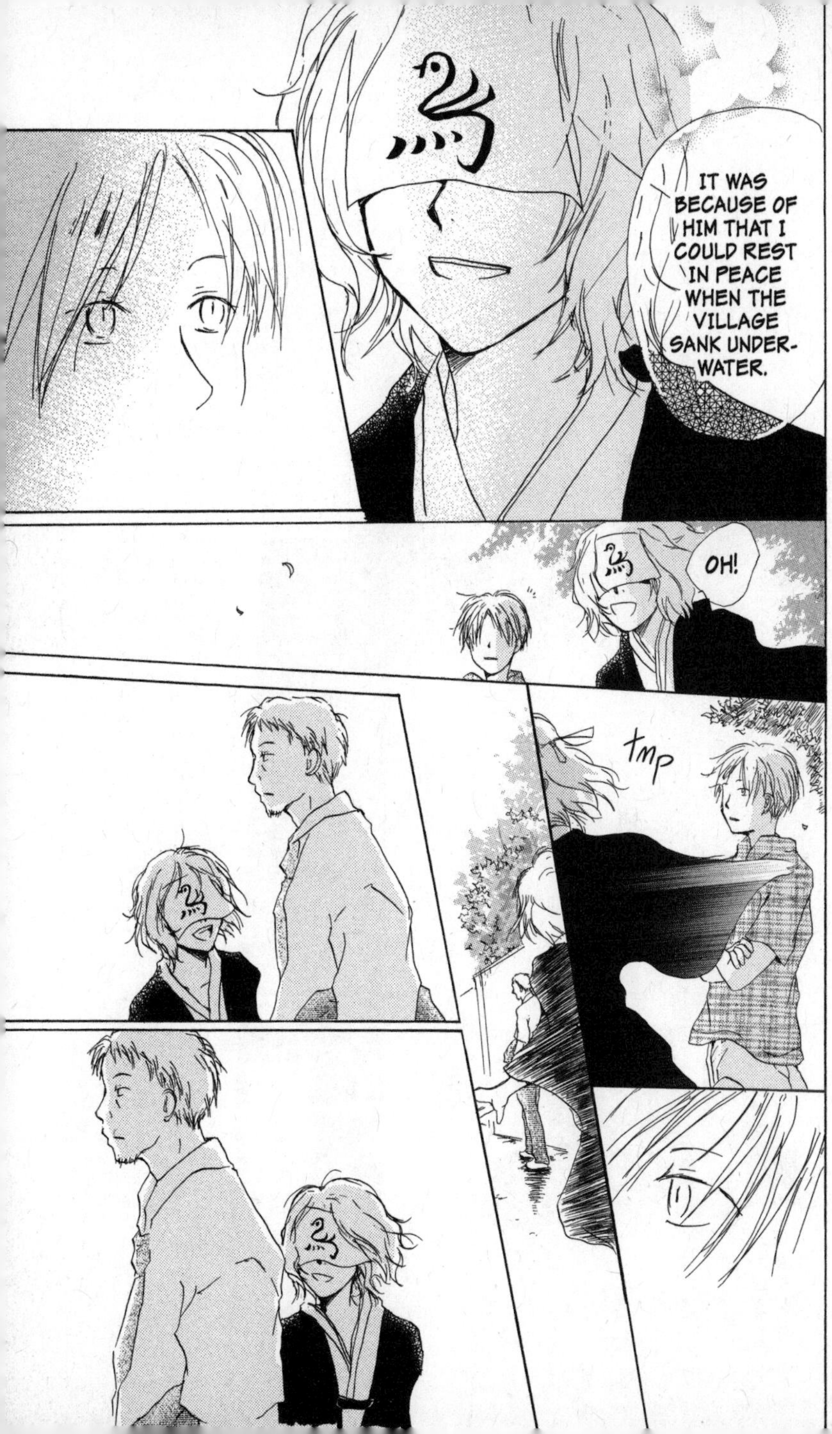
IT WAS BECAUSE OF HIM THAT I COULD REST IN PEACE WHEN THE VILLAGE SANK UNDER-WATER.
OH!
tmp

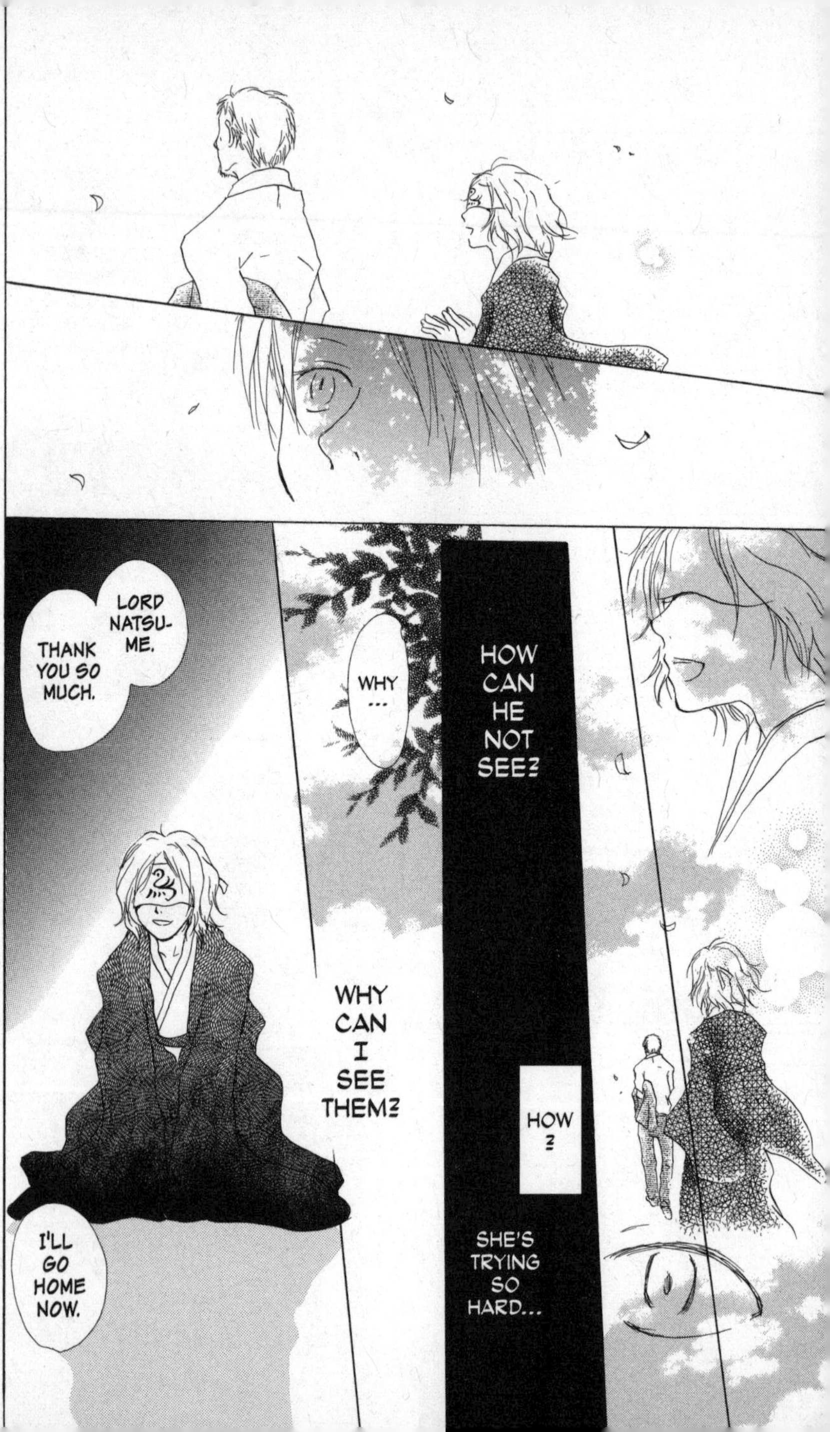
HOW CAN HE NOT SEE?
HOW?
SHE'S TRYING SO HARD...
WHY...
WHY CAN I SEE THEM?
LORD NATSUME. THANK YOU SO MUCH.
I'LL GO HOME NOW.

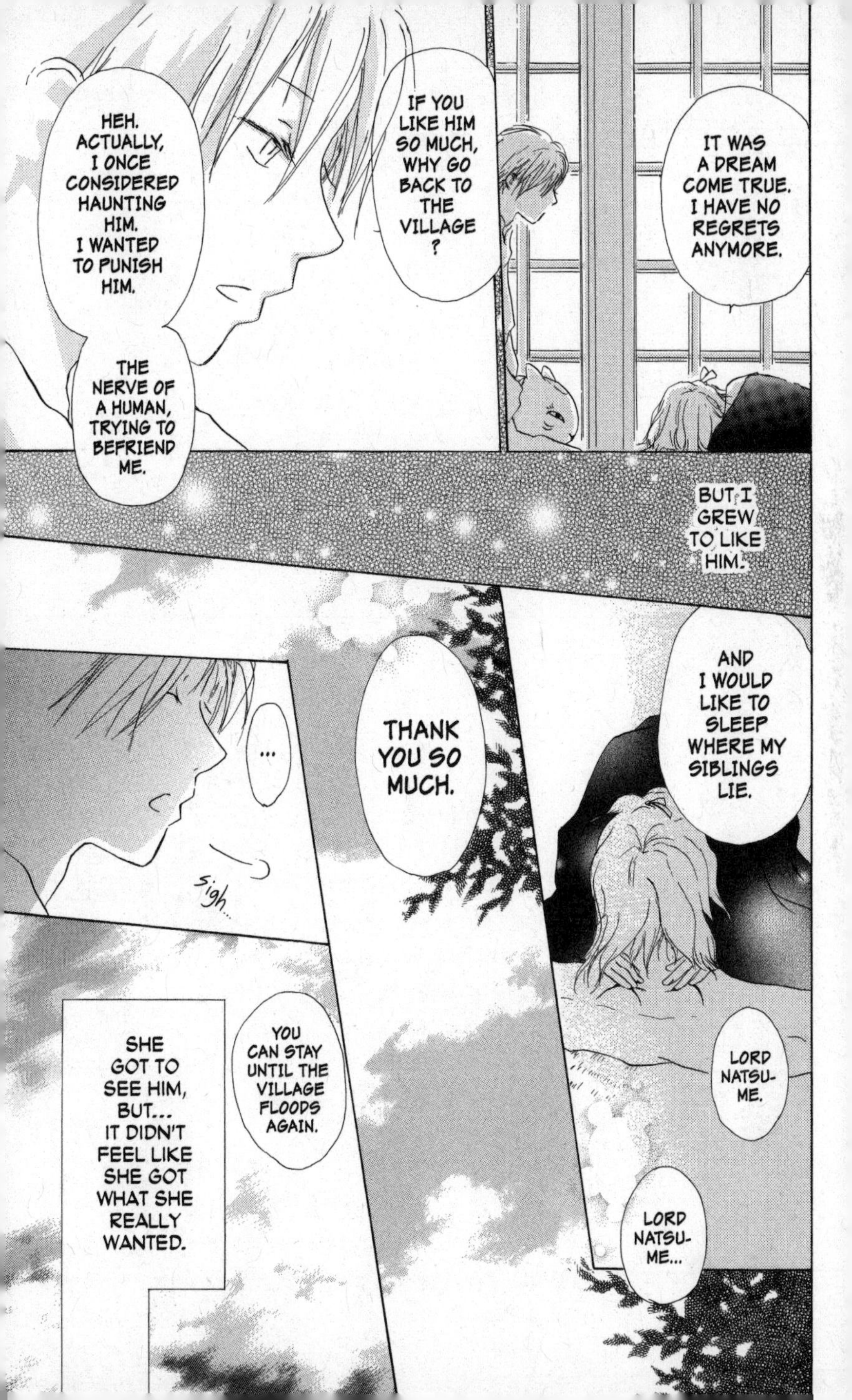
IT WAS A DREAM COME TRUE. I HAVE NO REGRETS ANYMORE.
IF YOU LIKE HIM SO MUCH, WHY GO BACK TO THE VILLAGE?
HEH. ACTUALLY, I ONCE CONSIDERED HAUNTING HIM. I WANTED TO PUNISH HIM.
THE NERVE OF A HUMAN, TRYING TO BEFRIEND ME.
BUT I GREW TO LIKE HIM.
AND I WOULD LIKE TO SLEEP WHERE MY SIBLINGS LIE.
LORD NATSU-ME.
LORD NATSU-ME...
THANK YOU SO MUCH.
...
sigh...
YOU CAN STAY UNTIL THE VILLAGE FLOODS AGAIN.
SHE GOT TO SEE HIM, BUT... IT DIDN'T FEEL LIKE SHE GOT WHAT SHE REALLY WANTED.

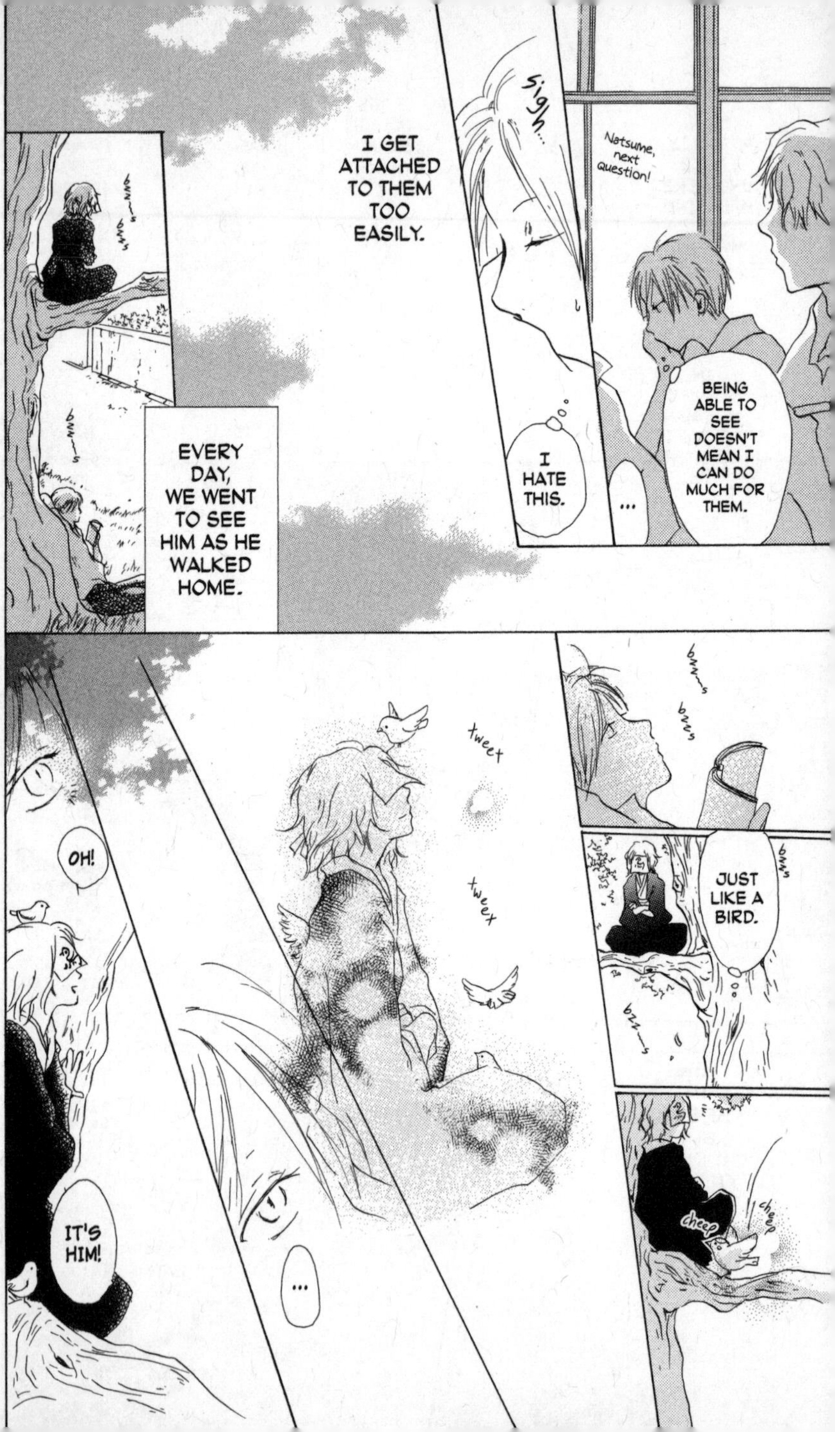
Natsume, next Question!
BEING ABLE TO SEE DOESN'T MEAN I CAN DO MUCH FOR THEM.
...
sigh...
I HATE THIS.
I GET ATTACHED TO THEM TOO EASILY.
EVERY DAY, WE WENT TO SEE HIM AS HE WALKED HOME.
JUST LIKE A BIRD.
cheep
cheep
tweet
tweet
...
OH!
IT'S HIM!

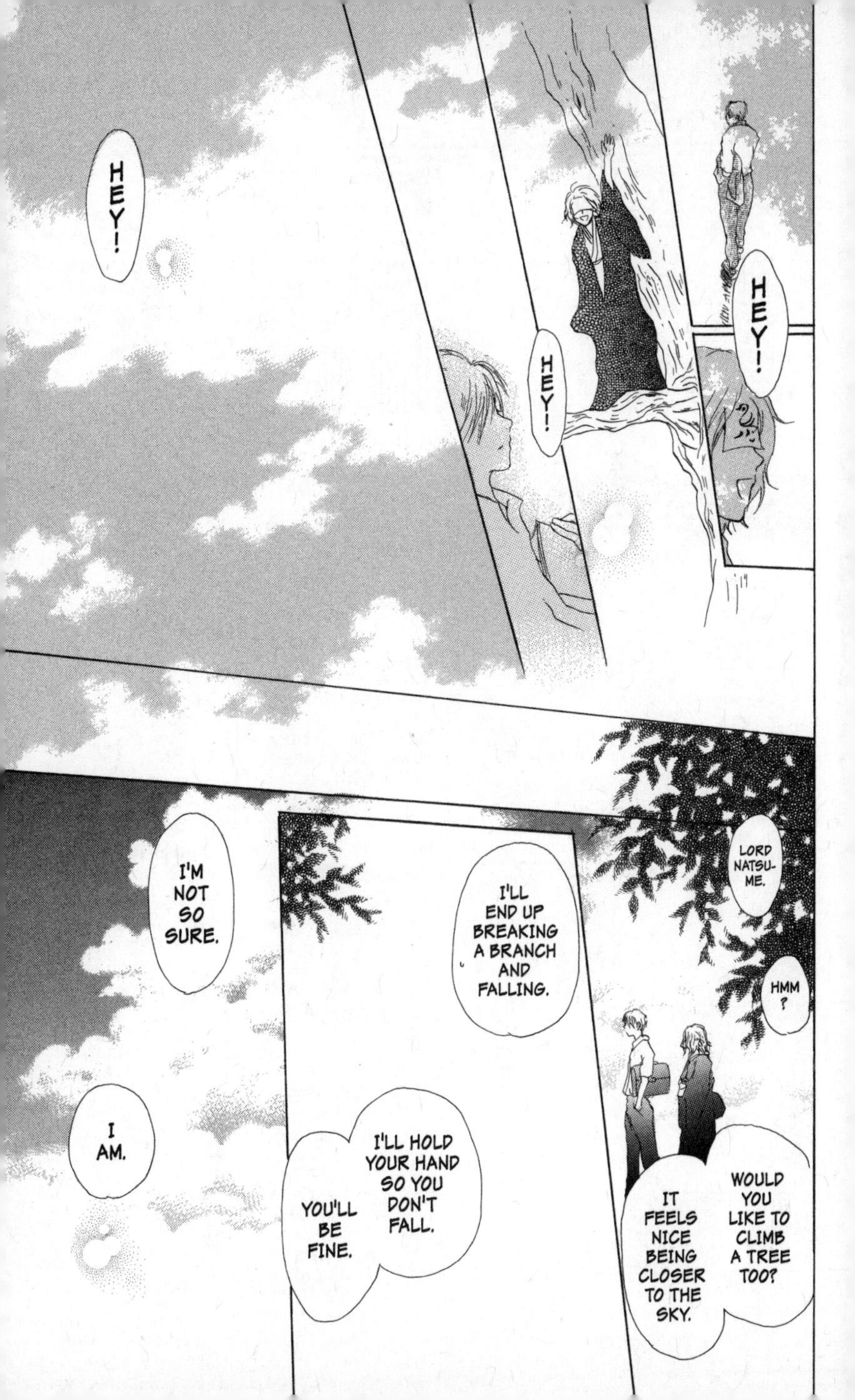
HEY!
HEY!
HEY!
LORD NATSUME.
HMM?
WOULD YOU LIKE TO CLIMB A TREE TOO?
IT FEELS NICE BEING CLOSER TO THE SKY.
I'LL END UP BREAKING A BRANCH AND FALLING.
I'LL HOLD YOUR HAND SO YOU DON'T FALL.
YOU'LL BE FINE.
I'M NOT SO SURE.
I AM.

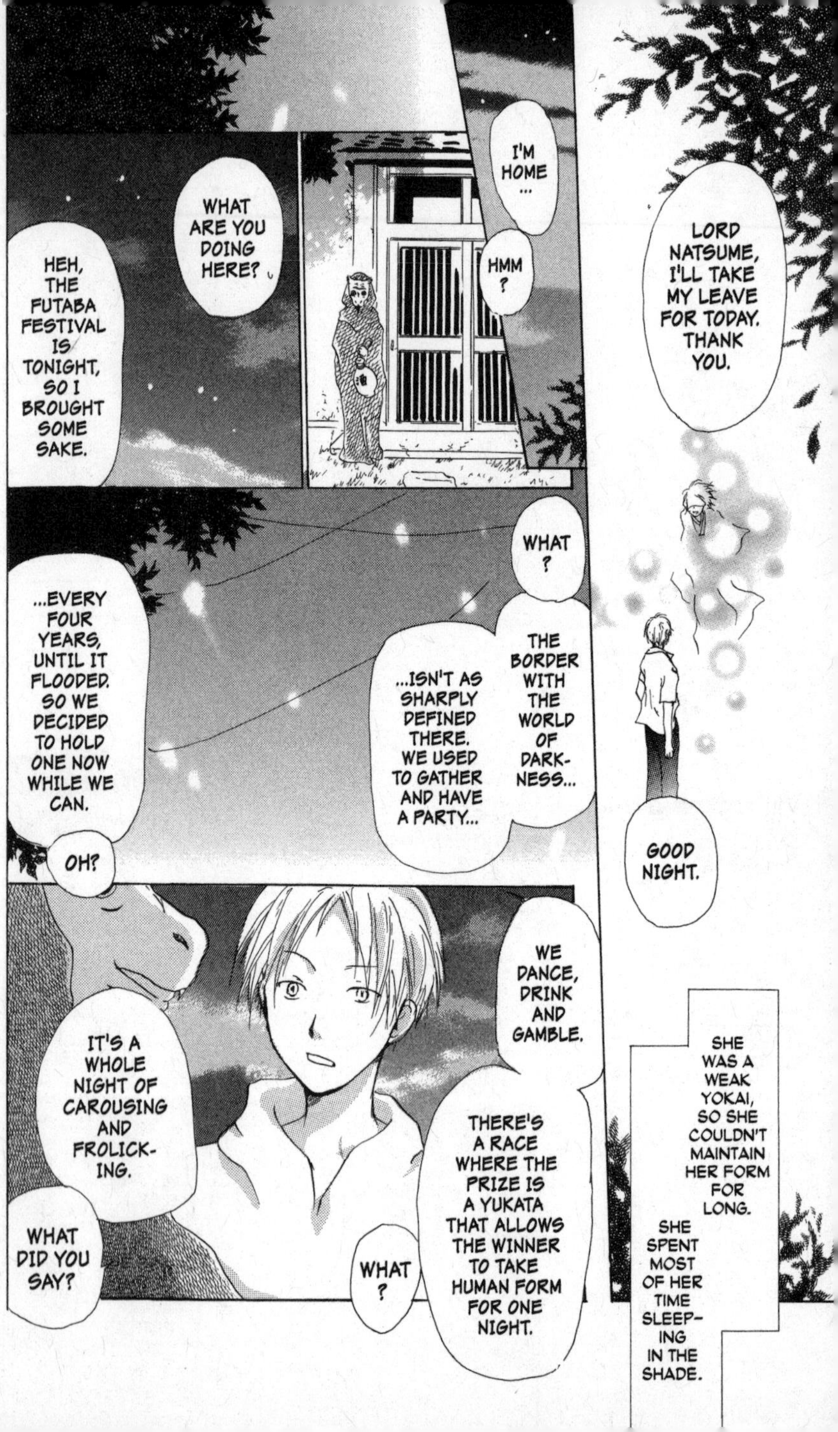
LORD NATSUME, I'LL TAKE MY LEAVE FOR TODAY. THANK YOU.
GOOD NIGHT.
SHE WAS A WEAK YOKAI, SO SHE COULDN'T MAINTAIN HER FORM FOR LONG.
SHE SPENT MOST OF HER TIME SLEEPING IN THE SHADE.
I'M HOME...
HMM?
WHAT ARE YOU DOING HERE?
HEH, THE FUTABA FESTIVAL IS TONIGHT, SO I BROUGHT SOME SAKE.
WHAT?
THE BORDER WITH THE WORLD OF DARKNESS...
...ISN'T AS SHARPLY DEFINED THERE. WE USED TO GATHER AND HAVE A PARTY...
...EVERY FOUR YEARS, UNTIL IT FLOODED. SO WE DECIDED TO HOLD ONE NOW WHILE WE CAN.
OH?
IT'S A WHOLE NIGHT OF CAROUSING AND FROLICKING.
WE DANCE, DRINK AND GAMBLE.
THERE'S A RACE WHERE THE PRIZE IS A YUKATA THAT ALLOWS THE WINNER TO TAKE HUMAN FORM FOR ONE NIGHT.
WHAT?
WHAT DID YOU SAY?

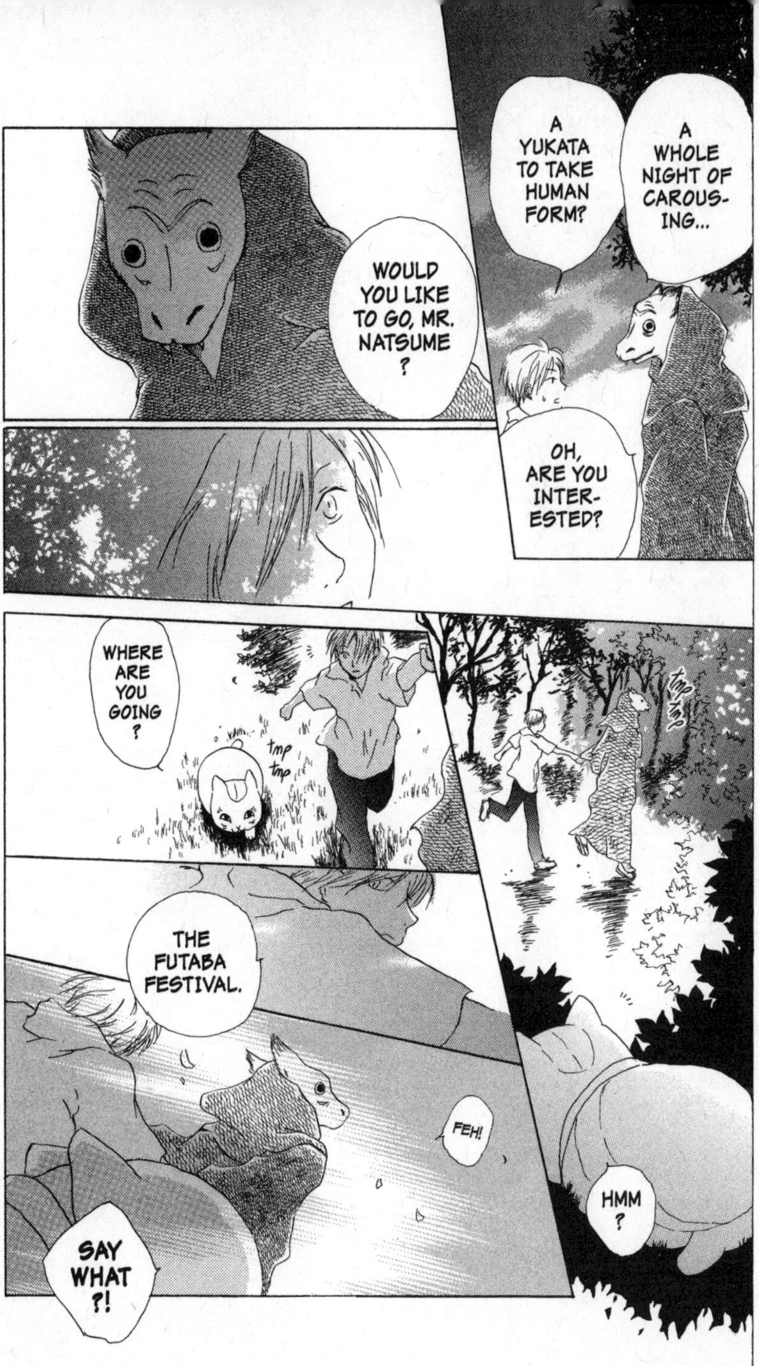
A WHOLE NIGHT OF CAROUSING...
A YUKATA TO TAKE HUMAN FORM?
OH, ARE YOU INTERESTED?
WOULD YOU LIKE TO GO, MR. NATSUME?
TMP TMP
HMM?
WHERE ARE YOU GOING?
TMP TMP
THE FUTABA FESTIVAL.
FEH!
SAY WHAT?!

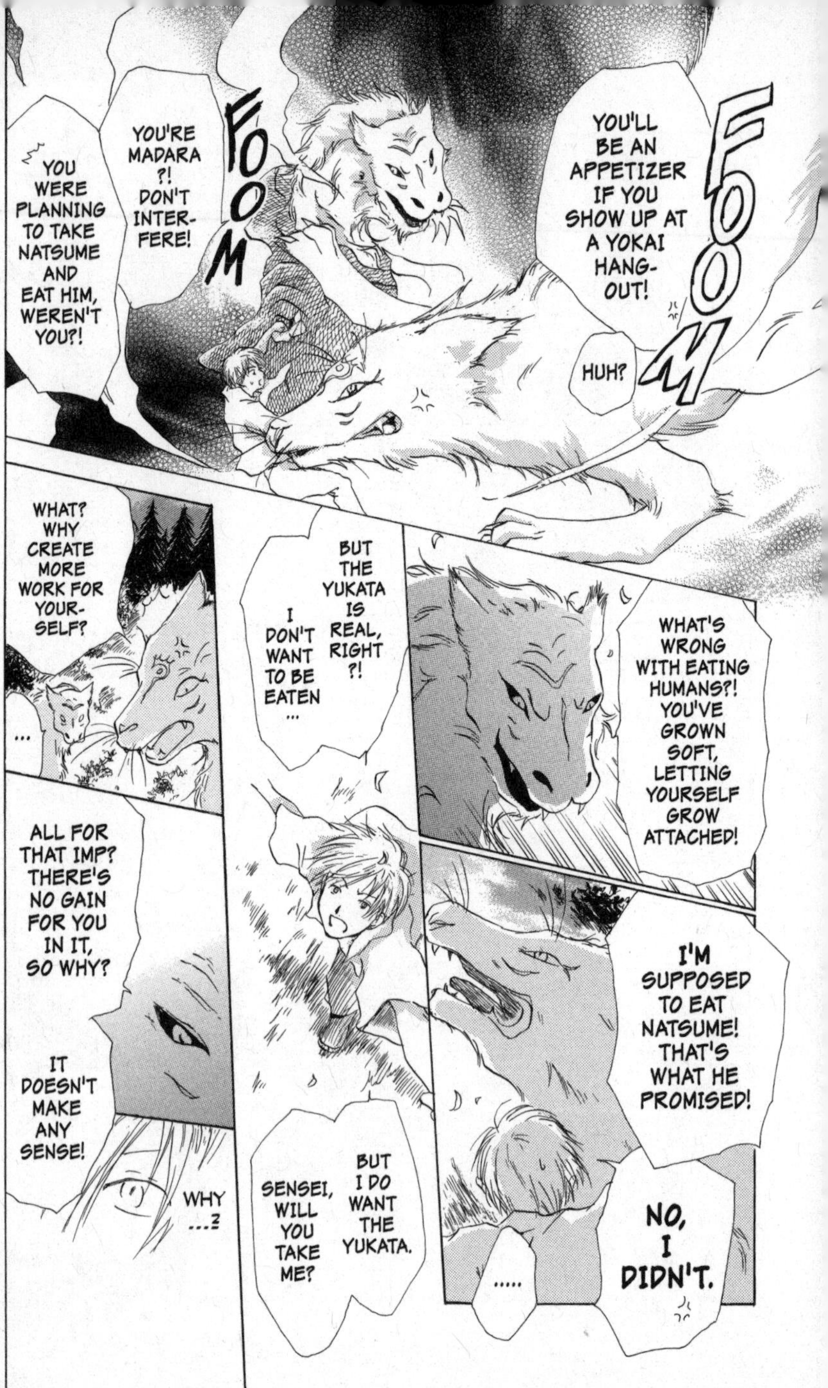
FOOM
YOU'LL BE AN APPETIZER IF YOU SHOW UP AT A YOKAI HANG-OUT!
HUH?
FOOM
YOU'RE MADARA?! DON'T INTER-FERE!
YOU WERE PLANNING TO TAKE NATSUME AND EAT HIM, WEREN'T YOU?!
WHAT'S WRONG WITH EATING HUMANS?! YOU'VE GROWN SOFT, LETTING YOURSELF GROW ATTACHED!
I'M SUPPOSED TO EAT NATSUME! THAT'S WHAT HE PROMISED!
NO, I DIDN'T.
.....
BUT THE YUKATA IS REAL, RIGHT?!
I DON'T WANT TO BE EATEN...
BUT I DO WANT THE YUKATA.
SENSEI, WILL YOU TAKE ME?
WHAT? WHY CREATE MORE WORK FOR YOURSELF?
...
ALL FOR THAT IMP? THERE'S NO GAIN FOR YOU IN IT, SO WHY?
IT DOESN'T MAKE ANY SENSE!
WHY...?

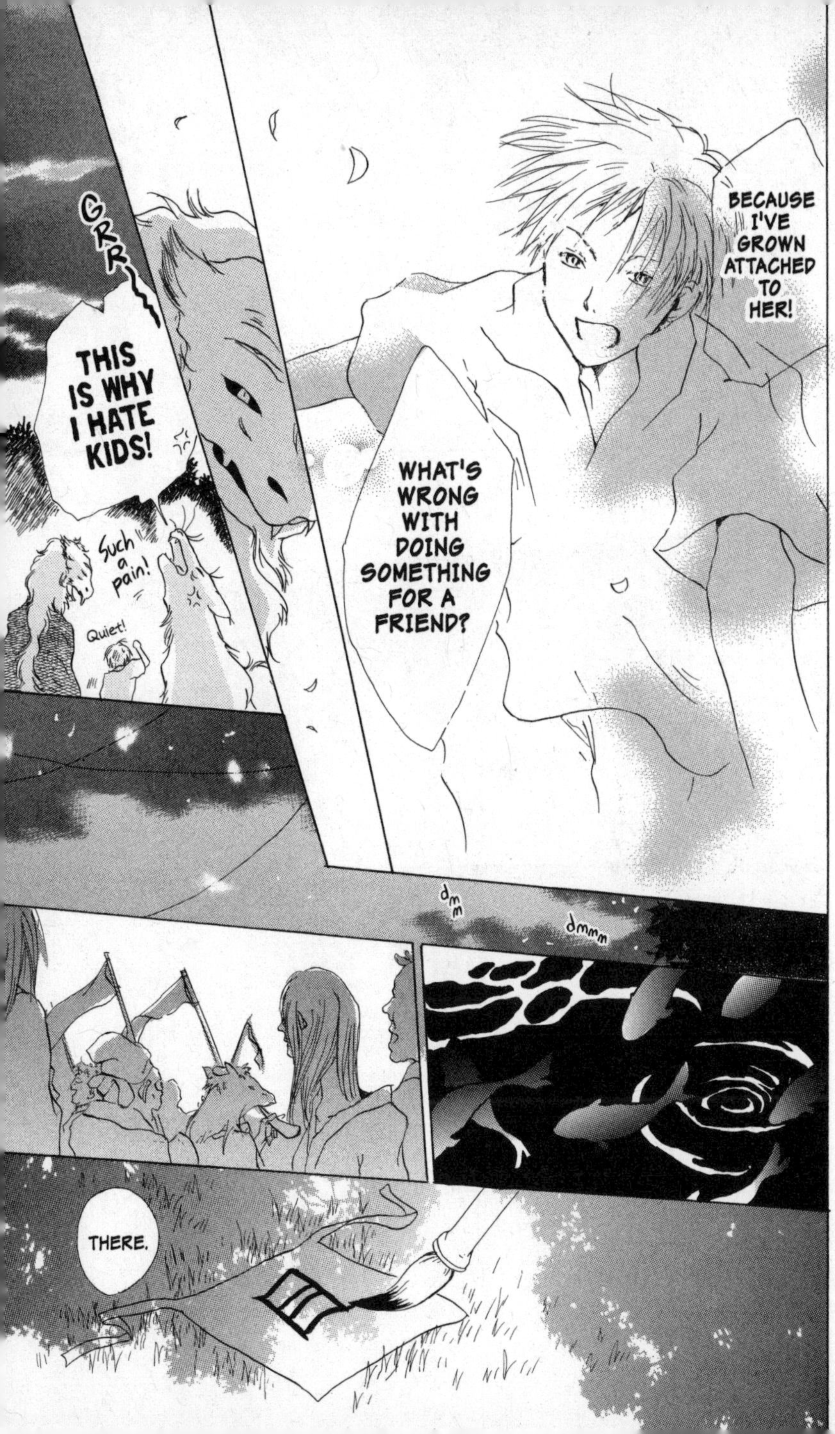
BECAUSE I'VE GROWN ATTACHED TO HER!
WHAT'S WRONG WITH DOING SOMETHING FOR A FRIEND?
GRR
THIS IS WHY I HATE KIDS!
Such a pain!
Quiet!
dmm
dmmm
THERE.

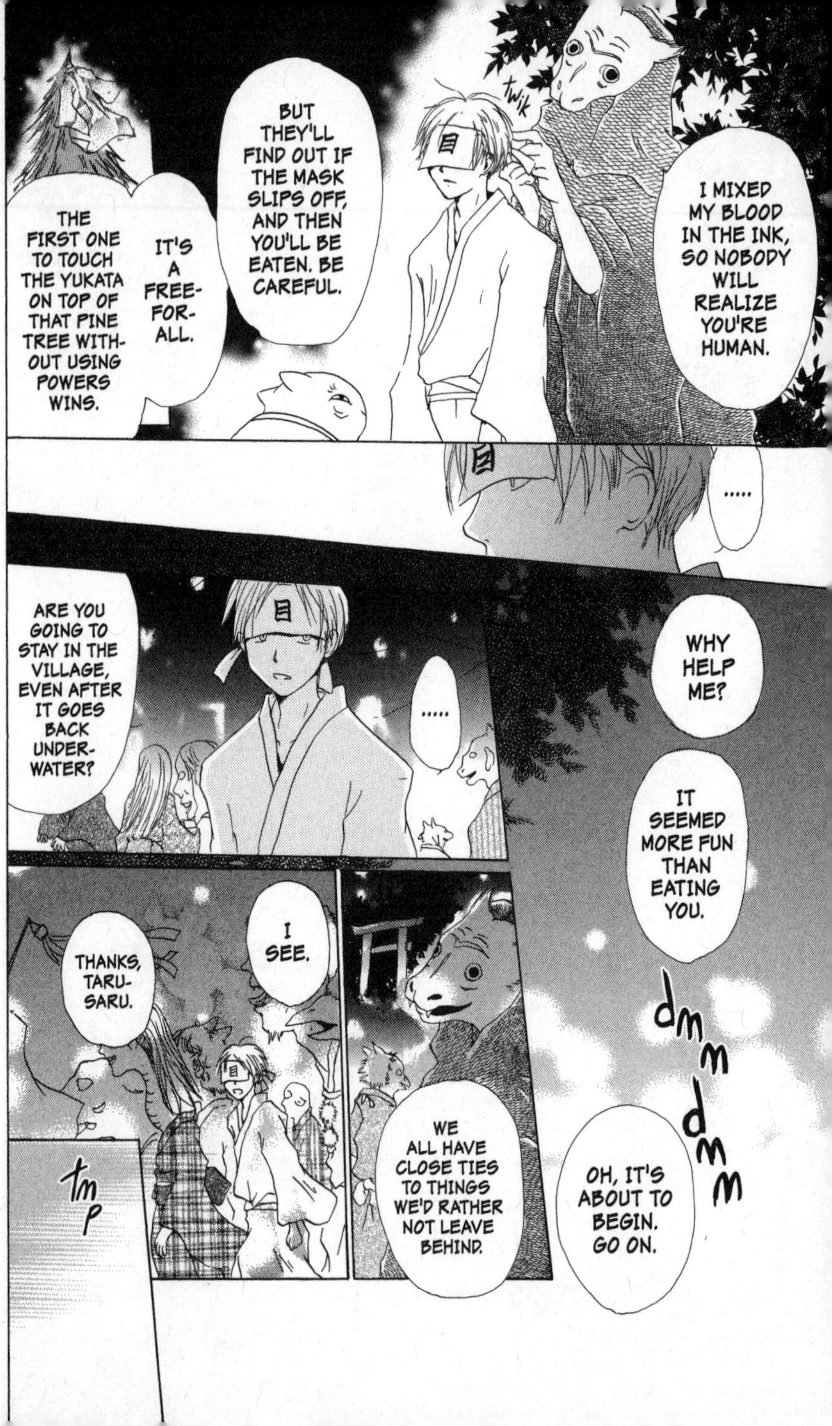
twik
I MIXED MY BLOOD IN THE INK, SO NOBODY WILL REALIZE YOU'RE HUMAN.
BUT THEY'LL FIND OUT IF THE MASK SLIPS OFF, AND THEN YOU'LL BE EATEN. BE CAREFUL.
IT'S A FREE-FOR-ALL.
THE FIRST ONE TO TOUCH THE YUKATA ON TOP OF THAT PINE TREE WITHOUT USING POWERS WINS.
.....
WHY HELP ME?
IT SEEMED MORE FUN THAN EATING YOU.
dmm dmm
OH, IT'S ABOUT TO BEGIN. GO ON.
.....
ARE YOU GOING TO STAY IN THE VILLAGE, EVEN AFTER IT GOES BACK UNDERWATER?
WE ALL HAVE CLOSE TIES TO THINGS WE'D RATHER NOT LEAVE BEHIND.
I SEE.
THANKS, TARU-SARU.
tmp

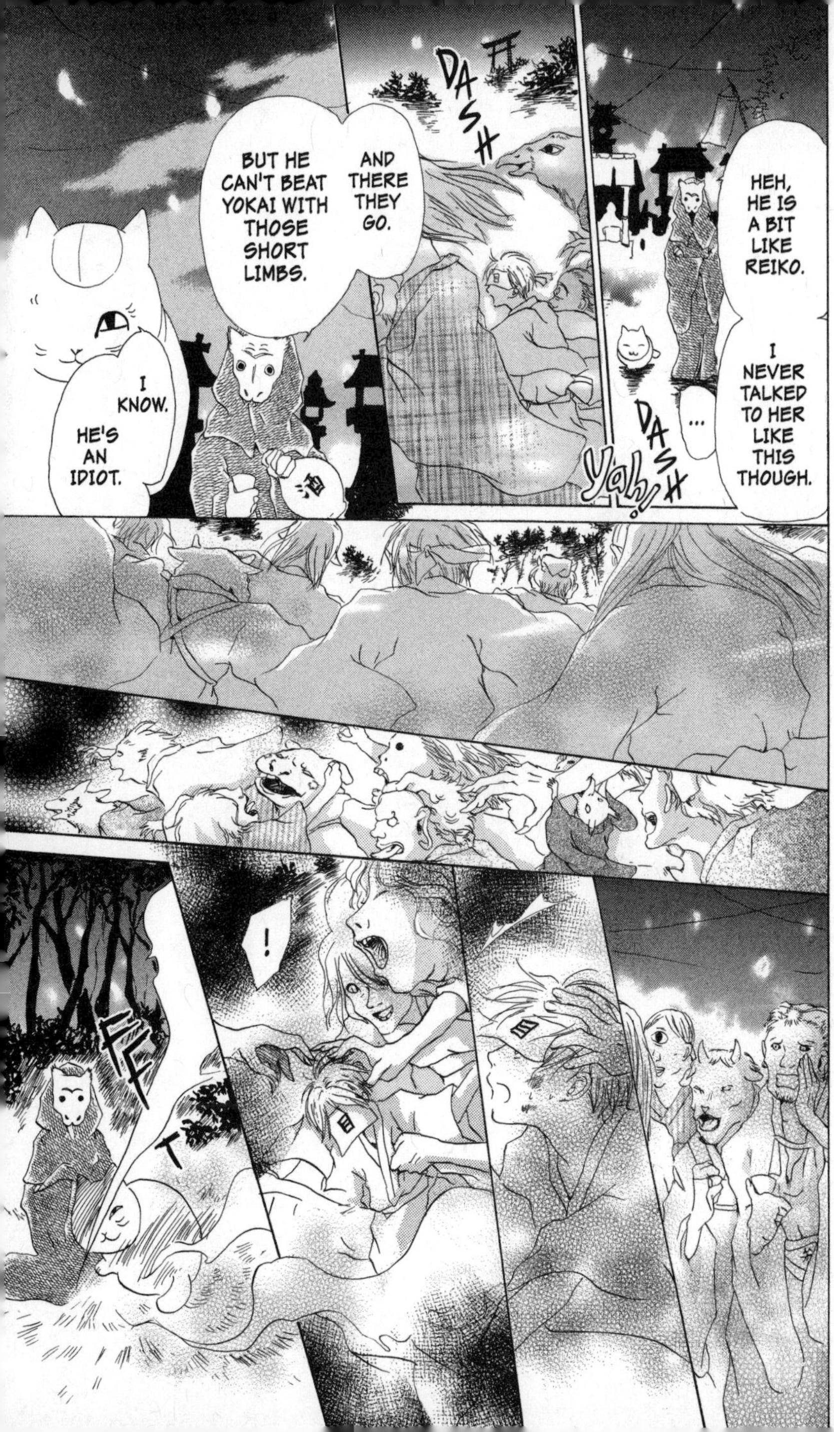
HEH, HE IS A BIT LIKE REIKO.
I NEVER TALKED TO HER LIKE THIS THOUGH.
...
DASH
Yah!
DASH
AND THERE THEY GO.
BUT HE CAN'T BEAT YOKAI WITH THOSE SHORT LIMBS.
I KNOW.
HE'S AN IDIOT.
酒
!
FF
T

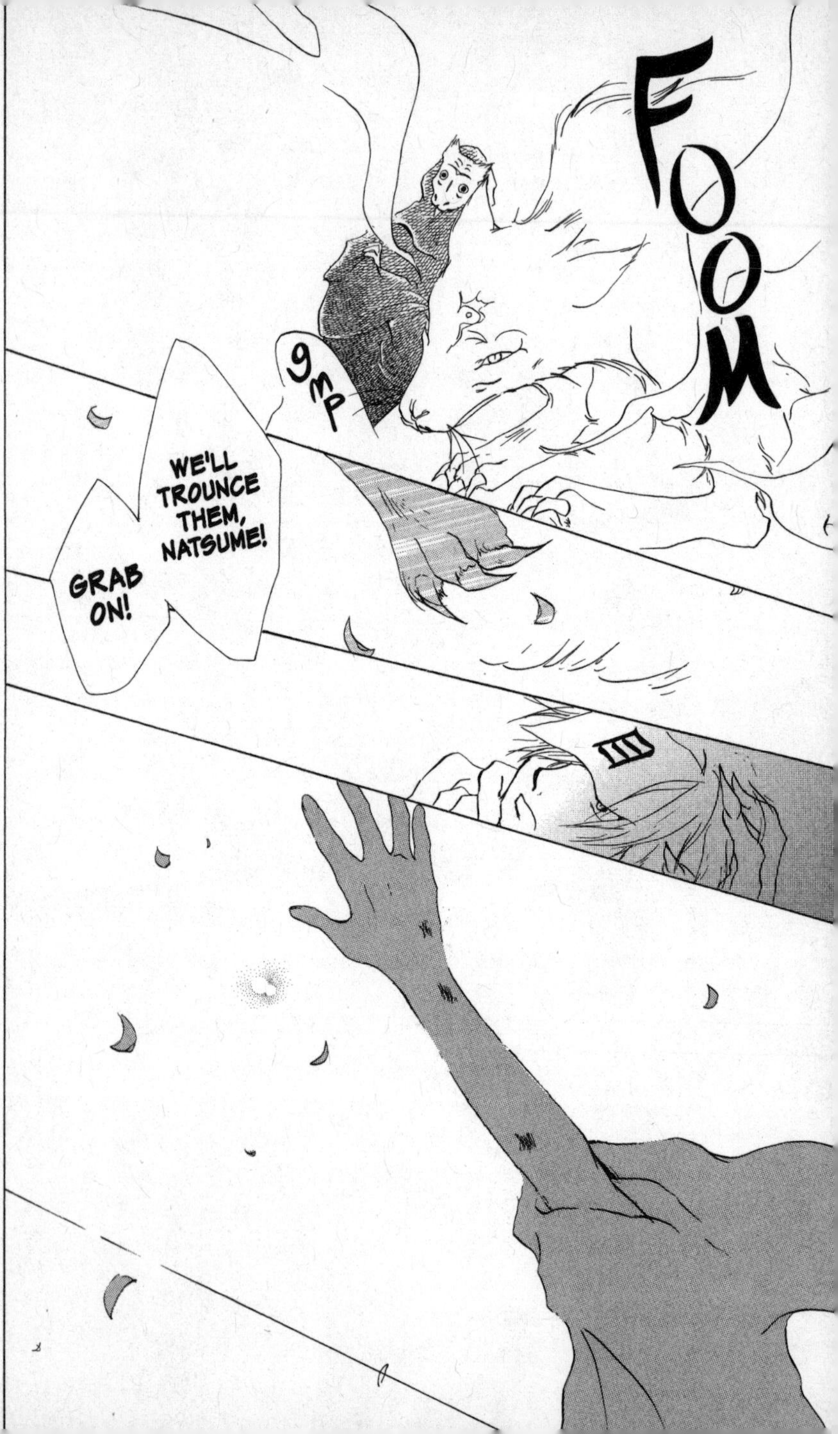
FOOM
GMP
WE'LL TROUNCE THEM, NATSUME!
GRAB ON!

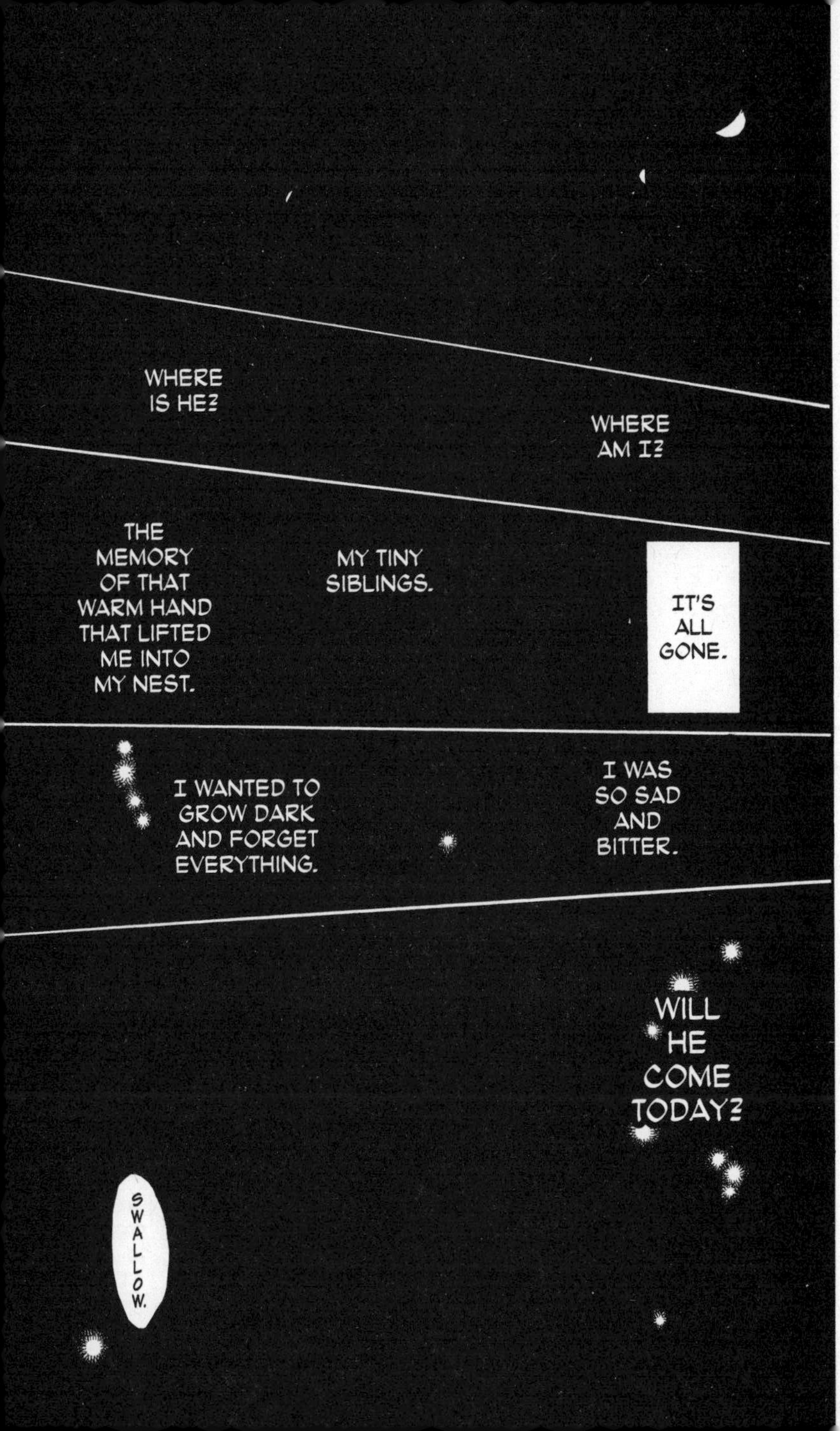
WHERE AM I?
WHERE IS HE?
IT'S ALL GONE.
MY TINY SIBLINGS.
THE MEMORY OF THAT WARM HAND THAT LIFTED ME INTO MY NEST.
I WAS SO SAD AND BITTER.
I WANTED TO GROW DARK AND FORGET EVERYTHING.
WILL HE COME TODAY?
SWALLOW.

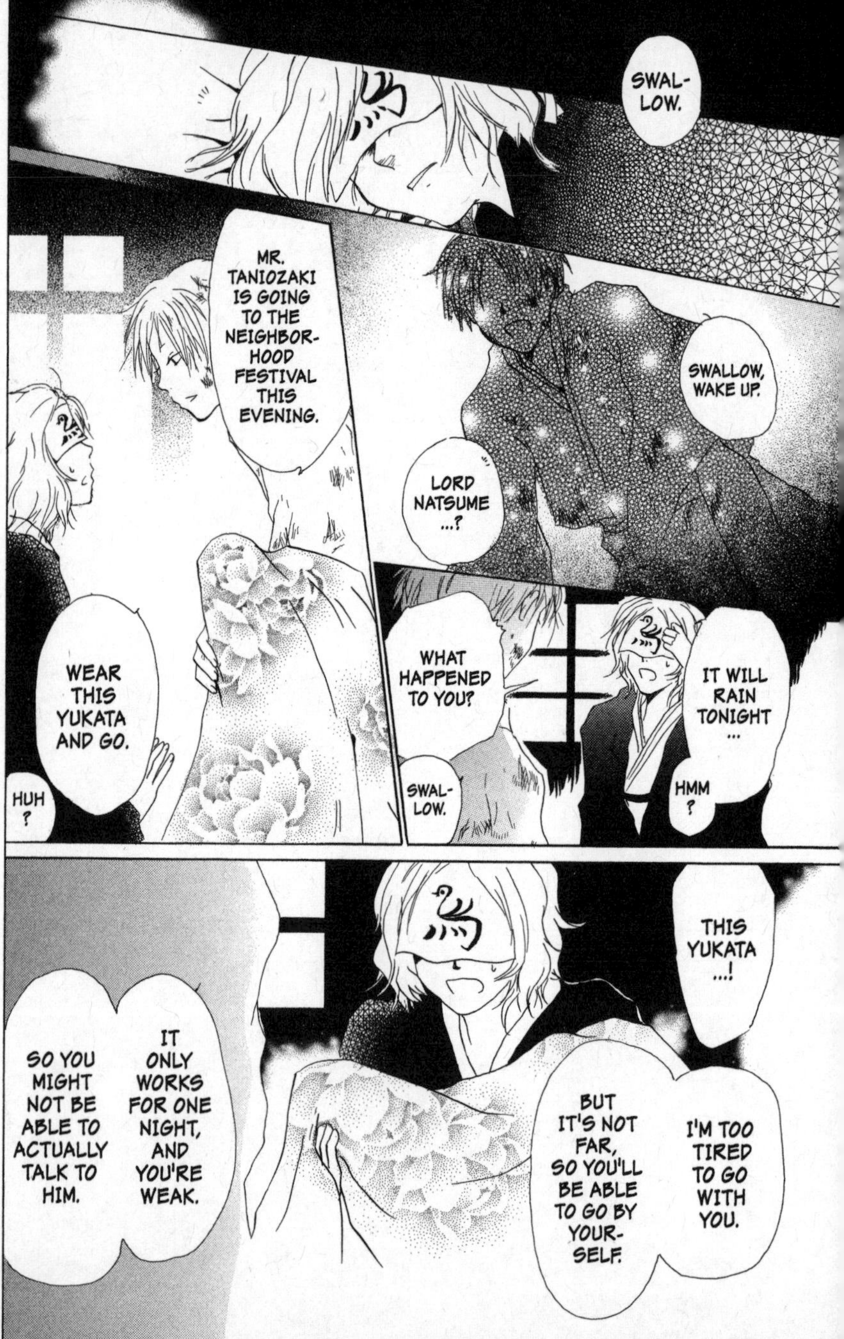
SWAL-LOW.
SWALLOW, WAKE UP.
LORD NATSUME ...?
IT WILL RAIN TONIGHT ...
WHAT HAPPENED TO YOU?
HMM ?
SWAL-LOW.
MR. TANIOZAKI IS GOING TO THE NEIGHBOR-HOOD FESTIVAL THIS EVENING.
WEAR THIS YUKATA AND GO.
HUH ?
THIS YUKATA ...!
I'M TOO TIRED TO GO WITH YOU.
BUT IT'S NOT FAR, SO YOU'LL BE ABLE TO GO BY YOUR-SELF.
IT ONLY WORKS FOR ONE NIGHT, AND YOU'RE WEAK.
SO YOU MIGHT NOT BE ABLE TO ACTUALLY TALK TO HIM.

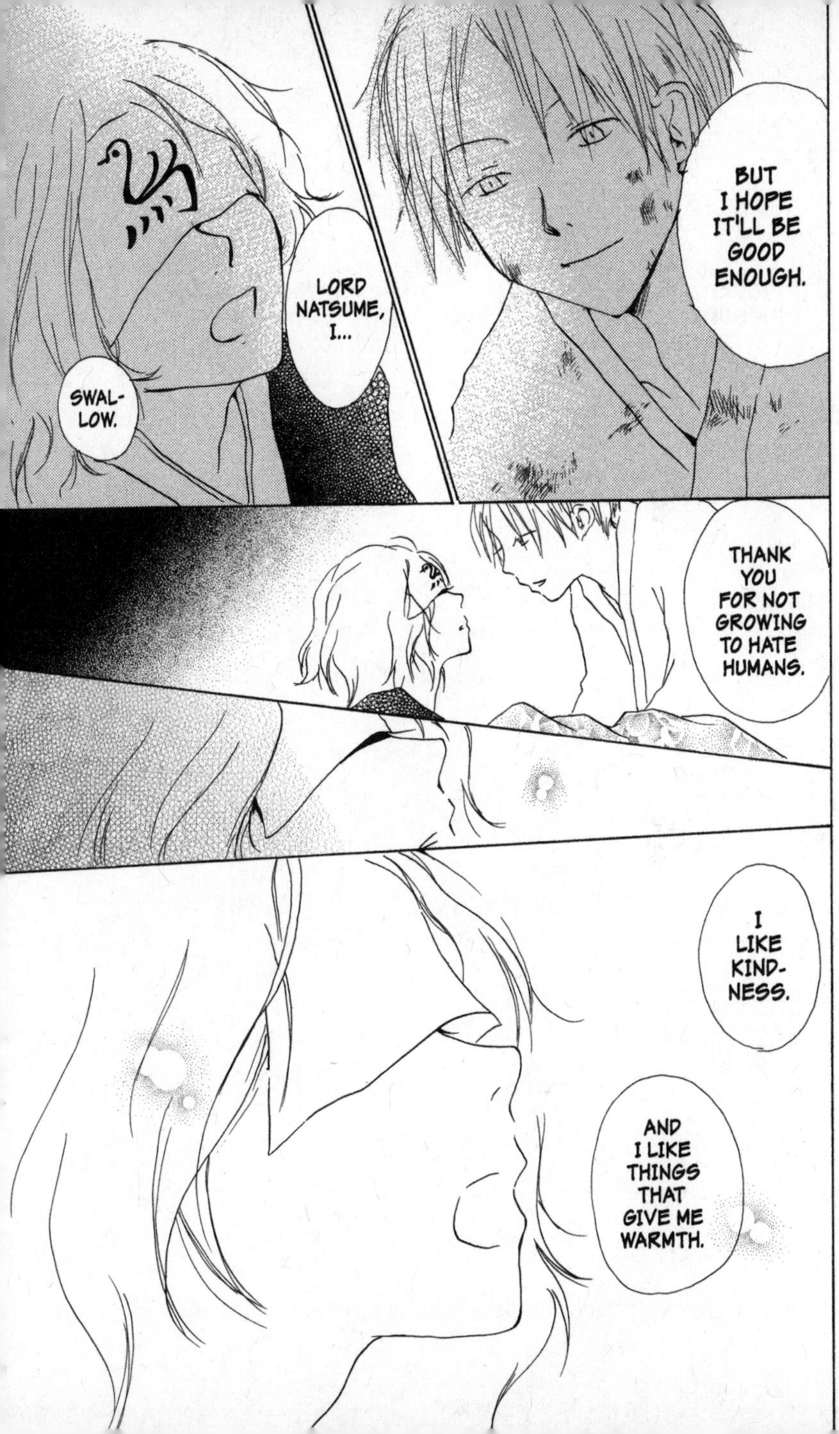
BUT I HOPE IT'LL BE GOOD ENOUGH.
LORD NATSUME, I...
SWAL-LOW.
THANK YOU FOR NOT GROWING TO HATE HUMANS.
I LIKE KIND-NESS.
AND I LIKE THINGS THAT GIVE ME WARMTH.

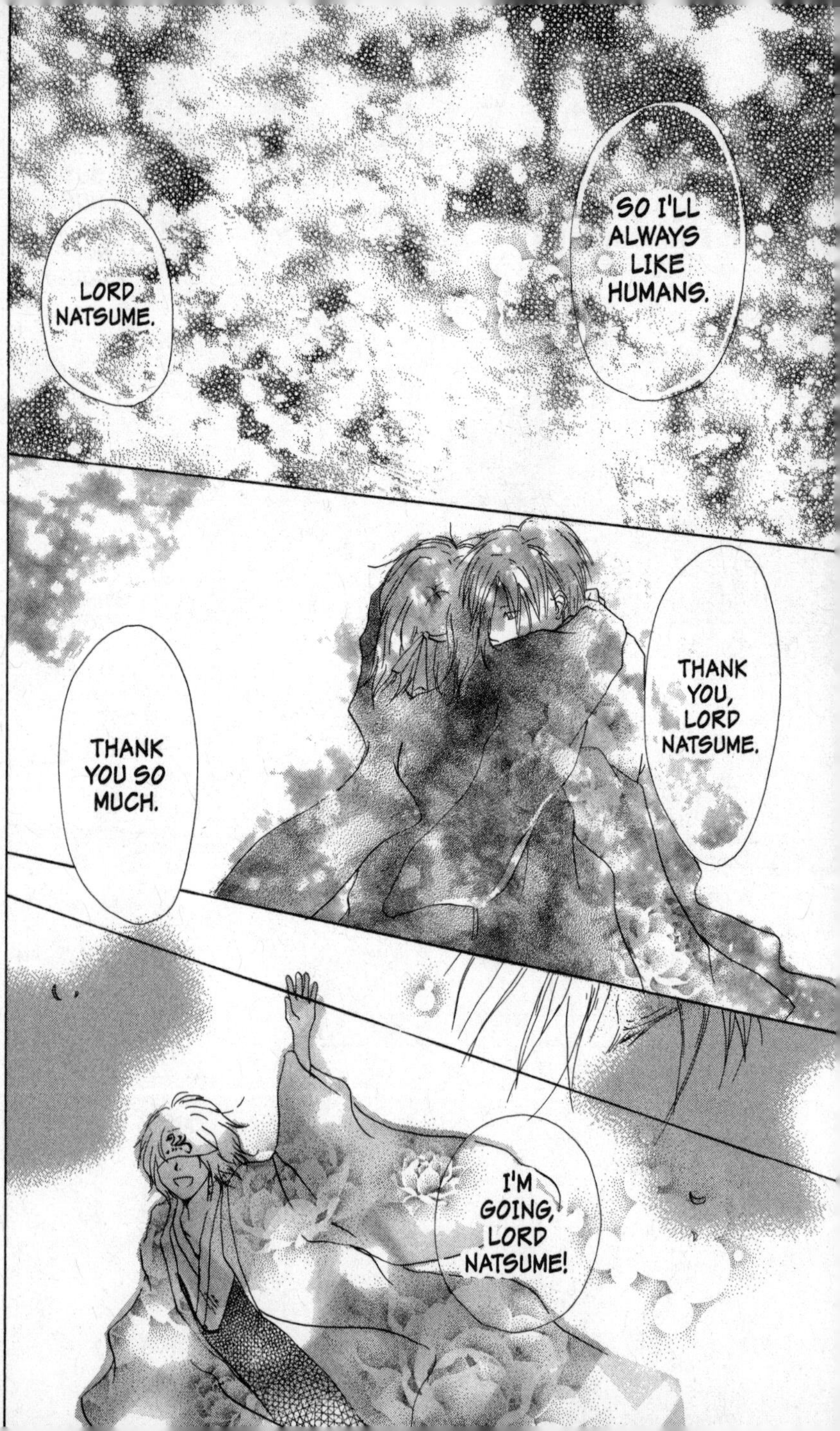
SO I'LL ALWAYS LIKE HUMANS.
LORD NATSUME.
THANK YOU, LORD NATSUME.
THANK YOU SO MUCH.
I'M GOING, LORD NATSUME!

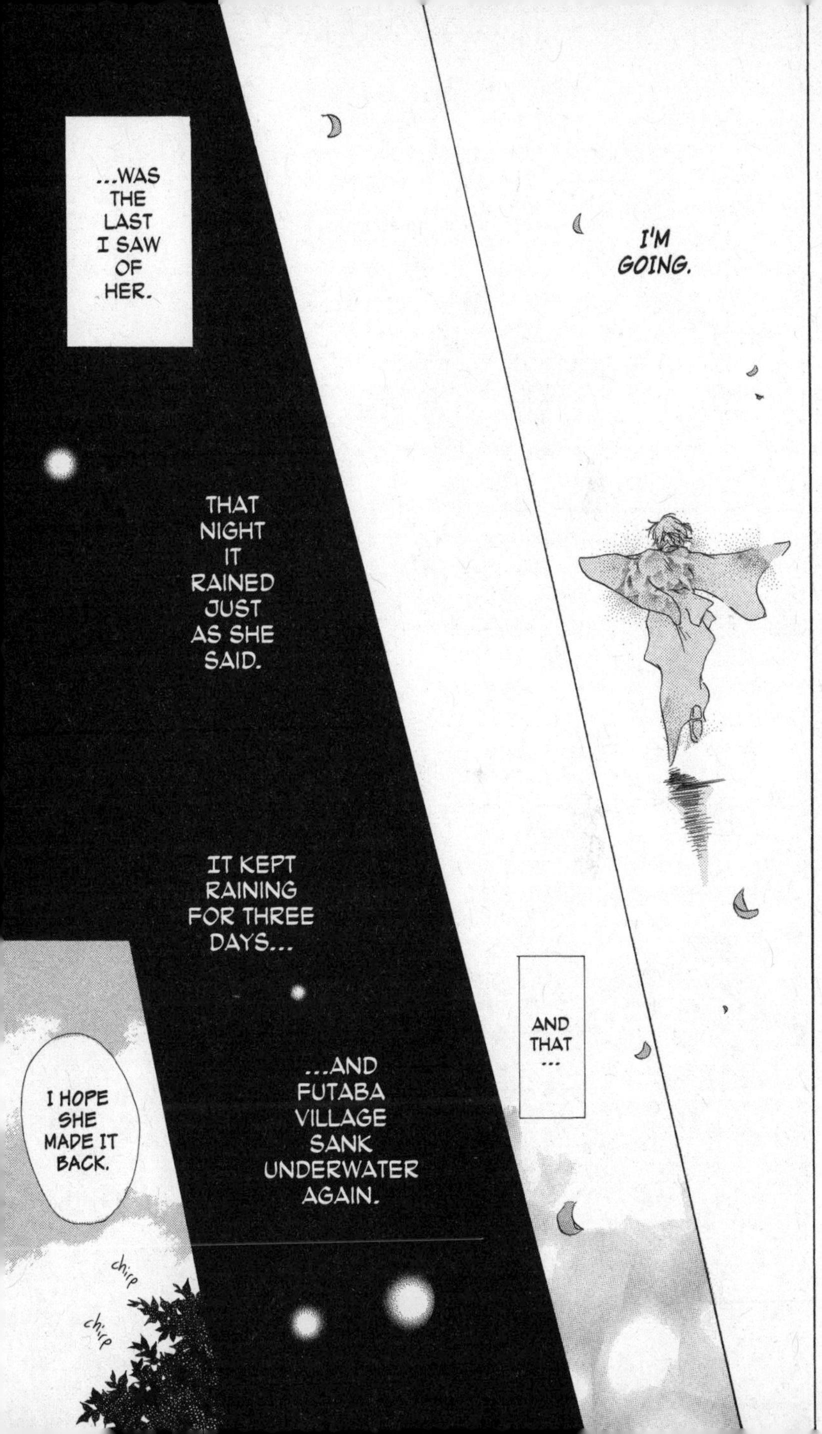
I'M GOING.
AND THAT...
...WAS THE LAST I SAW OF HER.
THAT NIGHT IT RAINED JUST AS SHE SAID.
IT KEPT RAINING FOR THREE DAYS...
...AND FUTABA VILLAGE SANK UNDERWATER AGAIN.
I HOPE SHE MADE IT BACK.
chirp
chirp

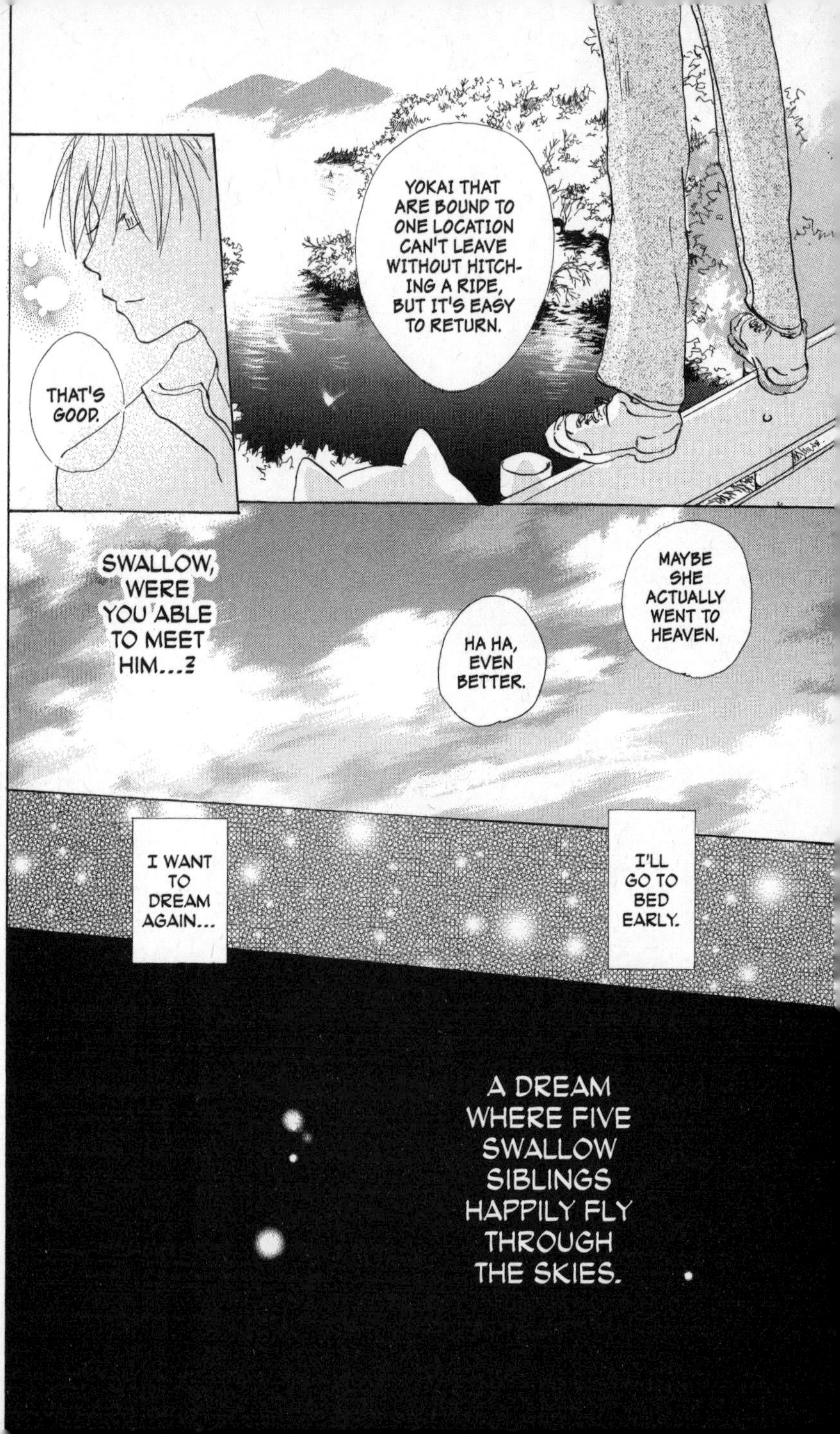
YOKAI THAT ARE BOUND TO ONE LOCATION CAN'T LEAVE WITHOUT HITCH-ING A RIDE, BUT IT'S EASY TO RETURN.
THAT'S GOOD.
MAYBE SHE ACTUALLY WENT TO HEAVEN.
HA HA, EVEN BETTER.
SWALLOW, WERE YOU ABLE TO MEET HIM...?
I'LL GO TO BED EARLY.
I WANT TO DREAM AGAIN...
A DREAM WHERE FIVE SWALLOW SIBLINGS HAPPILY FLY THROUGH THE SKIES.

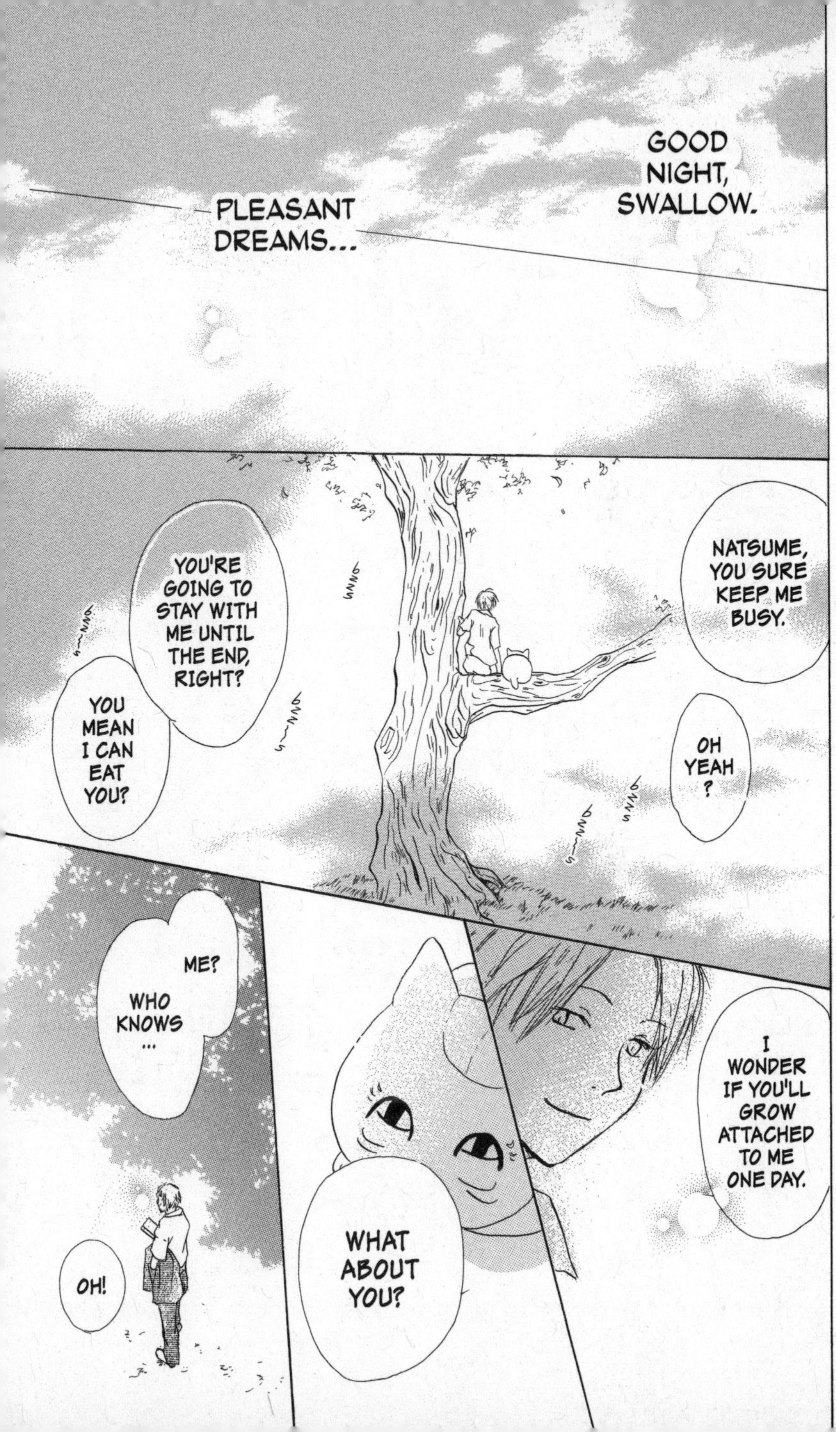
GOOD NIGHT, SWALLOW.
PLEASANT DREAMS...
NATSUME, YOU SURE KEEP ME BUSY.
OH YEAH?
YOU'RE GOING TO STAY WITH ME UNTIL THE END, RIGHT?
YOU MEAN I CAN EAT YOU?
I WONDER IF YOU'LL GROW ATTACHED TO ME ONE DAY.
WHAT ABOUT YOU?
ME?
WHO KNOWS...
OH!

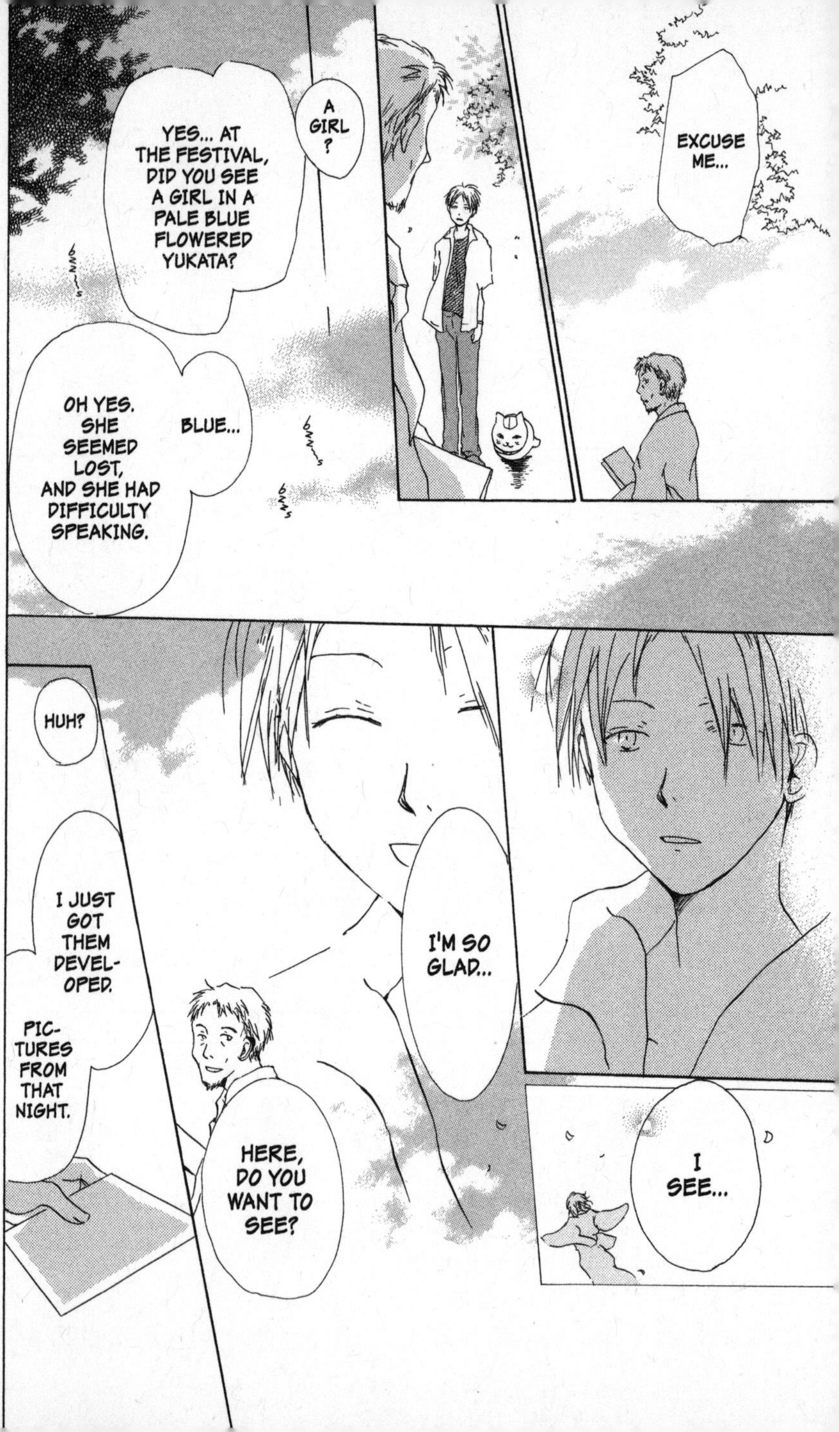

EXCUSE ME...
A GIRL?
YES... AT THE FESTIVAL, DID YOU SEE A GIRL IN A PALE BLUE FLOWERED YUKATA?
BLUE...
OH YES. SHE SEEMED LOST, AND SHE HAD DIFFICULTY SPEAKING.
I SEE...
I'M SO GLAD...
HERE, DO YOU WANT TO SEE?
HUH?
I JUST GOT THEM DEVEL-OPED.
PIC-TURES FROM THAT NIGHT.

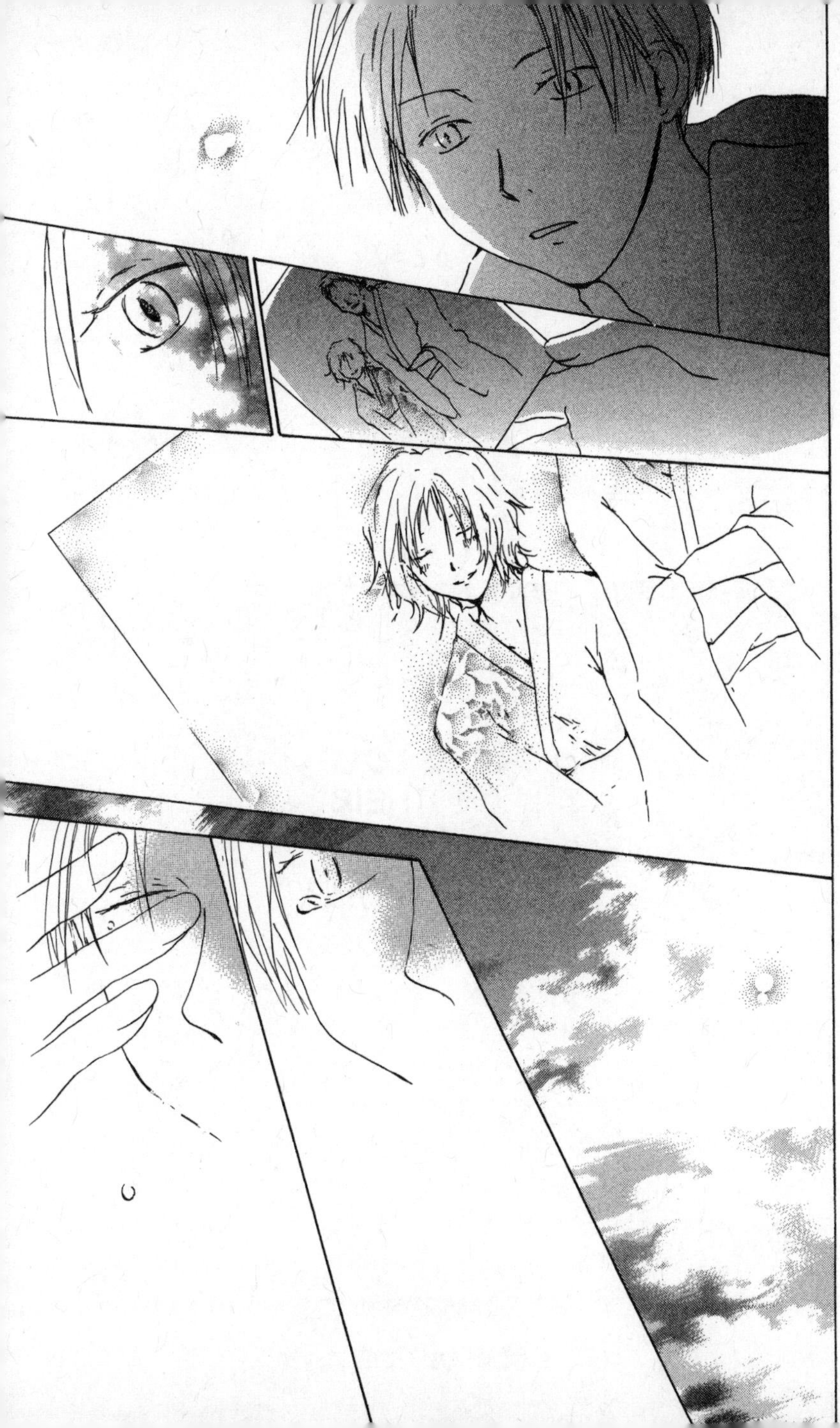

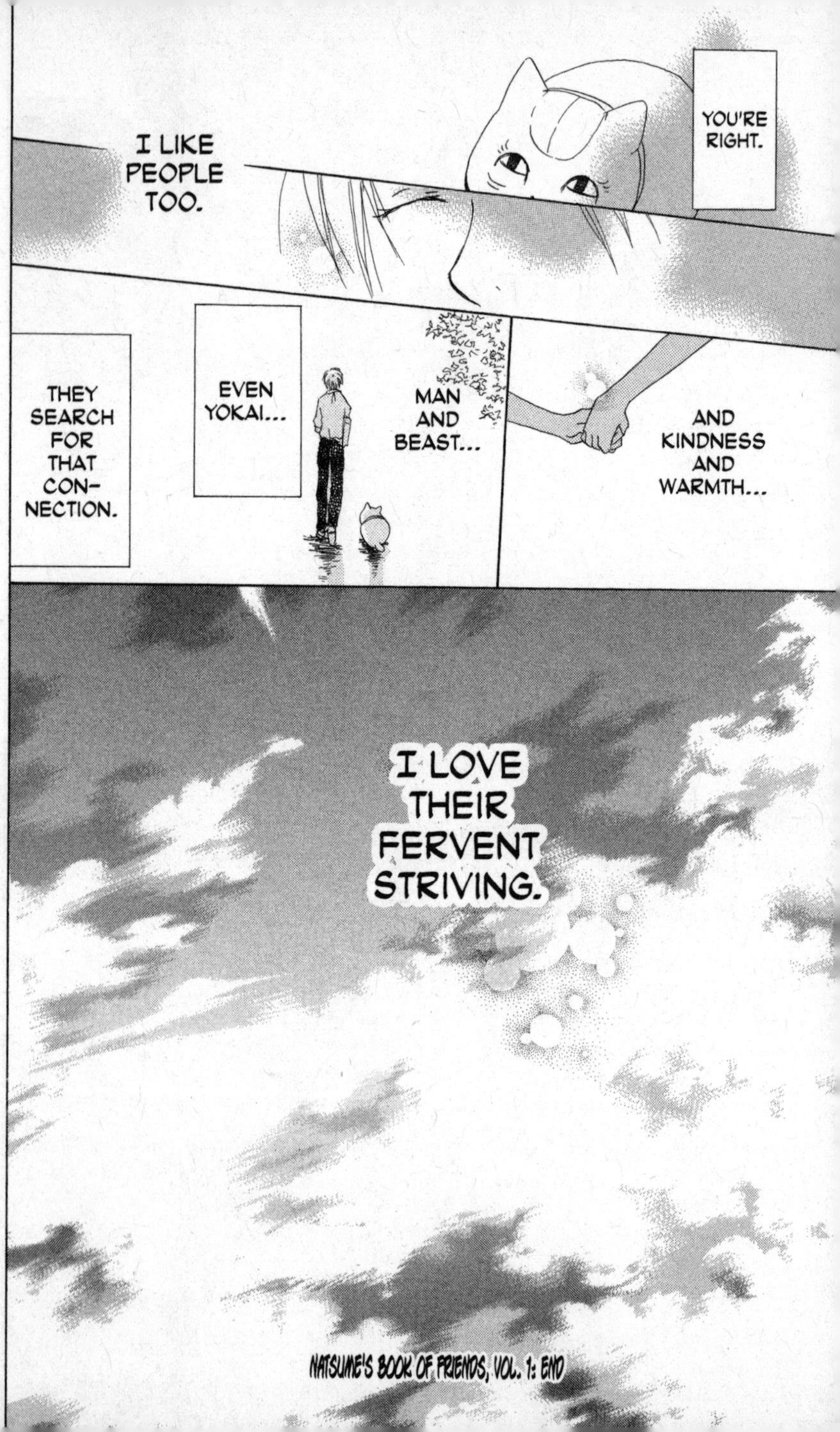
YOU'RE RIGHT.
I LIKE PEOPLE TOO.
AND KINDNESS AND WARMTH...
MAN AND BEAST...
EVEN YOKAI...
THEY SEARCH FOR THAT CON-NECTION.
I LOVE THEIR FERVENT STRIVING.
NATSUME'S BOOK OF FRIENDS, VOL. 1: END

AFTER-WORD

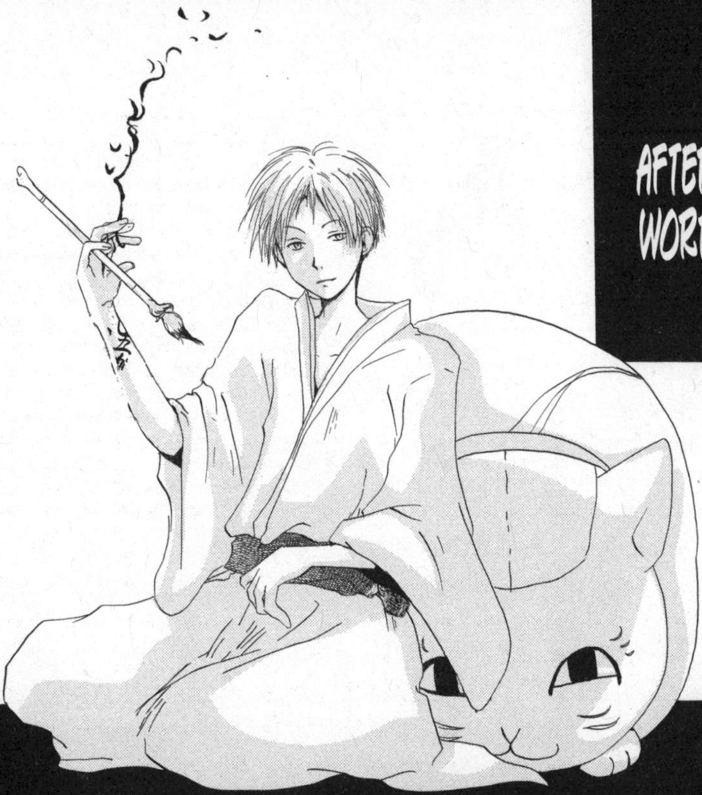

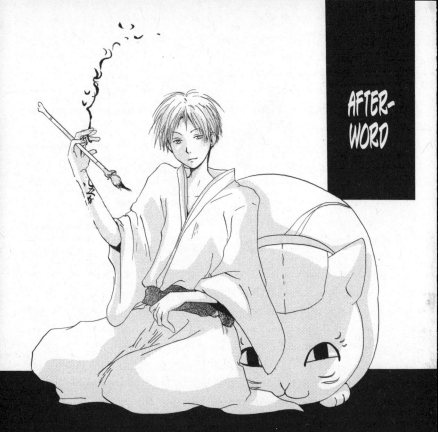

Thank you for reading. How did you like it? It was my first experience working on a series that is episodic in nature, published every once in a while. I floundered on a lot of things, but I'm also happy that readers will have an easier time picking up the story. I don't know how long I'll be able to continue like this, but I write each episode with the assumption that it could be the last. Compared to any of my previous characters, Natsume is rather less perceptive and more blunt, so he's not as rewarding for me as a writer. His lack of ability to express himself when asked for his thoughts rivals mine, so I keep wondering why I made him this way. But since he springs into action to compensate, I think he fits this story well. It's a story about a boy who tries to be a kind person.

CHAPTER 1

Nyanko Sensei's Grand Entrance!

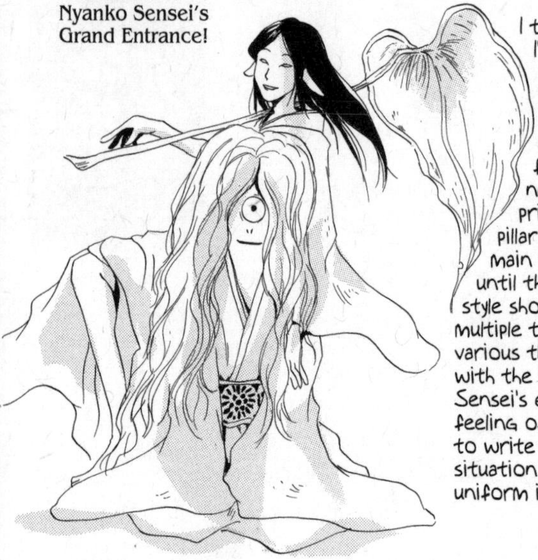

I told my editor that if possible, I'd like to do this as a series of stand-alone episodes. For this first episode, balancing the proportion of main to guest characters was difficult for both of us. I had almost never done a story where the principal character (the central pillar to the story) was also the main character, so I kept debating until the last minute how the drama style should be. I changed the beginning multiple times, experimenting with various things. But after I came up with the current flow to Nyanko Sensei's entrance, I think I grasped the feeling of this manga. I also wanted to write the tale of a boy in a curious situation where a young girl in a school uniform is his grandmother.

CHAPTER 2

The Dew God

I wanted to put in a bit of a romantic element. And I felt the pressure to include subtleties since I was given a whole 50 pages. (And whether it officially became a serial depended on this episode!) I came up with this story because whenever I see a little shrine buried among the bushes, I wonder if the resident god is lonely. Or if I see a tangerine offered once in a while, I imagine that the god will keep busy with his duties as long as at least this one person is around. But I also wanted to include the point that you shouldn't try to pledge yourself to something you can't commit to. I challenged myself to make it seem like the "Scrolls of Frolicking Animals" with little birds and beasts darting/scampering around. I became painfully aware that I need more practice illustrating cute but creepy things. Still, I had a lot of fun with this episode.

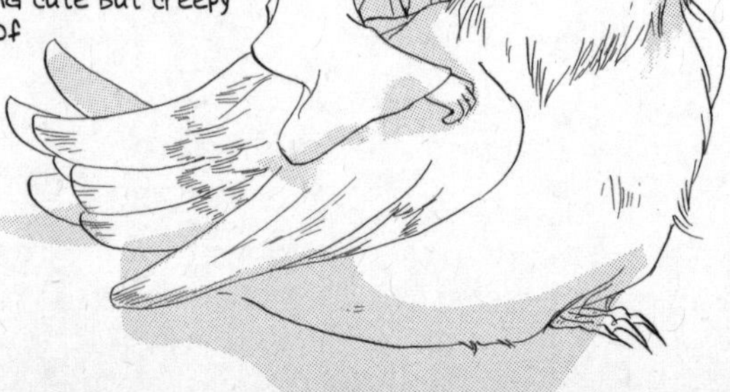

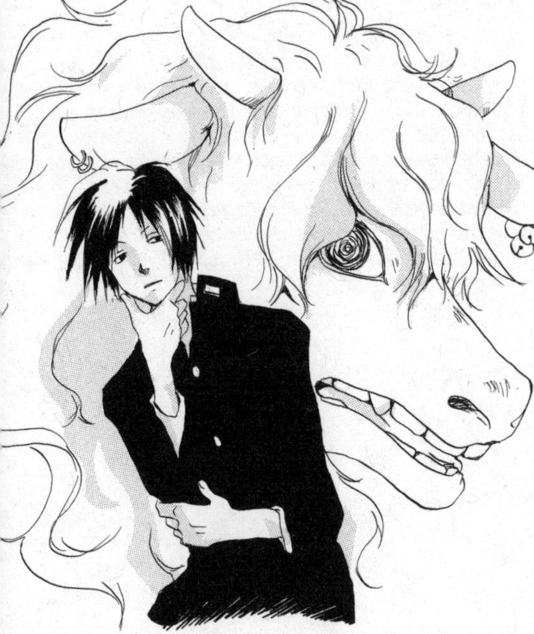

CHAPTER 3

Natsume vs. Human

I wanted a bit of a break, so I did this episode the way I wanted (one can only hope). A lot of stories about exterminating yokai exist, so I wanted to do a story about punishing humans. In chapters 1 and 2, Natsume spent more time with yokai than with humans, so having him make a friend was another one of my priorities. I wanted the reader, at the end of the episode, to be happy that he made a friend (Natsume would blush). So I hope it worked out. I hope I will be able to include stories like this sometimes.

CHAPTER 4

The Swallow Underwater

I lived in a region where a dam was a part of everyday life. Since it's a summer story, it's about the dam drying up, with a time limit until it rains again. So the yokai was a creature somewhat related to rain. I was nervous about going back to doing 40 pages. Even though Natsume acts cool and holds the powerful Book of Friends, he's still clumsy enough to get haunted. For the swallow, I started designing a girl with straight black hair, but it wasn't quite working right. It clicked for me when I went with lighter, fluffier hair. I wanted it to be creepy, so I limited her facial expressions. Looking back, a lot of yokai have wavy hair. Maybe because Natsume's hair is fine and slick.

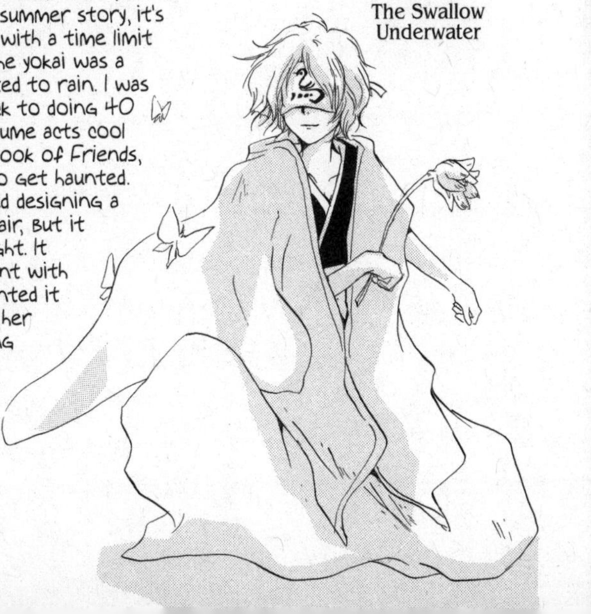

About Nyanko Sensei

When I was little, I received a ceramic lucky cat statue as a gift from an elderly couple who took care of me a lot. I loved it since the cat had such a charming face, but it broke. Sobbing, I glued it back together with modeling clay, and it's still sitting in my parents' house. I drew Nyanko Sensei while trying to remember its face. I thought Natsume should have a bird or a cat as his partner, and I chose a mysterious lucky cat.

Thank you so much for reading the whole thing. I'd like to go as far as I can with these characters. I'll treat it with the utmost care, so please continue with your support.

Let me hear your thoughts if possible!

Yuki Midorikawa
c/o Shojo Beat
295 Bay St
San Francicso, CA 94133

• Special thanks to: •
  Tamao Ohki
  Chika
  Mr. Sato
  My sister   Thank you so much.

I'll work hard so that you'll want to read my manga.
I hope we meet again.

Yuki Midorikawa
緑川 ゆき   Aug. 2005

Natsume's
BOOK OF FRIENDS

VOLUME 1 END NOTES

PAGE 10, PANEL 3: Yokai
Supernatural creatures, spirits and monsters in Japanese folklore.
Some are even ancient household items that have taken on a life of their own.

PAGE 10, PANEL 4: Shrine
When translating into English, a shrine denotes a Shinto place, and a temple is a Buddhist place.

PAGE 14, PANEL 8: Kekkai
A protective ward or barrier.

PAGE 15, PANEL 5: Cat statue
This is a Lucky or Beckoning cat (*maneki-neko*), and similar statues are often placed in front of stores to bring luck, money or customers. Lucky Cats are often depicted as bobtailed calicoes.

PAGE 23, PANEL 2: Sensei
A term than can mean teacher or master.

PAGE 24, PANEL 1: Nyanko
In Japanese, cats make the sound "nya" instead of "meow." A sort of cat dialect can be created by adding "nya" to words, so "Nyanko" means "neko" or "cat."

PAGE 71, PANEL 2: He looked like this.
The kanji on the yokai's chest can be read as an archaic form of "three" and might refer to the area where it lives, San-no-zuka (三ノ塚). "San" uses the modern kanji for "three."

PAGE 117, PANEL 8: Symbol the yokai are drawing
This is the kanji for *noroi*, which means "spell."

PAGE 162, PANEL 7: Symbol on the mask
This symbol is reminiscent of the ancient precursers to the kanji for "bird," which is 鳥.

PAGE 164, PANEL 2: Tanuki
An actual Japanese animal also known as a raccoon dog. They have a reputation for being quite plump.

PAGE 164, PANEL 3: Jug
The kanji means "sake."

PAGE 178, PANEL 6: Yukata
A lightweight, casual kimono often seen at summer festivals or hot spring inns. It literally means "bathing clothes."

PAGE 181, PANEL 7: Symbol on the mask
This is the kanji for *me*, which means "eye."

PAGE 196, PANEL 2: Scrolls of Frolicking Animals
Called Chōjū-jinbutsu-giga in Japanese, it is a set of four painted picture scrolls belonging to the Kozan-ji temple in Kyoto. They are sometimes credited as the first work of manga.

Yuki Midorikawa
is the creator of *Natsume's Book of Friends*, which was nominated for the Manga Taisho (Cartoon Grand Prize). Her other titles published in Japan include *Hotarubi no Mori e* (Into the Forest of Fireflies), *Hiiro no Isu* (The Scarlet Chair) and *Akaku Saku Koe* (The Voice That Blooms Red).

NATSUME'S BOOK OF FRIENDS

Vol. 1
Shojo Beat Edition

STORY AND ART BY Yuki Midorikawa

Translation & Adaptation Lillian Olsen
Touch-up Art & Lettering Sabrina Heep
Design Fawn Lau
Editor Pancha Diaz

Natsume Yujincho by Yuki Midorikawa
© Yuki Midorikawa 2005
All rights reserved.
First published in Japan in 2005 by HAKUSENSHA, Inc., Tokyo.
English language translation rights arranged with HAKUSENSHA, Inc., Tokyo.

Printed in the U.S.A.

Published by VIZ Media, LLC
P.O. Box 77010
San Francisco, CA 94107

10 9 8 7 6
First printing, January 2010
Sixth printing, July 2018

Don't Hide What's *Inside*

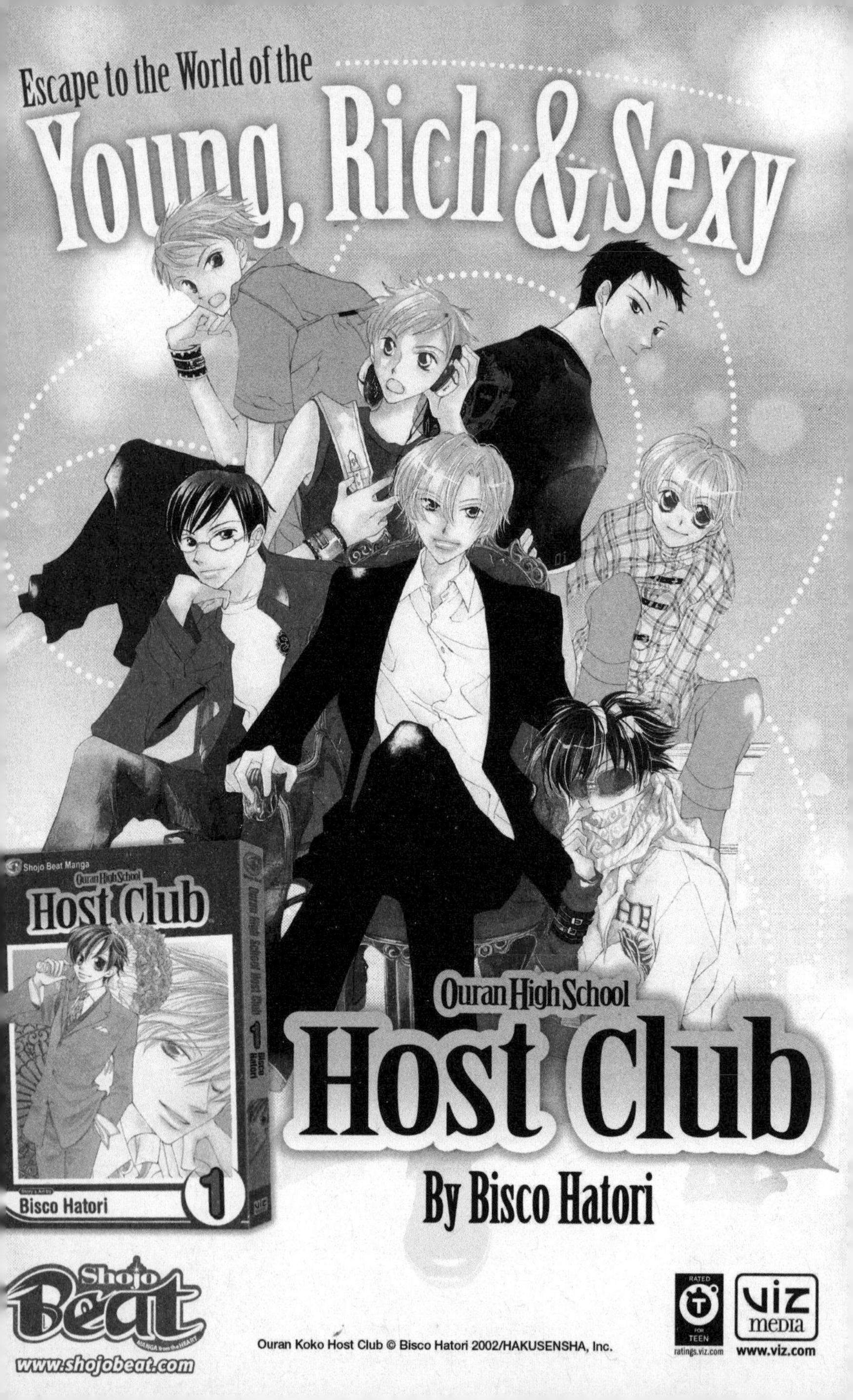
Escape to the World of the
Young, Rich & Sexy
Shojo Beat Manga
Ouran High School
Host Club
1
Bisco Hatori
Ouran High School
Host Club
By Bisco Hatori
Shojo Beat
www.shojobeat.com
Ouran Koko Host Club © Bisco Hatori 2002/HAKUSENSHA, Inc.
RATED
T
FOR
TEEN
ratings.viz.com
VIZ media
www.viz.com